Walking Britain's Rivers *and* Canals

Walking Britain's Rivers *and* Canals

Introduction by David Bellamy

Bartholomew

An Imprint of HarperCollinsPublishers

This edition published in Great Britain by Bartholomew
a division of HarperCollins Publishers Ltd in 1999
for Bookmart Ltd, Enderby, Leicester.

First published in 1997
by Collins Willow
an imprint of HarperCollins *Publishers*
London

© Julian Holland 1997
Introduction © Botancial Enterprises (Publications) Ltd 1997

1 3 5 7 9 8 6 4 2

A CIP catalogue record is available from the British Library

ISBN 0-261-67210-X

Designed and conceived by Julian Holland, Glastonbury, Somerset, UK

THE AUTHORS

THE BUDE CANAL
THE CAMEL TRAIL
THE LEE & STORT NAVIGATIONS
THE OXFORD CANAL
THE CHESHIRE RING
IN AND AROUND BIRMINGHAM
ACROSS THE PENNINES
THE LANCASTER CANAL
THE SWANSEA AND NEATH CANALS

Paul Atterbury trained as an art historian and has spent the last twenty years writing books and articles about many aspects of art and antiques, and about travel, with an empahasis on railways and canals. Co-author of the original *Nicholson Guides to Canals & Waterways of Britain*, he also wrote *See Britain by Train*, published by the AA and British Rail. Recent books include *Exploring Britain's Canals* (HarperCollins, 1994) and *Discovering Britain's Lost Railways* (AA Publishing, 1995). Paul is a regular member of the BBC TV's *Antiques Roadshow* team of experts.

THE BOUNDS OF AINSTY
THE EDEN WAY
THE WEARDALE WAY

Malcolm Boyes has walked extensively in all parts of Britain and is the author of over twenty books on walking and the north of England. He contributed to the AA's *Village Walks* and *Exploring Britain's Long Distance Paths*. **Hazel Chester**, his wife, is co-author with him of several books and is also an illustrator. They live in North Yorkshire.

THE ROYAL MILITARY CANAL
THE FEN RIVERS WAY
THE RIVER STOUR
THE RIVER ESK

Sue Gordon is a freelance editor and writer. She has edited numerous travel guides and books on Britain and is author of the AA's *Explore Britain's Villages*. Publications to which she has contributed include the AA's *Weekend Walks* and the *The AA Interactive Guide to Britain and Ireland* CD-ROM.

THE AVON WALKWAY
THE SEVERN WAY
THE THAMES & SEVERN WAY

Julian Holland is a book designer, living and working in Somerset. In his spare time he enjoys walking, photography and travelling by train. He has contributed to *Exploring Britain's Long Distance Paths*, published by the AA, and has written on canals, preserved railways and the villages of southwest England for the *AA Database of Britain*.

THE THAMES PATH
THE RIVER WEY AND ITS CONNECTIONS

Helen Livingston was born and brought up in Southern England and her love for walking in the region dates from her school days. As a freelance writer, she combines her interests in the countryside, history and literature. She is the author of *The Thames Path, Aerofilms Guide* (Ian Allan) and contributed to *Exploring Britain's Long Distance Paths* (AA Publishing).

THE SEVERN VALLEY WAY
THE WYE VALLEY WALK

Les Lumsdon has researched several cycling and walking books and writes a regular column for a Midlands newspaper. He is a consultant to *Getting About Britain* and Senior Lecturer in Tourism at Staffordshire Polytechnic. He contributed to *Exploring Britain's Long Distance Paths* (AA Publishing).

THE RIVER SPEY
THE CRINAN CANAL
THE RIVER DEE
THE UNION CANAL
THE RIVER TWEED

Roger Smith is a freelance writer and editor living in Scotland. He has written a number of books on walking, and wrote the walks in the Scotland section of *Exploring Britain's Long Distance Paths* (AA Publishing). Roger was formerly editor of the walkers' magazine *The Great Outdoors* and is a member of the Executive Committee of the National Trust for Scotland.

THE MONTGOMERY CANAL
THE MORFA MAWDDACH TRAIL

Nia Williams is a Welsh-speaking Cardiffian now living in Hampshire. She has worked as a freelance editor and writer since 1987, and has contributed to several books about Britain and France, including Michelin's *Green Guide to Wales*, the Consumer Association's *Great Days Out*, Thomas Cook's *On the Rails: France and the Benelux Countries* and *The AA Interactive Guide to Britain and Ireland* CD-ROM.

Title page photo
The magnificently retored Victorian warehouses at
Gloucester Docks, the northern terminus of the
Gloucester & Sharpness Canal

Contents

Map and List of Walks   6
Introduction by David Bellamy   7

The Walks

Southwest England   **10**
The Bude Canal   12
The Camel Trail   16
The Avon Walkway   20
The Severn Way   26
The Thames & Severn Way   32

South & Southeast England   **38**
The Thames Path   40
The River Wey and its Connections   56
The Royal Military Canal   64
The Lee & Stort Navigations   68
The Oxford Canal   72

Midlands & East Anglia   **76**
The Severn Valley Way   78
The Cheshire Ring   82
In and Around Birmingham   92
The Fen Rivers Way   100
The River Stour   102

North England   **106**
The Bounds of Ainsty   108
The Eden Way   112
The River Esk   120
The Weardale Way   124
Across the Pennines   132
The Lancaster Canal   140

Wales   **148**
The Wye Valley Walk   150
The Montgomery Canal   160
The Swansea and Neath Canals   164
The Morfa Mawddach Trail   168

Scotland   **170**
The River Spey   172
The Crinan Canal   176
The River Dee   178
The Union Canal   182
The River Tweed   186

Acknowledgements   192

Map and List of Walks

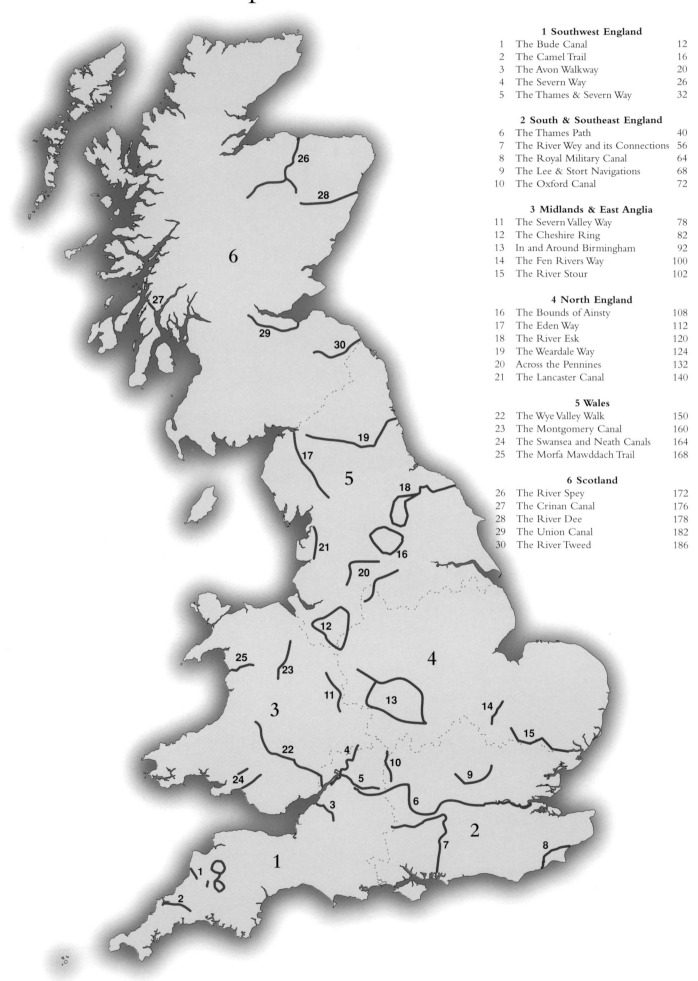

1 Southwest England

1	The Bude Canal	12
2	The Camel Trail	16
3	The Avon Walkway	20
4	The Severn Way	26
5	The Thames & Severn Way	32

2 South & Southeast England

6	The Thames Path	40
7	The River Wey and its Connections	56
8	The Royal Military Canal	64
9	The Lee & Stort Navigations	68
10	The Oxford Canal	72

3 Midlands & East Anglia

11	The Severn Valley Way	78
12	The Cheshire Ring	82
13	In and Around Birmingham	92
14	The Fen Rivers Way	100
15	The River Stour	102

4 North England

16	The Bounds of Ainsty	108
17	The Eden Way	112
18	The River Esk	120
19	The Weardale Way	124
20	Across the Pennines	132
21	The Lancaster Canal	140

5 Wales

22	The Wye Valley Walk	150
23	The Montgomery Canal	160
24	The Swansea and Neath Canals	164
25	The Morfa Mawddach Trail	168

6 Scotland

26	The River Spey	172
27	The Crinan Canal	176
28	The River Dee	178
29	The Union Canal	182
30	The River Tweed	186

Riverdance

Introduction by David Bellamy

AT THE HEART of every green landscape is a river that carries the sweet waters of life down towards the sea. Like all living things, a river passes through four stages of existence, birth, youth, maturity and old age. Springs, the first pulse of life, are among the most hallowed of places; holy, healing places where you may still drink water untainted even by the twentieth century. Rushing torrents, tumbling waterfalls and gurgling trout streams, the home of dippers and the spawning ground of river-run salmon, are the marks of ebullient youth. Kingfisher and heron patrol the swollen, but more tranquil, waters of maturity, where bridges span waterways that since the days of the Romans have acted as barriers to advance and attack. The majestic flood of memories that denotes old age is contained by reed-fringed meanders that slow the river's flow through the water meadows and flowery wetlands of its floodplains. And down the ages, shrines, forts, villages, castles, palaces, cathedrals, mills and manufactories have been built within our rivers' aegis. No wonder they have been an inspiration for artists, poets and writers.

Likewise our canals, the networkshop of the industrial revolution, were born to brass bands and civic celebration. In their youth they linked the corners of the nation with a system of transport for both muck and brass. Hard working in their maturity, they served the dark satanic mills that besmirched human lives and living landscapes, silver ribbons of hope for so much aquatic life. Sadly, forgotten in old age, some have passed away, most without jobs to do, without lock keepers, without anything to keep them in working order.

Old mills and the towpath on the Rochdale canal at Clegg Hall, near Milnrow.

Sadly too, few if any of our rivers survive in pristine state, and in places they are polluted, enriched and tamed out of all recognition. But the good news is that we are at last coming to our senses and many of our rivers and canals are being put back into more natural working order, ready to service the wildlife and the people of their catchment once again.

Otters and osprey, fingers on the pulse of a healthy, fishful river, and narrow boats, now plying a new trade, are making a comeback as NGOs, enthusiasts, river authorities, water companies, sport fishers and local government work together to clean up our act.

The green renaissance is at last getting under way and nowhere is it more obvious or important than in our waterways. So this wonderful and useful book could not be more timely. Here is a water wanderway that will allow you to steep yourself in all aspects of Britain's fantastic heritage, both natural and man made. Whether it is spring, summer, autumn or winter, there is always something to see by a waterway, an ever-changing panoply of interest. This is a book to be owned, read and enjoyed as a constant companion to homespun adventure. So, get yourself a pair of walking boots — and as you walk be careful where you put them. Wild flowers have rights, too.

David Bellamy
Bedburn 1996

The Gloucester & Sharpness Canal runs close to the east bank of the River Severn at Sharpness. In the distance are the scant remains of the Severn Railway Bridge, damaged beyond repair in 1960 when two barges hit one of the piers. The Severn Way passes the site.

Southwest England

The Bude Canal   12 – 15

The Camel Trail   16 – 19

The Avon Walkway   20 – 25

The Severn Way   26 – 31

The Thames & Severn Way   32 – 37

The Camel Estuary, looking towards Padstow

The Bude Canal

BUDE TO MARHAMCHURCH AND AROUND THE CANAL
12 MILES/20KM

THE walks described in this chapter are largely along the surviving towing paths of the once-extensive Bude canal system. Since its closure in the late 19th century, much of the canal and its associated works have disappeared. Some sections are now on privately owned land and well away from public footpaths and rights of way. As exploration is impossible by public transport, it is recommended that a car be used to link together the walkable sections and to visit other sites of interest.

The towing paths that are now in public use are well marked and in good condition and, with a car, most of the canal can be explored in one day. The changing nature of the landscape is particularly appealing, with many fine views over rolling farmland. By its very nature, and the elusive quality of its surviving elements, the Bude Canal offers a unique insight, in a remarkably rural setting, into early 19th-century attitudes towards industrialisation. It is a fragmented but fascinating walk.

WALKING GUIDES
Stalley, Jon, *The Bude Canal Trail* (North Cornwall District Council)
Young, Bill, *Walking Along the Old Bude Canal* This is full of information but the title is misleading, as walking along the Bude Canal is something that can, in reality, be done only occasionally.
A number of leaflets and guides to walks in the area are available at Bude Tourist Information Centre.

OS MAP
Landranger 190

LINKS
The Cornwall Coast Path passes through Bude.

The Bude canal network was one of the most remote and obscure in Britain. In 1774 plans were drawn up for a canal linking Bude and Plymouth, one of a number of ambitious schemes designed to link the north and south coasts of Cornwall and Devon. None came to fruition, but a simpler plan, to build a canal from Bude to Holsworthy and Launceston, was authorised by Parliament in 1819 and work began immediately under the control of the engineer James Green. Four years later the 35-mile network was complete. Complex and idiosyncratic, and designed for use only by 20ft-long tub boats that were horse-drawn in trains, the canal was created largely to transport sea sand, an important fertiliser at the time, to remote inland farms. Coal, building materials and farm supplies and produce were also carried, but sea sand remained the primary cargo throughout the canal's existence. Within six miles of Bude, the canal rose to 325ft above the sea, the changes in level being achieved by a series of six inclined planes, up which the loaded tub boats were dragged on wheels by clanking, and frequently breaking, chains driven by various forms of water or steam power. Despite chronic and long-lasting technical and financial difficulties, the canal continued in use until 1891.

Bude to Marhamchurch

BUDE TO MARHAMCHURCH
AND BACK

About 5 miles/8km
OS Landranger 190
*Start by the sea lock and lifeboat station in Bude
(grid reference 203 065)*

Originally a little fishing hamlet in the shadow of Stratton, Bude was really created by the canal and its harbour. From the 1820s ships of up to 300 tons could enter the canal basin through the sea lock at high tide, and the town grew rapidly, partly through industry and commerce and partly as a resort. Late Georgian cottages, Victorian villas and grand hotels determined the nature of the town, which continued to develop even more quickly after the arrival of the railway in 1898. Thundering Atlantic rollers and three miles of sandy beaches up to a mile in depth at low tide have given the town a lasting appeal, even though its makers, the canal and the railway, have gone. The sea lock survives, and at high tide large yachts and fishing boats can still find shelter in the extensive canal basin.

The lock stands high above the sandy beach and offers good views across the estuary and out to sea. Sections of old narrow-gauge railway can be seen on the beach, the remains of a once-considerable network used to bring the sand up to the quay. Here it was loaded into the tub boats prior to the long journey inland. At first quite large barges carried the sand inland for a couple of miles to Helebridge, where it was transshipped into the tub boats, but this was soon found to be unnecessarily complicated and the tub boats then came all the way to the basin. This, however, explains why as far as Helebridge the canal was built to a larger dimension and was equipped with wide locks. The quays and wharves still stretch far inland, but many of the buildings that once lined them have gone. One survivor houses the local museum, which tells the history of the canal, the town and local shipwrecks. There are also plenty of tea shops and cafés nearby. At the head of the basin is a road bridge and from here the towing path leads inland on the eastern side away from the town, past warehouses and the Tourist Information Centre.

As the path leaves the town behind there is an area of low-lying land, a legacy of the canal's construction that is now the Bude Marshes Local Nature Reserve. Canal and river run close together along the valley, sheltered by hedgerows. Across the valley is the overgrown embankment of the former railway. At Rodd's Bridge the towing path changes sides and then there is the first of the two large locks, well built from stone but now without their gates. Next is Whalesborough Lock and above it river and canal came briefly together, with a large spill weir to take the excess water into the river. Ahead are the hills and the white houses of Marhamchurch.

This is Helebridge and it is now necessary to cross the busy A39. Take great care. Turn left, take the fine old stone bridge across the canal and join the path again beyond the A39 road. Beneath the bridge, notice the grooves cut into the stone by the towing ropes. The towing path is on the northern side of the tree-lined basin. This was a busy place, where the large barges that had come up from Bude transshipped their 20-ton loads of sand into the smaller tub boats. A restored barge repair workshop, built in stone in the style typical of the canal, is an echo of those days. There is a small car park, with picnic tables.

Follow the towing path through the trees and soon the watered section of the canal comes to an end. This is the foot of the Marhamchurch inclined plane, the first of the six on the network. The chains that dragged the tub boats up the 836ft of the steep incline were powered by a huge waterwheel at the top. However, nothing remains to be seen. The actual track of the incline has disappeared beneath a pumping station and back gardens but parallel to it there is a broad path that climbs up to the village. Marhamchurch is a pretty village of colour-washed and stone houses with flowery gardens. At its heart, with fine views out to sea, is St Marwenne's Church, big and barrel-vaulted. It has a 17th-century pulpit, a carved coat of arms of Charles II and the floor is delightfully patterned with squares of slate set on end. The church has a strong bell-ringing tradition, evidenced by a display of certificates and awards.

For an alternative route back to Bude, retrace your steps down the track beside the incline and then, at the pumping station, turn right. The building on the left is the old foundry, where most of the ironwork for the canal was made, and further on, to the right, is Hele Mill. The footpath turns left before the mill, leads up the hill and across the field and then joins the old road. Pass the houses and turn left

into a lane that leads down to the A39. Cross this busy main road with great care and walk down the access road for the sewage works. The path goes to the left of the works and then joins the old railway embankment for a while before steps take it down into the valley and then along to join the minor road that leads to Rodd's Bridge. Turn left, rejoin the canal towing path and follow it back to Bude.

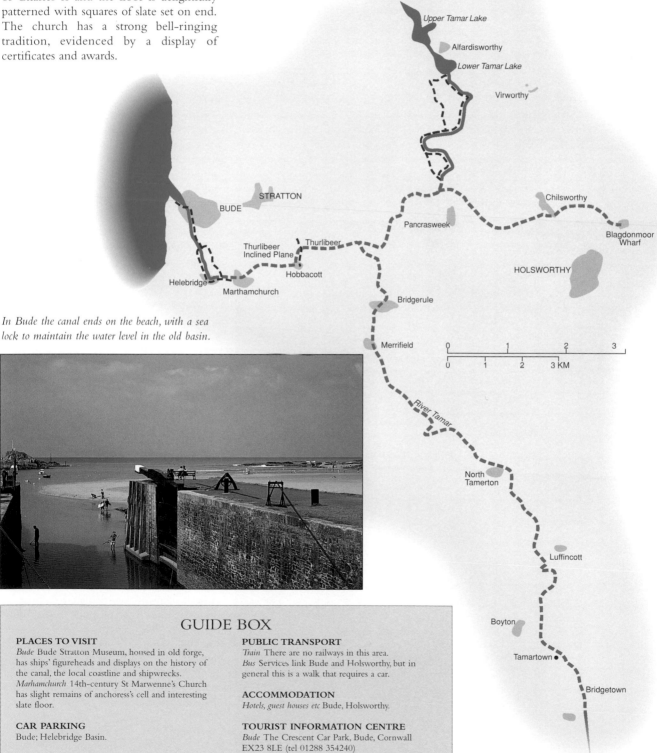

In Bude the canal ends on the beach, with a sea lock to maintain the water level in the old basin.

GUIDE BOX

PLACES TO VISIT
Bude Bude Stratton Museum, housed in old forge, has ships' figureheads and displays on the history of the canal, the local coastline and shipwrecks.
Marhamchurch 14th-century St Marwenne's Church has slight remains of anchoress's cell and interesting slate floor.

CAR PARKING
Bude; Helebridge Basin.

PUBLIC TRANSPORT
Train There are no railways in this area.
Bus Services link Bude and Holsworthy, but in general this is a walk that requires a car.

ACCOMMODATION
Hotels, guest houses etc Bude, Holsworthy.

TOURIST INFORMATION CENTRE
Bude The Crescent Car Park, Bude, Cornwall EX23 8LE (tel 01288 354240)

THE TAMAR LAKES AND THE VIRWORTHY BRANCH

About 6 miles / 10km
OS Landranger 190
*Start at the car park at the southern end
of Lower Tamar Lake
(grid reference 294 108)*

The 70-acre Lower Tamar Lake was created by the Bude Harbour and Canal Company to supply water to the Holsworthy and Launceston sections. The narrow canal that ran from the lake to join the Holsworthy branch to the east of Red Post was built as a navigable feeder. A wharf was built near Virworthy for the sand trade. When the canal was closed, the lake was retained as a reservoir, and it remained in use until 1971 when the larger Upper Tamar Lake was created. The Lower Lake is now a nature reserve popular with coarse fishermen, while the Upper Lake also offers fishing and has a sailing club. A footpath links the two lakes. Another footpath, recently re-established and likely to be extended, follows the towing path southwards from the Lower Lake.

From the car park take the well-marked path along the top of the dam, cross the bridge over the spill weir and join the towing path by the head of the feeder canal. The path is wide and well maintained and follows the meandering canal southwards. There is water in it, but the narrow channel is often overgrown and much loved by dragonflies. A bridge carrying a minor road marks the former head of navigation and beyond it is the wide expanse of Virworthy Wharf, restored sufficiently to give an idea of its appearance at the height of the sand trade. A former warehouse now houses a small museum.

From here the canal wanders southwards along a route across the fields that was determined by the need to follow a level contour line. It is a small waterway, with the bridges just wide enough to allow the passage of the tub boats, and its route has a secret intimacy that is particularly enjoyable. Initially it follows the Tamar but soon loops away into the woods and fields of rural Devon, its progress marked by the series of little bridges carrying minor roads or access tracks for farmers.

At the moment, the re-opened towing path ends at Brendon Bridge, on the minor road between Puckland and Lana, but there are plans to extend it further south. Walkers can now retrace their steps along the towing path to the lake or, for an alternative route that offers a quiet exploration of the remote farmlands of the

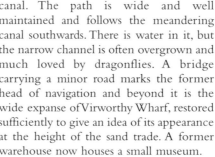

GUIDE BOX

PLACES TO VISIT
Virworthy Wharf Small museum.

CAR PARKING
There is ample car parking at the Tamar Lakes; cars can occasionally be left for a short time at sites of canal interest.

PUBLIC TRANSPORT
Train There are no railways in this area.
Bus There are services between Bude, Holsworthy and Launceston, but in general this is a walk that requires a car.

ACCOMMODATION
Hotels, guest houses etc Bude, Holsworthy, Launceston.

TOURIST INFORMATION CENTRES
Bude The Crescent Car Park, Bude, Cornwall EX23 8LE (tel 01288 354240)
Launceston Market House Arcade, Market Street, Launceston, Cornwall PL15 8EP (tel 01566 772321)

Devon-Cornwall border, they can leave the canal at Brendon Bridge, and follow the minor road northwards to Puckland, where it crosses the canal, and then continue on the minor road to Broomhill. Turn left here, onto a road that drops into the valley to cross the canal and the Tamar before climbing back up to Dexbeer. Continue along this road, bearing left at a junction and then shortly afterwards bear right at a larger one. After about ⅓ mile, turn right onto the road that leads back to the Lower Tamar Lake car park.

THE THURLIBEER INCLINED PLANE

About 1 mile / 1.5km
OS Landranger 190
*Start at the lay-by on the south side of the
A3072, just over 1 mile east of Stratton
(grid reference 244 052)*

The largest, and by far the most dramatic of the Bude Canal's six inclined planes was that built to carry the tub boats up the Hobbacott Downs at Thurlibeer. This, the second largest in Britain (the largest also being in Cornwall, at Morwellham), was 935ft long and raised the boats 225ft. Unlike the other waterwheel-powered Bude Canal planes, this one was built according to a plan developed by the American engineer Robert Fulton. Two shafts 225ft deep were sunk vertically from the top of the plane and each was equipped with a giant bucket, designed to hold 15 tons of water. When a bucket was full, it was lowered down the shaft. Its descending weight dragged up the iron rails on the plane a wheeled tub boat that was filled with about 5 tons of sand and attached to an endless chain. When the bucket of water reached the bottom of the shaft, and the

At Helebridge an old stone bridge crosses the canal, which remains full of water to the base of the Marhamchurch inclined plane, nearby.

tub boat the higher level of the canal, the water was released to flow along an adit into the canal at the lower level. The empty bucket was then hauled up to the top again and the whole process repeated. The weight of the empty tub boats descending the plane also acted as a counterbalance. The operation of this awesome machine was fraught with difficulties for the chains broke continuously, allowing loaded buckets to fall unchecked down the shafts and boats to rush headlong back down the plane and smash into others waiting at the bottom. At the same time, flailing sections of broken chain damaged other parts of the equipment and threatened the lives of those destined to operate it. Despite all this, and the serious financial problems that hindered the repairs, the plane remained in use for many years. A steam engine was installed to help operations but was rarely used because of its high running costs.

The tree-lined track of the plane rises steeply up the down, some canal buildings survive by the site of the basin at the top, and at the bottom are remains of the division of the canal into two – for the rising boats on the right and the descending ones on the left. All of this is on private land and there is no right of way along the track of the plane. However, a clearly marked footpath that starts from the lay-by on the A3072 runs initially down a track towards the top of the plane and then swings to the left to skirt the site of the basin and cross the bed of the canal. This allows adequate views of the surviving canal buildings and the top of the plane. It then becomes a field path that drops steeply into the valley, crosses a small stream and then climbs up the other side to Hobbacott Farm, on the minor road between Marhamchurch and Buttsbear Cross. The route of the path is roughly parallel to, but at a distance from, the inclined plane, whose lasting impact on the landscape can easily be seen. The steep line of the plane can also be seen clearly from a point on the minor road about 200yds west of Hobbacott Farm, shortly before a junction. There is nowhere to park a car on this road, other than briefly to admire the plane, so it is best to walk from the lay-by on the A3072 and then retrace the route.

OTHER BUDE CANAL SITES
OS Landranger 190

Realistically, the only way to explore the other surviving traces of the Bude Canal that are accessible to the public is by car.

There are several sites of interest in the Holsworthy area. A public footpath follows the route of the canal eastwards for about ½ mile from Chilsworthy, along the Chilsworthy embankment and across the River Deer, to the point where it meets another minor road by North Hogspark (grid reference 332 059 to 342 064). At Stanbury Wharf, on the A388 just north of

The line of the Thurlibeer inclined plane up the Hobbacott Downs can be clearly seen. An old stone warehouse stands at the top.

Holsworthy, the old warehouse, in typical Bude Canal style, survives along with traces of the basin and the wharf cottage, which is now a farm. For 60 years this wharf enabled Holsworthy to call itself a port, with the canal being the primary carrier to the town from Bude until the arrival of the railway. The buildings are private and parking is difficult (grid reference 349 051).

The long branch southwards towards Launceston was the first part of the canal to be completed, even though it stopped at Druxton Wharf, about 3 miles north of Launceston. The branch started near Red Post, just over 1 mile east of Thurlibeer, and then wandered southwards along the Tamar Valley, via Bridgerule, Tamerton and Boyton. There were three inclined planes, at Merrifield, Tamerton and Werrington, but their remains are on private land. The track of the Werrington plane, however, crosses a minor road that runs beside the Tamar between Tamartown and Bridgetown (grid reference 338 905). Other traces can be found, including bridges, buildings and lengths of canalbed, but access is restricted and local knowledge is required. In effect, the Launceston branch has more or less entirely disappeared.

The Camel Trail

PADSTOW TO POLEY'S BRIDGE
17 MILES/27KM

SUITABLE for walking, cycling and horse-riding, the Camel Trail is an easy and largely level route along 18 miles of former railway tracks that used to link Padstow, Wadebridge, Bodmin and Wenfordbridge. The Trail is formed of three main sections of about equal length, each of which is quite distinct in its character, its landscape and its historical background. First is the section from Padstow to Wadebridge. This is an elevated route along the south side of the beautiful tidal estuary of the Camel, built on the trackbed of the last few miles of the London & North Western Railway's north Cornwall line, which was completed in 1899. Next is the section from Wadebridge to Bodmin, through the winding and steeply wooded valley of the Camel along the route of one of Britain's earliest passenger-carrying railways, the Bodmin & Wadebridge, opened in September 1834. The third section is a gentle climb in beautiful woodland to Poley's Bridge, following the line of the mineral railway built to serve the claypits of Wenfordbridge.

It is an enjoyable and highly varied walk with Wadebridge or Bodmin making good places to break a two-day journey. However, the surface is very good and on a bicycle the whole route can easily be covered in a day. All kinds of cycles, as well as trailers to carry small children, can be hired in Padstow, Wadebridge and Bodmin.

WALKING GUIDES
The route is covered in a number of local guides and maps, but particularly good is the *Friendly Guide to the River Camel and the Camel Trail*, available in local Tourist Information Centres.

OS MAP
Landranger 200

LINKS
There are no links with other paths, but the upper waters of the Camel can be explored on an 8-mile footpath, the Camelford Way, between St Breward, 2 miles north of Poley's Bridge on the edge of Bodmin Moor, and Camelford. Cycling is not allowed on this path.

Padstow to Wadebridge

PADSTOW TO WADEBRIDGE
About 5¹/₂ miles/9km
OS Landranger 200
Start by the platform of the former station at Padstow, to the south of the harbour
(grid reference 921 749)

Former railways make wonderful tracks for walkers and cyclists, and this is one of the best. Padstow is a lively resort town of narrow streets, old houses and sheltered gardens with a traditional harbour, plenty of shops and restaurants, a fine medieval church and Prideaux Place, a grand Elizabethan mansion. During summer weekends the place is packed, the numbers swelled by the many cyclists using the Camel Trail. The start of the Trail is in the busy car park by the old station and the Shipwreck Museum with its turbulent lobster tanks. It is a muddle of meandering cars, cyclists and families out with prams, but it is all quickly left behind as the Trail sets off along the southern shore of the estuary. High on its embankment, the Trail immediately offers the first of a continuous series of splendid panoramic views out across the wide Camel Estuary, exciting at all states of tide. Across the water is Rock, linked to Padstow by a passenger ferry, and then there are miles of lovely hilly landscape, scattered farms and old houses half hidden by trees. It is a mecca for birds, especially at low tide when the waders pick their way over the sand bars. Breaking the panorama are short cuttings, with steep rocky walls covered in wild flowers and ferns, and sometimes overhung by bushes and trees. One such cutting leads to Little Petherick Bridge, three great spans of rusty iron girders striding over a creek. Instead of pounding locomotives hauling the Atlantic Coast Express on the last stage of its long journey from Waterloo, the bridge, in gentle retirement, now carries streams of cyclists quietly pushing their machines.

There are plenty of places where there are benches for a rest, a picnic and a look at the view. Sometimes in the summer an old-fashioned, cycle-mounted ice cream stall offers welcome refreshment. To the south are views over muddy creeks

Padstow, in the distance, is the start of a delightful walk alongside the tidal estuary of the Camel.

PADSTO

GUIDE BOX

PLACES TO VISIT
Padstow May Day 'Obby 'Oss procession. Tropical Bird Gardens. Shipwreck Museum – by start of Trail; Prideaux Place – Elizabethan mansion and 20 acres of deer park.

CAR PARKING
Padstow (old station); Wadebridge (off Eddystone Road in industrial section west of town centre).

PUBLIC TRANSPORT
Bus Services between Padstow, Wadebridge and Bodmin.
Train The Bodmin & Wenford Railway, a preserved steam line, operates limited services between Bodmin and the Trail at Boscarne Junction.

ACCOMMODATION
Hotels, guest houses etc Padstow, Wadebridge.

TOURIST INFORMATION CENTRES
Padstow The Red Brick Building, North Quay, Padstow, Cornwall PL28 8AF (tel 01841 533449)
Wadebridge Town Hall, Wadebridge, Cornwall PL27 7AQ (tel 01208 813725)

In summer an old-fashioned ice cream seller offers a welcome break for walkers and cyclists on the Camel Trail near Wadebridge.

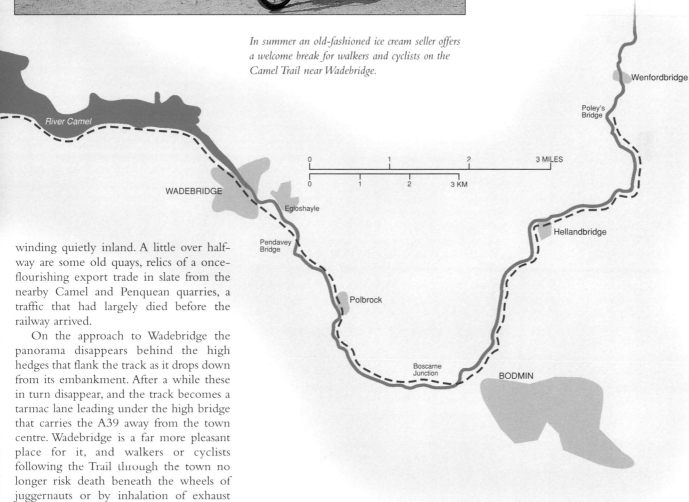

winding quietly inland. A little over half-way are some old quays, relics of a once-flourishing export trade in slate from the nearby Camel and Penquean quarries, a traffic that had largely died before the railway arrived.

On the approach to Wadebridge the panorama disappears behind the high hedges that flank the track as it drops down from its embankment. After a while these in turn disappear, and the track becomes a tarmac lane leading under the high bridge that carries the A39 away from the town centre. Wadebridge is a far more pleasant place for it, and walkers or cyclists following the Trail through the town no longer risk death beneath the wheels of juggernauts or by inhalation of exhaust fumes. The west end of the town is a kind of little industrial estate that has become home to a number of cycle hire bases, and this is where many people choose to start.

WADEBRIDGE TO DUNMERE JUNCTION (BODMIN)
About 5¹/₂ miles/9km
OS Landranger 200
Start at car park off Eddystone Road
(grid reference 991 724)

The centre of Wadebridge is compact, and close at hand are the 16 stone arches of the much rebuilt medieval bridge, whose construction was originally funded by wealthy farmers and wool merchants. The bridge forms an important visual barrier between the wide waters of the estuary and the emergence of the Camel as a regular river, twisting its way through the fields to the east of the town. The Trail runs parallel to the river through the town, passes the former railway station, now a day centre for the elderly dedicated to the memory of Sir John Betjeman, and then exits through modern suburbia to join the winding track of the old Bodmin & Wadebridge Railway. Opened before Victoria came to the throne, this was built to carry sea sand inland to fertilise the acid soils of Bodmin Moor, and to transport De Lank granite and china clay back down to Wadebridge harbour for export. It also carried passengers, thus securing its important place in railway history.

The Trail is immediately different, initially with views across the fields towards Egloshayle which, in the 18th century, was Wadebridge's smartest suburb. It then enters the woods that flank the river all the way to Bodmin. At Wadebridge Junction, just before Pendavey Bridge carries the track over the Camel, the trackbed of the former London & South Western main line sweeps away to the north along the valley of the River Allen to start its long tour of north Cornwall, via Delabole and Launceston. Much of this route is private and cannot easily be explored on foot or by bicycle.

Climbing gently most of the way, the Trail follows a delightful path through the woods, with the sparkling waters of the river close alongside, but at a lower level. Richly decorated with wild flowers and crossed by woodland footpaths, it is a hidden route, largely inaccessible by car and much used by horse-riders as well as

GUIDE BOX

PLACES TO VISIT
Bodmin Duke of Cornwall's Light Infantry Museum – armoury, medals, uniforms. Church of St Petroc – 15th-century saint's casket. Bodmin Farm Park – traditional farm animals.
Lanhydrock 17th-century house, 2¹/₂ miles southeast of Bodmin, rebuilt in grandiose style after fire in 1881; formal gardens, woodland..
Pencarrow 1¹/₂ miles west of Hellandbridge, elegant Georgian mansion, good paintings, furniture, china; palm house, ice house.
Camelford Museum of Historic Cycling, in old station building. North Cornwall Museum – local history and industries, including quarrying.

CAR PARKING
Wadebridge; Grogley Halt; Bodmin; Poley's Bridge; some of the roads that cross the Camel Trail offer limited parking but in general the route of the Trail is away from public roads.

PUBLIC TRANSPORT
Bus Services between Wadebridge, Bodmin and Camelford.
Train The Bodmin & Wenford Railway preserved steam line operates limited services between Bodmin and the Trail at Boscarne Junction.

ACCOMMODATION
Hotels, guest houses etc Wadebridge, Bodmin, Camelford.

TOURIST INFORMATION CENTRES
Wadebridge Town Hall, Wadebridge, Cornwall PL27 7AQ (tel 01208 813725)
Bodmin Shire House, Mount Folly Square, Bodmin, Cornwall PL31 2DQ (tel 01208 76616)
Camelford North Cornwall Museum, The Clease, Camelford, Cornwall PL32 9PL (tel 01840 212954)

cyclists and walkers. The appeal is universal, to every type of walker and cyclist, and to all age groups. Tough-looking mountain bikers, in brightly coloured tight-fitting costumes, take their time among the family parties wandering along with dogs and push chairs. Single platforms mark the sites of former halts, buried in the woods, and these make good places for a rest or a picnic. At one of these, Grogley Halt, where there is now a small car park, there was a branch line to serve a once-busy tin mine, to the south of Ruthernbridge. Just to the west of Nanstallon Halt, those in need of a cup of tea or an ice cream can stop at the Camel Trail Tea Gardens.

Shortly after this, walkers may be surprised by the sight of railway tracks and, from time to time, real trains. This is Boscarne Junction, reopened as a station in 1996 by the Bodmin & Wenford Railway to serve the Camel Trail. Trains from here run to Bodmin General Station, the Railway's headquarters, and there are services from there to Bodmin Parkway Station, on the main Paddington-to-Penzance line. It was this link, built by the Great Western Railway in the late 1880s, that finally ended the Bodmin & Wadebridge's long decades of isolation from the rest of Britain's railways.

Near Egloshayle the Camel Trail winds through the woods beside the river, a section popular with walkers, cyclists and horse-riders.

Next comes Dunmere Junction. Here, the right-hand path leads to Scarlet's Well and into Bodmin, ending by the old gaol, while the left marks the start of the third part of the journey, along the former clay line to Wenfordbridge.

DUNMERE JUNCTION (BODMIN) TO POLEY'S BRIDGE
About 6 miles/9km
OS Landranger 200
Start at Dunmere Junction, where the Camel Trail leaves the line to Bodmin (grid reference 044 675)

Once again there is an immediate change in the nature of the Camel Trail. Narrow, winding and now climbing more perceptibly, it is the perfect woodland route, high above the fast-flowing river that dances away through the trees. Always in the trees, it is a route marked by dappled light and rich displays of wild flowers, especially in the spring. The river, well below, is always accessible, rarely the case between Wadebridge and Bodmin. It is hard to believe that this delightful, twisting and completely secret route was in

use as a mineral railway as recently as the early 1980s, but there are signs – the typical cast-concrete gate and boundary posts, for instance, the tracks still in place where it bursts suddenly from the woods to cross roads, and the field gates that carry notices declaring 'Penalty for Not Closing the Gate £2'. Occasionally there are clearings with cottages and old-fashioned gardens, and at Hellandbridge, a tiny hamlet with a medieval bridge, the track emerges suddenly between two rows of houses, crosses a minor road, and then vanishes just as quickly back into the woods.

This journey of delights comes to a rather abrupt end at Poley's Bridge, where there is a large car park with a picnic site. Across the road are the sheds of the extensive English China Clay complex which stretches away beside the river towards Wenfordbridge, the line's original terminus. It was the clay and granite from this region that inspired the building of the railway in the first place, and it is still an important production centre, making, among other things, china clay powder for the paper industry. Delightful though this part of the Trail is, it might be better if it

The trail follows the old railway's secret route through the woods. Near Hellandbridge an old stone house sits in its pretty cottage garden.

were still a railway, sparing the little lanes of this remote region the impact of hundreds of thundering lorries.

THE CAMELFORD WAY

The road east and then northwards from the Poley's Bridge car park leads past the clay works towards St Breward, passing under an old bridge that used to carry the inclined railway link with the De Lank Granite quarry. South of St Breward is a path leading down to cross the river. This joins the Camelford Way, bypassing the village. Alternatively, carry on through the village to Churchtown and, where the road turns sharp left towards the river, go straight on and join the Camelford Way, which follows the river valley northwards to Camelford. The route explores the contrasting landscape of wooded river valley and moorland and passes the remote church at Advent and the Devil's Jump, a 50ft granite gorge jumped by the devil as he fled from Cornwall under the threat of being baked in a pasty.

The Avon Walkway

THE Avon Walkway is a 30-mile waymarked long distance path that follows the River Avon through contrasting landscapes from Pill, close to its confluence with the River Severn, to the Dundas Aqueduct southeast of Bath. En route it takes in the dramatic Avon Gorge and Brunel's famous suspension bridge, the historic Bristol Docks and Brunel's restored SS *Great Britain*, the architectural splendour of Georgian Bath, where the Walkway links with the Kennet & Avon Canal towpath, the water meadows of the Avon Valley and Rennie's classical Dundas Aqueduct.

PILL TO BRISTOL
About 8 miles/13km
OS Landranger 172
Start at car park in Pill
(grid reference 523 762)

The Avon Walkway starts at a car park on the south bank of the River Avon in the unprepossessing village of Pill, overlooked by the Avon motorway bridge and the north bank village of Shirehampton. Following the river bank eastwards for a short distance, the path veers inland around a hospital, then rejoins its riverside route at Chapel Pill Farm. The disued Bristol-to-Portishead railway line now keeps close company with the path on its route through the wooded Avon Gorge, paralleled on the north bank by the Portway. Clinging to the river bank, the path soon skirts the lower slopes of Leigh Woods, an area of leafy tranquillity set close to the city of Bristol. The woods are in the care of the National Trust who, in association with the Nature Conservancy

WALKING GUIDE
The Avon Walkway, a small leaflet originally published by the defunct Avon County Council and currently out of print may be re-issued by Bristol City Council.

OS MAP
Landranger 172

LINKS
The Bristol and Bath Railway Path shares part of the route between Keynsham and Bath. The Avon Cycleway meets the the Avon Walkway at Saltford. The Cotswold Way joins the walkway on the western outskirts of Bath.

Council, have designated this the Avon Gorge National Nature Reserve. A mixture of coniferous and broadleaf trees provides a protected habitat for many species of birds, as well as badgers, squirrels and foxes. Waymarked nature trails run through the woods, one of which links with the Avon Walkway. Clifton Down overlooks the gorge from a clifftop position on the north bank.

Soon the path passes directly beneath the graceful span of the Clifton Suspension Bridge. Various designs were submitted for the proposed bridge in 1829, but it was Isambard Kingdom Brunel's that was

The Avon Gorge, Brunel's Clifton Suspension Bridge and the entrance to Bristol Harbour.

finally chosen. Construction started in 1836, only to cease in 1840 when the project ran out of funds. Work eventually restarted in 1861 but in the meantime Brunel had died and he never saw his design translated into the bridge that, today, is one of his finest memorials. Completed in 1864, at a height of 250ft above high-water level and with a single span of 702ft, it incorporated iron chains from the old Hungerford Suspension Bridge in London.

A short distance up river from the suspension bridge the Avon Walkway runs along the northwestern outskirts of the Ashton Court Estate. The house, dating in part from the 15th century, and owned for centuries by merchants of Bristol, is one of the longest in the region. Set amidst wooded parkland, it is open to the public.

The Walkway now parts company with the disused Bristol-to-Portishead railway line and dives under a busy dual carriageway before entering Bristol Docks. Here, in the heart of Bristol, are the visible reminders of the city's prosperous sea-going past. Its growth as a port on the River Avon began in the 10th century and continued well into the 20th century. In 1497 John Cabot set sail from Bristol to

GUIDE BOX

PLACES TO VISIT
Bristol Harbour Restored SS *Great Britain*, the Bristol Industrial Museum and steam-hauled Bristol Harbour Railway.
Bristol 13th-century cathedral, Arnolfini Gallery, City Art Gallery, 18th-century Theatre Royal, Cabot Tower, Temple Meads Station.
Clifton Clifton Downs, Clifton Suspension Bridge, Bristol Zoo.

CAR PARKING
Pill (car park at start of Avon Walkway); Bristol Harbour; Bristol city centre.

PUBLIC TRANSPORT
Train Station at Bristol Temple Meads.
Bus Bristol-to-Portishead service stops at Pill.

ACCOMMODATION
Hotels, guest houses etc Bristol.
Camping West end of Bristol floating harbour.
Youth hostel YHA International Centre, 14 Narrow Quay, Bristol BS1 4QA.

TOURIST INFORMATION CENTRES
Gordano Welcome Break Services Junction 19 of M5, Portbury, Bristok BS12 9XG (tel 01275 375516)
Bristol St Nicholas Church, St Nicholas Street, Bristol BS1 1UE (tel 0117 926 0767)

discover Newfoundland and in 1552 the Society of Merchant Venturers was founded here. The port was soon importing raw materials from the far-flung corners of the growing British Empire. Today the port is mainly confined to leisure activities and has been much enhanced by the restoration of many of the dockside buildings. Commercial sea-going activities have, in recent years, been transferred to the nearby deeper water ports of Avonmouth and Portishead.

Nearby, in Great Western Dock, is the finely restored SS *Great Britain*. Designed by Isambard Kingdom Brunel, she was launched in 1843 and was the first ship in the world to be propelled solely by screw propulsion. In 1866 she was driven aground in a storm off the Falkland Islands, where she remained until 1970. After a long and arduous sea journey that brought her back to her home port of Bristol on a pontoon, the ship underwent extensive restoration and is now open to the public.

A short distance eastwards, the Bristol Industrial Museum houses a large transport collection with excellent ship and railway models. The adjoining Bristol Harbour Railway originally opened to the quayside in 1866 and the present operation of over half a mile of standard gauge track began in 1978. Steam trains operate on certain days along a harbourside track between Princes and Wapping wharves, overlooking the floating harbour. Passengers are carried in an open wagon and a brake van. The industrial museum also operates the restored steam tug *Mayflower* and a 35-ton steam crane. There are numerous dockside pubs and restaurants.

The Avon Walkway now crosses the swing bridge over the floating harbour, passing the Youth Hostel, the Arnolfini Gallery and the Theatre Royal before reaching Bristol Bridge. The present structure was built in the 18th century on the site of a medieval bridge. From here the path follows the north bank of the floating harbour through Castle Park before crossing the busy Temple Way and threading its way back to the north bank of the river. A short distance to the west is Temple Meads Station, opened in 1840 as the western terminus of Brunel's broad gauge Great Western Railway from Paddington.

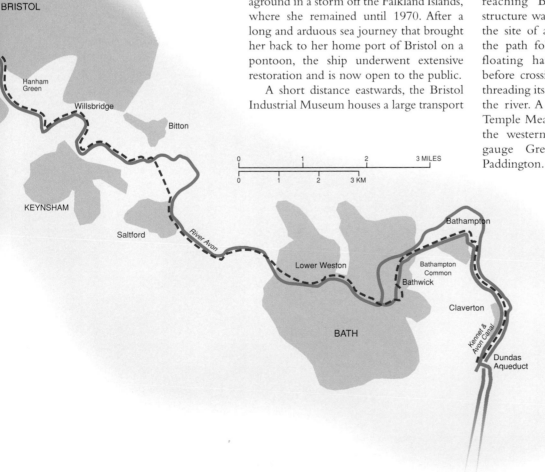

Bristol to Bath

BRISTOL TO KEYNSHAM
About 6 miles/10km
OS Landranger 172
Start at Bristol Temple Meads Station
(grid reference 599 725)

The Avon Walkway rejoins the north bank of the River Avon a short distance east of Brunel's Temple Meads Station. The path follows the riverbank through an industrial area before dipping under the Bristol-to-Paddington railway line and making a short detour through Netham, where it finally rejoins the river. The river now winds a course through the Bristol suburbs of St George, on the north bank, and St Anne's Park, on the south, to Conham. Here, in a bend of the river, is the Conham Country Park, where a ferry operates during summer months to Beese's Tea Gardens on the opposite bank. Within the park are car parks, picnic tables, fishing facilities for the disabled and a signed nature trail.

Reaching the southeastern suburbs of Bristol, the Avon Walkway passes along the wooded north bank of the river, through Hencliffe Wood and Bickley Wood before arriving at Hanham Lock, the upper tidal limit of the Avon. The rural tranquillity of this location is occasionally shattered by the passing of InterCity 125 trains on the Bristol-to-Paddington main line, which runs along the south bank. Situated close to the lock, the first of many between here and – via the Kennet & Avon Canal – Reading, are two riverside pubs, the Old Lock and Weir and the nearby Chequers. A brief diversion up the lane to the north takes the walker to the small 19th-century Christ Church and Hanham Court.

Leaving Hanham Lock and its hostelries behind, the path follows the winding River Avon through water meadows. Passing through Cleeve Wood, the path emerges opposite Keynsham Hams and the large Somerdale chocolate factory, built in 1881 and a notable local landmark. A short detour north from Cleeve Wood is the Avon Wildlife Trust's visitor centre at Willsbridge Mill. At the end of the horseshoe curve is Keynsham Lock, weir and bridge where the Lock Keeper is a popular pub. Keynsham is a useful point from which a return to Bristol can be made by taking a train from the nearby station. The Avon Vale Railway, a short preserved steam line, is located at Bitton, 1 mile northeast of Keynsham.

GUIDE BOX

PLACES TO VISIT
Conham Country Park Riverside location on the eastern outskirts of Bristol, with picnic tables, nature trail and (summer months) ferry.
Hanham Lock Two popular riverside pubs.
Hanham 19th-century Christ Church.
Willsbridge Mill Avon Wildlife Trust's visitor centre.
Keynsham Remains of 12th-century Augustinian Abbey in Abbey Park and 13th-century church.
Bitton Avon Vale Railway, a short preserved steam railway operating both sides of Bitton Station.
Saltford 17th-century church and access to Bristol and Bath Railway Path.
Bath Restored Green Park station now used as a covered car park for Sainsbury's supermarket. See page 24 for other major sites within the city.

CAR PARKING
Conham Country Park; Hanham Lock; Keynsham; Bath (city centre and railway station).

PUBLIC TRANSPORT
Train Stations at Keynsham, Oldfield Park and Bath Spa.
Bus Local services from Bath to Bristol via Saltford and Keynsham.

ACCOMMODATION
Hotels, guest houses etc Bath.
Camping Newton St Loe, on western outskirts of Bath.
Youth hostel Bathwick Hill, Bath BA2 6JZ.

TOURIST INFORMATION CENTRE
Bath Abbey Chambers, Abbey Church Yard, Bath BA1 1LY (tel 01225 462831)

The Chequers public house is attractively located on the north bank of the river near Hanham Lock.

KEYNSHAM TO BATH
About 8 miles / 13km
OS Landranger 172
Start at Keynsham Bridge
(grid reference 659 691)

Keynsham, familiar to adults of a certain age as the address of Radio Luxembourg's Horace Batchelor, is now an expanding dormitory suburb of Bristol. Within Abbey Park are the scanty remains of a 12th-century Augustinian Abbey which was dissolved in the 16th century. The Church of St John the Baptist dates in part from the 13th century, though its tower was rebuilt following an untimely collapse in 1632. The rest of the village is fairly nondescript, consisting mainly of a shopping centre, housing estates and industrial parks. From Keynsham Bridge the Avon Walkway heads east towards Bath, passing through low-lying water meadows for over 1 mile until it reaches the former railway bridge over the river. Here the Walkway temporarily joins company with the Bristol and Bath Railway Path.

The Bristol and Bath Railway Path is a 12½ mile permissive off-highway route, linking Bristol and Bath via Mangotsfield and created for the use of pedestrians, cyclists and wheelchair users. The traffic-free 'greenway' was constructed between 1979 and 1986, following the trackbed of old railway lines that had been closed during the 1960s.

Crossing the river on the old railway bridge, the Walkway and the Railway Path follow the trackbed as it takes a short-cut across a meandering bend of the river. The two paths part company on the outskirts of the village of Saltford, where the Walkway passes along the south bank of the river and the Railway Path continues over the river on an old railway bridge. A short detour in a northeasterly direction along the river bank takes the walker to Saltford Lock and the 18th-century Jolly Sailor pub. Saltford is a busy roadside village but it has the 17th-century Church of St Mary, the Bird in Hand country pub and Saltford Manor House. The latter (not open to the public) is reputed to be one of the oldest inhabited houses in England, with some parts dating back to Norman times.

Proceeding from Saltford, the Avon Walkway is sandwiched for a distance of over 1 mile between the south bank of the river and the Bristol-to-Paddington railway line. Following the river bank, the path veers northward and dives under an old railway bridge that carries the Railway Path. On the opposite bank are the landscaped grounds of Kelston Park. Soon

Keynsham Lock and, in the distance, the large Somerdale chocolate factory, built in 1881.

the outskirts of Bath are reached and the Walkway crosses to the north bank of the river, rejoining the Railway Path for a short distance. The last 2 miles before Bath through the suburbs of Weston Park and a final stretch through Green Park and along the north bank of the Avon leads to Bath Spa railway station. This is a convenient station for those who wish to return to either Keynsham or Bristol by train.

BATH GREEN PARK STATION

This was once the terminus of the Midland Railway's line to Bristol and the Somerset & Dorset Joint Railway's tortuous climb over the Mendips to Evercreech Junction and Bournemouth. The station, originally named Queen Square, was opened in 1870 by the Midland Railway Company and shared by the Somerset & Dorset from 1874. The wooden platforms and elegant single-span glass roof that covered the four tracks remained in use until 1966, when the railway was closed. The building was saved from demolition by Sainsbury's, who restored it to its former glory for use as a covered car park adjacent to their new supermarket.

Bath to Dundas Aqueduct

BATH TO DUNDAS AQUEDUCT
About 6 miles/10km
OS Landranger 172
Start at Bath Spa Station
(grid reference 752 643)

The final short section of the Avon Walkway from Bath to Dundas Aqueduct follows the towpath of the Kennet & Avon Canal from its junction with the River Avon at the bottom of the Widcombe flight of locks. The Walkway crosses from one side of the canal to the other several times during its route through the city. The city of Bath has much to offer the visitor and several days could be well spent visiting its many historic buildings. During the Roman occupation the city developed as a popular spa resort, using the warm springs that naturally occur in the area. Today, the superbly preserved Roman Baths and other remains from that period are one of the most popular tourist attractions in the city. During medieval times Bath became prosperous as an important centre of the wool trade. The present Bath Abbey was built between the late 15th century and the 19th century on the site of a Norman church. Of the other numerous architectural delights in the city, mention must be made of the terraces of grand Georgian houses – the curving Royal Crescent in particular, the Guildhall, the Pump Room and Pulteney Bridge. The latter, spanning the Avon a short distance upstream from the junction with the Kennet & Avon Canal, was built in 1770 to a design by Robert Adams and carries terraces of shops across the river.

The Avon Walkway heads eastwards out of the city, following the towpath past the flight of six locks at Widcombe, through the short Cleveland House Tunnel and alongside Sydney Gardens into the Sydney Gardens Tunnel. The River Avon and the Bristol-to-Paddington railway line soon come alongside the towpath and canal and they keep company for the next straight mile to Bathampton.

The Kennet & Avon Canal was built to link the two cities of London and Bristol. It is made up of three distinct sections: the first was the Kennet Navigation, from Reading to Newbury, completed in 1723; the second section, opened in 1727, was the Avon Navigation from Bath to Hanham; the third and last section was a 57-mile proper canal, designed by John

GUIDE BOX

PLACES TO VISIT
Bath The Roman Baths, one of the best-preserved remains in Europe; Bath Abbey, built on the site of a Norman church; late 18th-century Pump Rooms, where spa water can still be taken; the curving Royal Crescent, built in the 18th century by John Wood the Younger; the Theatre Royal, built as a house in 1720 by Beau Nash; Pulteney Bridge, designed by Robert Adam and completed in 1770, famous for its terraced shops running along both sides.
Bathampton 19th-century Church of St Nicholas and canalside pub.
Claverton Pumping Station John Rennie's unique 1813 waterwheel canal pump back in working order, open to the public occasional weekends.
Claverton Manor A museum of American decorative arts housed in an early 19th-century manor house overlooking Avon Valley.

CAR PARKING
Bath (city centre and railway station).

PUBLIC TRANSPORT
Train Stations at Bath Spa and Freshford.
Bus The service between Bath and Bradford-on-Avon service stops at Limpley Stoke.

ACCOMMODATION
Hotels, guest houses etc Bath.
Youth hostel, Bathwick Hill, Bath, BA2 6JZ.

TOURIST INFORMATION CENTRE
Bath Abbey Chambers, Abbey Church Yard, Bath BA1 1LY (tel 01225 462831)

The Kennet & Avon Canal, the Bath-to-Westbury railway line and the river all keep company along the Avon Valley south of Bath.

John Rennie's beautifully proportioned Dundas Aqueduct, opened in 1804, carries the Kennet & Avon Canal across the wooded Avon Valley.

wooded east bank of the river. Soon the path reaches Claverton Pumping Station, where the waterwheel pump is unique to British canals. It was designed by John Rennie to feed water into this long section of the canal and started operation in 1813. The pumping machinery has now been restored and can be seen in action on selected weekends. The nearby weir on the river is a pleasant spot to rest and watch the trains go by.

At Claverton Bridge a short lane leads to Claverton, a small picturesque village with mellow stone cottages and a 17th-century farmhouse. Claverton Manor, located on the steep hillside above the village, was built in the early 19th century and now houses the American Museum's collection of American decorative arts.

The final stretch of the Avon Walkway continues along the Kennet & Avon towpath in a southerly direction, passing Millbrook swing bridge, and crossing finally to the west bank at Dundas Bridge to end at the magnificent Dundas Aqueduct. The aqueduct was designed and engineered by John Rennie and opened in 1804. Its three beautifully proportioned arches carry the Kennet & Avon Canal across the River Avon. The entrance to the former Somersetshire Coal Canal and a short restored section, now used as a boatyard by the Bath & Dundas Canal Company, is located at the west end of the aqueduct.

Walkers wishing to return by train to Bath, Keynsham or Bristol can follow the canal towpath south to Limpley Stoke and from there follow lanes to the village of Freshford, a distance of about 1½ miles, where there is a riverside inn and a railway station.

Rennie and opened in 1810 to link the two river navigations. It included a number of fine architectural structures, but many physical and financial problems were encountered with the building of the last section and it has been constantly plagued by shortages of water supply. Initially, much of the commercial traffic was coal from the Somerset coalfields but competition from the railway, which ran parallel to the canal, soon brought a sharp decline in business. In 1852 the whole concern was sold to the Great Western Railway who, not surprisingly, made very little effort to maintain its commercial viability. The last remnants of local commercial traffic had ceased by 1930 and ten years later the canal was in a state of dereliction. The last through passage was made in 1951 and the waterway was then subsequently closed. Moves were made by the Kennet & Avon Canal Trust in 1962 to restore the canal completely, and their efforts culminated in an official reopening by the Queen in 1990. Due to the continuing problems

encountered with water supplies, certain lock sections, particularly at Caen Hill and Crofton, have had movement restrictions put on them.

At Bathampton the towpath, here sandwiched between the canal and the river and railway, takes a sharp bend around the base of Bathampton Down, its summit 670ft above sea level. Set on the downs above the wooded slopes are the modern buildings of the University of Bath and the 18-hole Bath Golf Club. The latter is located on the site of Caer Badun, a prehistoric hillfort which includes a section of the ancient Wansdyke. The canal passes through the village of Bathampton, where there is the mainly 19th-century Church of St Nicholas and the canalside George Inn. Continuing southwards, the towpath enters the picturesque and wooded valley of the River Avon, keeping close company with the river, railway and A36 road. After nearly 2 miles Warleigh Manor, an early 19th-century house built in the Tudor style, can be glimpsed on the

THE SOMERSETSHIRE COAL CANAL

Surveyed by John Rennie in the late 18th century, this narrow canal was opened in 1805 and linked the coalfields of North Somerset with the Kennet & Avon Canal. Because of the hilly terrain, the canal was never a success and was eventually sold to the Somerset & Dorset Railway in 1871. To cope with the severe inclines, a boat lift was built at Combe Hay but this was soon replaced by an inclined plane and then a series of locks. Faced with severe competition and a speedier service from the railways, the canal ceased operating in 1898. However, the first short section, from a lock gate close to Dundas Aqueduct on the Kennet & Avon Canal, has been restored and is used as a boatyard.

The Severn Way

THE River Severn is the longest river in the British Isles and has one of the highest tidal variations in the world. The Severn Way is a waymarked long distance path that follows closely the east bank of the river from the historic town of Tewkesbury through the city of Gloucester, with its magnificent cathedral and docks, and past Berkeley Castle, to end at an isolated riverside inn at Shepperdine, a few miles short of the first Severn crossing. The path was officially opened in the spring of 1989 and provides the walker with a fairly level route that takes in the slowly changing vistas and fast-flowing tides of this once-major waterway. Beyond, to the east, lies the sharp ridge of the Cotswold escarpment; to the west, the ancient Forest of Dean.

WALKING GUIDE
Gidman, S H, *Guide to The Severn Way East Bank* (Gloucestershire County Council, 1989).

OS MAPS
Landranger 150, 162

LINK The Thames & Severn Way (see pages 32–37) starts at Upper Framilode.

Tewkesbury to Gloucester

TEWKESBURY TO HAW BRIDGE
About 5 miles/8km
OS Landranger 150, 162
(162 for last ¼ mile only)
Start at the junction of Gloucester Road and Lower Lode Lane, Tewkesbury
(grid reference 885 322)

The Severn Way starts close to the 12th-century Benedictine Abbey of Tewkesbury at the junction of Gloucester Road and Lower Lode Lane. For a short distance, it shares the route with a local walk to the site of the Battle of Tewkesbury, fought in 1471 during the Wars of the Roses. The Way follows a short lane, at first skirting the east bank of the River Avon, until it reaches the floodbank of the Severn at Lower Lode. From here to Deerhurst, a distance of just over 1 mile, the route is along a bridleway on the top of the floodbank, passing en route the weir and lock at Upper Lode. Deerhurst, a small and picturesque village set on rising ground overlooking the river, has a remarkable group of old buildings and is well worth a short detour. The Priory Church of St Mary was founded in the 9th century and restored after the Viking invasions in the 10th century; the Priory House dates mainly from the 14th century but contains some 11th-century elements; Odda's Chapel, part of a medieval farmhouse, is one of the best-preserved Anglo-Saxon churches in the country.

From Deerhurst the Way passes through several fields, passing a sailing club and public house at Chaceley Stock on the opposite bank, still following closely the floodbank of the river as it comes to the riverside Coalhouse Inn near Apperley. Apperley village, a short detour away from the river, has several attractive half-timbered houses, 16th-century Apperley Court, the 19th-century Church of Holy Trinity and the popular Farmers Arms country pub.

The Way now follows the floodbank of the curving river for about 1 mile to Haw Bridge. Here, in 1958, a barge collided with the 19th-century cast-iron bridge and caused such extensive damage that a new one had to be built. To return to Tewkesbury, cross the bridge and follow the footpath along the west bank of the river to Mythe Bridge. Haw Bridge, on the B4213, is also the location for the New Bridge public house and the Haw Bridge Inn.

HAW BRIDGE TO GLOUCESTER
About 8 miles/13km
OS Landranger 162
Start at Haw Bridge
(grid reference 846 278)

Heading south from Haw Bridge, the Severn Way passes through a field before rejoining the floodbank. This is followed for nearly 1 mile to the junction with the derelict Coombe Hill Canal. The canal was opened in 1796 to carry coal for nearby Cheltenham and runs eastward from the river for a distance of nearly 3 miles. Following floods in 1875, it was abandoned and lay derelict for many years. It is now a linear nature reserve owned by the Gloucestershire Trust. After crossing a footbridge over the canal, the Way joins a lane as far as the riverside Red Lion Inn and campsite at Wainlode, dominated by cliffs cut into the river bank and overlooked by nearby Wainlode Hill.

Continuing south from Wainlode, the Way passes through woods before crossing several fields close to the floodbank until it reaches Rodway Lane. This marks the point at which a chain-ferry once operated across the river to Ashleworth Quay and where the old river towpath transferred from the east to the west bank. Ashleworth Quay, tantalisingly close but not now accessible from the east bank, is a secluded riverside village with a superb 15th-century pub. The Severn Way continues along the eastern riverbank south of Rodway Lane for about 1 mile until two former claypits, now a nature reserve, are reached close to the village of Sandhurst. The village is a short detour inland and has several timber-framed buildings and the 14th-century Church of St Lawrence.

The Severn Way continues along the river bank and the old towpath with the tower of Gloucester Cathedral now dominating the view to the south. The surrounding area is often prone to severe flooding during the winter months and care should be taken during this period of the year. At Upper Parting the river splits, its western arm flowing over Maisemore Weir before rejoining the eastern arm at

---

GUIDE BOX

PLACES TO VISIT
Tewkesbury 12th-century Benedictine abbey famous for its vast Norman nave. 13th- and 14th-century inns and many fine 17th- and 18th-century buildings.
Battle of Tewkesbury Site of a 1471 Yorkist victory in the Wars of the Roses, close to A38 on the southern outskirts of the town.
Deerhurst Anglo-Saxon Church of St Mary and Odda's Chapel, close to the Severn Way.
Coombe Hill Canal Nature Reserve A footpath follows both banks of the derelict Coombe Hill Canal, now operated as a linear nature reserve.
Gloucester Historic Roman city, until the 20th century the lowest crossing of the Severn. Dominated by the cathedral that dates back to the 11th century, famous for its 14th-century east window and the tomb of King Edward II. City Museum traces Gloucester's Roman origins.
Gloucester Docks National Waterways Museum and Museum of Advertising & Packaging.

CAR PARKING
Tewkesbury; Gloucester.

PUBLIC TRANSPORT
Train Stations at Ashchurch (for Tewkesbury), Gloucester.
Bus Services between Tewkesbury and Gloucester; limited service between Haw Bridge and Tewkesbury.

ACCOMMODATION
Hotels, guest houses etc Tewkesbury, Gloucester.
Camping Tewkesbury, Wainlode.

TOURIST INFORMATION CENTRES
Tewkesbury 64 Barton Street, Tewkesbury, Gloucestershire GL20 5PX (tel 01684 295027)
Gloucester St Michael's Tower, The Cross, Gloucester GL1 1PD (tel 01452 421188)

The restored Victorian warehouses at Gloucester Docks, northern terminus of the Gloucester & Sharpness Canal. One is now home to the National Waterways Museum.

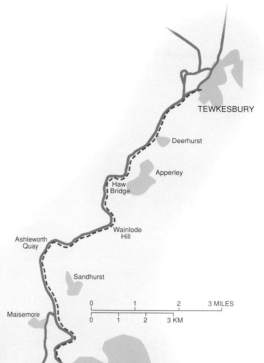

TEWKESBURY

Deerhurst

Apperley

Haw
Bridge

Wainlode
Hill

Ashleworth
Quay

Sandhurst

Maisemore

0   1   2   3 MILES
0   1   2   3 KM

GLOUCESTER

Minsterworth   Hempsted

Elmore
Back

Elmore

Stonebench

Longney

Newnham

River Severn

Epney

Arlingham

Upper
Framilode

Fretherne

Gloucester & Sharpness Canal

Saul

Hock Cliff

Stroudwater Canal

Frampton
on
Severn

River Severn

Wildfowl and
Wetlands Trust

Shepherds
Patch

Purton

Slimbridge

Sharpness

Berkeley

Power
Station

Windbound Inn

Shepperdine

GLOUCESTER DOCKS

The docks form the northern terminal of the Gloucester & Sharpness Canal, which was built to bypass the notoriously dangerous lower reaches of the River Severn. Construction of the 15-mile-long canal began at Gloucester in 1794, but financial shortages called work to a halt after only 5½ miles had been built. However, in 1817 Thomas Telford was asked by the government to make a feasibility study for the completion of the route and on his recommendations the government then provided sufficient funds for the work to be finished. When opened in 1827 it was, for a while, the widest and deepest ship canal in the world and for this reason it is still used by commercial shipping to Gloucester and, via the River Severn, to Worcester.

One of the handsomely restored warehouses at Gloucester Docks is now home to the National Waterways Museum, opened in 1988 and housed on three floors of a Victorian warehouse. Here the 200-year story of inland waterways is told with working models, archive film, interactives and hands-on exhibits. Outside, around two sides of the quay, are boats of all shapes and sizes, as well as old railway wagons and wagon turntables. Boat trips are operated from the museum aboard *Queen Boadicea II*, built in 1936 as a Thames passenger ship and used at the evacuation of Dunkirk in 1940. Every day between April and October, 45-minute trips run on the Gloucester & Sharpness Canal, and longer day cruises go to Sharpness or Tewkesbury. In the summer months evening cruises can be taken up the River Severn.

Lower Parting, 1½ miles to the south. Continuing towards Gloucester, the old river towpath passes a former brick works and crosses a footbridge before coming to Globe House, once a riverside inn. It soon passes another one-time riverside inn, the Jolly Waterman, then dives under the Gloucester northern bypass and the Gloucester-to-Cardiff railway line. The Way arrives in the northwestern outskirts of the city at Westgate Park. From Westgate Bridge it is short stroll along The Quay past HM Prison, built on the site of Gloucester Castle, to the North Lock and the restored warehouses of Gloucester Docks.

Gloucester to Frampton on Severn

GUIDE BOX

PLACES TO VISIT
Hempsted 14th-century church and medieval village cross.
Longney 13th-century church.
Upper Framilode 19th-century church and junction of derelict Stroudwater Canal.
Wick Court Well-preserved 16th-century moated manor house, open by appointment.
Arlingham 14th-century church.
Freetherne 19th-century church with fine spire.
Frampton on Severn Picturesque village with exceptionally large green; 14th-century church.

CAR PARKING
Gloucester; Frampton on Severn (small car park at Splatt Bridge, south of St Mary's Church).

PUBLIC TRANSPORT
Train Station at Gloucester.
Bus Between Gloucester and Frampton on Severn.

ACCOMMODATION
Hotels, guest houses etc Gloucester.

TOURIST INFORMATION CENTRE
Gloucester St Michael's Tower, The Cross, Gloucester GL1 1PD (tel 01452 421188)

GLOUCESTER TO UPPER FRAMILODE
About 13 miles / 21km
OS Landranger 162
Start at North Lock, Gloucester Docks
(grid reference 827 184)

Gloucester Docks and its Victorian warehouses mark the northern limit of the Gloucester & Sharpness Canal. From the North Lock, the Severn Way passes along Severn Road, on the western boundary of the docks, and then into Llanthony Road before reaching the partially restored remains of Llanthony Priory. The Augustinian Priory was built in the 12th century but all that remains now is the 14th-century gatehouse and tithe barn adjacent to a timber-and-stone Tudor house. A short distance after the Priory, the Severn Way turns right to reach the river bank overlooking Llanthony Weir and a disused lock. Turning left, the path skirts a small industrial estate before reaching fields and the junction of the east and west arms of the river at Lower Parting.

The Way now follows the river bank for nearly 2 miles before passing a large refuse tip close to the village of Hempsted. A short detour can be made to the village to inspect the 14th-century Church of St Swithun, the medieval village cross and 17th-century Hempsted House. The Severn is now making wide, sweeping loops across the landscape and the Way hugs the east bank through Stonebench, formerly the site of a riverside inn, towards the hamlet of Elmore. In the village are attractive timber-framed cottages and 16th-century Elmore Court, set on rising ground overlooking the river. Elmore Back, a small group of riverside timber-framed cottages, is a short distance on along the floodbank. On the opposite bank is the pretty village of Minsterworth and the Church of St Peter, rebuilt in 1870 by Henry Woodyer.

The path continues for several miles along the floodbank, flanked inland by numerous apple and pear orchards. This area once supplied cider and perry to the boatmen of the Severn through many long-vanished riverside drinking houses. The small village of Longney, with its 13th-century Church of St Laurence, is but a short detour inland. A further mile brings the Severn Way to the Anchor Inn at Epney before it continues along the lane to the village of Upper Framilode, the site of the junction of the semi-derelict Stroudwater Canal with the river. Here, the 18th-century Church of St Peter marks the start of the Thames & Severn Way, which follows the course of the Stroudwater and Thames & Severn canals to Lechlade (see pages 32–37).

The broad expanse of the River Severn looking north from the Anchor Inn at Epney.

UPPER FRAMILODE TO FRAMPTON ON SEVERN

About 8 miles/13km
OS Landranger 162
Start at the Church of St Peter, Upper Framilode (grid reference 750 704)

Continuing in a westerly direction from Upper Framilode Church, the Severn Way follows the riverside lane past the Darell Arms and, as the lane veers sharply away from the river, crosses a stile into a field. Wick Court, a short detour up the lane, is a well-preserved 16th-century moated manor house that is open to the public by appointment. The Way continues through several fields until it rejoins the floodbank. For the next 4 miles the River Severn executes an enormous loop, with the path following the top of the floodbank all the way. To the south lies Arlingham village and its 14th-century Church of St Mary, set in the centre of a flat peninsula formed by the river's loop and reached by a footpath from the Severn Way. A 19th-century scheme to build a canal through the neck of the peninsula, thus shortening boat journeys by several miles, never came to fruition.

Following the loop of the river, the Severn Way passes the unusual red and green Garden Cliff on the opposite bank and finally reaches the isolated Old Passage Inn set opposite the village of Newnham. The village, perched on red-coloured cliffs, was for many centuries linked to the inn by a ferry and in the early 19th century work started on the construction of a tunnel. This soon came to grief after flooding and was abandoned. A floating bridge was built after the Second World War but within a year this, too, was abandoned due to the damage caused by the high tides. From the Old Passage Inn a drovers' road leads to the village of Arlingham.

The Severn Way continues to follow the loop of the river, skirting south of Arlingham until it comes to a stretch of woodland and a nature reserve above Hock Cliff is reached. Hock Cliff, consisting of alternate bands of clay and limestone, is gradually being eroded by the river and, in the process, layers of fossils are being exposed. From the top of the cliff there are splendid views southwards of the ever-widening River Severn and the two road bridges in the distance. The Way now bypasses the village of Fretherne and its magnificent spired Church of St Mary, leaving the floodbank behind before crossing several fields to a lane that leads to Fretherne Bridge and the Gloucester & Sharpness Canal.

The next 7 miles of the Severn Way to Sharpness follow the level towpath of the canal but a short detour at Fretherne Bridge leads to the picturesque village of Frampton on Severn. The village boasts the largest village green in England, its 22 acres containing three ponds and a cricket pitch. The green is lined on one side by attractive half-timbered and Georgian houses, a shop and the Bell Inn, while the other is overlooked by 18th-century Frampton Court and its orangery. The 14th-century Church of St Mary lies at the end of a tree-lined avenue on the southern outskirts of the village, adjacent to the Gloucester & Sharpness Canal.

Boats stranded by the low tide near Newnham, viewed from the east bank of the Severn at Old Passage Inn, site of a long-abandoned river crossing.

THE RIVER SEVERN

The River Severn has been an important waterway since the Middle Ages, linking the Bristol Channel with the Midlands, and by the early 1800s boats could travel as far north as Bewdley and Welshpool. However, due to the strong tidal nature of the river and its shifting sand banks, the passage of commercial traffic became increasingly difficult and dangerous, with barges being hauled up river by gangs of men. The southern stretch from Sharpness to Gloucester was bypassed by the Gloucester & Sharpness Canal, opened in 1827. With the opening of the Worcester & Birmingham and Staffordshire & Worcestershire canals, the Severn's navigation was improved with large-scale dredging and the building of locks to bypass weirs. Commercial traffic, including coal, timber and more recently oil, was relatively heavy until the 1970s but this has since declined. It is now used as an important linking route for leisure craft between the Midland canals, the River Avon and the Gloucester & Sharpness Canal.

The river has one of the highest tidal variations in the world, sometimes in excess of 40ft. The highest tides are spring tides, which occur when the earth, moon and sun are in a straight line. When there is a particulary strong spring tide a wall of water, sometimes several feet high and known as the Severn Bore, sweeps up the narrowing estuary of the Severn, creating a natural spectacle that is watched by thousands of onlookers on the river bank. Nowadays many intrepid surfers and canoeists take part in the dangerous act of riding the Bore up the river. One of the favourite locations to see the Bore is at Stonebench, near Elmore.

Frampton on Severn to Shepperdine

GUIDE BOX

PLACES TO VISIT
Slimbridge Wildfowl & Wetlands Trust The world's largest collection of wildfowl, best seen in winter.
Slimbridge village 13th-century church.
Sharpness Public viewing area overlooking docks and entrance to Gloucester & Sharpness Canal.
Berkeley 11th-century castle, 12th-century Church of St Mary, Georgian buildings.

CAR PARKING
Frampton on Severn (adjacent to Splatt Bridge); Sharpness Docks (public viewing area); Berkeley.

PUBLIC TRANSPORT
Train Station at Cam & Dursley, 1½ miles southeast of Slimbridge.
Bus Occasional service between Gloucester and Sharpness; limited services between Bristol and Berkeley and Thornbury, south of Shepperdine.

ACCOMMODATION
Hotel, guest houses etc Berkeley.
Camping Shepherd's Patch, near Slimbridge.
Youth hostel Shepherd's Patch, near Slimbridge.

TOURIST INFORMATION CENTRE
Stroud The Subscription Rooms, George Street, Stroud, Gloucestershire GL5 1AE (tel 01453 765768)

FRAMPTON ON SEVERN TO SHARPNESS
About 9 miles / 14km
OS Landranger 162
Start at Splatt Bridge, Frampton on Severn
(grid reference 743 068)

After the short detour to Frampton on Severn, the Severn Way rejoins the Gloucester & Sharpness Canal west bank towpath at Splatt Bridge. Adjacent to the lifting bridge is one of the single-storey classical-style bridge-keeper's houses whose style is unique to this canal. The towpath continues in a southerly direction, passing the outlet of the River Cam that supplies water to the canal shortly before Cam Bridge. The Tudor Arms country pub is to be found near the canal crossing at Shepherd's Patch, where there is also a camp site and Slimbridge Youth Hostel. Half a mile to the northwest is the Slimbridge Wildfowl and Wetlands Trust, while Slimbridge village lies ¾ mile to the southeast.

Founded by the late Sir Peter Scott in 1946, the Slimbridge Wildfowl and Wetlands Trust is home to the world's largest and most varied collection of wildfowl. The best time to visit is during the winter, when thousands of wild geese seek sanctuary in the Severn Estuary. In Slimbridge village the 13th-century spired Church of St John is one of the finest examples of the Early Gothic style in the country.

Proceeding now in a southwesterly direction, the Severn Way follows the towpath along the west bank of the Gloucester & Sharpness Canal. To the west, the floodbank of the river comes ever closer. The towpath passes a large waterworks shortly before reaching the riverside hamlet of Purton, the Berkeley Arms riverside pub and another of the distinctive bridge-keeper's cottages. The canal now runs parallel and close to the east bank of the Severn before reaching the site of the former 21-span Severn Railway Bridge. Opened in 1879, the bridge carried the Berkeley Road Junction-to-Lydney railway line over the river until one foggy night in October 1960 when two barges struck the piers and brought down two spans. The remaining spans were eventually demolished in 1970.

The bridge-keeper's house at Splatt Bridge on the Gloucester & Sharpness Canal near Frampton.

As it enters Sharpness Docks, the Severn Way forks right along the Marina towards the Old Dock House, which stands like a lonely sentry overlooking the river. The path now takes a winding route through the docks to the site of the former railway station and the old Severn Bridge & Railway Hotel. It then takes Oldminster Road, turning right after the Pier Head Hotel, to reach a public viewing area and car park overlooking the sea basin.

The importance of Sharpness Docks was greatly increased following the completion of the Gloucester & Sharpness Canal in 1827. Although commercial traffic to Gloucester and beyond has now dwindled, the docks still handle large quantities of imports and exports from and to all over Europe and can handle ships up to 5,000 tons. The immediate hinterland now contains many factories and warehouses but the small village of Sharpness itself consists mainly of dockworkers' cottages.

SHARPNESS TO SHEPPERDINE
About 7 miles/11km
OS Landranger 162
Start at public viewing area, Sharpness Docks
(grid reference 667 022)

From Sharpness Docks the final section of the Severn Way follows the floodbank for about 1 mile until it reaches the mouth of Berkeley Pill. The Severn at this stage in its journey to the sea is over a mile wide and at low tide large expanses of treacherous sand and mud are revealed. On the opposite bank the entrance to Lydney Harbour can be seen, with the wooded slopes of the ancient Forest of Dean rising to the west. Ahead are the massive concrete towers and chimneys of Berkeley nuclear power station.

At Berkeley Pill the Way veers inland, following the north bank before reaching a lane midway between the historic town of Berkeley and the power station. Berkeley, a short and worthwhile detour inland from the Way, as well as being home to the famous Berkeley Hunt, has much of interest to the visitor. Berkeley Castle, the keep and bailey of which dates from the 11th century, was where King Edward II was murdered in the dungeons in 1327. His tomb can be seen in Gloucester Cathedral. The nearby Church of St Mary dates from the 12th century although the tower was rebuilt in the 1900s. Edward Jenner, the discoverer of cowpox vaccination, was born in the village and, in 1823, was buried in the chancel of the church. The main street is wide, overlooked by attractive Georgian houses and the 18th-century Berkeley Arms Hotel.

Back on the Severn Way, the route follows the road westwards to the entrance of Berkeley power station. This 20th-century concrete edifice was one of the first commercial nuclear power stations in Britain. Work began in 1957 and the station started generating electricity for the National Grid in 1962, finally ceasing operation in 1989. It is currently being decommissioned, a procedure which will take many years to complete. The Severn Way skirts the eastern and southern perimeter of the complex before passing through several fields to rejoin the river floodbank. This, in turn, becomes a massive sea wall overlooking the dangerous waters and sand banks of the river. The Way passes the isolated Severn House Farm and, about 2 miles on, remote Chapel House before finally reaching the aptly named Windbound Inn, close to the hamlet of Shepperdine.

Although this is the official end of the Severn Way, the sea wall can be followed southwards, past Oldbury nuclear power station, to the soaring span of the Severn Road Bridge at Aust.

Near the southern end of the Severn Way as it reaches the Windbound Inn near Shepperdine.

SLIMBRIDGE WILDFOWL & WETLANDS TRUST

Located $^1/_2$ mile west of the Severn Way and the Gloucester & Sharpness Canal, the Trust was established as a sanctuary for wildfowl by the late Sir Peter Scott in 1946. Since then it has grown to become the world's largest collection of wildfowl, with over 150 different species resident. The Trust's vast water meadows, lying close to the Severn Estuary, also attract thousands of migrating birds during the winter months. These enormous numbers of birds, including geese, Bewick swans, ducks and waders, can be viewed from towers within the Trust's land. In addition to providing a permanent or temporary home to these birds, the Trust also carries out important research into migratory patterns and ecological aspects and is proud to have played a vital part in saving many species of wildfowl from extinction. It is open to the public all year except Christmas Day.

The Thames & Severn Way

UPPER FRAMILODE TO LECHLADE
36 MILES/57KM

THE Thames & Severn Way is a long distance footpath over the Cotswold Hills, linking the rivers Thames and Severn and following closely the route of two canals, the Thames & Severn and the Stroudwater, currently being restored by the Cotswold Canals Trust. Much of the Way makes use of the old towpaths but when this is not possible nearby footpaths or lanes are used. The Trust's aim is that all the towpath will eventually be accessible to the public. The route of the path takes in the flat farmland of the Severn Vale, former mills and the junction of the two canals at Stroud, the beautiful Golden Valley, the summit pound at Daneway, Sapperton Tunnel entrances, the source of the River Thames, the Cotswold Water Park and, finally, the picturesque town of Lechlade.

WALKING GUIDE
A leaflet and further information are available from the Cotswold Canals Trust, 44 Black Jack Street, Cirencester, Gloucestershire GL7 2AA.

OS MAPS
Landranger 162, 163

LINKS
The Severn Way (see pages 26–31) passes through Upper Framilode. The Thames Path (see pages 38–53) starts at Thameshead. The Cotswold Way meets the Thames & Severn at Ryeford.

Upper Framilode to Stroud

[Map showing the route from River Severn, Upper Framilode, Saul, Saul Junction, Whitminster, Westend, Stonehouse, Eastington, Ryeford, STROUD, Brimscombe, Golden Valley, Chalford, Frampton Mansell, Daneway, Sapperton, Sapperton Tunnel, Coa...]

THE GLOUCESTER & SHARPNESS CANAL

Work on the 15-mile long Gloucester & Sharpness Canal started at Gloucester in 1794, but the money ran out with only 5½ miles built. In 1817 the government commissioned Thomas Telford to look into the feasibility of completing the route, essential if the treacherous lower reaches of the River Severn were to be bypassed. Telford managed to convince the government that they should provide the funds to complete the work and the canal was eventually opened in 1827. For a while it was the world's widest and deepest ship canal, and today boats still travel up as far as Gloucester and, via the River Severn, to Worcester. There is no restriction on the height of vessels as all bridges are of the lifting or swinging type. The junction at Saul with the Stroudwater Canal was particularly important and is now the subject of complete restoration. The restored warehouses and docks at Gloucester are home to the National Waterways Museum.

UPPER FRAMILODE TO STROUD
7½ miles/12km
OS Landranger 162
Start at St Peter's Church, Upper Framilode
(grid reference 750 104)

The Thames & Severn Way starts on the east bank of the River Severn at St Peter's Church, Upper Framilode, where it links with The Severn Way long distance path (see pages 26–31). From here to Stroud the footpath follows the route of the Stroudwater Canal, opened in 1779 to link the wool-producing town of Stroud to the navigable River Severn. Commercial traffic ceased in 1941 and the canal was formally abandoned in 1954. Since 1972 the Cotswold Canals Trust has been steadily restoring locks and dredging sections of the canal.

The route leads away from the church towards the site of Framilode Bridge, with the infilled basin to the left. The old towpath passes the Ship Inn and then the canal ends abruptly a short distance beyond Moor Street Bridge. From here to just before Saul Junction the walker must follow the course of the River Frome. Saul Junction, on the Gloucester & Sharpness Canal, has a busy boatyard, pedestrian swing bridge and a cottage that saw busier days as the Junction Inn.

Crossing the Gloucester & Sharpness Canal, the path leads to Walk Bridge, which until the canal was abandoned in 1954 was a swing bridge, and continues along the left bank of the Stroudwater Canal until the water ends again at Whitminster Lock. The lock is currently under restoration by the Cotswold Canals

GUIDE BOX

PLACES TO VISIT
Upper Framilode Mid-19th-century church with Romanesque-style tower, set on the banks of the River Severn close to the western end of the Stroudwater Canal.
Eastington Wharf, near Stonehouse A slipway on a restored and dredged section of the Stroudwater Canal. The Cotswold Canals Trust operates public trips on the *Phoenix* in summer.
Stonehouse 14th-century St Cyr's Church, rebuilt in the 1800s, on the bank of the Stroudwater Canal.
Selsley (¾ mile south of canal near Stroud) 1862 church with windows by William Morris, Burne-Jones, Philip Webb, Rossetti, Ford Madox Brown.

CAR PARKING
Upper Framilode (limited); Stonehouse; Stroud.

PUBLIC TRANSPORT
Train Stations at Stonehouse and Stroud.
Bus Between Gloucester and Frampton on Severn (2 miles south of Upper Framilode).

ACCOMMODATION
Hotels, guest houses etc Stroud.

TOURIST INFORMATION CENTRE
Stroud The Subscription Rooms, George Street, Stroud, Gloucestershire GL5 1AE
(tel 01453 765768)

The restored Blunder Lock on the Stroudwater Canal near Eastington.

Trust and will have a guillotine gate connecting into the River Frome. The path now follows the right bank of the Frome before rejoining the old canal towpath close to the site of Stonepits Swing Bridge. This is currently a causeway but there are plans to replace it with a high-level fixed bridge. The towpath continues eastwards, past Occupation Bridge, a recently restored humpback bridge, before ending at a roundabout on the A38. During the construction of the M5 the canal was infilled for the next ½ mile, but restoration of the waterway under the motorway is feasible in the long term.

The Thames & Severn Way now temporarily leaves the route of the old canal, following footpaths over a field to a motorway bridge. After crossing the bridge and following the lane through the hamlet of Westend, it goes over a further field and the A419 before rejoining the canal at Westfield Bridge. The bridge and Westfield Lock are temporarily stranded in a field awaiting restoration. The path now resumes eastward alongside the right bank of the canal to Meadow Mill spillweir. A coal wharf was once located here to supply the woollen mills of nearby Eastington. The towpath continues past Dock Lock to the Pike Lock road crossing, where it alters course to the left bank of the canal. This section of the canal is now navigable for small boats, and during the summer months public boat trips are operated by the Cotswold Canals Trust from Eastington Wharf. From here the towpath continues past the restored Blunder Lock and Newtown Lock to Newtown Roving Bridge.

The canal is now entering the Stroud Valley. Cotswold stone houses and cottages are scattered along its hillsides and former woollen mill buildings are strung along the valley bottom. From Newtown Roving Bridge the towpath reaches the world's first plastic lifting bridge at Bonds Mill, then burrows under the Birmingham-to-Bristol main railway line, past picturesque St Cyr's Church and under Nutshell Bridge to the Ship Inn, on the outskirts of Stonehouse. From here the towpath passes under the former Midland Railway skew bridge, which once carried the Stonehouse-to-Nailsworth branch line, and comes to Ryeford Bridge. This section of the canal has been dredged by the Canal Trust and is a popular spot for anglers. The Thames & Severn Way shares its route with the Cotswold Way long distance footpath from Ryeford to the recently restored Ebley Mill. From Ryeford Double Lock the canal has been infilled, but water re-appears at Ebley Mill. After passing Hilly Orchard footbridge, Dudbridge Lock and Foundry Lock, the canal ends at Wallbridge close to the centre of Stroud. The former canal basin is now infilled but some original buildings still exist.

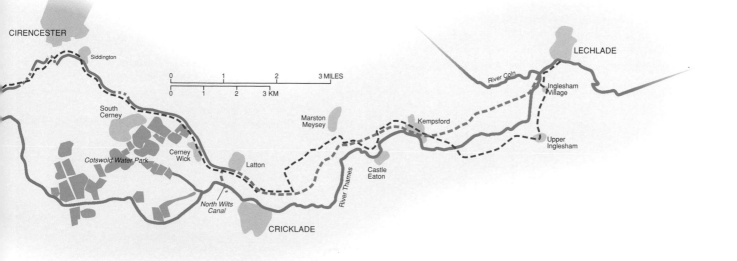

Stroud to Siddington

STROUD TO SAPPERTON
About 7 miles / 11km
OS Landranger 162, 163
Start at Wallbridge, Stroud
(grid reference 846 051)

From Stroud to Lechlade the Thames & Severn Way follows closely the towpath of the Thames & Severn Canal. This heavily engineered canal was opened in 1789 and, with the Stroudwater Canal, formed a link between the rivers Severn and Thames. Because the locks were built to accommodate only Thames barges, all through-loads from the Stroudwater, built to take the wider Severn Trow, had to be transshipped into smaller boats at Brimscombe Port. Dogged by water supply problems and faulty engineering work, the canal was never a success. Very little through-traffic was carried and by 1911 it had ceased altogether. The last section to close, in 1933, was between Stroud and Chalford. The Stroudwater canal was officially abandoned in 1954. However, since 1972, the Cotswold Canals Trust has been restoring many sections with the long-term aim of reopening the whole canal to navigation.

From Wallbridge in Stroud follow the footpath to Wallbridge Lower Lock and continue along the towpath, crossing the A46, to Wallbridge Middle Wharf and then to the restored Wallbridge Upper Lock.

Shortly after this lock, the path follows an infilled section of the canal, passing under the GWR viaduct, until it rejoins the towpath at the River Frome aqueduct. The towpath passes, in quick succession, Bowbridge Lock, Griffin Mill Lock and Ham Hill Lock before reaching the Air Plants factory, site of Hope Mill Lock and a former boatyard. Continuing in a south-easterly direction, the towpath passes Goughs Orchard Lock before reaching the Ship Inn at Brimscombe. Here the towpath is temporarily left behind as a detour is made around factories and offices to the site of Brimscombe Port. Here there were warehouses and a major transshipment basin, 700ft long. The site is now covered by industrial buildings, but a plaque records the position.

Following the River Frome, the Way soon rejoins the canal towpath at Bourne Lock before burrowing under a railway viaduct to Beales Lock and St Mary's Lock, close to St Mary's Mill. A railway embankment now blocks the canal, but the towpath is quickly rejoined and the route continues past Illes Lock and the infilled Ballingers Lock to the Chalford Round House – the first of five conical-shaped houses on the canal. Soon the canal disappears, a result of road improvements in the 1950s, but the towpath remains and passes the infilled Chapel Lock before crossing the A419 to the infilled Bell Lock,

GUIDE BOX

PLACES TO VISIT
Daneway, near Sapperton A very popular country pub with a garden overlooking the Thames & Severn Canal and the wooded valley of the River Frome. Built in the 18th century for the navvies working on Sapperton Tunnel.
Sapperton A picturesque village, country pub, Church of St Kenelm.
Tunnel House, Coates Isolated country pub, reached along a rough track, close to the eastern portal of Sapperton Tunnel; once frequented by the canal 'leggers'. Camping facilities available.
Thames Head A simple incribed stone marks the official source of the River Thames.

CAR PARKING
Stroud; Sapperton (on-street); Siddington (on-street).

PUBLIC TRANSPORT
Train Stations at Stroud and Kemble.
Bus Services between Stroud and Gloucester, Stroud and Cirencester, Cirencester and Swindon.

ACCOMMODATION
Hotels, guest houses etc Stroud, Cirencester.

TOURIST INFORMATION CENTRES
Stroud The Subscription Rooms, George Street, Stroud, Gloucestershire GL5 1AE
(tel 01453 765768)
Cirencester Corn Hall, Market Place, Cirencester, Gloucestershire GL7 2NW (tel 01285 654180)

Clowes Bridge and Red Lion Lock. The latter is marked with a stone inscription carved by a stone mason in 1784. The canal, perched on the side of the valley, soon becomes wider and thick with reeds, fed by the many springs that flow out of the

The view of the Thames & Severn Canal from Frampton Mansell, looking towards Sapperton.

hillside. Valley Lock, set close to a former mill leat, marks the start of the picturesque Golden Valley and the beginning of the steep climb to the summit pound at Daneway. This is, naturally, a very heavily locked section of the canal and the towpath passes, in quick succession, Bakers Mill Locks, Puck Mill Locks, Whitehall Locks, Bathurst Meadows Lock and Siccarage Wood Locks before reaching the Daneway Locks. The nearby 18th-century Daneway Inn, built for the navvies constructing Sapperton Tunnel, marks the start of the summit pound, 310ft above sea level. The towpath wends its way along the wooded hillside to the Daneway Portal of Sapperton Tunnel. This gothic structure has been restored by the Canal Trust and English Heritage. From here a footpath covers the short distance to pretty Sapperton village.

SAPPERTON TO SIDDINGTON
About 8 miles/13km
OS Landranger 163
Start at Sapperton village
(grid reference 946 034)

From Sapperton village the Thames & Severn Way follows a series of lanes and footpaths before rejoining the canal towpath at the Coates Portal of the Sapperton Tunnel. Passing St Kenelm's Church and the Bell Inn, the path soon leaves the village behind and passes along a lane close to clumps of beech trees on mounds which mark the dangerous entrances to construction shafts to the canal tunnel. The track then crosses a field and the A419 and passes through Hailey Woods and under the railway line before reaching the isolated Tunnel House Inn and the Coates Portal of the tunnel. The grand portal was restored by the Canal Trust in 1977 and it forms the logo for the Thames & Severn Way. The towpath recommences here and passes along Kings Reach to the restored Coates Round House before passing under a bridge to Coatesfield Bridge. Here the towpath ceases to be a public right of way and the Way follows a lane before crossing two fields to the official source of the Thames at Thameshead. This is also the starting point of the 178-mile Thames Path to Woolwich (see pages 40–55).

Unfortunately, the greater part of the Thames & Severn Way from Thames Head to Siddington is along country lanes and, for a short distance, a main road, but it never strays far from the course of the canal. From Thames Head, cross more fields to join the A433. Turn left along this road, passing over the canal, and turn right at the next cross roads, noting the remains of the Smerril Aqueduct on the right, just

The eastern portal of Sapperton Tunnel at Coates, restored by the Cotswold Canals Trust.

before reaching the A429. Turn right for a short distance along this road and then turn left towards Ewen, passing under the closed Kemble-to-Cirencester railway line at Ewen Wharf. To the left is Halfway Bridge, named because of its equidistance from Stroud and Lechlade. The Way follows a track to the bridge, where it rejoins the restored towpath for the next $^{1}/_{2}$ mile, then crosses a lane before rejoining the towpath towards Siddington. At this point the course of the canal is lost in a field and the Way rejoins the lane. Soon, Bluehouse Farm, once a canal lengthman's cottage, is reached and after a short distance the village of Siddington beckons the walker with its flight of locks and the Greyhound country pub. The centre of Cirencester is 1 mile northwest.

SAPPERTON TUNNEL

The major engineering feature of the Thames & Severn Canal, at 3,817yds in length, was, and is, one of the longest canal tunnels in England. It was completed in time for the canal's opening in 1789 and was constructed by sinking 25 vertical shafts in the grounds of the Bathurst Estate. Boats were propelled through by 'leggers', men who lay on top of the canal boats pushing with their legs against the tunnel roof. The eastern portal at Coates, now restored, is decorated with Doric columns, while the western portal at Daneway, now also restored, has an embattled parapet. Water shortage problems at the nearby summit soon involved the construction of a pumping station at Thames Head. Initially this was operated by a windpump, but this was soon replaced in 1792 by a Boulton & Watt steam engine. In 1844 this, in turn, was replaced by a Cornish beam engine, which was not scrapped until the Second World War.

Siddington to Lechlade

SIDDINGTON TO CRICKLADE
5 miles/8km
OS Landranger 163
Start at Siddington village
(grid reference 034 995)

From Siddington the Thames & Severn Way follows the canal towpath as far as Latton. Starting at the humpback bridge at Siddington, the towpath passes what was a four-lock flight; a house has been built over the bottom lock. After crossing over the Ashton Keynes road, the path continues along a stretch of canal in water to Cowground Bridge. Here, the humpback bridge is currently being restored by the Canal Trust. The towpath continues on an embankment over the water meadows of the River Churn, which in the 16th century were drained by a series of water channels. A wooden footbridge now replaces the earth embankment, blown up for practice in the Second World War, where the canal crossed the culverted river. The Way soon passes through a cutting and emerges at a lane at the top lock of the South Cerney flight.

The canal now disappears for a short distance, but the Way follows the course across a field where the remains of lock chamber walls and pounds can still be traced. At Northmoor Lane a section of the canal has been carefully restored by the Canal Trust, the Dig Deep Organisation and the Waterways Recovery Group. From here to Latton the canal is often water-filled and the towpath passes the restored Boxwell Spring Lock and Upper and Lower Wildmoorway Locks. The latter lock is unique in having a side pond, the remains of which can be seen next to the lock chamber. The section of canal between this lock and Spine Road, built during the excavation of the nearby Cotswold Water Park, was dredged during 1995. After crossing the Spine Road, the towpath passes the Water Park Visitor Centre and car park and follows the overgrown canal to restored Cerney Wick Lock and another round house. The Way crosses a lane and then continues to the site of Latton Basin, the former junction with the North Wilts Canal.

The Thames & Severn Way now continues along a public footpath, following the north bank of the River Churn, with the shallow depression of the canal visible to the left. Soon all traces of this disappear because the course of the canal was obliterated for a short distance during the building of the Cricklade bypass. The public footpath leads to the old road where, after a short distance, the former Cricklade wharfhouse can be seen.

GUIDE BOX

PLACES TO VISIT
Cirencester Corinium Museum holds one of the country's finest Roman collections, with reconstructions of mosaic craftsman's workshop, dining room and kitchen.
Cotswold Water Park, South Cerney Nearly 100 lakes, created by gravel extraction, provide facilities for water-based activities; tours on Edwardian-style launch to view wildlife.
Down Ampney Church has associations with Knights Hospitallers and World War II airmen. Vaughan Williams was born in the Old Vicarage.
Cricklade Good 17th- and 18th-century buildings dominated by magnificent wool church.
Lechlade Beautiful Georgian streets; fine wool church inspired Shelley's *Summer Evening in a Churchyard*.

CAR PARKING
Siddington; Cotswold Water Park (beside Thames & Severn Way at Visitor Centre); Lechlade.

PUBLIC TRANSPORT
Bus Services between Cirencester and Swindon via Cricklade and between Lechlade and Swindon or Cirencester.

ACCOMMODATION
Hotels, guest houses etc Cirencester, Cricklade, Lechlade.
Camping South Cerney, Lechlade.

TOURIST INFORMATION CENTRE
Cirencester Corn Hall, Market Place, Cirencester, Gloucestershire GL7 2NW (tel 01285 654180)

Turn left to cross the A419, following this road to the right for 100 yards, before turning left over stiles to rejoin the towpath of the Thames & Severn Canal.

Looking towards Wildmoorway Lower Lock.

CRICKLADE TO LECHLADE
About 8¹/₂ miles/14km
OS Landranger 163
Start at canal towpath on A419 opposite Cricklade Wharf (grid reference 102 945)

From the A419 at Cricklade the towpath can be followed on a low embankment for ¹/₂ mile as far as Ampney Brook. However, at this point, the embankment totally disappears and the Thames & Severn Way follows the brook and then a track towards Eysey Manor. The entrance to the manor is flanked by two canal mileposts which were removed when the canal was infilled. From here to Lechlade there is very little of the towpath that is a public right of way and so the Thames & Severn Way meanders along lanes and footpaths, occasionally catching glimpses of the course of the old canal and its remains.

From the entrance to Eysey Manor the route crosses over the infilled canal, once the site of a humpback bridge, and follows a lane northwards until it reaches the Kempsford lane. It then turns right and joins the lane for about 1 mile. After passing the turning for Marston Meysey, the Way takes a track on the right that leads down towards Marston Meysey Round House. Skirting this to the left, the track then follows the course of the infilled canal across several fields until turning right towards a caravan park near the small

village of Castle Eaton. A short southerly detour can be made to the village, set on the south bank of the River Thames, and the Red Lion country pub.

The Thames & Severn Way turns left up the lane to the site of Crooked Bridge and rejoins the Kempsford lane. Turn right onto the lane towards Kempsford and after ¹/₂ mile Oatlands Bridge can be seen to the right, standing isolated in the middle of a field. A brick in the parapet of the bridge has the inscription 'Stonehouse Brick Company' cast into it, a reminder that the bricks for the bridge were carried by canal boat, via the Stroudwater Canal, from Stonehouse.

The route continues through the village of Kempsford, where the Anchor Inn offers refreshment, until it comes to the site of the old canal crossing at Kempsford Bridge. Just before the crossing, turn left into Ham Lane and a gravel track. With gravel workings to the left, turn right to the site of Green Lane Bridge and then on to Hannington Lane. There are no public rights of way along the route of the canal at present and the Thames & Severn Way follows the lane over the River Thames and joins the Thames Path (see pages 40–55) as it turns left along a track to a bridle path. This path continues for about 2 miles to the village of Upper Inglesham, where the route of the Way turns left and follows the A361 northwards for 1¹/₄ miles.

Marston Meysey Round House, close to the route of the infilled canal.

Before Lechlade, turn left to the picturesque 11th-century Inglesham Church and the site of a medieval village. The Way now follows the banks of the River Thames to the end of the Thames & Severn Canal and its junction with the rivers Coln and Thames. From the footbridge over the river there is a good view of the end of the canal hidden amongst reeds and willow trees. From here it is but a short distance along the bank of the Thames to Halfpenny Bridge and the charming village of Lechlade.

NORTH WILTS CANAL

Built as a link between the River Thames, the Thames & Severn Canal, the Wilts & Berks Canal and the Kennet & Avon Canal, the North Wilts Canal was opened between Latton Basin and Swindon in 1819. Traffic, including coal from the North Somerset coalfields, was never heavy and the advent of the railways in the 1840s started its inevitable decline. All commercial traffic had ceased by 1906, the canal was officially abandoned in 1914 and since then much of the route in built-up areas has been covered over. The Brunel Shopping Centre in Swindon now covers the site of the junction between the North Wilts and the Wilts & Berks Canals.

South & Southeast England

The Thames Path   40 – 55

The River Wey and its Connections   56 – 63

The Royal Military Canal   64 – 67

The Lee & Stort Navigations   68 – 71

The Oxford Canal   72 – 75

Along the River Thame from the Thames Path, near Dorchester

The Thames Path

THAMES HEAD TO WOOLWICH
178 MILES/285KM

THE Thames Path, Britain's newest National Trail, encompasses a remarkable range of scenery, from meadowland and marshland to attractive villages and the noise and excitement of Greater London. The river itself has been described as 'liquid history' and the path passes through such notable historic places as Oxford and Windsor, as well as countless less urban spots written large and small in the book of time. The path follows the River Thames from its source to the Thames Barrier at Woolwich. Wherever possible, it keeps to the river banks, following the towpath created in the canal era when the river was a working waterway. Above Lechlade the path has been extended along the attractive little headstream to the spring at Thames Head. Similarly, below Putney a riverside route has been created to take the walker alongside 'London River' towards the wide estuary and the sea.

WALKING GUIDES

Geo Projects *Thames: the river and the path* (map).
Jebb, Miles *A Guide to the Thames Path* (Constable, 1988).
Livingston, Helen *The Thames Path*, Aerofilms Guide (Ian Allan, 1993).
Sharp, David *The Thames Path* (Ordnance Survey/Countryside Commission and Ramblers' Association, 1996).

OS MAPS

Landranger 163, 164, 174, 175, 176, 177

LINKS

The Thames & Severn Way (see pages 32–37) meets the Thames Path at Thames Head and near Cricklade.
The Ridgeway Path (roughly on the line of the Icknield Way) crosses the Thames Path at Goring.
The Bristol-to-London Long Distance Path crosses the Thames Path at Reading.
The Oxfordshire Way joins the Thames Path at Henley on Thames.
The London Countryway follows the line of the Thames Path from Marlow to Windsor.

Thames Head to Lechlade

THAMES HEAD TO CRICKLADE

About 12 miles/19km
OS Landranger 163
Start at Thames Head Inn
(grid reference 981 995)

The delightful first section of the Thames Path follows the main headwater stream of the River Thames, a slim streamlet that slips between meadows and woodlands. The path itself begins in the middle of a Gloucestershire meadow at the river's source, Thames Head, close to the overgrown embankment of the Thames & Severn Canal. Tradition names the meadow Trewsbury Mead and says that the Romans fought a battle here for the possession of the nearby British stronghold of Trewsbury Fort. Their great road, Foss Way, runs nearby and the easiest route to Thames Head is to follow the Thames Path from this main road (A433), and then retrace your steps along the sinuous grassy hollow which marks the course of the infant River Thames. This can be followed downstream to a point where a culvert takes it under the Foss Way and across the meadows past the Lyd Well – reputedly Roman – and so to the A429 at the point where the old Kemble branch line crossed both road and river.

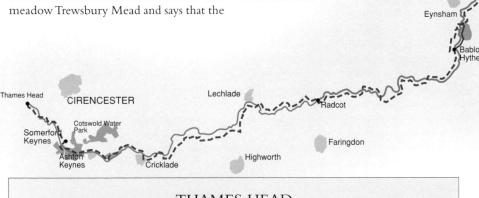

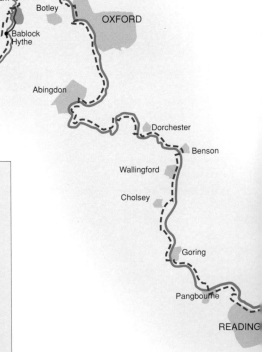

THAMES HEAD

The source of the River Thames at Thames Head is a haunting, magical spot; a ring of stones, said by some to mark the site of a Roman well, shaded by a large ash tree. It is also remarkably unassuming, since for six months a year there is rarely any water to be seen, though winter rains bring it bubbling up through the ring of stones to overflow down the meadow. This lack of water has led to the source being disputed in favour of Seven Springs near Cheltenham, fount of the tributary river, the Churn. But the Churn is a separate river, and Thames Head is the true source. To mark this, the Thames Conservators once set up a reclining statue of Father Thames here. This is now at St John's Lock, Lechlade, and the monument at Thames Head is a simple inscribed stone.

The Thames Path continues to Parker's Bridge and Mill Farm, once the highest of the many watermills on the Thames, and so to Ewen, a tiny place. From here onwards there is water in the Thames even in dry weather. The path follows the youthful river alongside Upper Mill Farm to Somerford Keynes, where it turns away from the village past the ancient church. This is worth visiting for its Saxon porchway and early 11th-century carvings. The path rejoins the Thames at Kemble Mill and proceeds to Neigh Bridge. From here it shadows the river as it picks its way through the Cotswold Water Park, one of the largest wetlands in Britain, covering 12,000 acres, and enters the village of Ashton Keynes along Church Walk.

Emerging from Ashton Keynes, the path crosses fields to rejoin the river briefly at Waterhay Bridge. It passes the game fishing area of Manorbrook Lake before returning to the river bank, going under the old railway bridge and across the line of the North Wiltshire Canal, to arrive at Cricklade's magnificent 114-acre North Meadow. Today this meadow is managed as a nature reserve, with a crop of hay organically grown allowing for lush growth of meadow flowers. Between 12 August and 12 February there is free access to the meadow and all Cricklade householders possess grazing rights. For the other six months, while the hay crop is growing and being harvested, access is on specified footpaths only. The sea of fritillaries in late spring is a glorious and, today, sadly rare sight.

You can easily detour into the ancient town of Cricklade. Its present layout dates back to the late 9th century when a Saxon burgh was created, probably by Alfred the Great. This was a square earthwork enclosure, later fortified by stone town walls. The Norman St Mary's Church is built on the line of the northern wall and

may include part of one of the gatehouses. In the High Street a group of houses is all that is left of a priory founded in 1231 by the Knights Hospitallers. The buildings are said to be connected by tunnel with St Mary's Church. Today, Cricklade is dominated by the magnificent 16th-century turreted tower of St Sampson's Church, one of the great Cotswold wool churches.

CRICKLADE TO LECHLADE
About 9 miles/14km
OS Landranger 163
Start at Cricklade town centre
(grid reference 101 935)

Beyond Cricklade the Thames Path goes under the Roman road, Ermin Way, now the A419, and crosses the Thames at Eysey footbridge. It keeps to fields above the river, which it recrosses at Water Eaton, before following a lane to Castle Eaton and the pleasant Red Lion Inn. In Norman times this little Thames-side village had a castle belonging to the Zouche family. Today all traces of that edifice have vanished, but the church still keeps two Norman doorways (one carved with dragons) and a font of the same era. During

the Victorian restoration the old sanctus bell was found hidden among the rafters and it has been set in its own little bellcote.

From Castle Eaton the Thames Path follows a lane south of the river as far as Blackford Farm and then crosses fields to Upper Inglesham, a hilltop village. From here it runs along the busy A361 to Inglesham, a flourishing wool village during the Middle Ages that has dwindled to a couple of cottages beside the 11th-century church. The adjacent field, where the Thames Path runs, is scarred by humps and hollows, all that remains of the rest of the village. The church is a gem, beautifully restored 100 years ago and one of the marvels of the Thames Path: a haven of peace, with its great stone step worn hollow by the passage of countless feet. Inside are fragments of wall paintings and on the south wall a strangely moving Anglo-Saxon sculpture of the Virgin and Child. There is peace at Inglesham of the kind that makes one stronger to face the world.

Beyond Inglesham the River Coln and the Thames & Severn Canal join the Thames, and the Thames towpath begins running along the river bank to Halfpenny Bridge at Lechlade.

Lechlade to Bablock Hythe

GUIDE BOX

PLACES TO VISIT
Kelmscott Manor William Morris's home.
Buscot Park 18th-century house with good
collection of Old Masters and pre-Raphaelite
paintings; water gardens; kitchen garden.

CAR PARKING
Buscot; Radcot (by bridge); Tadpole Bridge;
Bablock Hythe (at riverside).

PUBLIC TRANSPORT
No satisfactory public transport.

ACCOMMODATION
Hotels Buscot.
Camping Standlake.

TOURIST INFORMATION OFFICE
Faringdon 7a Market Place, Faringdon,
Oxfordshire SN7 7HL (tel 01367 242191)

LECHLADE TO RADCOT
About 7 miles / 11km
OS Landranger 163
*Start at Lechlade Halfpenny Bridge
(grid reference 214 993)*

Lechlade's handsome Halfpenny Bridge was built in 1792 to replace a ferry, the pedestrian toll of a halfpenny giving the bridge its name. Lechlade lies on the opposite bank to the Thames Path, its skyline dominated by the spire of St Lawrence's Church, built in 1474 and one of the finest Cotswold wool churches. Its soaring spire inspired the poet Shelley when he stayed here in 1815.

During the summer, Lechlade's little wharf, once busy with commercial barge traffic, buzzes with the bustle of holidaymakers. Just downstream is St John's Lock, the highest on the river, and since 1974 home to the reclining statue of Father Thames, an exhibit at the Great Exhibition of 1851. The path crosses the river by St John's Bridge and passes the Trout Inn which stands on the site of the medieval priory of St John the Baptist. Passing along a lane and past a large mill on the tributary River Leach, from which Lechlade derives its name, the path returns to the Thames to follow the towpath alongside open meadows and the tranquil river to Buscot Weir.

Buscot, now run by the National Trust, was built as a model village in 1879 by an eccentric Australian squire. He practically ruined himself by his fanatical introduction of up-to-date farming technology, which included steam ploughs that worked at night illuminated by limelight flares. Nearby Eaton Weir footbridge is on the site of the last of the Thames flashlocks, which operated until 1936. In the 1830s the lock was kept by a Mr Hart, a member of a famous Thames family, who kept kegs of contraband spirits hidden in the river close by, secured by long chains.

The next village downstream is Kelmscot, famed as the 'Nowhere' in William Morris's *News from Nowhere*. Morris lived at Kelmscott Manor for 25 years and loved the place dearly, describing his home as 'heaven on earth'. He moved here in 1871 with his wife, Jane, and the artist Dante Gabriel Rossetti, but Rossetti, after pursuing Janey Morris and alienating the locals, complained that the place was boring and returned to London.

Beyond Kelmscot, the Thames Path continues along the old towpath to Grafton Lock and so to Radcot, a lonely riverside inn at a spot which has witnessed two battles, one in 1387, when Henry Bolingbroke (later Henry IV) defeated the Earl of Oxford who had declared for Richard II, and another in 1645, during the Civil War, when a contingent of Prince Rupert's men fought off the Parliamentarians. At Radcot the Thames flows in two channels – the original one and a cut made in 1787 to improve the navigation for barge traffic heading to and from the new Thames & Severn Canal. The bridge over the cut was built that same year, but the three-arched bridge over the old river course is the oldest spanning the Thames. It dates from about 1280. The two pointed outer arches of the bridge are original, but the rounded central one was rebuilt after the battle in 1387, when Bolingbroke's troops had destroyed it, trapping the Earl of Oxford's men between themselves and the river.

The sole remaining ford on the Thames at Duxford, a delightful place beside the Thames Path.

RADCOT TO BABLOCK HYTHE
About 13 miles/21km
OS Landranger 164
*Start at car park by Radcot Bridge
(grid reference 285 995)*

The river now flows through a remote and lonely landscape of large fields, a region that was formerly a great tract of marshland where there are still but few settlements and the wind blows keenly. In winter months the walker can tramp in delightful solitude past Radcot Lock and Rushey Lock, both of which in summer are alive with the bustle and noise of pleasure cruisers, narrow boats and their crews. The towpath is at times overgrown as it shadows the lonely winding river between wide meadows dotted with grazing cattle to Tadpole Bridge and the Trout Inn. There used to be a large coal wharf here, where now the pleasure cruisers moor. Beyond comes Tenfoot Bridge (once the site of a 10ft flash lock) where the Thames Path crosses the river to go over the fields to the little hamlet of Duxford. Duxford lies on a great meander

loop of the river that was abandoned as a delightfully sequestered backwater when Shifford Lock Cut was opened in 1898. Here is the last true ford on the Thames, a magical spot of shallow rippling water and overhanging greenery.

Remote and lonely Shifford stands on the opposite bank of the river. This tiny place is no more than a couple of cottages and Old Shifford Farm, and gives little hint today of its past glories. It was once a royal borough, where tradition claims that Alfred the Great held one of the first English parliaments – in a field still known as 'Court Close'.

The six-arched bridge at Newbridge, at the confluence of the Thames and the River Windrush, was built by Benedictine monks in the late 13th century, making Newbridge the second oldest bridge on the river, though it was renovated in the 15th century and again in 1801. On 1 June 1644, during the great Civil War, there was skirmish at Newbridge, but today the spot is well known for its two inns, the Maybush on the right-hand bank and the Rose Revived on the left.

The view along the Thames Path to the 13th-century bridge at Newbridge.

Hart's footbridge, about a mile below Newbridge, stands at the site of Hart's or Rudge's Weir. Here, during the 18th century, one of the most charming of Thames-side love stories was played out. The lock-keeper, Mr Rudge, had a daughter called Betty who fell in love with a student from nearby Oxford who often came to fish the river hereabouts. He was the 2nd Viscount Ashbrook and it must have seemed to Betty that there could be no happy ending to their relationship. This did not trouble the young man who proposed and was accepted and then sent Betty to learn the social graces with some nearby gentlefolk. The happy pair were married in Northmoor Church in 1766 and lived together in great contentment until the viscount's death 18 years later. The old weir where this romance started was replaced by Northmoor Lock in 1859. Below Northmoor Lock the path continues to Bablock Hythe, site of an ancient river crossing.

Bablock Hythe to Abingdon

BABLOCK HYTHE TO GODSTOW LOCK, OXFORD
About 7 miles/11km
OS Landranger 164
Start at Bablock Hythe, car park by river
(grid reference 434 042)

There has been an important river crossing at Bablock Hythe from at least Roman times, and the ferry here is mentioned by Matthew Arnold in his great poem *The Scholar Gipsy*. As late as World War II a vehicle ferry worked here, but traffic dwindled and in 1986 it stopped operating and the adjacent Ferryman Inn closed down. Happily a new landlord reopened both the inn and the ancient river crossing; he now runs a passenger ferry service during pub hours. This little ferry has allowed the resumption of another tradition: it is said that if you throw four coins into the river from the Bablock Hythe ferry, they will be returned to you sevenfold. The towpath from Bablock Hythe to Pinkhill Lock runs on the eastern side of the river and walkers wishing to follow it will need to make use of the ferry. It is advisable to telephone the inn (tel 01865 880028) to check that it is available.

Walkers who do not use the ferry must keep to the western side of the river. Here the path heads through the meadows close to the village of Stanton Harcourt, until 1711 the seat of the Harcourt family. Their great house was demolished in about 1750, leaving only the medieval domestic kitchen and one of the towers, known as Pope's Tower since the poet Alexander Pope spent the summer of 1718 there writing his famous translation of Homer's *Iliad*. This path returns to the river which it crosses at Pinkhill Lock. Here, the eastern bank of the river is dominated by the great grassy bank surrounding Farmoor Reservoir. In dry weather its water is used to top up the level of the Thames.

The path makes a short detour by road, rejoining the towpath at the Oxford Cruisers Boatyard. The wooded Oxford Heights make a backdrop for the next stage of the Thames Path as it follows the winding river through rich meadowlands to Eynsham (Swinford) Bridge, built in 1777 as part of a turnpike road scheme. It is one of only two toll bridges remaining on the river. Beyond Eynsham (Swinford) Lock the path carries on through the edge of Wytham Great Wood, passing the

GUIDE BOX

PLACES TO VISIT
Stanton Harcourt Manor Medieval kitchen, Pope's Tower, domestic chapel.
Oxford Colleges – usually open most afternoons, but times vary; several museums and attractions, including the Ashmolean and the Oxford Story; Botanic Gardens.

CAR PARKING
Bablock Hythe (near river); Eynsham (Swinford) Bridge; Godstow (Port Meadow); Oxford (St Ebbe's car park is near Folly Bridge); Sandford (village street and at King's Head by the river).

PUBLIC TRANSPORT
Train Stations at Oxford, Radley.
Bus City Link London to Abingdon and Oxford; local buses Oxford to Eynsham.
Boat Summer services between Abingdon and Oxford.

ACCOMMODATION
Hotels, guest houses etc Stanton Harcourt, Eynsham, Oxford, Sandford on Thames.

TOURIST INFORMATION OFFICE
Oxford The Old School, Gloucester Green, Oxford OX1 2DA (tel 01865 726871)

confluence with the River Evenlode. Continuing along the towpath round the big meander, the walker arrives at King's Lock. On the other side of the river is

The ruins of Godstow Nunnery set in their peaceful Thames-side meadow and dominated by the infirmary chapel.

Duke's Cut, excavated by the Duke of Marlborough in 1789 to link the Thames and the new Oxford Canal.

The riverside towpath turns south under the A34 and past the site of the original Oxford University paper mill at Wolvercote and so to Godstow Bridge. This bridge gets a mention in Arnold's *The Scholar Gipsy* and is well known today for the Trout Inn, that haunt of Oxford undergraduates. Yet, here are the romantic ruins of Godstow Nunnery, burial place of Henry II's tragic and beautiful mistress, 'Fair Rosamund'. She died here in 1176, poisoned, some say, by the jealous queen.

GODSTOW LOCK, OXFORD, TO ABINGDON

About 13 miles/21km
OS Landranger 164
Start at Godstow Bridge
(grid reference 484 092)

South of Godstow Lock, the path continues opposite the vast unenclosed Port Meadow to Binsey, where the ghost of a sailor is said to haunt the Perch Inn. From Binsey you can detour along a raised causeway to the church and St Margaret's Well, which has a reputation for curing eye ailments. At Medley, just beyond Binsey, the path crosses the river and follows the left-hand river bank behind Oxford Station – on the site of Osney Abbey – and continues behind houses and gardens to reach Osney Bridge.

From Osney Bridge, the path runs along the right-hand bank past the Waterman's Arms to Osney Lock and continues round a big meander loop and past Folly Bridge. Soon famous Christ Church Meadow sweeps down to the river close to the confluence with the River Cherwell, and the path continues to Iffley, a little haven hemmed in by Oxford's suburban spread. It has a magnificent Norman church, built in 1170–80. It is a massive building with a square tower rising in three stages, an imposing nave and doorways carved with animals, birds and fish. The black marble font also dates from the 12th century. Iffley Lock, beside the poplar trees, was one of the first locks constructed on the Thames, though the present lock dates from 1924.

South of Iffley comes Sandford, a manor given to the Knights Templar by Thomas de Saunford in 1240. Temple Farm hints at this connection and the Templars' chapel is preserved as an old barn. You can turn right to visit deep and dangerous Sandford Pool on the weir stream, where over the years five undergraduates, all from Christ Church, have met death by drowning. The fact that all the fatalities were from Christ

New housing next to the lock stands on the site of Sandford's former mill, descendant of the mill first built here in 1294. The last mill here, whose chimney was a landmark for miles around, closed in the 1980s.

Church is sometimes connected with the fate of George Napier, Jesuit scion of the manor in the reign of Elizabeth I. In 1568 he was captured and executed at Oxford, his head being displayed on the front of Christ Church. On Christmas Eve his ghost is said to drive a shadowy coach from Temple Farm to Oxford, searching for his lost head.

Sandford Lock, another of the earliest Thames locks, is the deepest on the river above Teddington, with a fall of 8ft 10ins. Sandford Mill, first built in 1294, used to stand beside the lock and was working into the 1980s producing coloured paper. Sadly, the site has been razed and replaced by smart housing.

South of Sandford the Thames Path runs along a tranquil and untroubled reach of the river increasingly enclosed by high banks. Radley, with its public school, lies uphill to the right, and the Thames Path passes by the school's boathouse. On the opposite bank stands Nuneham House, built in 1756 by Lord Harcourt.

The river swings westwards below Nuneham and the path follows it into open meadows and so to Abingdon Lock. The Thames Path crosses the river here and follows the towpath to Abingdon Bridge, with good views of riverside Abingdon on the opposite bank.

FAIR ROSAMUND

Godstow Nunnery was an aristocratic foundation where Rosamund Clifford was educated and where she met Henry II, whose love for her has passed into legend. He made her a bower in the grounds of his palace at Woodstock, where he would visit her clandestinely, but when she died tragically young she was buried here at Godstow. At first her tomb stood before the High Altar, but when the bishop, St Hugh, learned who was buried amid such state he ordered her sealed coffin to be moved elsewhere. Even so, her grave became a place of pilgrimage, and for centuries prayers were said for her soul. When, at the Dissolution, Rosamund's tomb was taken up and opened, a glorious scent of spices and perfumes wafted around those present, so even in death there seemed to be nothing but sweetness surrounding her. Today the ruins of Godstow Nunnery are a haunting sight, a few crumbling stone walls alongside the Thames Path.

Abingdon to Pangbourne

ABINGDON TO WALLINGFORD
About 13 miles/21km
OS Landranger 164, 175
**(175 only for last ½ mile into
Wallingford)**
*Start at Abingdon Bridge
(grid reference 500 968)*

Abingdon is a beautiful Thames-side town, with a gracious old stone bridge, quaint almshouses, a magnificent town hall, and St Helen's Church with its soaring spire. The town grew from the stalls of various traders set up in front of the Benedictine abbey, of which only the grand old gatehouse and a couple of other buildings remain. Nonetheless, other works of the monks remain, notably the present main stream of the river, thought to have been dug by the monks who diverted the river from its old course along the Swift Ditch. The emergence of Abingdon as a wool market during the Middle Ages led to bitter in-fighting between town and abbey. The merchants formed a guild, the Fraternity of the Holy Cross, and started to improve their town, building the Church of St Helen, the almshouses, Abingdon Bridge, the causeway across Andersey Island and Culham Bridge over the Swift Ditch on land obtained by Royal Charter from the Abbot of Abingdon in 1416.

From Abingdon Bridge the Thames Path crosses the western entrance to the Swift Ditch and continues along the towpath, seemingly heading for the vast cooling towers of Didcot Power Station, before bearing left into Culham Cut, a navigational channel constructed in 1809 to bypass Sutton Mill.

The path arrives at Culham Lock and carries on downriver to Clifton Cut and Clifton Lock. Shortly after the lock, the path crosses the river at the handsome red-brick Clifton Hampden Bridge. This seven-arch bridge dates from 1857 and was designed by Sir George Gilbert Scott. Nearby stands the Barley Mow pub, parts of which date from 1350. Turning left, the Thames Path continues around a sweeping meander loop with the brick-and-timber cottages and colourful gardens of the village of Clifton Hampden clinging to the rocky river cliff opposite.

At Day's Lock, site of the main gauging station for the flow of the upper Thames, the towpath recrosses the river. The Sinodun Hills, crowned by their clumps of trees, lie to the right, brooding over this reach of the river. To the left is the ancient town of Dorchester on Thames. The Thames Path crosses the tributary River Thame near its confluence with the Thames and continues to Shillingford,

GUIDE BOX

PLACES TO VISIT
Abingdon County Hall Particularly fine; built in 1682 when Abingdon was County Town of Berkshire.
Wallingford Castle Gardens Haven of peace on the site of the Norman castle destroyed by Cromwell.
Beale Pakr (Childe Beale Wildlife Trust) Birds and rare breeds.
Basildon Park Classical 18th-century Bath stone house, plasterwork decorations; unusual Octagon Room; decorative Shell Room.

CAR PARKING
Abingdon (near bridge); Culham (beside bridge over lock); Clifton Hampden (by bridge); Shillingford; Wallingford (by bridge); Goring.

PUBLIC TRANSPORT
Train Stations at Didcot (6 miles from Abingdon, 4 miles from Clifton Hampden), Goring, Pangbourne.
Bus Oxford City Link, London to Wallingford, Dorchester, Shillingford and Abingdon.
Boat Summer services between Abingdon and Oxford.

ACCOMMODATION
Hotels, guest houses etc Abingdon, Dorchester on Thames, Wallingford, Streatley, Goring on Thames.

TOURIST INFORMATION OFFICES
Abingdon 25 Bridge Street, Abingdon, Oxfordshire OX14 3HN (tel 01235 522711)
Wallingford Town Hall, Market Place, Wallingford, Oxfordshire OX10 0EG (tel 01491 826972)

The Thames Path runs through lush meadowland as it approaches Clifton Hampden Bridge.

where it briefly leaves the river, rejoining the towpath at Shillingford Bridge, a graceful three-arch structure built in 1827 as part of a turnpike road.

Beyond Shillingford is Benson, shadowed today by its RAF base but actually a place of antiquity, being a tribal capital in Saxon times and the site of a great battle where Offa, king of Mercia, repelled the West Saxons. Here the path detours briefly from the river to go through the outskirts of Benson and then crosses the river at Benson Lock and continues to Wallingford.

WALLINGFORD TO PANGBOURNE
About 11 miles/18km
OS Landranger 175, 174
Start at Wallingford Bridge
(grid reference 610 895)

Wallingford was founded by the Romans at a point where they could ford the River Thames. In Saxon times it became a 'burgh', was sacked by the Danes – a common occurrence in this part of England – and further fortified by a massive castle under William the Conqueror. He was also responsible for the first Wallingford Bridge. The present 17-arched bridge is basically medieval, but was rebuilt and widened in 1809. The scanty remains of the castle consist of the grassy mound to the right of the Thames Path on the northern side of the town. Many English monarchs visited the castle, including King Stephen, who gave Wallingford its first charter in 1155. St Peter's Church stands close to the town end of the bridge, and has an impressive spire rising from an octagonal lantern.

South of Wallingford comes Cholsey Marsh Nature Reserve, an area of damp water meadows managed by traditional methods close to the site of the former Little Stoke ferry, where until the mid-19th century laden corn wagons were ferried over the river. The Thames Path follows the main road through Moulsford to turn left down Ferry Lane and regain the river at the Beetle and Wedge Hotel. It was here that HG Wells wrote *The History of Mr Polly* and the pub itself was the model for the Potwell Inn.

The towpath continues downstream past Cleve Lock to Streatley. Here the path turns left and crosses the Thames by the famous Swan Hotel to Goring, Streatley's twin village. This is the crossing point of the Icknield Way, most famous of all prehistoric trackways. South of Goring the towpath heads into the beautiful Goring Gap, the deep wooded valley by which the River Thames passes through the Chiltern Hills. The path follows the river under the

The Dyke Hills alongside the Thames Path at Dorchester on Thames are defensive earthworks dating back to the Iron Age.

railway bridge near Gatehampton, built in 1840 and designed by Brunel. On the opposite side of the river is 14th-century Basildon Church. The valley steepens and narrows where Hartslock Wood crowds down to the water's edge. Opposite is the Childe Beale Wildlife Trust and Beale Bird Park, home to rare and endangered creatures. The Thames Path turns away from the river to head uphill through the woodland onto the chalk downland. Look back and you will see Basildon Park, a fine 18th-century National Trust property, on the hillside.

The Thames Path continues past Coombe Farm and soon arrives on the outskirts of Whitchurch. Here it turns right down the steep village street, detours past the church and reaches the second tollbridge over the River Thames, connecting Whitchurch to its twin village, Pangbourne.

DORCHESTER ON THAMES

This quaint and attractive town, with picturesque cottages, speaks of its long history. The earliest phase of Dorchester's history is marked by the 'Dyke Hills', the defensive double banks of an Iron Age fort in the low-lying Thames-side meadows between the rivers Thames and Thame. An area of 114 acres is enclosed and would have provided a safe haven in times of danger for the Iron Age tribe and its livestock. Later, the Romans built a camp and then a town here, part of whose town walls still stand. Important in Roman times as a trading post on the river, Dorchester continued to flourish under the Saxons and in the 7th century an important Bishopric was established here. In AD635 St Birinus founded Dorchester Abbey, which is justly famous. Its large and richly decorated church, dating from 1170, was saved at the Dissolution to act as parish church for the town. It has a particularly fine Jesse window with stone branches and figures in stone and glass. The 12th-century lead font is also notable, and the lychgate is by Butterfield.

Pangbourne to Marlow

PANGBOURNE TO
LOWER SHIPLAKE
About 14 miles/22km
OS Landranger 175
Start at Pangbourne Bridge
(grid reference 632 767)

Pangbourne, where the little River Pang flows into the Thames, is best known as the home in his declining years of Kenneth Grahame, author of that Thames-side classic *The Wind in the Willows*. He died here in 1932. Less well known is that Pangbourne was granted its charter in the 9th century. The Thames Path runs through Pangbourne Meadow (now National Trust), a traditional water meadow of waving grasses and flowers, and continues along the riverbank opposite Hardwick House. Elizabeth I visited there and so did Charles I, who played bowls on the great lawn which slopes southward to the river.

Sadly, there is no right of way over Mapledurham Lock to the tiny village of Mapledurham, so walkers on the Thames Path must content themselves with looking across the river to the little church, the working watermill, which today is open to the public and produces stone ground flour, and the mellow house where Alexander Pope stayed with the Blounts.

From Mapledurham Lock the path detours from the river through the Purley Park Estate and returns to the river down steps at the Roebuck Inn. This diversion dates from 1777 when the landowner, Mr Worlidge of Purley, refused to sell the necessary strip of land for the towpath. In the end a short length of towpath was established on the opposite bank (marked on the OS map) with a horse ferry operating at either end to carry the beasts over! This stretch is not accessible to walkers as the ferries no longer exist and so the Thames Path still has to skirt Mr Worlidge's field, even though it is now a housing estate.

Returning to the riverside below the Roebuck Inn, the towpath heads towards Reading through a pleasant region of meadows, allotments, open land and public gardens. Reading is known today as an industrial and commercial centre, but it has a venerable history with Iron Age and Roman antecedents, though modern Reading grew from a Saxon settlement on the River Kennet. During the Middle Ages Reading developed into an important centre of the cloth industry. Henry I founded a great Cluniac abbey here and was buried in its great church in 1135. The gatehouse and a few broken walls in Forbury Park are all that remain of the massive abbey. The gatehouse was once used as a school and Jane Austen was one of the pupils.

The Thames Path takes a brief detour away from the river at Shiplake.

The Thames Path arrives at the riverside promenade in Reading and continues past Caversham Bridge, Reading Bridge and Caversham Lock to enter King's Meadow, now open playing fields but once the site of jousting tournaments. The towpath crosses the mouth of the River Kennet by Horseshoe Bridge and enters the Thames Valley Country Park, formerly rough meadows beside the river where it is thought that the 13th-century monk from Reading Abbey, John de Fornsete, was inspired to write 'Summer is icumen in', the earliest known piece of harmonised secular music.

The stretch of the river between Reading and Sonning is particularly lovely, with meadows and woods coming down to the waterside. Sonning Lock is famed for its brightly coloured floral displays, while Sonning itself is a quaint and most attractive place of brick-built houses and rustic cottages. It was centre of a diocese covering Berkshire and Wiltshire in the 10th and 11th centuries and even at the Reformation the Bishop of Salisbury still lived in Sonning's old Bishop's Palace. This has now almost entirely vanished. The old Deanery has also disappeared, save one stretch of wall used in the building of the new house, Deanery Gardens, by Sir Edwin Lutyens in 1901.

The path crosses the Thames at Sonning Bridge and then turns right over the millstream to join the towpath on the left-hand bank of the river. There has been a mill at Sonning since at least the 14th century and the present building, of 1797, has been converted into a 200-seat theatre.

Beyond Sonning comes Shiplake, perched on a river cliff above the towpath. The church is known for its 15th-century stained glass saved from the sack of the abbey church at St Omer during the French Revolution and as the place where Lord Tennyson married his Emily in 1859 after 14 years' courtship. The path turns inland at Shiplake Lock, crossing fields to Lower Shiplake and Shiplake Station.

LOWER SHIPLAKE TO MARLOW
About 11 miles/18km
OS Landranger 175
Start at Shiplake Station
(grid reference 776 797)

The Thames Path follows a road from Shiplake Station, returning to the river past Bolney Court. Marsh Lock, a short distance along the towpath, is well known for its long wooden causeways which give an excellent view of the churning white waters of the weir against a backdrop of dark trees. Beyond Marsh Lock the towpath approaches Henley on Thames, famed for its annual regatta in early July. This was first held in 1839 and today attracts rowing crews from all over the world. The path approaches Henley along a wide promenade, crosses the river on Henley's famous bridge and continues alongside the regatta course.

The towpath continues past Temple Island, where the races begin and where

A pleasure boat enters Marsh Lock alongside the causeway right next to the weir.

stands a mock temple, set up in 1771. Rounding the great meander bend, the path passes the weirs at Hambleden, where there has been a mill since before Domesday Book. The present 16th-century mill building has now been converted into flats, but its white weatherboarded bulk alongside the foaming weirs still makes for a beautiful riverside scene.

At the site of the old Aston ferry, the Thames Path turns away from the river to Aston, a cluster of cottages and the Flower Pot Hotel. It turns left along a private road, passing across the lower lawn of the splendid mansion, Culham Court, perched high above the river. Beyond Culham Court the path rejoins the river and continues opposite Medmenham Abbey. Once a cell of Woburn's Cistercian Abbey, it was consecrated in 1200, but became notorious for the activities of the Hellfire Club, which held its obscene orgies here in the mid-18th century.

The Thames Path arrives at Hurley, with its green and prosperous riverside, and continues past Hurley Lock. It crosses the river by the lock bridge and runs along the right-hand bank to the new Temple footbridge. Here the Thames Path crosses back over the river to run along the left-hand bank past Temple Lock and, on the opposite bank, Bisham Abbey, now the National Sports Centre, to Marlow.

Marlow to Staines

MARLOW TO MAIDENHEAD
About 8 miles/13km
OS Landranger 175
Start at Marlow suspension bridge
(grid reference 852 861)

The pleasant old market town of Marlow has several interesting buildings and many literary connections, since Shelley, Peacock and, over a century later, TS Eliot all lived here for a while. The elegant suspension bridge was built in 1831 and on the other side of the river is the famous Compleat Angler restaurant. The Thames Path does not cross the river here but goes through the churchyard and a series of narrow alleys and paths to Marlow Mill. Beyond the green, the path goes under the A404.

The official path continues along the left-hand bank past the former and once-important Spade Oak ferry to Bourne End. A pleasant alternative is to cross the river by the modern road bridge in Marlow and turn left along the road before climbing the path through the thick deciduous woodlands of Quarry Wood to emerge on the top of Winter Hill. This magnificent open area belongs to the National Trust and offers fine views over the Thames Valley and Chiltern Hills. This alternative route now goes downhill to return to the river at Ferry Cottage, site of the Spade Oak ferry, and then follows the

river round a large meander bend opposite Bourne End, along the edge of Cock Marsh (National Trust), a tract of wet lowland managed as a nature reserve, to rejoin the official route at Bourne End railway bridge.

The official route crosses the Thames at Bourne End, alongside the railway bridge and continues to Cookham. Here it turns through the churchyard passing close to the grave of the artist Stanley Spencer (1891–1959). The church was mentioned in Domesday and Cookham itself is an ancient place with a wide and pleasing High Street. The path passes the diminutive Stanley Spencer Gallery and rejoins the river at the former My Lady ferry. Here it turns right to follow the Thames to Maidenhead, with the hanging beechwoods on the opposite bank towering 200ft above the river for the 2-mile stretch. Above the woods is Cliveden House, formerly seat of the Duke of Westminster and then of Lord Astor and his American-born wife, Nancy, the first woman MP. Later the house was the scene of 20th-century political scandals and it is now let as a hotel by the National Trust.

The towpath joins the riverside road leading into Maidenhead and passes Boulter's Lock, one of the most famous on the river, thanks to the well-known picture, painted in 1895 by Gregory, in

GUIDE BOX

PLACES TO VISIT
Cookham, Stanley Spencer Gallery Small gallery dedicated to the local painter.
Eton Eton College – famous public school founded by Henry VI.
Windsor Castle – State apartments and St George's Chapel, Savill Garden (Windsor Great Park); Legoland; Windsor Royalty and Empire Exhibition.

CAR PARKING
Marlow; Cookham; Maidenhead (near Boulter's Lock); Windsor; Runnymede.

PUBLIC TRANSPORT
Train Stations at Marlow, Cookham, Maidenhead, Windsor, Staines.
Bus Green Line from London to Windsor and to Staines.
Boat Summer services at Cookham, Maidenhead, Windsor and Runnymede.

ACCOMMODATION
Hotels, guest houses etc Marlow, Maidenhead, Windsor, Datchet, Staines.

TOURIST INFORMATION OFFICES
Marlow Court Garden Leisure Complex, Pound Lane, Marlow, Bucks, SL7 2AE (tel 01628 483597)
Maidenhead The Library, St Ives Road, Maidenhead, Berkshire SL6 1QU (tel 01628 781110)
Windsor 24 High Street, Windsor, Berkshire SL4 1LH (tel 01753 852010)

which the lock is crowded with all manner of craft. It is still a busy place, fascinating to watch, as it bustles with motor cruisers and their holidaying crews.

The panoramic view over the Thames Valley and the Chiltern Hills is worth the detour from the path and the climb up steep Quarry wood.

MAIDENHEAD TO STAINES
About 14 miles/22km
OS Landranger 175, 176
Start at Maidenhead Bridge
(grid reference 899 813)

At Maidenhead Bridge, a graceful stone structure of 1772–7, the path crosses the river on the A4 and then continues along the left-hand bank. Skindles Hotel stands beside the bridge, famous as the scene of many an assignation during the golden age of the Thames. Brunel's spectacular low-arched railway bridge lies ahead. Built in 1839, this bridge achieved fame through Turner's great painting *Rain, Steam and Speed*. The towpath passes under one of the two main arches, known as 'the sounding arch' because of the echo.

Bray, on the opposite river bank, is the village made famous by the legendary vicar of easy conscience who changed his brand of Christianity to suit the times. Bray is also famous for Michel Roux's Waterside Inn, which lies at the bottom of Ferry Lane. Nearby is Bray Lock and its attractive garden, and just beyond is the M4 bridge, built in 1961, which has a footway for those who wish to detour into Bray. The Thames Path follows the left-hand bank along Dorney Reach, where a detour along the Barge Path leads to Dorney Church and the Tudor mansion, Dorney Park. Here, during the reign of Charles II,

John Rose, head gardener, grew the first pineapple to be produced in England. The pub at Dorney celebrates the event – it is called The Pineapple. On the opposite bank are Bray Studios.

Dorney's enormous Thames Meadow lies on the left and the towpath runs alongside it past Boveney's tiny church, the Chapel of St Mary Magdalen. There has been a place of worship here since Saxon times and even today the church is lit only by candles. The village, a large one scattered about a green, lies away from the river bank. Boveney Lock lies beyond the church. On the opposite bank is Windsor Racecourse and beyond that the great solid outline of Windsor itself, crowding up the hill to the royal stronghold.

The towpath passes under the A355 and then the railway bridge to arrive at Eton. It passes the Eton College boathouse and turns right to cross the river to Windsor. The towpath does not pass through Windsor itself, but runs along the quayside and Romney Walk, with a brief glimpse across the river to Eton College Chapel, to arrive at Romney Lock. Beyond the lock the path follows the big meander under the railway bridge and across playing fields to Victoria Bridge. Here it crosses the Thames and passes through Datchet to recross the river at Albert Bridge.

From Albert Bridge the towpath continues past Old Windsor Lock to Old

The chapel of St Mary Magdelen at Boveney, where there has been a place of worship since Saxon times.

Windsor, an ancient place despite its modern suburban dress. There was a Saxon palace here in the 9th century, and even after the Norman Conquest it was used as a royal residence. Henry I moved his court to Windsor Castle in 1110 and the old Saxon palace fell into disrepair. Now we do not even know exactly where it stood. But Old Windsor Priory remains, as does the 13th-century parish church, restored in 1863. A little further on is the Bells of Ouzeley pub, named after the bells of Ouzeley Abbey, which are said to have been lost in the river hereabouts during the Reformation.

The Thames Path continues along the riverside road to Runnymede, where King John was forced to sign the Magna Carta on 15 June 1215. Runnymede (National Trust) is broad green riverside parkland, a haven of tranquillity and peace. Behind, as a superb backdrop, are the wooded slopes of Cooper's Hill, topped by the RAF memorial built in 1953 by Sir Edward Maufe. Nearby is the Kennedy Memorial on an acre of land given to the American people by the Queen.

The towpath continues to Bell Weir Lock and the M25 road bridge, completed in 1978, and follows the river to Staines.

Staines to Kew

STAINES TO HAMPTON COURT

About 12¹/₂ miles/20km
OS Landranger 176
Start at Staines Bridge
(grid reference 032 714)

The Thames Path crosses Staines Bridge, where in Roman times there was an important river crossing, and turns right past the Riverside pub into Clarence Street before returning to the riverside promenade. It continues across the mouth of the tributary River Colne and into the riverside gardens and carries on to Penton Hook Lock Cut, which bypasses a goose-neck meander on the river. This is a land of riverside bungalows, each with its own patch of river frontage, bright with flowers. Ellen Terry (1848–1928) the actress lived at Penton Hook for a time.

The towpath gives way to a gravelled walk at Laleham and then joins a pleasant riverside road, appropriately named Thames Side. Laleham is known for its connections with Dr Thomas Arnold the famous headmaster, who ran a small private school here prior to his appointment at Rugby, and with his poet son, Matthew, who was born, lived and died here. Laleham Park, once the grounds of Laleham House, the ancestral home of the Earls of Lucan, is a pleasant open space beside the river. The towpath passes under the M3 and runs alongside Chertsey Lock to Chertsey Bridge. On the opposite side of the river along this reach once stood the now almost entirely vanished Chertsey Abbey, one of the greatest of the many Thames-side monastic houses.

Chertsey Bridge is an elegant structure reflecting much of Chertsey's own refined 18th-century atmosphere. The custom of ringing the curfew still survives; it is rung daily between Michaelmas and Lady Day on the 14th-century Abbey Bell, a survivor of the abbey now set in the 19th-century church tower.

The path continues on the left-hand bank past the bridge to Shepperton Lock on the edge of the maze of waterways at the confluence with the River Wey. Here the walker can either follow the roads which shadow the main stream of the Thames through its double meander at Shepperton to cross the river at Walton Bridge, or cross the Thames by ferry and follow the towpath alongside the deep artificial Desborough Cut, which was excavated in 1935 to ease navigation. Beyond the Desborough Cut the towpath

GUIDE BOX

PLACES TO VISIT
Hampton Court Palace Started early 16th century, expanded by Henry VIII and later monarchs – Tudor kitchens, orangery, vine, maze.
Ham House – lovely Stuart (1610) house and 17th-century garden.
Kew Royal Botanic Gardens – world-famous gardens and research centre.

CAR PARKING
Staines (near bridge); Chertsey (near bridge); Walton-on-Thames (near bridge); Hampton Court Palace; Kingston upon Thames; Ham House; Richmond.

PUBLIC TRANSPORT
Train Stations at Staines, Chertsey, Weybridge, Walton-on-Thames, Hampton, Kingston, Richmond (London Transport and BR), Kew (LT), Kew Bridge.
Bus Green Line from London to Staines, Hampton and Kingston. London Transport buses to Richmond and Kew.
Boat Summer services at Hampton Court, Kingston, Richmond and Kew.

ACCOMMODATION
Hotels, guest houses etc Staines, Walton-on-Thames, Hampton Court, Hampton Wick, Richmond.

TOURIST INFORMATION OFFICES
Richmond Old Town Hall, Whittaker Avenue, Richmond, Surrey TW9 1TP (tel 0181 940 9125)
Twickenham Civic Centre, 44 York Street, Twickenham, Middlesex TW1 3BZ (tel 0181 891 1411)

passes through the open space called Cowey Stakes, held by local tradition to be the spot where Julius Caesar crossed the Thames in 55BC, and meets up with the route through Shepperton at Walton-on-Thames.

The towpath, on the right-hand bank, passes beneath Walton Bridge, where an iron bridge has replaced the brick one of 1864, the subject of another painting by Turner, while the earlier wooden latticework bridge on the site was once painted by Canaletto. The towpath runs alongside the river to Sunbury Locks. Sunbury itself, with its Byzantine-style church built in 1752, lies on the opposite bank. Swan-upping, the annual marking of the year's cygnets to establish ownership, starts at Sunbury in the third week of July. It is a tradition that goes back 800 years and is presided over by the Queen's Swan Keeper, resplendent in his scarlet livery.

The towpath passes the former Hurst Park Racecourse and Molesey Lock. On the opposite bank stands the village of Hampton, still served by a ferry which sets out from just below St Mary's Church, a large building of 1831. Garrick House was the home of the great actor David Garrick, who bought the place in 1745. In Molesey, a settlement named in Domesday, the towpath merges with the riverside road and reaches Hampton Court Bridge beside the railway station.

A narrow boat passes through Chertsey Lock.

HAMPTON COURT TO KEW
About 10¹/₂ miles/17km
OS Landranger 176
Start at Hampton Court Bridge
(grid reference 154 685)

The Thames Path crosses over the river by Hampton Court Bridge and rejoins the towpath on the north bank in Hampton Court Park, close to the famous palace.

At Kingston Bridge the path crosses the river to Kingston upon Thames, a modern-looking place that has a long and noble history. Seven Saxon kings were crowned here and their coronation stone is still preserved outside the 1930s Guildhall. Beyond Kingston the towpath runs along the banks of the river, with trees and open spaces crowding down to the water's edge, to Teddington Locks (there are three of them), which mark the highest point upriver at which tides are felt. The locking system at Teddington, rebuilt in 1931, is the largest on the river, with the 650ft barge lock designed to accommodate a tug and six barges. Not far below the locks a stone obelisk marks the boundary of jurisdiction between the Environment Agency (formerly the National Rivers Authority) and the Port of London Authority. Below this point the Thames can truly be called 'London River', the tidal highway on which the great city came into being.

During the 18th century Twickenham, on the opposite bank, was a fashionable land of villas and parkland. Nearby Eel Pie Island, one of the largest on the river, retains its reputation as a trendy place, with studios and clubs as well as boatbuilders, repair yards and bungalows.

A little further down the river, and on the same side as the Thames Path, stands Ham House, a superb Jacobean mansion built in 1610. The Thames Path passes through the car park close to a landing stage from which a ferry crosses to Twickenham, and continues through Petersham Meadows to Richmond Terrace and graceful Richmond Bridge. The royal palace, where Queen Elizabeth I died in 1603, has long since vanished, but Richmond still has something of the atmosphere of a well-to-do town of Georgian times. Richmond Park was the subject of a famous lawsuit in 1758 when there was an unsuccessful attempt to exclude the public, as a result of which the

Looking down to the Thames from the wooded heights of Richmond Hill.

public have the right to free use of the park for all time. The towpath passes by Richmond Lock and rounds the meander bend opposite Isleworth to arrive at Kew.

HAMPTON COURT

Said to be the most magnificent secular building in England, Hampton Court Palace was begun by Cardinal Wolsey in 1514 and was presented by him to Henry VIII in an attempt to retain the king's favour. The king courted Anne Boleyn here and their joint initials are inscribed in a love-knot over the gateway. The Great Gate House, the Clock House and the Great Hall date from this time. Later, in the reign of William and Mary, the east front and south front were added by Sir Christopher Wren. At the same time, the famous maze was first planted. Hampton Court was the residence for 12 successive monarchs, the last being George II. During those years several historic events occurred here, including the second trial of Mary, Queen of Scots, and the famous conference, held under Mary's son, James I, which led to the King James Authorised Version of the Bible.

Kew to Woolwich

KEW TO WESTMINSTER

About 12 miles/19km

OS Landranger 176

Start at Kew Bridge

(grid reference 190 778)

This final stretch of the Thames Path gives an unusual and rewarding view of London, for from Kew downstream the Thames is increasingly an urban river with the great city standing astride its banks. Kew itself centres on its triangular-shaped green, surrounded by Georgian houses and the Church of St Anne (1710–14), with the main entrance to the Royal Botanic Gardens at the apex of the triangle.

The towpath passes under Kew Bridge. On the other side of the river is the fascinating Kew Bridge Steam Museum and, along the bank east of the bridge, the quaint old fishermen's cottages of Strand on the Green, and the elegant Georgian river frontage of Chiswick. Then comes Chiswick Bridge, Mortlake, famous during the 17th century for its tapestry works, and the elegant 18th- and 19th-century houses with attractive iron verandas and balconies that face the river at Barnes Terrace. Rounding the big meander bend, the Thames Path arrives at Hammersmith Bridge, built in 1887, and continues beside Barn Elms Park and its school playing fields to Putney Embankment and its boat houses. The view over the river from here is to Fulham Palace, main residence of the

Bishop of London. Every spring the Oxford and Cambridge Boat race is rowed between Putney Bridge and Mortlake.

The towpath ends at Putney Bridge, and from this point the Thames Path is still being created. Eventually a route will be available on both sides of the river, but the many bridges mean that it is in any case easy to cross from one bank to the other to see the sights. The route given below mostly follows the present official south bank path.

The Thames Path runs alongside the river in Wandsworth Park before following a well-signed route across the River Wandle. Wandsworth was, until the 19th century, a little village famous for its silk and hat industry, and the urban stream that gave it its name was a renowned fishing river. The path goes under the Wandsworth Bridge approach and returns to the Thames. Along this riverside route, with views to Lots Road Power Station and the Chelsea Harbour development, the riverscape is changing fast as the old warehouses disappear and flats spring up in their place, but St Mary's Church, surviving flotsam from the wreck of the 18th-century village of Battersea, stands serene even if somewhat overshadowed by the end of the 20th century. Built in 1775, with a big porchway, St Mary's is another of those unexpected Thames-side gems, a moment of reflection and communion with the past on the banks of a river that

GUIDE BOX

PLACES TO VISIT

Royal Botanic Gardens, Kew – world-famous gardens.

Kew Bridge Steam Museum Victorian pumping station with steam engines and six beam engines.

St Mary's Church, Battersea 18th-century haven of peace.

Chelsea Physic Garden On opposite side of river – second oldest botanic garden in England, begun 1673, an oasis.

Royal Hospital, Chelsea On opposite side of river – chapel, great hall, museum; pensioners' parade Sundays at 10.30.

Museum of Garden History, St Mary-at-Lambeth – includes accurately recreated 17th-century garden.

Houses of Parliament On opposite side of river – House of Commons, House of Lords, Big Ben.

Westminster Abbey On opposite side of river – every coronation since 1066 has taken place here; tombs and memorials of many famous people.

South Bank Arts Complex includes Festival Hall and National Theatre; Museum of the Moving Image.

St Paul's Cathedral On opposite side of river – Wren's masterpiece.

Southwark Cathedral Gothic glory.

HMS Belfast. World War II big gun armoured warship.

Tower Bridge World-famous landmark.

Cutty Sark Greenwich – fastest tea clipper ever built (1869).

Royal Naval College Greenwich – built by Wren as a naval hospital; splendid Painted Hall and chapel.

Queen's House Greenwich – focal point of Royal Naval College by Inigo Jones.

National Maritime Museum Greenwich – the story of Britain and the sea.

Thames Barrier Visitors' Centre Woolwich – world's largest movable flood barrier.

CAR PARKING

Car parking is difficult in central London and it is best to use public transport.

PUBLIC TRANSPORT

Train Stations at Kew Gardens (BR and LT), Kew Bridge (BR), Barnes Bridge (BR), Putney (BR), Putney Bridge (LT), East Putney (LT), Wandsworth Town (BR), Vauxhall (BR and LT), Waterloo (BR and LT), Blackfriars (BR and LT, on opposite side of river), Cannon Street (BR and LT, on opposite side of river), London Bridge (BR and LT), Rotherhithe (LT), Island Gardens (Docklands, on opposite side of river), foot tunnel to Greenwich Pier, Charlton (BR).

Bus Numerous London Transport bus routes.

Boat Summer services at Kew.

ACCOMMODATION

Hotels, guest houses etc Wide variety of choice with prices to suit all pockets.

TOURIST INFORMATION OFFICES

London Tourist Board 26 Grosvenor Gardens, London SW1W 0DU (tel 0171 730 3488)

Greenwich 46 Greenwich Church, Street, Greenwich SE10 9BL (tel 0181 858 6376)

seems to sweep all too inexorably into the future.

Beyond St Mary's the Thames Path continues past Battersea Bridge and Albert Bridge into Battersea Park with its peace pagoda and views across the river to Chelsea Physic Garden and the Chelsea Royal Hospital. From Chelsea Bridge the south bank path follows the road away

The Thames at the Pool of London, looking to the World War II big gun armoured warship, HMS Belfast, and the river's most famous crossing point, Tower Bridge, ahead.

from the river to Vauxhall, but the north bank route runs along the riverside opposite the sad bulk of Battersea Power Station to Vauxhall Bridge. From here the south bank route runs along the Albert Embankment with views across the river to Millbank, dominated by the 378ft Millbank Tower, built in 1963. Close to Lambeth Bridge is Lambeth Palace, official residence of the Archbishop of Canterbury since the 12th century. Then comes the famous view over the river to the Houses of Parliament.

WESTMINSTER TO WOOLWICH
About 11 miles/17km
OS Landranger 177
Start at Westminster Bridge
(grid reference 307 796)

The Thames Path marches along the famous riverside promenade alongside the South Bank Arts Complex and under Waterloo Bridge, with the familiar London vista unfolding on the other side – the tree-lined Embankment and the great dome of St Paul's Cathedral. Beside Blackfriars Bridge is the Doggetts Coat and Badge, a pub named after the famous Thames Watermen's rowing race – the longest in the world – started in 1715 by Thomas Doggett, an Irish comedian. The path continues along Bankside Reach to Cardinal's Wharf and a house reputedly inhabited by Sir Christopher Wren while he was building St Paul's. It is more likely that it was an inn at that time, for since the 16th century Bankside was the resort of inns, amusement gardens and theatres. The Globe, the Rose and the Swan were all here, as the newly built replica of the Globe Theatre reminds us.

Continuing under Southwark Bridge and along Bankside, the Thames Path swings away from the river past the site of the Clink prison and the sparse remains of 13th-century Winchester Palace, to return to the river at the Thames-Side Inn. The path runs beside Southwark Cathedral, originally built in 1206 as part of the Augustinian priory of St Mary Overie and surely the most inspiring piece of true Gothic architecture in London.

The path crosses the London Bridge approach and descends steps to the riverside terrace. London Bridge stands at London's ancient bridging point, until 1749 the site of the only bridge spanning the Thames in London. The Thames Path arrives at the Pool of London and continues to Tower Bridge. Beyond Tower Bridge the path arrives at Shad Thames, which it follows alongside St Saviour's Dock, returning to the river at Cherry Garden Pier. Here ships sound a signal if

they need Tower Bridge raised for their passage, and here it was that Turner painted *The Fighting Temeraire* as she was towed to the breaker's yard.

The path will eventually follow the riverside through Rotherhithe but at present it detours through the former Surrey Docks to climb Stave Hill, with its views across the river to the Isle of Dogs, dominated by the vast 800ft skyscraper at Canary Wharf. The path ambles on to Deptford Strand, from where Sir Francis Drake set sail, and turns inland past the noble old Church of St Nicholas, before working its way back to the Thames near Greenwich Pier and the famous tea clipper, *Cutty Sark*.

Greenwich is known for the gracious façade of its former Royal Naval College, whose superb buildings overlook the river. Once beyond them, the Thames Path truly reaches industrial Thames-side and crosses over the entrance to the Blackwall Tunnel to reach the Tideway Sailing Centre. A broad riverside walk runs from here past the Hope and Anchor pub to the route's destination, the Thames Barrier.

The Canary Wharf tower is seen in the distance from the Thames Barrier at Woolwich, where the Thames Path ends.

THE POOL OF LONDON

The river reach between London Bridge and Tower Bridge is known as the Pool of London, historically a safe anchorage guarded on the opposite bank by the massive bulk of the Tower of London. Today this reach of the river is open and tranquil, but once it was a bustling, busy place, regarded by many as the heart of the British Empire. Here the great conveyors of commerce departed to and arrived from the four corners of the globe. Until a hundred years ago The Pool was a great forest of masts, more recently it throbbed with the engines of steam ships and barges discharging cargo and taking cargo aboard. Now The Pool is quiet, dreaming of its past, and the old wharf buildings have been restored and turned into shops, pubs and restaurants. HMS *Belfast*, the cruiser converted to a floating naval museum, lies anchored here. Tower Bridge, now the most famous bridge in London, was built in 1894.

The River Wey and its Connections

THE RIVER WEY: WEYBRIDGE TO GODALMING
19 MILES/30KM
THE BASINGSTOKE CANAL: WEST BYFLEET TO GREYWELL
31 MILES/50KM
THE WEY & ARUN CANAL: SHALFORD TO AMBERLEY
33 MILES/53KM

THERE is unhurried and pleasant walking along the towpaths of the River Wey and its two branch canals, the Basingstoke and the Wey & Arun. The River Wey flows into the Thames at Weybridge, and the River Wey Navigation, which opened in 1653 and follows it south to Guildford, is the oldest locked waterway in England. The Godalming Navigation, of 1760, continues the waterway south to Godalming. Both navigations now belong to the National Trust. The Basingstoke Canal, which climbs up across the Surrey heaths and into Hampshire, opened in 1794 and had become almost completely derelict before restoration began in the 1970s. The partly restored Wey & Arun Canal, which heads south through rural Surrey and Sussex from Shalford, between Guildford and Godalming, to Amberley, opened in 1816 but was never a successful commercial route, and closed in 1871.

The River Wey

GUILDFORD TO GODALMING
19 MILES/30KM

WEYBRIDGE TO GUILDFORD
About 13 miles/20km
OS Landranger 176, 187, 186
Start at Thames Lock, Weybridge
(grid reference 072 654)

Weybridge stands at the confluence of the rivers Wey and Thames, and is the starting point for this walk along the Wey, an 'improved river', with sections of canal which cut across the necks of sweeping meander bends. Although close to London, the River Wey is astonishingly rural, with many historic buildings nearby. It was a prosperous waterway carrying timber, bound downstream for London via the Thames as well as pottery from Farnham, paper, hoops, bark, flour and corn. Goods were carried to Guildford as late as the 1960s, and there was a brief renewal of transport upstream to Coxes Mill in the early 1980s.

The walk begins at Thames Lock and turns upstream to the former Coxes Mill and Coxes Lock. Beyond this the towpath continues past New Haw Lock and the White Hart Inn, and opposite the entrance to the Basingstoke Canal into Byfleet, famous today for the banked racing circuit at Brooklands, now a museum. South of Byfleet the towpath runs between meadows and a belt of woodland to the Anchor Inn and Pyrford Lock. To the east the attractive group of Wisley's Church Farm and early Norman church stands in splendid isolation on the lane to Wisley village and the Royal Horticultural Society's famous gardens.

Beyond Pyrford Lock come Walsham Flood Gates and square-shaped Walsham Lock, one of the last turf-sided locks in Britain, with grass going right down to the water's edge. Pyrford, on the west bank, is renowned for its humble little Norman church, while Ripley, on the eastern bank, was originally a coaching village on the Portsmouth Road. On the far side of the river beside the Abbey Stream are the lovely ruins of Newark Priory, founded in the late 12th century.

Beyond the priory the walk continues past Papercourt Lock to Tanyard Bridge at Send, a string of hamlets along the River Wey. It passes the New Inn and Cart Bridge to reach Worsfold Gates and then runs past Triggs Lock, a delightful part of the walk. Beyond Send footbridge the walk adjoins the grounds of Sutton Place, built by Sir Richard Weston, protégé of Henry VIII. The house is unusual in its terracotta ornamentation. In later years it was the home of Sir Richard's descendant, another Sir Richard Weston, who with three partners founded the Wey Navigation in 1651.

At Broad Oak Weir the towpath runs alongside moorings for river craft, with wooded slopes on the opposite bank, and so arrives at Bowers Lock. Next comes Old Bucks Weir and the towpath continues along the river banks into Guildford, with glimpses ahead of the imposing 20th-century cathedral (completed in 1966) on Stag Hill. The river flows under the Guildford bypass, where walkers must cross the river to return to the towpath.

WALKING GUIDES
Wey Navigation
National Trust *River Wey Navigations* (leaflet includes information for walkers).
Basingstoke Canal
Basingstoke Canal Towpath Trail, free leaflet from Basingstoke Canal Centre, Mytchett Place Road, Mytchett, Surrey GU16 6DD (tel 01252 370073).
Map of the Basingstoke Canal Geo Projects.
Wey & Arun Canal
Mackintosh, Aeneas *Wey-South Path*, available from Wey & Arun Canal Trust, 24 Griffiths Avenue, Lancing, Sussex BN15 0HW (tel 01913 753099).

OS MAPS
Wey Navigation
Landranger 176, 186, 187
Basingstoke Canal
Landranger 186
Wey & Arun Canal
Landrangers 186, 187, 197

LINKS
The Thames Path lies across the Thames by ferry from Weybridge, at the start of the Wey Navigation. The North Downs Way crosses the Wey Navigation at St Catherine's Bridge, south of Guildford. The Blackwater Valley Path crosses the Basingstoke Canal near Ash. The Greensand Way crosses the Wey & Arun Canal south of Wonersh. The Sussex Border Path crosses the Wey & Arun Canal near Loxwood. The South Downs Way crosses the River Arun at Amberley.

GUILDFORD TO GODALMING
About 6 miles/10km
OS Landranger 186
Start at Guildford, just east of the station
(grid reference 495 993)

Guildford was founded at the point where the River Wey breaches the North Downs, at a convenient point for a ford. It was already established as west Surrey's main town by the time of Domesday, shortly after which the royal manor was embellished by a Norman castle, today set incongruously in municipal gardens. The town is reputed to be the Astolat of the Arthurian legends and has for long been praised for its beautiful setting on the steeply sloping hills bordering the river.

Certainly the view of the Mount from the steep High Street, with its Tudor Abbot's Hospital and its famous clock jutting out from the façade of the Guildhall, is something that not even the gyrating latter end of the 20th century can mar.

The river is spanned by four bridges in close succession. At Guildford Wharf above

be held. This fair was far-famed and may well have been the original of Bunyan's Vanity Fair in *Pilgrim's Progress*, for Bunyan once lived in a house on the common.

The towpath passes opposite the entrance to the Wey & Arun Canal. A rural and wooded section follows, leading past

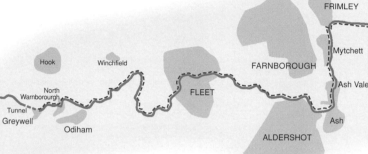

the new Friary Bridge, the Wey Navigation ends and the Godalming Navigation begins. Beyond the Town Mill, now the scenery workshop for the Yvonne Arnaud Theatre, the towpath arrives at Millmead Lock and continues opposite the busy Guildford Boat House to enter the beautiful Wey Gap through the chalk downland. Water meadows stretch down to the river on the opposite bank, and the path runs under the lee of St Catherine's Hill. Here is the old crossing point of the Pilgrim's Way, now followed in part by the North Downs Way. The footbridge is on the site of the former St Catherine's Ferry, which carried the pilgrims over the river.

St Catherine's Lock and Riff Raff Weir follow, and then comes Broadford Bridge, with its pub and cottages. A detour left leads to the cottagey village of Shalford on the Guildford-to-Horsham road. In the 17th century, the vicar here was William Oughtred, a famous mathematician who in 1631 introduced the use of an 'x' as the multiplication sign. Close by stands Shalford Mill, while further along is the large common where Shalford Fair used to

Unstead Lock and Catteshall Lock to Farncombe, well-known for its boathouse, which hires out all manner of river craft.

Godalming, its church carrying a huge lead spire, centres on narrow streets which curve towards the 'pepperpot' market hall of 1814, an attractive townscape. The path arrives at Godalming Wharf and the Town Bridge, head of the old Godalming Navigation. A footpath continues along the river to Boarden Bridge, near Godalming Railway Station and the end of the walk.

Thames Lock, at Weybridge.

GUIDE BOX

PLACES TO VISIT
Elmbridge Museum Displays include Wisley canoe.
Brooklands Museum Tells the story of motor racing and aviation at Brooklands (open by appointment).
Wisley, Royal Horticultural Society Garden – variety of different gardens cover 250 acres; church – simple Norman church (undedicated) standing beside Church Farm, an attractive group.
Pyrford, St Nicholas' Church – an unaltered Norman church, rare in Surrey.
Guildford Guildford Wharf, upper limit of Wey Navigation – restored treadmill crane; museum; castle – ruined shell of Norman castle; cathedral – southern England's only 20th-century cathedral; guildhall; Guildford Boat House – river trips and cruising restaurant; canoes, rowing boats for hire.
St Catherine's Chapel Ruinous early 14th-century chapel on St Catherine's Hill, south of Guildford on Pilgrim's Way.

Shalford Mill Original waterwheel and machinery at this restored 18th-century watermill on River Wey.

CAR PARKING
Weybridge; Byfleet; Guildford; Shalford (limited parking near Stonebridge and at station); Godalming (near Godalming Wharf).

PUBLIC TRANSPORT
Train Stations at Weybridge, Byfleet and New Haw, Guildford, Shalford, Godalming.
Bus Between Weybridge and Guildford.

ACCOMMODATION
Hotels, guest houses etc Guildford, Godalming.

TOURIST INFORMATION OFFICE
Guildford 14 Tunsgate, Guildford, Surrey GU1 3QT (tel 01483 444333/4)

The Basingstoke Canal

WEST BYFLEET TO GREYWELL
31 MILES/50KM

The Basingstoke Canal was constructed in 1794 to link Basingstoke, then a little market town, with the great market of London, via the Wey Navigation. It ran through what was then an intensely rural area, and as nothing came of the grandiose plans to link it to the Channel coast at the big commercial port of Southampton, it was only ever used to carry local goods. The materials needed to build the London & South Western Railway were shipped along it, as were bricks and timber for the Aldershot Military Camps established in the 1850s. Then in 1895 the new owner established a brickworks at Up Nately and transported his product to London down the canal. The brickworks was forced to close in 1908 because the bricks were of inferior quality. After World War I the canal declined and was effectively bisected by the collapse of the Greywell Tunnel in 1932. By the 1970s it was derelict. Restoration of the canal between the collapsed tunnel and the Wey Navigation began in 1973 and was complete by 1988 with the official opening in 1991.

In many respects the Basingstoke Canal is the walkers' canal *par excellence*, for canal traffic is limited to conserve water, particularly through the Deepcut Lock flight, but the towpath is well trodden and much used. The restricted traffic means the canal is also noted for its wildlife (see opposite page).

WEST BYFLEET TO ASH VALE
About 14 miles/22km
OS Landranger 187, 186
(187 only for first ⅓ mile in West Byfleet)
Start at Woodham Junction, West Byfleet (grid reference 055 620)

The walk starts at Woodham Junction where the Basingstoke Canal joins the Wey Navigation just beyond New Haw Lock. Almost immediately the canal rises through a flight of six locks and then passes through Sheerwater and under Chertsey Road Bridge to Woking. The towpath keeps to the south side of the canal through the town, where trips are available on the traditional narrow boat *Painted Lady*.

There is another flight of locks, four this time, at St John's. Then, passing under Kiln Bridge, the canal arrives at an attractively sylvan reach with trees and rhododendrons coming down towards the water on the verge of Hook Heath. The towpath continues along the south bank to Brookwood Bridge. Here the towpath crosses to the northern bank, passes the flight of three locks and climbs above the 150ft contour. Brookwood Cemetery lies to the south.

GUIDE BOX

PLACES TO VISIT
Basingstoke Canal Centre Mytchett Place Road, Mytchett – houses canal exhibition, tea room, adventure playground; boat trips.
Aldershot Military Museum – military life behind the scenes; Airborne Forces Museum – the parachute forces' story.

CAR PARKING
Woodham Locks; West Byfleet (station); Woking (town centre and at Kiln Bridge above St John's Locks); Mytchett (Basingstoke Canal Centre); Aldershot (Farnborough Road Bridge and Claycart Bridge); Fleet (Pyestock Hill beside Norris Bridge); Crookham (Crookham Wharf); Winchfield Hurst (Barley Mow Bridge); Odiham (Colt Hill and village centre); Greywel (limited parking in village).

PUBLIC TRANSPORT
Train Stations at Byfleet and New Haw, West Byfleet, Woking, Brookwood, Ash Vale, Ash, Aldershot, Fleet.
Bus Local bus services from Byfleet, Woking, Aldershot and Fleet.
Boat Canal trips from Basingstoke Canal Visitor Centre, Woking and Colt Hill, Odiham.

ACCOMMODATION
Hotels, guest houses etc Woking, Fleet, Odiham
Camping Basingstoke Canal Centre, Mytchett Place Road, Mytchett.

TOURIST INFORMATION CENTRE
Aldershot Military Museum, Queen's Avenue, Aldershot, Hampshire, GU11 2LG
(tel 01252 20968)

At Pirbright Bridge the towpath returns to the southern bank just before Deepcut Locks, the major flight of locks on the canal, 14 of them, which raise the canal by 90ft in only 2 miles. This is thickly wooded scenery and brings the walker to the top of the Surrey heathlands. The canal passes through the long cutting known as Deep Cut, 1,000yds long and up to 70ft deep, secluded and remote, overhung by mature trees. Beyond the cut the canal swings through 90 degrees to head south, crossing the London-to-Southampton railway by aqueduct.

At Guildford Road Bridge the walker crosses the canal to follow the towpath southwards on the western bank. Cross the canal by the road bridge at Mytchett to visit the Basingstoke Canal Centre. This houses an exhibition, gift shop and tea room and is the headquarters of the Basingstoke Canal Authority. It is also the departure point of the trip-boat *Daydream* and the floating restaurant *Lady of Camelot*.

South of the Basingstoke Canal Centre the canal broadens into Mytchett Lake, a reservoir probably enlarged from a natural hollow, and then heads south through some delightful scenery into Ash Vale, passing another reservoir, Greatbottom Flash, well known for its water plants, dragonflies and water birds including great crested grebe and dabchick. Opposite is Ash Vale Boat Yard.

The peaceful solitude of St John's Lock.

the famous Farnborough Air Show. In fact, the runway stops just short of the canal and in 1913 the first seaplane trials were undertaken here at Eelmoor Flash. The towpath passes through the edge of Pyestock Wood and so arrives at Fleet. It passes Pondtail and Reading Road Bridges and Reading Wharf to emerge in the countryside again passing Crookham Village. Crookham Swing Bridge is the last remaining swing bridge on the Basingstoke Canal, while Chequers Bridge stands beside the former Crookham Wharf, now a car park. This was one of the ten wharves along the Basingstoke Canal through which timber and coal were shipped to and from London.

Along the final reach the canal twists and turns. On the opposite side of the waterway are Coxmoor Wood and Dogmersfield Park. The canal turns northwards and here is the Great Wall of Dogmersfield, a 60yd-long retaining wall built in 1983 to reinforce the unstable bank opposite Tundry Pond. The village of Dogmersfield lies to the east. The canal rounds a further bend by the village of Winchfield Hurst and continues past Odiham Common (opposite Broad Oak) and past the Odiham bypass bridge under the lee of Colt Hill. Across the canal on the southern side are Odiham and North Warnborough, but the towpath keeps to the northern bank past a couple of pleasant waterside inns to Odiham Castle.

Shortly after this the limit of navigation is reached, but the towpath continues a bit further to the eastern portal of Greywell Tunnel and the end of this walk along the Basingstoke Canal.

ASH VALE TO GREYWELL
About 17 miles/27km
OS Landranger 186
Start at Ash Vale Station
(grid reference 892 533)

A mile or so south of Ash Vale Station, the canal swings west again in another right angle bend, to cross the valley of the river Blackwater near Ash. The canal originally crossed the valley on Ash Embankment, built of the material excavated from Deepcut, but this had breached before restoration of the canal began. Today the new Blackwater Valley Relief Road (A331) runs north–south along the valley parallel to the little river and the canal crosses on the new Blackwater Aqueduct. The

The end of the walk: the eastern portal of the collapsed Greywell Tunnel, site of an internationally important bat roost.

waterway flows between Aldershot and Farnborough, quintessentially army land, and past Ash Lock, a single lock at the start of the last pound and now the last working lock on the restored Basingstoke Canal.

The canal passes close to several of Aldershot's army museums and under Farnborough Bridge to Aldershot Wharf, which served the army camp when it was being built in 1854–9. Later the garrison at the camp used the canal for recreation, for fishing, swimming and pleasure boating, and annual regattas were held. To the north is Farnborough Airfield, for long home to

WILDLIFE ON THE BASINGSTOKE CANAL

The Basingstoke Canal is famous as the home of some of the most important wildlife sites in Britain. Because it was derelict for many years, and even today traffic on the canal is relatively light, wildlife has been allowed to flourish. It is well known for its variety of aquatic plants, waterbirds, including great crested grebe and dabchick, and animals. In addition, the canal is one of the best dragonfly habitats in Britain. At the western end, in the collapsed and impassable Greywell Tunnel, there is a bat roost of international importance. If the canal ever returns to Basingstoke, then a new stretch of canal, avoiding the tunnel, will probably be built in order not to disturb the bats' home.

Much of the canal has recently been designated as a Site of Special Scientific Interest, and the local councils are working closely with English Nature to ensure that this important role of the canal is preserved for the enjoyment of future generations.

The Wey & Arun Canal: The Wey-South Path

SHALFORD TO AMBERLEY
33 MILES/53KM

GUIDE BOX

PLACES TO VISIT
Brewhurst Lock Close to the Onslow Arms at Loxwood – restored lock, canal boat trips (times posted at the Onslow Arms).
Alfold, St Nicholas' Church (detour from the path) – Wealden church of about 1300AD with grave of Huguenot glass-maker, Jean Carre.
Dunsfold, The Countryways Experience – farm park family attraction.

CAR PARKING
Shalford (limited parking near Stonebridge and at station); Run Common (limited parking off road); Three Compasses (along road); Loxwood (limited parking on village street and near Onslow Arms)

PUBLIC TRANSPORT
Train Station at Shalford
Bus Local buses from Guildford
Boat Canal boat trips at Brewhurst Lock, Loxwood

ACCOMMODATION
Hotels, guest houses etc Cranleigh

TOURIST INFORMATION OFFICE
Guildford 14, Tunsgate, Guildford, Surrey GU1 3QT (tel 01483 444333/4)

This secretive, half-forgotten waterway slides furtively among the meadows and wooded hills of Surrey and Sussex. The canal, which had opened amid great celebrations and general hope for the future in 1816, closed in 1868 due to competition from the railways and problems with water supply. It was abandoned in 1871, and the three aqueducts and 26 locks were left to decay. Nonetheless, much of the line of the old canal remains and is actively under restoration by the Wey & Arun Canal Trust. The Trust has devised a splendid walk, the Wey-South Path, which shadows the canal as closely as possible.

The Wey & Arun Canal consists of two parts, the Wey & Arun Junction Canal, which opened in 1816 and which connects Shalford on the River Wey with Newbridge on the River Arun, and the older Arun Navigation, an 'improved' river of 1787, which runs from Newbridge Wharf, Billingshurst, southwards via Amberley to the coast at Littlehampton. The Wey & Arun Canal was designed to provide an inland waterway that connected London with the English Channel ports, thus eliminating the need to carry goods round the coast, a dangerous option during the Napoleonic Wars. It is ironic indeed that the through route, now frequently dubbed 'London's Lost Route to the Sea', opened the year after Napoleon's defeat at the battle of Waterloo.

Shalford to Loxwood

SHALFORD TO CRANLEIGH
About 6¹/₂ miles/10km
OS Landranger 186
Start at Shalford (grid reference 996 465)

The Wey & Arun Junction Canal branched from the River Wey at Shalford, where the Wey-South Path begins. Here, at 'Gun's Mouth' – so named because of a large gunpowder factory that once stood on the site – and Stonebridge Wharf, there is a small length of canal. It is full of moored boats, but runs only as far as the main road, where the old canal bridge has been bricked up and the walker must follow the public right of way along the line of the disused Guildford-to-Horsham Railway. This runs between the line of the canal and the Bramley Stream. Soon both railway and canal cross the stream, but as the old

A tranquil stretch of the Wey & Arun Canal near Dunsfold.

railway bridge has gone, the path crosses the stream along the Gosden Aqueduct, which formerly carried the canal over the little river. It rejoins the old railway on the farther side and passes the site of Bramley and Wonersh Station, continuing parallel to a restored section of canal. The path crosses the Greensand Way on its way from Shamley Green to Hascombe, and continues past Rushett Farm.

The path turns left over Run Common to join the canal and turns south along it on the farther bank for a short distance before leaving it again to head for Rowly Farm. A stony track leads to an isolated cottage and the old railway embankment from where you can detour into Cranleigh. There is no railway station but there are bus services to Guildford and Godalming.

CRANLEIGH TO LOXWOOD
About 8¹/₂ miles/13km
OS Landranger 176, 187, 186
Start near Rye House Farm
(grid reference 038 397)

The Wey-South Path rejoins the canal near Rye House Farm and along the next section plays at hide-and-seek with the canal; following the towpath for a short length and then veering away across the fields to bypass a section of towpath with no public right of way, only to return to the canalside a few fields on. All the way from Shalford the path has been slowly climbing onto the sandy Surrey Hills and finally reaches the canal's summit level, 163ft OD, near Cranleigh. The summit level extends southwards for 5 miles.

Once across Elmbridge Road near Cranleigh, the route lies along the old towpath for one field's length before turning from the waterway opposite the new 'Elmbridge Village' of retirement homes, near the site of the former wharf that served Cranleigh. The path passes the glasshouses of West Cranleigh Nurseries and turns right down Alfold Road. It returns to the canal along the drive to Uttworth Manor but leaves it again at Mill Farm and detours through fields back onto Alfold Road. A short distance along the road, the route crosses Flash Bridge over the upper waters of the Bramley Stream and then runs alongside the canal to Fast Bridge, hidden amid the trees on the right beside the A281. Just beyond, the summit level is fed by water from Vachery Pond, a reservoir a few miles to the east created by enlarging an ornamental pond.

The path crosses the A281 to follow the grassy trackway on the farther side of the main road, keeping close to the canal, but not alongside it, to the Three Compasses

Restoration work in progress on Brewhurst Lock on the Wey & Arun Canal in June 1996.

Inn. This was the venue, in 1816, for the official opening celebrations of the canal. To the west, on the other side of the canal, is Dunsfold Airfield.

Beyond the Three Compasses the path follows the lane towards Dunsfold through bluebell woods and past the entrance to 'The Countryways Experience' farm park. It turns off along the bridleway near the Forestry Commission car park. The bridleway arrives at the side of the old canal and the Wey-South Path turns left onto the towpath for over 1 mile. Here the canal passes through Sidney Wood – an industrial site long before the canal was dug, for during the reign of Elizabeth I there was a glass-making furnace here, part of the extensive medieval and 16th-century Wealden glass industry.

The right of way along the towpath stops shortly before reaching a large pink house. The Wey-South Path detours past the drive to Lock House, now a private property but formerly the headquarters of the Canal Company. It crosses over the canal at High Bridge before returning to the towpath which it follows through woodland and meadow for the next 4 miles. The summit level came to an end in Sidney Wood, and the old canal descended steeply through a series of nine locks. All

the locks were blown up during World War II as an exercise in demolition and have yet to be restored.

The towpath crosses the Surrey/Sussex border and reaches the B2133 at Loxwood opposite the Onslow Arms.

RESTORING THE WEY & ARUN CANAL

Ever since the closure of the Wey & Arun Canal – shortly after the publication of JB Dashwood's famous account of a journey over it in 1867, *The Thames to the Solent* – many people have expressed regret at its closure and have hoped that one day it could be reopened. At the beginning of this century, the writer Hilaire Belloc bemoaned the canal's fate and argued for its restoration, albeit anonymously. His voice went unheard; and it seemed as though the canal would disappear for ever.

The revival of interest in Britain's waterways saw the formation of the Wey & Arun Canal Society in 1970, an organisation dedicated to restoring the canal throughout. The task seemed monumental, if not impossible, but slowly the society has restored various stretches of the route, and many of the locks. Many problems, including the reinstatement of aqueducts, still remain, but the outlook is promising. Loxwood and the Onslow Arms look set once again to become an exciting hub of activity, as 'London's Lost Route to the Sea' is found again, and a waterway once more links London and the English Channel.

Loxwood to Amberley

LOXWOOD TO NEWBRIDGE
About 6 miles / 13km
OS Landranger 186, 187, 197
Start at Loxwood
(grid reference 041 312)

At Loxwood the towpath passes behind the Onslow Arms along a renovated stretch of canal to restored Brewhurst Lock, below which canal boat trips are available. The walk continues along the towpath following the winding canal to the site of Drungewick Aqueduct, which formerly carried the canal across the River Lox, a tributary of the River Arun. The aqueduct has all but completely vanished and for the next couple of miles there is no right of way along the towpath. The Wey-South Path heads south along Drungewick Lane for about $1/2$ mile past the moated site of Drungewick Manor. The path then runs along a pleasant tree-lined track and over fields to Malham Farm, passing among the farm buildings. Beyond the farm the path continues over the fields, running at first along a causeway between two lakes, part of the former water supply for the canal, and then passes through the edge of a woodland to reach the B2133.

A short stretch of roadwalking follows, necessitating great care as the road is both busy and fairly narrow. At Newpound Common the path turns off left along the bridleway to Loves Farm, going round the buildings and through the belt of woodland to reach the canal at Loves Bridge. Here the walk turns south along the towpath passing fully restored Rowner Lock and Northlands Lift Bridge. Nearby is the site of the demolished Rowner Mill. The path continues along the towpath across the wide breezy fields of the

GUIDE BOX

PLACES TO VISIT
Stopham Bridge Beautiful medieval bridge spanning River Arun, rebuilt in stone 1423, central arch raised in 1822 for river traffic.
Amberley Chalk Pits Museum Working museum in the former Amberley Chalk Pits, with a display on the history of the Wey & Arun Canal.

CAR PARKING
Loxwood (limited parking near Onslow Arms); Newbridge (limited parking by bridge on A272); Stopham Bridge (near bridge); Greatham Bridge (by bridge); Amberley (museum and limited parking in village)

PUBLIC TRANSPORT
Train Stations at Billingshurst, Pulborough, Amberley
Bus Local bus services from Billingshurst, Pulborough and Amberley

ACCOMMODATION
Hotels, guest houses etc Newbridge, Pulborough, Arundel

TOURIST INFORMATION CENTRE
Arundel 61 High Street, Arundel, West Sussex BN18 9AJ (tel 01903 882268)

broadening Arun Valley to the A272 at Newbridge, terminus of the Wey & Arun Junction Canal and beginning of the older Arun Navigation. It is just over 1 mile's detour from here to Billingshurst, where there is a railway station and accommodation.

NEWBRIDGE TO AMBERLEY
About 12 miles / 20km
OS Landranger 197
Start at Newbridge parking area
(grid reference 069 259)

The Wey-South Path continues on the south side of the A272, running along the towpath past the wharf basin and opposite the magnificent restored warehouse that is now used as holiday accommodation. The canal converges with the river and the towpath runs along the verdant neck of land between them, in spring and summer a carpet of colourful wild flowers. There is a sharp right turn at the point where the canal seems to disappear and the river continues on its way, for here the canal turned abruptly across the field, but it has now been infilled. On the far side of the field the canal crossed the river by Orfold Aqueduct, and the towpath still does so. To the south of the aqueduct is Lording's Lock, its brick walls clearly visible. Beyond this lock the towpath continues alongside the derelict canal, first on one side and then on the other, until the concrete bridge near Haybarn.

From this point south there is no right of way along the towpath and the Wey-South crosses the canal and continues along a farm track to recross the canal on a causeway and the river by a bridge. The

The trip-boat on the restored Wey & Arun Canal below the Brewhurst Lock.

path runs over the meadowland to Pallingham Lane, a private road, and Furnace Pond Cottage, the name a clear reminder of the former Wealden iron industry which displaced the earlier glass-making industry of the region.

The Wey-South Path follows the track along a little valley to Fittleworth Road. Here it turns along the narrow country lane and follows it southwards for about ½ mile before turning left along a track towards Pallingham Quay Farm. A left turn, ignoring the farm, takes the walker back over the River Arun and to a restored reach of the Arun Navigation. It is possible to cross the canal bed just north of Pallingham Lock Cottage and then turn south parallel to the canal past Pallingham Lock. The lock is on private land, but it marks the start of the Arun Navigation and is at the tidal head of the River Arun. The Wey-South Path follows the track to join a little lane at Pickhurst Farm and then turns south along it for about 1 mile before turning off along a bridleway. This is initially a sunken lane but soon rises to give splendid views ahead to the South Downs.

Passing through Pulborough Park, the route rejoins the River Arun near Stopham Bridge where the graceful 15th-century stone structure is now overshadowed by a thundering modern concrete one. This is an ancient bridging point, with that ageless combination of great house – Stopham House, on the far side of the bridge, ancestral home of the Barttelots – bridge, and inn, the popular White Hart. The six outer arches of the old bridge date back to its rebuilding in stone in 1423, while the higher central arch was raised in 1822 as an aid to shipping.

The path heads briefly along the road before turning south to cross the river on a lattice footbridge. To the west is part of the Rother Navigation, constructed in 1794 to link Petworth and Midhurst to the Arun. Beyond, the Wey-South crosses the Rother on a concrete bridge and heads past the waterworks. It turns right and crosses the line of Stane Street, the Roman road between London and Chichester, just to the east of the mangled remains of a Roman posting station wrecked by the building of the now dismantled Pulborough-to-Midhurst railway. The Wey-South Path follows this line for some 200yds. An iron lattice bridge takes the walker across the main line railway to the A29.

On the farther side of the main road the route leads downhill, crossing the line of

Looking north along the River Arun from Greatham Bridge.

the Roman road known as the Sussex Greensand Way and close to Hardham Priory. It reaches the canal, which emerges from the now impassable Hardham Tunnel (the southern portal with its blocking metal grid can be seen), and follows the towpath to the road near Greatham Bridge. A left turn takes the walker along the road and over the Arun at Greatham Bridge from whence a pathway heads south, initially along the river bank and then over the wide expanse of Amberley Wild Brooks, the water meadows famed for their varied wildlife. Ahead lies Amberley, guarded by the bulk of its low-lying Norman castle, now a hotel, and overlooked by the white ramparts of the erstwhile chalk pits that now house an excellent working museum.

The path heads steeply up to Amberley, a pleasant village, where the Wey-South turns right to cross the busy main road and climb up Mill Lane, along the route of the South Downs Way. A right turn along High Titten leads back to the main road, Arundel railway station and the Chalk Pits Museum, where there is a display relating to the Wey & Arun Canal.

The Royal Military Canal

SEABROOK (HYTHE) TO PETT LEVEL
27 MILES/43KM

Walking in solitary peace along the edge of the Romney Marshes beside a canal that is little more than a rich wildlife habitat, it is hard to credit the thinking behind its creation as a barrier to keep Napoleon's marauding troops at bay. In fact, of course, the French never came, and the whole thing now looks somewhat like an eccentric military folly.

The Royal Military Canal Path is currently open for 5 miles west of Hythe and for 15 between Warehorne and Pett Level, near Hastings, but there are plans to establish a canalside path along its entire length. With level, fairly easy walking and places like Appledore, Rye and Winchelsea to stop at, it makes a very pleasant weekend or two-day break.

WALKING GUIDE
Royal Military Canal, a guide book published by Kent County Council.

MAPS
OS Landranger 189, 199 (199 needed for ³/₄ mile at Cliff End only).

LINKS
The Saxon Shore Way shares the RMC route between Stutfall Castle and Bilsington and, with Sussex Border Path also, between Iden Lock and Rye.

When William Pitt the Younger began his second term as Prime Minister in 1804, the threat of invasion by Napoleon was serious and the defence of the coast a crucial issue. It was thought the French would try to land on the flat beaches between the cliffs of Hastings in the west and Folkestone in the east. The suggestion was made that a canal be built from Shorncliffe, near Folkestone to the River Rother north of Rye. Troops could be transported quickly in barges while a parallel road, screened by the bank created with the soil dug out from the canal, would also enable troops to be moved safely. The Rother and then the Brede would continue the line of defence to Winchelsea and from there another section of canal would be built to Pett Level, near Hastings.

Pitt, recently Lord Warden of the Cinque Ports, greeted the proposal with enthusiasm and swiftly persuaded the local landowners that the canal was not only vital to the defence of the realm, but would also provide proper drainage of the marshes in winter and a controlled water supply in summer. John Rennie was appointed consultant engineer and work started in the autumn 1804. However, flooding and storms caused delays, so that it was 1806 before the canal was ready for use between Shorncliffe and the River Rother, and 1809 before the entire length was completed. By this time the French fleet had long since been destroyed at Trafalgar, Napoleon had fallen, and the canal, constructed at an immense cost of £230,000, was of no military value.

In an effort to recoup the cost of construction, the canal commissioners opened it to the public. Freight- and passenger-carrying traffic operated until the mid-19th century, but was never busy and from 1851 the railway between Ashford and Hastings took most of it away and the canal fell into disuse early in the 1900s. Today it is protected as one of the largest linear defensive monuments in Britain.

Seabrook to Warehorne

SEABROOK TO STUTFALL CASTLE
5 miles/8km
OS Landranger 189
Start at Seabrook (grid reference 188 349 or at car park, grid reference 178 347)

The canal starts unremarkably at Seabrook, alongside the A259 Hythe-to-Folkestone road, where it meets the road that runs along the seafront. A grassy bank edges the turning basin, a popular spot for local lads with fishing rods. There is an alternative access point with a parking area a few hundred yards west.

The RMC path follows the north side of the canal, with private gardens on the right. As it comes to the centre of Hythe, a pleasant Cinque Port town, the canal is lined with flowers and trees, and in summer rowing boats can be hired from the public gardens, a tradition that dates back to Edwardian days.

West of the town the canal follows the contour of the steep escarpment that centuries ago was a high cliff towering over the English Channel. Meanwhile, close to the canal's southern bank, the little trains of the Romney, Hythe & Dymchurch Railway run out across the Romney Marshes to Dungeness. Characteristically, the edges of the canal are lined with patches of small yellow waterlilies, and swans, moorhen and the occasional canoeist glide quietly through the duckweed. Two miles on, the canal passes under the cast-iron bridge at West Hythe while the path (now a bridleway) crosses the road to a car parking area in some trees. Trees and bushes line the northern bank fairly densely, giving only glimpses of the water to the left and, to the right, the village of Lympne with its castle and Norman church standing proud on top of the escarpment. This was a seaport

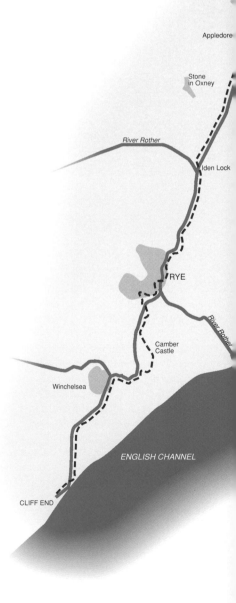

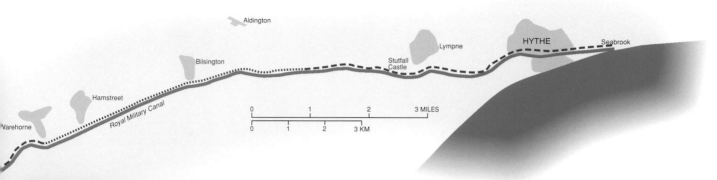

Water lilies line the canal near Port Lympne.

in Roman times and in the fields beneath the village are the ruins of the Roman fort, Lemanis, now called Stutfall Castle.

The tree cover breaks temporarily at West Hythe sluice, a reminder that the canal is still used to irrigate the Romney Marshes in summer and to prevent flooding in winter. The footpath narrows as the RMC Path and the Saxon Shore Way continue west through more trees and undergrowth. Views of the canal are restricted but the Port Lympne Wild Animal Park on land immediately to the north brings a touch of the exotic with sounds of elephants calling and sightings of bison and antelope.

A footpath leads off to the right up to the top of the hill and back to West Hythe, and a little further on a bridge taking a dead-end minor road over the canal provides the first crossing point since West

Hythe. From here a path along the southern bank makes an alternative return route to West Hythe.

STUTFALL CASTLE TO WAREHORNE
OS Landranger 189

The opening of a public footpath along the 6 miles of canal between Marwood Farm (grid reference 081 342), 2½ miles east of Bilsington, and Warehorne is, at the time of writing, subject to a public enquiry. For the time being, walkers should continue with the Saxon Shore Way, running through trees beside the canal for another mile or so and then turning north to Honeypot Cottage and threading through Aldington and Ham Street to Warehorne.

The canal, meanwhile, away from the steep escarpment and with the trees thinning out, runs peacefully on through an agricultural landscape; pastureland and old

orchards are grazed by sheep. Parallel and a little to the north, the B2067 passes through the villages of Bilsington, Ruckinge and Hamstreet on its way to Warehorne, with several minor roads leading off it down to and over the canal.

The first of these crosses the canal at a point where the old Royal Military Road can be seen as a private road running east through farmland along the northern bank. South of Bonnington, the little 13th-century St Rumwold's Church is close to the canal. At Ruckinge there is a good view of one of the kinks built every 500yds to allow a clear line of fire. A pillbox survives from World War II, when the land adjoining the canal, sold into private hands in 1935, was requisitioned by the War Office. Hamstreet has a useful railway station just over 1 mile from the start of the next section of the path canal at Warehorne.

GUIDE BOX

PLACES TO VISIT
Romney, Hythe & Dymchurch Railway 15-inch gauge railway with one-third full size steam and diesel locomotives runs across the Romney Marshes between Hythe and Dungeness. *Port Lympne* Wild Animal Park.

CAR PARKING
Hythe; West Hythe; Hamstreet; Warehorne (street parking only).

PUBLIC TRANSPORT
Trains Nearest mainline station to Hythe is Sandling, on the Ashford-to-Folkestone line. Warehorne is 1 mile from Hamstreet Station, on the Ashford-to-Hastings line. See above for Romney, Hythe & Dymchurch Railway. *Buses* Serve Hythe, Lympne, Hamstreet.

ACCOMMODATION
Hotels, guest houses etc Hythe, Appledore Station (5 minutes on the train from Warehorne).

TOURIST INFORMATION CENTRES
Hythe En Route Travel, Red Lion Square, Hythe, Kent CT21 5AZ (tel 01303 267799)
Folkestone Harbour Street, Folkestone, Kent CT20 2PJ (01303 258594)

Warehorne to Cliff End

WAREHORNE TO RYE

About 9 miles/5km

OS Landranger 189

Start at road bridge 1/4 mile south of the village (grid reference 991 320)

The Royal Military Canal between Warehorne and Appledore is National Trust property and their sign marks the access point off the minor road south of the village. There is a public footpath along the former towpath on the south bank, but the RMC Path takes the grassy strip between the bank and the back drain. For the most part disturbed only by the occasional canoeist, the Royal Military Canal is rich in watery wildlife and while the eye may be drawn first to the waterlilies, dragonflies and waterbirds of the canal itself, this ditch is in its own right rich in colourful plantlife. Fields of barley or sweetcorn lie on the either side.

Swans inhabit the canal at several points, but most notably at Appledore, the next village on the route. Here it is well worth diverting up the road into the village, a pretty, unhurried place, with shops and pubs, that a long while back stood on the banks of the Rother – until a storm in 1287 diverted the river's course. The lush grass of the Romney Marshes has always supported large flocks of sheep and in medieval times Appledore was a wealthy weaving centre.

From here to Rye the old Military Road beside the canal is still in use, making this the best stretch to appreciate fully the scale of the whole operation. From the path on top of the bank, one can see to the left the canal, the towpath and the front drain beyond it, and to the right the military road and the back drain. Walking along in peace and quiet, in the company of sheep resting beneath the spreading lime

GUIDE BOX

PLACES TO VISIT
Rye Ypres Tower; Rye Castle Museum, housed in Ypres Tower; Lamb House, home of Henry James; church – clock, Burne-Jones window.
Winchelsea Cinque Port; St Thomas's Church; Court Hall and Museum.
Camber Castle, Pett Level. Can be reached on foot only.
Romney Marsh Churches See below.

CAR PARKING
Hamstreet; Warehorne (roadside); Appledore (roadside and Appledore Dam); Rye; Winchelsea; Cliff End.

PUBLIC TRANSPORT
Trains Hamstreet, Appledore, Rye, Winchelsea are on the Ashford-to-Hastings line.
Buses Hamstreet, Appledore, Rye, Winchelsea, Cliff End.

ACCOMMODATION
Hotels, guest houses etc Hamstreet, Appledore Station, Rye, Winchelsea, Cliff End.

TOURIST INFORMATION CENTRES
Rye The Heritage Centre, Strand Quay, Rye, East Sussex TN31 7AY (tel 01797 226696)
Hastings 4 Robertson Terrace, Hastings, East Sussex TN34 1EZ (tel 01424 718888)

trees or grazing the grassy bank, and with only the odd bicycle or car passing along the road, it is hard to imagine how anyone ever imagined this might have been the scene of invasion and bloody battle. The occasional concrete pillbox is a reminder of a more recent unfulfilled threat of invasion across the Channel.

A mile or so south of Appledore, the isolated village of Stone in Oxney can be seen to the west, on the northern face of the hill, once an island, known as the Isle of Oxney. Round the other side, the rocky outcrop of Stone Cliff overlooks the valley of the Rother. Stone Bridge provides fishermen with access to the eastern bank. Beyond them lie ploughed fields and the pastures of the Romney Marshes.

Iden Lock, disused and green with duckweed, marks the point where the canal runs into the River Rother. The old lock-keeper's cottage stands empty and overgrown. The RMC Path crosses to the east bank of the Rother here, joining the Saxon Shore Way and the Sussex Border Path. Following the edge of the field, the path passes a short stretch of private mooring used by motorboat owners with their caravans and then arrives at Scots Float Sluice and the buildings of the Environment Agency (formerly NRA).

South of Scots Float, the Rother is tidal. The path follows the raised floodbank as the river winds through grassland (more sheep) with Rye's church and castle silhouetted ahead. On the outskirts of the town, the path passes under the railway

A characteristic stretch near Appledore, with swans, one of the dog-legs constructed every 500 yards to allow a clear line of fire along any section, and a World War II pillbox.

line and meets the bridge that takes the A259 over the river and along the quay, busy with fishing boats, into the town centre. Rye is delightful and its steep streets are full of ancient nooks and crannies but, as a result, it gets very crowded and accommodation over summer weekends can be difficult to find.

RYE TO CLIFF END
About 5¹/₂ miles/9km
OS Landranger 189, 199
(199 for last ³/₄ mile only)
Start at Rye Harbour Road bridge off A 259
(grid reference 919 198)

The Royal Military Canal Path runs off at right angles to the Rye Harbour road where it crosses the River Brede. On one side of the bridge is the marina, where smart boats jostle for space; on the other the abandoned canal, its green duckweedy surface broken only by scuttling moorhen. The path soon wanders off onto the levels between Rye Harbour and Winchelsea to pass Camber Castle, the impressive ruins of

a polygonal blockhouse built by Henry VIII in 1538 in defence of the coastline. It features in some of Paul Nash's paintings.

At Castle Farm the path joins the road into Winchelsea, another Cinque Port, built by Edward I on a grid plan. Set high on a hill and rich in history and beautiful buildings – from weatherboarded houses to the splendid Decorated church, it makes an excellent stopping point.

Down at the foot of the hill, the next stretch of the Royal Military Canal – with the RMC Path and the Saxon Shore Way on its eastern bank – runs south from the River Brede. To the west is a gently undulating landscape of farms and villages, while to the east Pett Level stretches for a mile or so to the sea, flat pastureland criss-crossed with drainage ditches and a group of lakes populated by waders and waterfowl. The canal ends up in Cliff End, a undistinguished settlement separated from its shingly beach by a high, protective sea wall. On the far side of the canal, tall houses have large windows on the top floor giving views over the seawall. The

Near Stone Cliff. The bank on the left once provided a parapet for picking off invaders and also screened the military road.

canal below is lined with bullrushes, purple loosestrife and willowherb, and dragonflies and damselflies dart hither and thither.

ROMNEY MARSH CHURCHES

Flat, windswept and remote, Romney Marsh, bounded by the Royal Military Canal on one side and the sea on the other, has an atmosphere of its own; some might say atmosphere is what it is all about. It is a corner of Britain that is loved by many, and not least for its 20 or so medieval churches. Many of them are gems of Norman architecture, built by wool merchants whose wealth derived from the sheep that thrive on Marsh's fertile grassland. An illustrated booklet, *Romney Marsh Churches*, produced by the Romney Marsh Historic Churches Trust and available from local bookshops and Tourist Information Offices, describes them all.

The Lee & Stort Navigations

HERTFORD TO BISHOP'S STORTFORD
20 MILES/32KM

THIS is a gentle 20-mile walk along the towing paths of two of England's old river navigations. Before the large-scale development of the canal network in the late 18th century, much of the country's economy was dependent upon river navigations such as these. Many have subsequently been lost and these two waterways, still fully navigable and in a good state of repair, are a rare survival. The Lee Navigation is the older of the two, having been used regularly by boats at least since the Roman period. Under an Act of 1571 the navigation was greatly improved and the first pound lock built. Over the succeeding centuries further improvements gradually brought the river and its locks to the point where it could handle 100-ton barges. The Stort, always a quieter river, was turned into a navigation in the 18th century, largely to serve the needs of agriculture.

The towing paths are in good condition and the walk described here could be completed in one day. Alternatively, it can be spread over two days, so as to enjoy to the full the changing nature of the Constable-like landscape and the many old mills and maltings that line the banks of both rivers. The whole route is well served by railways. No cycling on the towpaths without a permit from British Waterways.

WALKING GUIDES
There is no published guide as such, but all the information required by walkers is contained in *Nicholson's Ordnance Survey Guide to the Waterways Book 1: South.*

OS MAPS
Landranger 166, 167

LINKS
Part of the route is now called the Stort Walkway and another part the Lee Valley Walk, and the route is crossed by or linked to a number of other official walks, including the New River Walk, the Three Forests Way, the Chain Walk and the Harcamlow Way. West of Hertford the River Lee is followed as far as Luton by the Lee Valley Walk; unclear in its waymarking, and with some sections along quite busy roads, this is not a particularly enjoyable walk.

Hertford to Roydon

HERTFORD TO ROYDON
About 8 miles/13km
OS Landranger 166, 167
Start at Mill Bridge, at the head of navigation in the centre of Hertford
(grid reference 327 128)

Hertford is still a pleasant and traditional county town, whose centre has largely survived the assaults of the motor car. It has the remains of a medieval castle, some fine churches, an 18th-century shire hall and plenty of pubs, as befits a river famous for its maltings. The castle stands near the head of navigation, while one of the pubs, the Old Barge Inn, with its well-painted sign, is on the towing path near the start of the walk. Initially beneath trees and in a quiet urban setting, the path is flanked by terraces of old cottages with flowery gardens looking out across the river, and then by some allotments. The path curves round Kings Meads, passing moored boats and, to the left, the River Rib in its parkland setting. It crosses to the southern bank and after the first lock gradually leaves the town behind. Never far away is the New River, created early in the 17th century by Sir Hugh Myddleton to carry fresh water to north London, its route southwards marked by old pumping stations. The New River Walk follows much of this route, and offers an alternative for walkers.

The New River and the Lee flow together towards Ware in a wide valley, crossed by the huge viaduct that carries the A10. The approach to Ware is attractive, and the town looks its best from the river,

which flows through its centre, skirting the site of the 14th-century priory and passing a series of delightful 18th-century garden gazebos that project over the water between the trees. In the distance is the tall spire of St Mary's Church. Some old maltings are also still standing, their distinctive architectural features echoed in the nearby modern buildings. Maltings are a recurring theme along both the Lee and the Stort.

To the east of Ware the river divides, with the straight cut of the navigation branching off to the southeast, easily identified by the towing path that follows it. The old course of the river meanders away to the east, to flow through water meadows and flooded gravel workings. This is an attractive section, wild and wooded, and with a network of paths and bridleways leading off in several directions. The Amwell Walkway, for instance, follows initially the route of the old branch line to Buntingford. There is also a wildlife reserve where avocet, great crested grebe and bittern have been seen. At the southern end of this section is St Margaret's Station, a good starting place for many of the walks. Nearby is Stanstead Lock, and across the river on the valleyside is Stanstead Abbots, a pretty village whose fine church has an unusual timber porch.

Flanked by water meadows and reservoirs, the river skirts the suburbs of Hoddesdon on its way to Rye House, famous for a failed assassination attempt on the life of Charles II and his son, James. The house has disappeared, but a splendid gateway survives, richly decorated in Tudor

brickwork, and set in a park. Rye House Marsh is an RSPB nature reserve. There is limited parking by the gatehouse. Just to the south is Feilde's Lock and Weir, where the River Stort meets the Lee.

It is possible to continue southwards beside the River Lee and through the Lee Valley Country Park to north London, but our walk follows the River Stort from the

junction. Cross over the Lee and join the towpath on the southern side of the Stort.

The different character of the Stort is immediately noticeable. Narrow, winding and rural throughout its route, it is claimed to be one of the prettiest river navigations in England. Against a backdrop of hills, the river winds towards Roydon through a landscape of small fields patterned by groups of trees. At Roydon, the old mill is now the centre of a large caravan park and leisure centre. The towing path changes sides at Roydon, the first of several cross-overs between here and Bishop's Stortford. Roydon village spreads up the hill from the pretty railway station, which is now a restaurant, to the small medieval church. The lock cottage, just beyond the village and the low railway bridge, carries the shield of Sir George Duckett, who created the Stort Navigation in the 18th century.

The Lee Navigation starts in Hertford, the towing path flanked by the Old Barge Inn and traditional cottages.

GUIDE BOX

PLACES TO VISIT
Ware Scott's Grotto – remarkable folly built in 1776 with rooms and passages 67ft under ground; decorated with shells and pebbles (take torch).
Great Amwell Museum of Street Lighting – collection of columns and lanterns from 200BC. Water Gardens near church commemorate Hugh Myddleton's scheme to carry water to north London in 1609.
Stanstead Abbots Rye House, ruins with Gate House; RSPB Reserve.

CAR PARKING
Hertford; Rye House Gateway (limited); Roydon (on street).

PUBLIC TRANSPORT
Train Stations at each end of this section, Hertford East, Ware, St Margaret's, Rye House, Roydon.
Bus Services between Hertford and Roydon via Hoddesdon.

ACCOMMODATION
Hotels, guest houses etc Hertford, Ware.

TOURIST INFORMATION CENTRE
Hertford The Castle, Hertford, SG14 1HR (tel 01992 584322)

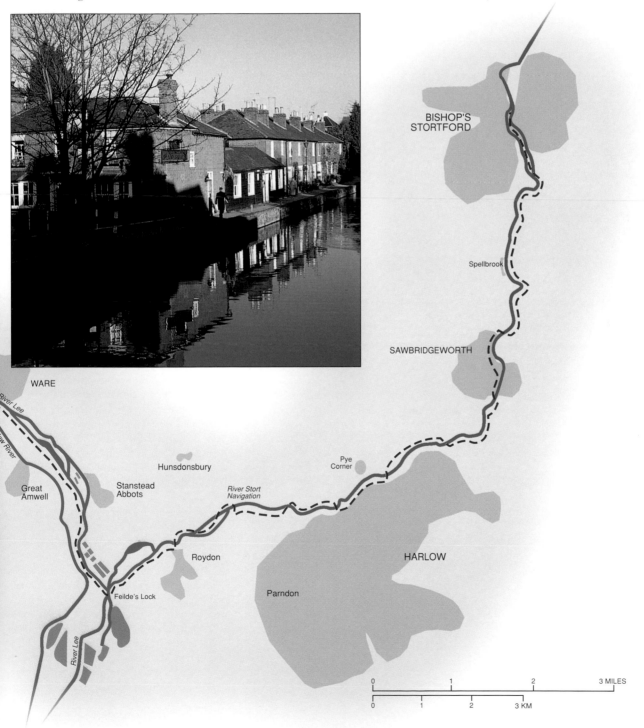

Roydon to Bishop's Stortford

ROYDON TO SAWBRIDGEWORTH
12 miles/19km
OS Landranger 167
Start at ornamental bridge carrying B181
across the Stort, by Roydon Station
(grid reference 406 105)

The course of the River Stort east of Roydon is a delight, with the river winding its way through water meadows against a background of green hills. To the north is Briggens Park, formerly a private estate and now a country house hotel. The first lock, Hunsdon Mill, is hidden among trees at the end of a tiny road that leads only to a group of private houses, one of which is the former mill. There is no public parking here. Just to the west of the

lock is a lush meadow, now a nature reserve and filled with wild flowers in spring. The Harcamlow Way follows the river from Hunsdonbury to Sawbridgeworth.

Rural seclusion continues for a while, the peace and quiet threatened only by the sometimes very close proximity of the busy A414 dual carriageway. The river turns south away from the road to Parndon Lock, where a large white weatherboarded mill stands by the river, something that is a characteristic feature of the Stort. Moored pleasure boats fill the mill cut in place of the old grain barges that used to supply the mill and, set on a lower level, is a handsome early 19th-century former mill-owner's house. It is a lovely setting, its peace marred only by the trains on the nearby line. It is

GUIDE BOX

PLACES TO VISIT
Sawbridgeworth Church of St Mary the Great, mainly 14th-century with interesting font and pulpit; excellent brasses and monuments.
Bishop's Stortford Rhodes Memorial Museum and Commonwealth Centre, in birthplace of Cecil Rhodes, details his life and career in South Africa.

CAR PARKING
Harlow; Sawbridgeworth; Bishop's Stortford.

PUBLIC TRANSPORT
Train Stations at Roydon, Harlow Town, Harlow Mill, Sawbridgeworth, Bishop's Stortford.
Bus Services between Roydon and Harlow; Harlow, Sawbridgeworth and Bishop's Stortford.

ACCOMMODATION
Hotels, guest houses etc Harlow, Sawbridgeworth, Bishop's Stortford.

TOURIST INFORMATION CENTRE
Bishop's Stortford The Old Monastery, Windhill, Bishop's Stortford, Berkshire CM23 2ND (tel 01279 652274)

hard to believe that the great sprawl of Harlow New Town is just to the south. A track from the lock leads between high hedges to the A414 and across it to Eastwick, a remote hamlet with a church by Sir Reginald Blomfield that is approached by a fine yew avenue.

From Parndon the river skirts Harlow, hidden from the town by banks of trees, and so it is with some surprise that it suddenly reaches Burnt Mill Lock adjacent to Harlow Town Station, an ambitious but slightly battered expression of 1960s modernism. Winding along its private valley, accessible only by boat or on foot, the Stort continues eastwards, passing Latton Lock and Harlow Lock. The latter provides the best access point for Harlow Old Town, where 18th-century houses and a Norman chapel survive.

The river then swings to the south of Pishiobury Park, allowing good views of this castellated late 18th-century mansion developed by James Wyatt from a smaller Tudor house. Its fine grounds were landscaped in characteristic style by Capability Brown around a long, curving lake. To the south of the park is the remote Feakes Lock.

After so much rural seclusion, Sheering Mill Lock comes as something of a shock. Here, beside the river, is a huge new development of malting-style buildings, mostly for residential use. The vernacular language and details of the traditional maltings have been exploited in a bizarre, decorative but ultimately meaningless way, in a kind of post-modern glorification of 19th-century industrial architecture. The real thing, huge, brick-built and timber-clad, exists in profusion a little further on, near to Sawbridgeworth Station. Long

At Parndon Lock, on the River Stort, the traditional mill buildings survive, giving a hint of the navigation's busy past.

detached from their original use, these have mostly been converted, but their presence underlines the curious fact that Sawbridgeworth was once Britain's second largest malting town.

Commercial barge carrying to the maltings ceased years ago, but a boatyard and moorings cater for modern leisure boating. The handsome town, full of fine buildings dating from the 16th to the 19th century, rises up the hillside to the west of the river. At its heart is the great church, notable for monuments, brasses and 18th-century gravestones.

SAWBRIDGEWORTH TO BISHOP'S STORTFORD
About 5 miles/8km
OS Landranger 167
*Start at bridge near Sawbridgeworth Station
(grid reference 489 150)*

From Sawbridgeworth the river curves northwards through woods and water

meadows to the delightfully remote Tednambury Lock, set in the middle of a field and well away from its old mill, now a restaurant. The former mill cut houses a boatyard and extensive moorings. The next lock is Spellbrook, adjacent to the prehistoric Walbury Camp, unfortunately well-hidden and on private land, and then the rural pleasures of the Stort come to an end at Twyford Lock. Ahead are the suburbs and industrial estates that flank Bishop's Stortford, but the approach to the town is not unpleasant past South Mill Lock. The walk continues along the towing path, under the railway bridge, to follow the river's quiet entry into the town.

It can end just by the bridge that carries the A1184 across it, a short walk from the railway station, or it can carry on into the town centre, along an urban stretch lined with fine old maltings and rather indifferent modern buildings. The head of navigation is adjacent to a large and convenient riverside car park, accessible via

Near Spellbrook the frozen River Stort makes its way through a wintry landscape. Such conditions posed great problems during its commercial days.

a footbridge, and useful for those wanting to start the walk in Bishop's Stortford. The busy market town, noted for its timber-framed inns and as the birthplace of Cecil Rhodes, is just to the west of the car park.

Early in the 19th century there was a plan to connect the Stort at Bishop's Stortford with the River Cam via a 30-mile canal. Had this grand scheme ever got off the ground, it would have created a link between the waterways of Cambridge and the Fens and the rest of the English network of navigable waterways. Bishop's Stortford could, as a result, have been a very much busier place. Instead, it is just the end of a delightfully rural navigation, a minor waterway that was never busy even in its commercial heyday, and whose survival offers rare pleasures to boaters and walkers today.

The Oxford Canal

COMPLETE ROUTE
OXFORD TO HAWKESBURY JUNCTION
77 MILES/123KM
SECTION COVERED
OXFORD TO BANBURY
27 MILES/43KM

THIS is an easy 27-mile walk that follows a well-signposted Canal Walk route along the towing path of one of Britain's oldest canals. The path is generally in good condition, and the walk described here can be completed quite easily in two days. Walkers may want to spend longer, however, taking time to explore Oxford and the canal's links with the Thames, enjoying the Cherwell Valley landscape and visiting places of interest along the route, or extending the walk northwards from Banbury for a further 4½ miles to the village of Cropredy. The route between Oxford and Banbury is well served by the railway, with intermediate stations at Tackley, Heyford and King's Sutton. No cycling without towpath permit from British Waterways.

WALKING GUIDES
Nicholson's Ordnance Survey Guide to the Waterways Book I South contains all the information required by walkers for the whole of the Oxford Canal's 77-mile route to the Midlands. Pearson, JM *Canal Companion* covers the Oxford Canal in the same volume as the Grand Union Canal.

OS MAPS
Landranger 164, 151

LINKS
The Thames Path passes through Oxford but does not connect directly.

Authorised in 1769 as part of a grand scheme to forge a waterway link between London and the Midlands, the Oxford Canal was originally surveyed by James Brindley and its winding, contour route is typical of that canal pioneer's work. Construction began at its northern end and in March 1778 the first load of Midlands coal was unloaded in Banbury. Financial problems then caused delays, but work resumed in 1786 and in 1790 a fleet of boats entered Oxford's new wharf to the accompaniment of the Oxford Militia Band. Rapidly successful, the Oxford Canal Company was paying its shareholders a 25 per cent dividend by 1810. Increasing competition in the 1820s encouraged the canal to improve its meandering route and, under the direction of the engineer Charles Vignoles, 13½ miles were cut from the original 91. Railway competition caused further problems, and the latter part of the 19th century saw a steady decline in traffic and revenue. However, its close links with the Midlands collieries kept the canal alive and as late as the 1930s the company was still able to pay an 8 per cent dividend. By the 1950s traffic was so reduced that the canal was considered for closure, but its future was secured after a fierce campaign by the Inland Waterways Association, and now the Oxford Canal is one of England's most attractive cruising waterways.

The Hythe Bridge terminus of the canal in Oxford.

Oxford to Tackley

OXFORD TO KIDLINGTON
About 5½ miles/9km
OS Landranger 164
*Start at canal terminus by Hythe Bridge
(grid reference 505 064)*

From the station, turn left towards the city centre, then bear left into Hythe Bridge Street. The canal is beyond the Isis River Bridge. The terminus of the Oxford Canal is a leafy backwater, where the waterway comes to a rather abrupt end, parallel to but slightly above the fast-flowing Isis. Until the 1940s the canal continued under the road to two large city basins, both buried under modern development.

For the walker, the first experience of the canal is the long line of moored boats stretching along the towing path into the distance, a colourful ribbon beneath the trees. Many are residential, complete with letter boxes and other paraphernalia, maintaining a tradition long associated with Oxford's canal. The towing path, a well-surfaced embankment keeping canal and Isis apart and much used by walkers, shoppers, joggers and cyclists, offers an intimate view of the vagaries of canal boat life. A cast-iron bridge lifts the path over Isis Lock, the start of the short Sheepwash channel that leads via the Isis and under the railway to the Thames. Opened in 1796, this became the major link between the canal and the Thames for commercial craft, allowing narrow boats to travel southwards along the Thames to London or onto the Kennet & Avon Canal at Reading, and northwards to Lechlade and the junction with the Thames & Severn Canal. Thus, in the early 19th century, Oxford could be seen as the hub of a far-reaching waterway network.

North Oxford suburbia now take over, with interesting gardens flanking the canal, and then there is a burst of canalside industry as the path swings to the east of Port Meadow, accompanied by the busy railway. Characteristic are the lift bridges, some in the original form designed by Brindley with wooden balance beams, and some more modern in steel. One, linking a factory that straddles the canal is even operated by electricity. After Port Meadow comes Wolvercote Lock, with the village, formerly noted for its paper mills, to the west. Under 1 mile away is the famous Trout Inn on the Thames and the ruins of Godstow Nunnery. In a rather wild and unresolved landscape the canal passes under first the arches of the elevated A34 and then the Woodstock Road to reach the isolated Duke's Lock, with its cottage and arched towpath bridge. Below the lock is the Duke's Cut, a narrow and overgrown link with the Thames created in 1789 at the behest of the Duke of Marlborough to enable Midlands coal to be brought directly to his Wolvercote paper mill.

Turning away from the railway for a while, the canal enters a more rural and isolated stretch that takes it between Yarnton and Kidlington. Seclusion comes to an end by the burgeoning housing estates of Kidlington, followed by the industrial estates to the north of the town.

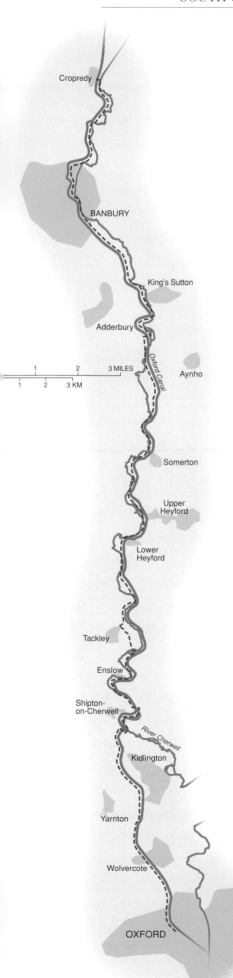

Kidlington makes a suitable break point, with accommodation and buses back to Oxford or on to Banbury. Cross the canal on the road bridge.

KIDLINGTON TO TACKLEY
About 6 miles/10km
OS LANDRANGER 164
Start at Yarnton Bridge
(grid reference 489 134)

The canal passes under the railway to the west of Kidlington and then runs closely with the A423 for a while, until a sharp turn to the east takes it away from the road and into Thrupp, a pretty canal village with a famous pub, a terrace of traditional stone cottages, a lift bridge, a British Waterways Yard and plenty of moored boats. The towpath crosses over to the eastern bank at the lift bridge. Another sharp turn takes the canal beside the Cherwell, and from this point river and canal are never far apart.

From here it is a short walk along the tree-lined towing path to Shipton-on-Cherwell, where the church stands high above the canal and the bridge. To the east are the fields of the Cherwell Valley, bisected by the railway embankment. It is worth a short detour across these fields to visit the lovely isolated church at Hampton Gay. Buried in the churchyard are some of the victims of a railway disaster that occurred on Christmas Eve 1874, when a crowded train left the rails by the canal bridge and fell into the frozen waters below. Beyond the church are the spectacular, but dangerous, ruins of Hampton Gay Manor, destroyed by fire in the late 19th century. Another, longer detour from Shipton can be made to Woodstock and Blenheim, 2½ miles west.

Curving round to Shipton Lock, built broad and hexagonal-shaped to pass sufficient water down into the canal, the two waterways now come together for a while. Absorbed into the Cherwell's

sinuous curves and willow-lined banks, the canal becomes delightfully pre-industrial and natural, like a scene in a Constable painting. At the next lock, in an isolated setting overshadowed by the old Bunker Hill quarry, canal and river separate again, with the towing path crossing the river on a cast-iron bridge. The canal now curves sharply round to Enslow, passing under the A4095 by the Rock of Gibraltar pub. Old wharves here used to serve the stone and coal trades, and more recently were used for the transport, by boat and rail, of cement from the canalside works nearby. The last stretch, pleasantly isolated in the now well-defined Cherwell Valley, leads to Pigeon's Lock. A path from here leads round the old mill, across the Cherwell and left onto a track. At the next junction turn right, and follow the track across the fields and beside the railway to Tackley Station.

A boat heads north from a lock near Kidlington.

Tackley to Banbury

TACKLEY TO SOMERTON
About 6¹/₂ miles/10km
OS Landranger 151, 164
Start at Tackley Station
(grid reference 485 206)

Following closely the winding course of the River Cherwell, the Oxford Canal skirts a hill to the east of Tackley, and cannot be seen from the village. Direct access to the canal is made difficult by the Cherwell, which lies between village and canal. Walkers can therefore either retrace steps to Pigeon's Lock, to the south, or take a more interesting route to the north. For this, walk up Nethercote Road through the village, passing the pub, and at the junction at the end of the road turn right. This road shortly turns to the left. Ignore this, and keep straight on up a track. At the top, turn left into the field and follow a path across the field, with the panorama of the Cherwell Valley spreading out beside you. The view of the broad sweep of the valley, with cows drifting about in the riverside fields, is magnificent, and includes the Cherwell, with an old oxbow bend, a canal bridge, and the waterway's curving route away through the trees. In the foreground the railway adds another dimension. At the end of the field go through a gate and follow a track that crosses the railway, and then curves down into the valley. This leads to the river and a

handsome stone bridge whose arches of different periods have been merged to span both river and canal. Nearby is a lock, half hidden in the trees. This is Northbrook. Turn left onto the towing path, and walk through the delightfully remote and undisturbed woods that frame the canal.

Soon, the river swings away to the west and the landscape opens out, with another lock isolated in the middle of the fields. River and canal come close together again, separated by the railway, and then the river swings away to play its part in the landscaped park of Rousham House, visible across the fields to the west. Ahead now is the bridge carrying the B4030, and immediately beyond it Heyford Station and a boatyard housed in traditional canal buildings. Lower Heyford village is spread over the hillside, and the canal curves round it, with good views of the church and a variety of pretty stone buildings.

An essential detour (under 1 mile each way) is to leave the canal at the bridge by the station, follow the road across the valley, turn left at the crossroads after the river and walk up the hill to the drive leading to Rousham House. Here, complete and virtually unchanged, is one of the earliest of England's landscape gardens, created by William Kent early in the 18th century. It is on a small scale and easily explored, but in its classical buildings, its careful landscaping, its dramatic use of

water and its contrived naturalness it contains the foundation upon which were built the great late 18th-century gardens, such as Blenheim or Stowe. A visit to Rousham explains so much about the landscape tradition in Britain, and it puts in context the lasting appeal of the Cherwell Valley which is, after all, a man-made landscape on a grand scale.

From Lower Heyford the canal continues through water meadows and trees to Upper Heyford, another stone-built village, with a church overlooking the canal. The huge, former American air base up above the village is now, thankfully, quiet and its blasting F-111s just an unpleasant memory. With the Astons overlooking the valley from the western hillsides, the canal now follows a rural route beside the Cherwell, its own river-like meanders interrupted by remote locks and bridges and by the close presence of the railway. Somerton is another quiet stone hillside village, which once had a busy wharf.

SOMERTON TO BANBURY
About 8¹/₂ miles/14km
OS Landranger 164, 151
Start at Somerton Bridge
(grid reference 290 496)

North of Somerton village comes Somerton deep lock, with its remarkably isolated canal cottage. After the lock, with the canal briefly entering Northamptonshire, railways begin to dominate the valley, two lines coming together after a flurry of embankments and viaducts at a complicated junction west of Aynho. At one time, each line had a separate station here, but both closed years ago. A more recent arrival in the Cherwell

A feature of the Oxford Canal are the old wooden lift bridges. A boat navigates a more modern one near Lower Heyford.

Valley is the M40, whose noisy presence beside the canal starts south of Aynho and continues until beyond Banbury, with three crossings of the canal's meandering route in a few miles. The B4031 crosses the canal at Aynho Bridge, passes over and under the two railway lines and climbs the hill on the eastern side of the valley for 1 mile or so to Aynho.

Aynho is a soft stone village of great appeal, and a worthwhile detour. At its heart is Aynho Park, a fine expression of formal 18th-century classicism. Adjacent, and rather more light-hearted, is the classicised church. Back on the canal, beside the B4031, Aynho Wharf is now a busy boatyard and restaurant. The moored boats are now left behind, and canal and river wind their way northwards. At Aynho Weir Lock, the Cherwell crosses the canal on the level, a relatively unusual event in canal terms, and something that can cause excitement for boaters when the river is in full spate.

The peace of the countryside is now increasingly shattered by the presence of the M40. By comparison, the railway and even the B4100, which crosses the canal on top of the very narrow old Nell Bridge, seem well-mannered and restrained. Here the towing path changes sides. Soon comes the first of the M40 crossings, with the motorway striding across the valley. Ahead now above the trees is a tall church spire, dominating the valley for miles around and

apparently changing its position as the canal pursues its wandering course. This is King's Sutton Church, at the centre of a particularly appealing stone village.

A sequence of old wooden lifting bridges follows before the canal swings west towards the M40, which crosses over it and then sweeps away to the east of Banbury. Despite the motorway, this part of the canal retains a distinctly rural atmosphere and seems a natural component in the landscape of the broad valley, unlike its aggressive modern rival. It is hard now to maintain a sense of historical context and appreciate the enormous upheaval in social and environmental terms caused by the building of first the canal and then the railway along the hitherto undisturbed Cherwell Valley. Perhaps a century from now the motorway will be as much a part of the landscape as those two early invaders are now.

The canal's route into Banbury is through fields, which keep at bay for some time the town's outlying suburbs and industrial parks that spread over the valley's western slopes. With river and canal close together, industry finally takes the upper hand and the last stretch into the town is rather gloomy, and not really indicative of Banbury's real qualities. Old warehouses and new industrial developments accompany the canal into the town centre, passing the railway station. The best place to

Surrounded by autumnal fields, the canal winds along the wide Cherwell Valley near Somerton.

leave the canal is the town lock, now set in an area greatly improved by new developments. The track from the lift bridge leads directly into the town centre, passing the bus station on the way. Just beyond the lock is a boatyard, housed in an old single-storey building famous for its association with Nurser's, formerly one of the country's best-known builders of traditional wooden narrow boats.

The canal's northern exit from Banbury is altogether more appealing, past back gardens and suburban houses, and then along beside the A423 for a while. It then turns to the east, passing under the railway and the M40, and reaches a delightful and secluded part of the Cherwell Valley. It is 4¹/₂ miles from Banbury to Cropredy, and walkers may like to add this to the main route. A return can be made along the canal towing path, south along the lanes via Great Bourton and Little Bourton and thence to the canal, or by bus to Banbury. Cropredy is a pretty brick village of wandering streets that all seem to lead to the canal. A plaque on the town bridge over the Cherwell describes the Civil War battle of June 1644 when a small force of Royalist cavalry managed to scatter a large Cromwellian force under General Waller, thus protecting the route to Oxford.

Midlands & East Anglia

The Severn Valley Way   78 – 81

The Cheshire Ring   82 – 91

In and Around Birmingham   92 – 99

The Fen Rivers Way   100 – 101

The River Stour   102 – 105

Gas Street Basin on the Birmingham Canal Network

The Severn Valley Way

COMPLETE ROUTE
SEVERN BEACH TO PLYNLIMON
(part of the extended Severn Way)
220 MILES/354KM
SECTION COVERED
STOURPORT TO IRONBRIDGE
27 MILES/43KM

THE River Severn rises at Plynlimon in Mid Wales and flows for almost 220 miles to the Bristol Channel. It has always been important to the places through which it passes, no more so than at Stourport, which grew up as a junction with the Staffordshire & Worcestershire Canal, and Bewdley and Bridgnorth, which also enjoyed a flourishing trade from the river in earlier times.

Above all else, the Severn is a beautiful river, rich in wildlife. You are likely to see swans, duck and heron on the water and kingfisher and pied wagtail, especially on the quieter sections between Bridgnorth and Ironbridge. The World Heritage Site at Ironbridge has to be one of the finest attractions in the United Kingdom and makes a splendid place to conclude two days of gentle walking in Worcestershire and Shropshire.

> **WALKING GUIDES**
> There is currently no one guide to this part of the Severn Valley, but as the Severn Way is developed accompanying literature will follow. There are, however, a number of local walking books available at tourist information offices.
>
> **OS MAPS**
> OS Landranger 127, 138
>
> **LINKS**
> The walk crosses the Worcestershire Way at Arley, a splendid route from Kinver Edge to the Malvern Hills. At Coalbrookdale it also joins with the Silken Way, an urban walk and cycle trail through to Telford and Wellington.

Stourport to Bridgnorth

STOURPORT TO ARLEY
About 7½ miles/12km
OS Landranger 138
Start at Canal Basin, Stourport
(grid reference 710 811)

There is a small car park at the Stourport Canal Basin and several others in town. All buses from Kidderminster stop just around the corner in York Street.

Looking across the canal basin, it is not difficult to imagine how congested it would have been when the town was the major inland port for the area. Stourport owes its very existence to the promoters of the Staffordshire & Worcestershire Canal who, despite receiving rival claims from nearby towns, decided that this should be where their canal met the navigable

Severn. In the end Stourport gained at Bewdley's expense. Walk by what must be one of the largest public houses for miles, the Tontine, to the riverside and turn right.

Pass beneath the town bridge, a fine structure dating from 1870, and past amusement parks, trip boats and parks to reach the countryside in a short while. The Way is easy to follow as it is waymarked with the Severn Way logo, a Severn trow, or flat-bottomed boat, suited to the shallows of these upper reaches. Pass near the Manor Gardens at Lickhill and through fields to Blackstone Rock. Here the path deviates to skirt the outcrop and then you cut left again to walk beneath the new bypass.

Within 1 mile you reach Bewdley, coming out into Stourport Road by a new housing complex. Go left here to Bewdley

Bridge, which spans the river and leads into the town centre. This masterpiece was designed by Thomas Telford and completed in 1798. It offers an exceptionally good view of the quayside, built to meet the growing river trade in the 18th century. The handsome Georgian buildings along Severnside reflect the prosperity of the time. Bewdley first developed in medieval days, initially as a bridging point of the Severn on the road to Wales and then through a gradual impovement of trade along the river. It also became the centre of a number of local industries, such as rope and clay-pipe making as well as the many wood crafts of the nearby Wyre Forest. The museum tells the full story in a well-constructed display, while a town trail takes you around the back streets.

Those who have little time for pavements should cross back over the bridge to the eastern shore and go first left along a road by offices and cottages to a barred gate. Here you will see a Severn Valley Way marker once more. The route to Bridgnorth is waymarked throughout. It soon joins the riverside and within 1 mile passes beneath the remaining pillars of the old railway line to Tenbury Wells. There are excellent views of the Wyre Forest, a royal hunting forest well known in the past for its charcoal burning, wood working and basket making. In the 16th century charcoal burning became so prevalent that the forest was almost completely depleted,

The historic canal basin at Stourport, once a major inland port.

but the government later insisted on a system of coppicing and matters improved for a few hundred years. Charcoal burning continued until the mid-20th century.

The path moves closer to the Severn Valley Railway at Northwood to pass by riverside dwellings. It then regains its position by the river and by reservoirs at Trimpley. The path runs through woodland beneath the Victoria Railway bridge. This was built by Sir John Fowler, who is better known for his Forth Bridge in Scotland. Continue for less than 1 mile into the pretty village of Upper Arley. A quarter of a mile away across the river is Arley Station, which featured in the television series *Oh! Dr Beeching*. From here you can return to Bewdley or Kidderminster by steam train.

ARLEY TO BRIDGNORTH
About 10 miles/16km
OS Landranger 138
Start at Arley Bridge
(grid reference 766 801)

Arley is a very pleasant quarter, owing much to its church and hall. At one time the river was crossed by ferry but now there is a footbridge. Once over it, go right along the western river bank through pastureland to the village of Highley, approximately 2½ miles ahead. Half-way, you cross the tributary Borle Brook at

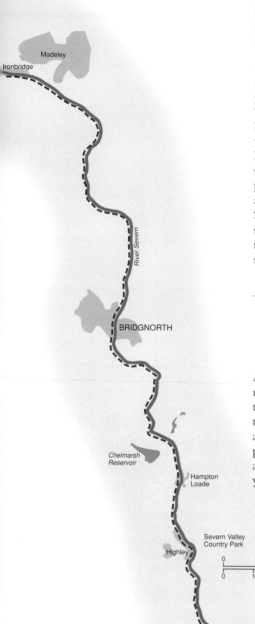

Brooksmouth. There was a wharf here at one time and a narrow gauge tramway that followed the brook to a small working at Billingsley.

Carry on along the river bank, reaching the Ship Inn below Highley railway station. Continue by the river to the Severn Valley Country Park, an area reclaimed after 100 years of mining and quarrying. Cross the river over the Miners Bridge if you wish to walk up to the Visitor Centre (generally open weekends only). The park is a good example of bringing what was a derelict area back to nature. Otherwise, keep ahead to Hampton Loade, where you will find the last remaining chain ferry on the river. There is also a stop here on the Severn Valley Railway line.

The route through to Bridgnorth follows the river's edge for the best part of 5 miles. As you near the town you will see to your left Daniel's Mill, a water-powered mill restored to grind corn. Just ¼ mile ahead go under the bypass and then continue to Bridgnorth Low Town. You can cut left to rise up to the Severn Valley Railway or to walk into High Town, perched 200ft up above the river.

Bridgnorth to Ironbridge

BRIDGNORTH TO IRONBRIDGE

About 9¹/₂ miles/15km

OS Landranger 138, 127

Start at the Castle Hill Railway, Low Town
(grid reference 718 929)

Bridgnorth is a town of curiosities, with seven sets of steps winding between the High Town and Low Town and an unusual funicular (Castle Hill Railway) too. The Norman castle keep leans more violently than the Tower of Pisa, and the High Street is packed with half-timbered and Georgian houses of real character. It is simply England at its best and very much a place to be enjoyed on foot.

From the Castle Hill Railway (lower station) in Low Town go left into Cartway and right into Riverside by the exquisite timbered Bishop Percy's House, built in 1580. The road runs between new housing and the river, passing the site of an old medieval Franciscan friary.

You are soon out into the countryside, edging by Bridgnorth Golf Club. You then walk through a succession of fields with the occasional farm. You will see to the left the old railway trackbed of the Severn Valley Railway. On the opposite bank is a cave carved out of the sandstone Winscote Hills, one of many to be seen in this area.

The highlight of the walk is the delightful Victorian bridge leading to Apley Hall, the home of the landowning Whitmore family in the 1820s. To the left is a group of dwellings, including the old Linley station house. Proceed ahead through pockets of woodland as the valley narrows. You pass near farmsteads but there are few landmarks in this isolated part.

Walk along the edge of cornfields to a dwelling, Balls Foundry, where a track leads off to the left to the old railway trackbed. Follow this and go right to walk along the trackbed towards Coalport. Pass by Maws Craft Centre and Jackfield Tile Works, with its impressive display of wall and floor tiles. Keep going along the old railway line, signposted Severn Valley Walk, through woodland to Ironbridge Gorge, often heralded as the birthplace of the Industrial Revolution. Its pioneering work in cast iron, of which the Iron Bridge is the finest of exhibits, has made this part of the Severn Valley a very special place to visit. Much of its rich past has been brought to life in the Gorge Museums and the entire area has justifiably been designated a World Heritage site.

The beautifully ornate Victorian bridge which leads to Apley Hall.

GUIDE BOX

PLACES TO VISIT
Ironbridge Birthplace of the Industrial Revolution – museums include the Museum of Iron at Coalbrookdale, the Jackfield Tile Museum, Blists Hill Open Air Museum, and the China Museum and Tar Tunnel at Coalport.

CAR PARKING
Bridgnorth; Ironbridge (but because of congestion in summer visitors are encouraged to park and ride).

PUBLIC TRANSPORT
Bus A service runs between the far end of the Iron Bridge and Bridgnorth.

ACCOMMODATION
Hotels, guest houses etc Bridgnorth, Ironbridge.

TOURIST INFORMATION CENTRES
Bridgnorth Listley Street, Bridgnorth, Shropshire WV16 4AW (tel 01746 763358)
Ironbridge The Wharfage, Ironbridge, Telford, Shropshire TF8 7AW (tel 01952 432166)

The cast-iron Iron Bridge – a masterpiece of early engineering and the finest exhibit in the World Heritage Site of Ironbridge Gorge.

THE SEVERN VALLEY RAILWAY

Steam first ran on the metals of the Severn Valley Railway in 1862. By all accounts, it was seen as a promising railway among a plethora of no-hope proposals placed before Parliament. It carried passenger traffic for just over 100 years and freight on certain sections for a few years longer. In 1965 the Severn Valley Railway was born and the first scheduled train ran on the original tracks in 1970. Since then it has become one of the major steam railways in the country, carrying hundreds of thousands of passengers a year along the 16 miles between Kidderminster Town Station (adjacent to the main line station) and Bridgnorth. Its flower-decked stations are restored in full GWR style and near Northwood the line crosses the Severn on the famous Victoria Bridge, whose 200ft cast-iron span was the longest in the world when completed in 1861.

For most of the route, the railway follows the river through the hills and so in the months that it operates (March to October) it is an ideal way for walkers to gain access to the Valley. With stations at Bewdley, Northwood Halt, Arley, Highley, Severn Valley Country Park Halt, Hampton Loade and Eardington, it is useful for anyone wanting to make a return journey to the start point. The full one-way journey takes about 1 hour 10 minutes.

A busy scene at Bewdley Station.

The Cheshire Ring

A CIRCULAR WALK FROM MANCHESTER, VIA MARPLE, MACCLESFIELD, HARDINGS WOOD, MIDDLEWICH, PRESTON BROOK AND LYMM
97 MILES/155KM

THE Cheshire Ring has for years been the most popular canal cruising circuit in Britain, and this walk, now established as the Cheshire Ring Canal Walk, follows the towing paths of the canals that make up the circle. These are the Ashton, the Peak Forest, the Macclesfield, the Trent & Mersey and the Bridgewater.

A substantial 97-mile walk, this a fascinating exploration of the heart of the waterway network created from the middle of the 18th century to fuel Britain's industrial revolution. Included are some of the earliest of England's major artificial waterways, the Bridgewater and the Trent & Mersey, along with one of the last to be built, the Macclesfield. The walk therefore encompasses the history of the canal age. The landscape that surrounds the canals of the Cheshire Ring is highly varied. It ranges from the pastoral to the squalid, is frequently spectacular and always interesting.

After many years of neglect, the towing paths are now in good condition and the going is quite easy. If spread out over five days, the walk is not too demanding. Access is generally good and much of the route is well served by public transport. No cycling without towpath permit from British Waterways.

WALKING GUIDES
All the information required by walkers can be found in Pearson's *Canal Companion to the Cheshire Ring*, and in *Nicholson's Ordnance Survey Guide to the Waterways Book 3: North*. Shorter walks based on Manchester and the Cheshire Ring are detailed in Perrott, David, *Walk the Waterways Around Manchester* and Quinlan, Ray, *Canal Walks of England and Wales*.

OS MAPS
Landranger 108, 109, 117, 118

LINKS
The Staffordshire Way and the Mow Cop Trail both pass over The Cloud, 2 miles east of Congleton. The Middlewood Way is an 11-mile walk along a disused railway line that comes close to the Macclesfield Canal between Higher Poynton and Macclesfield. The South Cheshire Way crosses the canal 1 mile northeast of the Mow Cop.

Ashton-under-Lyne to Marple

ASHTON-UNDER-LYNE TO MARPLE
About 8 miles/13km
OS Landranger 109
Start at Portland Basin,
south of Ashton-under-Lyne town centre
(grid reference 935 984)

Portland Basin is the meeting point of three canals, the Ashton, the Huddersfield Narrow and the Peak Forest, a major canal junction in an area bounded by old mills and railway lines. For years a place of squalor and decay, the basin has now been brought back to life by the revival of its canals. Mills and warehouses are being converted into offices and flats and waterside pubs and other facilities are making their own contribution. One now houses the Tameside Industrial Heritage Centre.

The Peak Forest Canal near Hyde.

From Portland Basin walkers can set off westwards along the Ashton Canal towards the centre of Manchester, eastwards along the restored section of the Huddersfield Narrow Canal to Staley Wharf, or southwards along the Peak Forest Canal. The towing path is on the southern side of the basin and it is carried over the Peak Forest on a handsome stone bridge. Cross this and then turn left down onto the Peak Forest's towing path, which almost immediately accompanies the canal across the River Tame on a hefty stone aqueduct. From here the Peak Forest follows a quiet but unremarkable route at first along the valley of the Tame, passing to the west of Dukinfield, and then southwards towards Hyde, surrounded by the remains of industry and suburban development. This was an area famous for its textile mills, great gaunt buildings built to exploit the waters of the Tame and now lingering on from the time when cotton was king. Rural pockets survive, adding variety to the walk. A long bridge carries the motorway, and then, with trees increasingly shielding it from its setting, the canal pursues a wandering route to the west of Hyde and Romiley. Both towns are hidden from view but access to them is easy. Their former dependence upon the canal is underlined by the fine brick warehouse at Hyde Wharf. Here, the towing path crosses briefly to the eastern bank. Between Hyde and Romiley, with the canal's rather secret route hidden by trees, is the short Woodley Tunnel, complete with towing path. The Tame swings away to the west but the railway is never far away, with convenient stations at Hyde, Woodley, Romiley and Marple for those wanting a shorter walk.

Completed in 1800, the Peak Forest was built initially for the carriage of limestone from quarries in the Derbyshire hills. The engineer was Benjamin Outram and there are many features that reflect his dramatic approach to canal building. Notable are the fine stone bridges and warehouses, and the well-engineered route. However, Outram's masterpiece is the great aqueduct over the River Goyt, a magnificent classical structure in well-cut stone that carries the canal 100ft above the thickly wooded Goyt Valley. The approach is excellent, through woods and cuttings and past the Hyde Bank Tunnel. There is no towing path, so walkers follow the old

horse-path across the top. Emerging from the woods, the canal seems suddenly to fly across the valley on Outram's great stone arches. The best view of the aqueduct is from a train on the parallel, but higher railway viaduct. There is a footpath that leaves the towing path beyond the aqueduct to lead down into the Goyt Valley, but views from this are limited by the dense woods. Once out of the woods, the aqueduct's fine proportions and the delicacy of its pierced form can be enjoyed from below.

After the aqueduct come the locks, a flight of 16 to raise the canal over 200ft into Marple. These are splendid locks, finely constructed, richly detailed and beautifully flanked by trees, and it is no surprise that the towing path is often

GUIDE BOX

PLACES TO VISIT
Manchester See page 90.

CAR PARKING
There is ample public and street parking in urban areas along the route.

PUBLIC TRANSPORT
Train Good service between Manchester and Macclesfield; also stations near the canal at Ashton-under-Lyne, Hyde North, Hyde Central, Romiley, Marple.
Bus Services between Manchester and Marple.

ACCOMMODATION
Hotels, guest houses etc Manchester, Marple.

TOURIST INFORMATION CENTRE
Manchester Visitor Centre, Town Hall Extension, Lloyd Street, Manchester M60 2LA (tel 0161 234 3157/8)

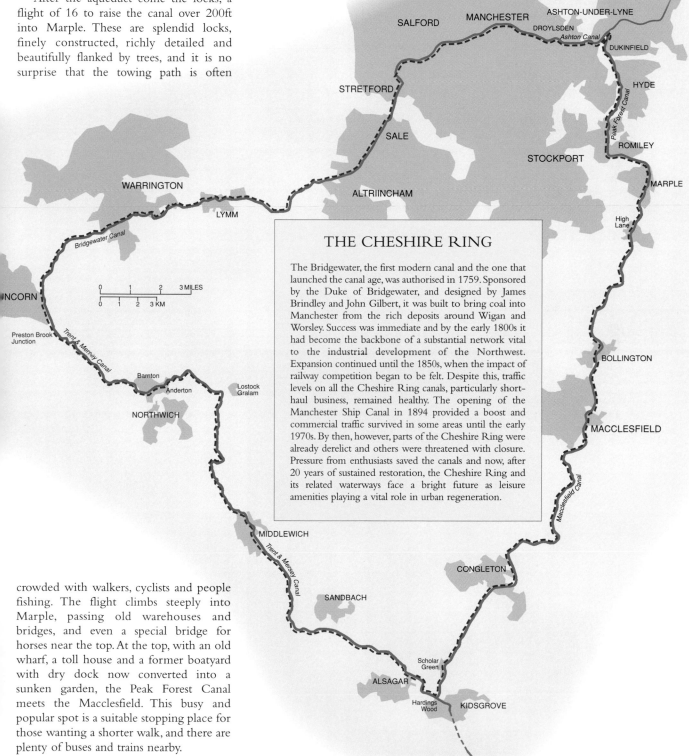

THE CHESHIRE RING

The Bridgewater, the first modern canal and the one that launched the canal age, was authorised in 1759. Sponsored by the Duke of Bridgewater, and designed by James Brindley and John Gilbert, it was built to bring coal into Manchester from the rich deposits around Wigan and Worsley. Success was immediate and by the early 1800s it had become the backbone of a substantial network vital to the industrial development of the Northwest. Expansion continued until the 1850s, when the impact of railway competition began to be felt. Despite this, traffic levels on all the Cheshire Ring canals, particularly short-haul business, remained healthy. The opening of the Manchester Ship Canal in 1894 provided a boost and commercial traffic survived in some areas until the early 1970s. By then, however, parts of the Cheshire Ring were already derelict and others were threatened with closure. Pressure from enthusiasts saved the canals and now, after 20 years of sustained restoration, the Cheshire Ring and its related waterways face a bright future as leisure amenities playing a vital role in urban regeneration.

crowded with walkers, cyclists and people fishing. The flight climbs steeply into Marple, passing old warehouses and bridges, and even a special bridge for horses near the top. At the top, with an old wharf, a toll house and a former boatyard with dry dock now converted into a sunken garden, the Peak Forest Canal meets the Macclesfield. This busy and popular spot is a suitable stopping place for those wanting a shorter walk, and there are plenty of buses and trains nearby.

Marple to Hardings Wood

MARPLE TO MACCLESFIELD
About 10 miles/16km
OS Landranger 109, 118
Start at Marple Junction
(grid reference 962 885)

Completed in 1831, the Macclesfield was a latecomer on the canal scene. Originally surveyed by Thomas Telford but built under the direction of William Crosley, the canal was designed for the carriage of coal, stone, grain, textiles and other materials, and it offered a more direct, but heavily locked route into Manchester from the south. Direct beneficiaries included the mill owners of Bollington, Macclesfield and Congleton. Even today, it has the air of a modern canal, with a direct and well-engineered route, large and handsome warehouses, and fine stone bridges whose flowing curves enabled horses to cross from one side of the canal to the other without being unhitched from their barges. For all that, the route is remarkably remote, and often in cuttings and on embankments as it makes its way southwards across the increasingly hilly terrain. Mills are a feature of the canal,

notably the magnificent one in red and cream bricks, Goyt Mill, by Bridge 3, just south of the junction. The route south, through a former coal mining region, passes between High Lane and Poynton, with the Lyme Park Country Park spread over the wooded hills to the east. Mount Vernon wharf, near Poynton, was formerly an important feature of the coal trade on the canal, but leisure boating has long taken over. Also related to the coal industry are the flat-topped bridges, easily raised to overcome any subsidence caused by mining.

The canal continues southwards, closely accompanied by the Middlewood Way, an 11-mile footpath that follows a former railway line. Its close presence to the west offers a range of circular routes. Next comes Bollington. The canal curves round this old stone mill town on a high embankment and a tall aqueduct giving excellent views across the rooftops below. Empty textile mills litter the landscape, gaunt and impressive memorials to a lost industry. Views are a feature of the Macclesfield Canal, bounded as it is by the Derbyshire Peaks to the east and the

GUIDE BOX

PLACES TO VISIT
Lyme Park (1½ miles southeast of Middlewood) Tudor house with later additions, Gibbons carvings, English clock collection; historic grounds used for BBC's Pride & Prejudice.
Adlington Hall (1½ miles west of canal, near Adlington) Timber-framing in fine Cheshire tradition, with large 17th-century organ in hammer-beamed roofed Great Hall.
Macclesfield Paradise Mill – demonstrations of silk handloom weaving in former silk mill. Silk Museum – tableaux, audio-visuals etc tell story of silk.
Gawsworth Hall (1½ miles west of canal, southwest of Macclesfield) Tudor manor house with rare Elizabethan pleasure garden; birthplace of Shakespeare's 'dark lady', Mary Fitton.
Astbury Battlemented Norman church with Jacobean painted roof in pretty village.
The Cloud 700ft climb from the canal rewarded with views (on a clear day) as far as Wales.
Little Moreton Hall (4 miles west of Congleton, 20 minutes' walk from Bridge 86) Britain's finest example of a timber-framed moated house, dating from 1450; Long Gallery, Great Hall, Knot Garden.

CAR PARKING
There is ample public and on street parking in Marple, Macclesfield, Congleton, Kidsgrove; also at Higher Poynton (grid reference 943 833) and north of Wood Lanes (grid reference 942 826); limited street parking at Hardings Wood.

PUBLIC TRANSPORT
Trains Link Macclesfield, Congleton and Kidsgrove; also stations at Marple, Middlewood, Adlington.
Bus Routes serve Adlington, Bollington, Macclesfield, Congleton, Kidsgrove.

ACCOMMODATION
Hotels, guest houses etc Macclesfield, Congleton and the Kidsgrove area.
Camping North of Wood Lanes.

TOURIST INFORMATION CENTRES
Macclesfield Council Offices, Town Hall, Macclesfield, Cheshire SK10 1DX (tel 01625 504114)
Congleton Town Hall, High Street, Congleton, Cheshire CW12 1BN (tel 01260 271095)
Stoke-on-Trent Potteries Shopping Centre, Quadrant Road, Hanley, Stoke-on-Trent, Staffordshire ST1 1RZ (tel 01782 284600)

Cheshire Plain to the west, and its high route across the hilly landscape allows ample opportunity to enjoy both. Beyond Bollington is the pointed peak of White Nancy, a great feature that dominates the canal for miles. From Bollington southwards into Macclesfield, the surroundings are more industrial in a modern sense, but trees keep the most boring aspects at bay. The canal's approach is to the east, clinging to the steep hillside, but its raised route allows plenty of interesting views over the streets and rooftops of Macclesfield. Mills and marinas take the canal into this handsome silk town, with its fine stone buildings. The best access point is from Bridge 37, which carries the A537. This leads directly to the station and the town centre, a few minutes' walk away.

The towpath of the Marple Flight of 16 locks, lifting the Peak Forest Canal up from the Goyt Valley, is perennially popular with local families.

MACCLESFIELD TO CONGLETON
About 10¹/₂ miles/17km
OS Landranger 118
Start at Macclesfield Station
(grid reference 920 736)

From the station walk eastwards away from the town along the A537 Buxton Road, and join the towing path where the road crosses the canal. Southwards from Macclesfield, the canal follows an increasingly rural route. The main line railway and the A523 are never far away and yet they do not seem to intrude on the canal's sense of seclusion as it crosses the foothills of the Derbyshire Peaks. Old quarries high in the hills, and a patchwork of drystone walled fields decorate the landscape to the east, while to the west the farmland stretches away into the distance. At Bosley the canal's 12 locks are grouped into a flight, beautifully placed in a remote setting among the trees and remarkable in the quality of their engineering. The local gritstone chambers with their double gates are particularly attractive. The locks carry the canal down into the Dane Valley, below the huge Bosley Reservoir to the east from which the canal draws its water. At the bottom lock the canal passes under a bridge which used to carry the old North Staffordshire Railway's scenic line to Leek, and then swings west to cross the River Dane on a grand aqueduct, a classically elegant structure in stone. It now follows the River Dane in a broad loop westwards towards Congleton, with the views to the east dominated by the high peak of The Cloud, 1,126ft above sea level and well worth the long climb up to its summit. The best approach from the canal is from Bridge 61, which carries the A54.

The town of Congleton itself is rather hidden from the canal behind a suburban screen, and then the high embankment that carries the canal across Bath Vale makes it seem rather inaccessible. The best approach is from Bridge 75, carrying the A527. This is close to the station for those wanting a direct train back to Macclesfield, and a little under 1 mile from the town centre, to the west.

CONGLETON TO
HARDINGS WOOD
About 5¹/₂ miles/9km
OS Landranger 118
Start at Congleton Station
(grid reference 873 623)

South from Congleton, the canal passes briefly through spreading suburbia and then enters a rural landscape once more, less dramatic perhaps but still pleasantly pastoral. A worthwhile detour is the short

The view across the Cheshire Plain from The Cloud, with the Macclesfield Canal and the railway crossing a green landscape.

walk from Bridge 81 to Astbury's fine church and pretty village, ¹/₂ mile away to the west.

Increasingly dominant now is the tall hill to the east crowned with what apears to be a ruined castle. This, the summit of a long gritstone escarpment, is Mow Cop, and the castle an is eyecatcher folly created in 1754 by the owner of nearby Rode Hall. A number of footpaths lead from the canal up to Mow Cop, the best of which is the South Cheshire Way, joined from the minor road that crosses the canal at Bridge 83. Mow Cop is also famous as the setting for the first Primitive Methodist open air camp meeting, in May 1807, the start of a powerful nonconformist movement in the region.

A little further on, at Bridge 86, another footpath leaves the canal, this time westwards across the fields to Little Moreton Hall, the most famous timber-framed mansion in Britain and now in the care of the National Trust. Immediately beyond the bridge are the grounds of Ramsdell Hall, a country house of a later era whose lawns sweep down to the canal and turn it into a kind of ornamental waterway to separate the garden from the parkland beyond the towing path. This is a delightful stretch, with the canal raised above the farmland that rolls away to the west, but it soon ends in the domestic suburbia of Scholar Green. From here onwards the canal is in a deep cutting that hides it from the surrounding houses. At

Hall Green there is a stop lock, with accompanying lock cottage and former stables. This was originally a barrier to make sure the water belonging to the Trent & Mersey Company did not flow into the Macclesfield, and vice versa, a legacy of the fierce rivalry that existed between canal companies early in the 19th century. The canal then leaves the cutting, crosses the A50 on a sturdy stone aqueduct, and crosses the Trent & Mersey Canal on another aqueduct before turning east to run parallel to the Trent & Mersey for some distance to Hardings Wood Junction. Here the two canals finally meet, having anticipated by some 150 years the kind of slip road connection commonly used on motorways. From the junction the Trent & Mersey continues westwards, dropping down the Red Bull Locks that lower it beneath the Macclesfield's aqueduct and on towards Alsager. To complete this walk, walk eastwards from the junction, alongside the Trent & Mersey, for a short while to the next bridge. This gives access to Kidsgrove Station and the town. A little further on, with the water stained ochre red by iron deposits, is the entrance to the famous Harecastle Tunnel, and beside it the old portal of its forerunner, designed by James Brindley and long since closed by mining subsidence.

Hardings Wood to Wincham Wharf, Lostock Gralam

HARDINGS WOOD TO SANDBACH
About 9 miles/14km
OS Landranger 118
Start at Hardings Wood Junction
(grid reference 835 547)

The Trent & Mersey is a canal of distinctive character, tough, stone-built, and fitting well into the landscape. It bears the stamp of its famous engineer, James Brindley, for whom it was the Grand Trunk Canal, half of the great cross of waterways he planned to link the Mersey, the Humber, the Thames and the Severn. Opened in 1777, it was one of the first of the long-distance waterway routes to be completed and its structures still have an 18th-century feel about them.

The walk starts at the junction with the Macclesfield Canal, and immediately there is the first of the 26 locks in 7 miles that carry the canal down onto the Cheshire

Plain. This long and demanding flight has always been known, as anyone who has worked a boat up or down will appreciate, as Heartbreak Hill. The locks come steadily as the landscape unrolls, and many are set in pairs. The whole flight was doubled in the 1830s at the instigation of Thomas Telford to speed up the flow of traffic, and a number still survive as pairs. The second pair of locks lower the Trent & Mersey under the Macclesfield Canal, and then the descent into the broad landscape is rapid and continuous, past Red Bull, where the British Waterways maintenance depot is housed in a former Pickford's warehouse, and curving down past Church Lawton.

The battlemented peak of Mow Cop forms a distant backdrop to the east, while to the west is Alsager, 1 mile's walk from the bridge carrying the A50 over the canal, just past the small Snapes Aqueduct. Next come Rode Heath and the Thurlwood Locks, in a setting that brings together farmland, suburbia and echoes of former industry, mainly coal mining and salt extraction. As the canal approaches Hassall Green, the landscape becomes hillier, with woods breaking up the pattern of the fields, and then another lock lowers the canal beneath the M6 motorway. This noisy intruder is quickly forgotten, but the sense of rural isolation is soon diminished, first by a large golf course at Malkin's Bank, built over a former chemical works, and then by encroaching industry around Wheelock and Sandbach. The canal passes well to the south of this old town, best known for its vehicle plants. The bottom of the lock flight is at Wheelock, and from here the canal follows a winding course parallel to the River Wheelock, passing

A typical Trent & Mersey bridge, complete with original carved stone number, on Heartbreak Hill near Alsager.

underneath the main railway line by Ettiley Heath. Bridge 160, two bridges further on, carries a minor road that leads to Sandbach Station, ½ mile to the east. There are trains from here back to Kidsgrove, via Crewe.

SANDBACH TO WINCHAM WHARF, LOSTOCK GRALAM
About 10 miles/16km
OS Landranger 118
Start at Sandbach Station
(grid reference 738 615)

From here the nature of the canal changes, with the waterway often raised on an embankment above the surrounding landscape. Originally, when the canal was built, everything was on the level, but centuries of salt extraction has caused continuous subsidence, and the canal has been steadily raised to compensate. The approach to Middlewich, the salt capital of England since the Roman period, is adjacent to the busy A533, and rather in the shadow of chemical and salt works, and other large-scale industries. Middlewich is

a busy canal town, with a drydock, plenty of moored boats, a sequence of locks, and the junction with the branch that leads south-westwards across a remote and attractive agricultural landscape to join the Shropshire Union Canal network at Barbridge. The centre of Middlewich is close at hand, and easily reached from a number of town bridges. There is no railway station, but buses are available for those wanting a shorter walk. The final lock in Middlewich, and the last on this part of the canal, is a broad one, built to enable larger salt barges to reach Middlewich. Shortly afterwards the Croxton Aqueduct carries the canal over the River Dane. This too was originally built to a broader gauge, but it has since been narrowed.

The canal now follows the meandering, tree-lined course of the Dane for some time, crossing a quiet landscape isolated from any roads. Adjacent to the canal, and sometimes merging with it, is a series of lakes, or flashes. In the 1950s, when canal carrying was coming to an end, these were used as graveyards for redundant narrow

West of Middlewich, in the Dane Valley, the Trent & Mersey is delightfully rural.

boats, and many old working craft, with their memories, still lurk beneath the surface. The canal winds round Whatcroft Hall, and then turns eastwards away from the River Dane, flanked by remote woodlands. After a railway crossing, it turns north again, making the most of the landscape before meeting the outlying suburbs that surround Northwich.

From here on, past Rudheath and Broken Cross, housing and industry take over, with the chemical works dominant. The A530 runs beside the canal on this final stretch, which ends at Wincham Wharf. Here there is a convenient pub and restaurant, and a marina offering boat trips. A short walk eastwards from here along the A559 leads to Lostock Gralam, where there is a station. Trains run from here to Northwich and Manchester, but there is no direct link with lines southwards to Crewe, and so buses are more useful for those wanting to return to the start point.

Wincham Wharf to Lymm

WINCHAM WHARF TO PRESTON BROOK JUNCTION

About 11 miles/18km

OS Landranger 118, 117, 108

*Start at Wincham Wharf, Lostock Gralam
(grid reference 685 746)*

Salt works and other industries accompany the canal as it curves round to the east of the Northwich complex. At Marston, the former Lion Salt Works, the last in Britain to have made salt by the process of evaporation in open brine pans, stands right by the canal. This is now a museum and discovery centre, and nearby is the site of one of the largest of the old salt mines. The canal then makes a brief escape from the surrounding industry, passing through a remote area of woods and lakes, now part of the Marbury Country Park. The suburbs soon encroach again as the canal approaches Anderton, but there are extraordinary views down to the huge chemical complex to the south in the

Weaver Valley. It is an impressive and dramatic sight, and a suitable backdrop for the Anderton boat lift, one of the greatest wonders of the waterways.

Opened in 1875, this prehistoric-looking structure in rusty iron was designed to raise and lower loaded boats vertically between the Trent & Mersey Canal and the River Weaver Navigation in the valley below. There were two great iron tanks, each capable of holding two narrow boats, and they worked originally on a counterbalance system, aided by hydraulics and a steam engine. Later, electricity took over and the tanks were made to operate independently. With some hiccups, this monster continued to operate until 1983, but it has been silent and partially stripped down ever since, with vital parts of its machinery lying in overgrown heaps in the surrounding field. Full restoration is promised, thanks to contributions from the National Lottery, and so the experience of taking a boat vertically from one waterway

GUIDE BOX

PLACES TO VISIT
Marston Lion Salt Works and Discovery Centre tells story of local salt industry.
Anderton Boat Lift – amazing device for raising or lowering boats, in tanks of water, 50ft between Trent & Mersey Canal and Weaver Navigation.
Daresbury Birthplace of Lewis Carroll, whose *Alice in Wonderland* characters are celebrated in stained-glass in the church.
Runcorn Norton Priory – displays tell the story of its life, from medieval priory to Tudor manor house to Georgian mansion.
Higher Walton Walton Hall and Gardens – grounds with children's zoo.

PARKING
Wincham Wharf (limited); street parking in the villages en route; Lymm.

PUBLIC TRANSPORT
Train This section of the Cheshire Ring is poorly served by railways, the relevant local lines having been closed during the Beeching era.
Bus Routes serve Lymm, Runcorn, Warrington, Altrincham.

ACCOMMODATION
Hotels, guest houses etc Northwich, Runcorn, Warrington.

TOURIST INFORMATION CENTRES
Runcorn 57 Church Street, Runcorn, Cheshire WA7 1LG (tel 01928 576776)
Warrington Polltax House, Rylands Street, Warrington, Cheshire WA1 1BN (tel 01925 442180)

to another should one day be possible once again. From the top, the lift looks insubstantial, and unclear in its function. Walk down the paths beside it leading down into the Weaver Valley to appreciate its full splendour. There is a small car park at the top, but access to the bottom is only on foot. The best views are probably from the chemical works across the Weaver.

After the excitement of the lift, the canal becomes suburban again as it approaches the little portal of Barnton Tunnel. This, wide enough for one boat only, and without a towing path, is quickly followed by the slightly longer Saltersford Tunnel, equally narrow and also without a towing path. Walkers follow the old horse paths over the top in each case. The western approach to Barnton Tunnel is delightfully wooded, and there are views through the woods down across the broad Weaver Valley to the south. Unlike the rural Trent & Mersey, the Weaver is still a busy navigation, carrying large ships inland to the chemical plants around Northwich and Winsford, and the sight of a ship passing through the huge locks and the swing bridges, and sailing through fields of cows, is always exciting.

Woods accompany the canal round Little Leigh, but it then enters a more open landscape, its route through fields on the northern side of the Weaver Valley, with

The remarkable Anderton Boat Lift transported loaded boats from the higher level of the Trent & Mersey down to the River Weaver.

views across the river meadows to the hills beyond. This continues past Dutton Hall, where there are exciting views of the huge locks and bridges of the Weaver, and then the canal enters a wooded stretch that takes it away from the Weaver and to the southern end of the long Preston Brook Tunnel. There is a stop lock built to protect the Trent & Mersey's water supplies. The tunnel was one of the first to be built under James Brindley's direction and it is narrow and rather meandering in its route. There is no towing path and walkers must take the old horse track over the top for the whole of the 1,239yds of the tunnel. This and the two shorter tunnels were always a bottleneck, even after steam-powered tugs were introduced at Preston Brook in 1865.

Beyond the tunnel is the short stretch of canal leading to Preston Brook Junction. This is technically the Preston Brook branch of the Bridgewater Canal, the Trent & Mersey officially ending at the northern portal of the tunnel. This explains the sharp V shape of the actual junction. Until the 1950s this was one of the busiest canal ports in England, where the larger boats of the Bridgewater, sailing from Manchester or Runcorn Docks, transshipped their loads onto narrow boats for the onward journey along the Trent & Mersey. Today, it is a rather gloomy spot, overshadowed by the M56 motorway, with only a boatyard and marina to hint at past glories. A bridge carries the towing path across to the Bridgewater.

PRESTON BROOK JUNCTION TO LYMM

About 10 miles/16km
OS Landranger 108, 109
Start at Preston Brook Junction
(grid reference 568 807)

Buses from Runcorn along the A56 cross the canal at this point. There is limited parking by the junction. Unfortunately, the nearby stations offer only the most convoluted journeys, except to and from Manchester.

From the junction, the Bridgewater Canal quickly becomes more rural in its immediate surroundings, and there are striking views to the north out across the Mersey Estuary via a complex network of roads, railways and pylons. In the distance is the Manchester Ship Canal, a dramatic contrast in scale and yet equally moribund in commercial terms. At least the meandering Bridgewater is well established as a leisure waterway. Up on the wooded hillside to the east is Daresbury, where Charles Dodgson, alias Lewis Carroll, was born. Leave the canal at Keckwick Bridge

for a short detour to the church where Alice and other characters from his books feature in the stained-glass windows. The canal continues to wind its way past Moore to Walton, where the old Hall, up above the canal, is now open to the public, with a children's zoo in the grounds. The setting here is attractive, and then the route becomes more suburban, with back gardens and allotments flanking the towing path as the canal cuts through Stockton Heath and the outer fringes of Warrington.

In Stockton, at London Bridge, the bridge carrying the A49, old steps show where passengers in the 18th century waited for the high-speed packet boats running between Manchester and Runcorn, a service made possible by the Bridgewater's lack of locks. The age of the canal is also shown by the old brick bridges, and it is hard in its present context to remember how revolutionary and dramatic it must have seemed when it was built in the middle of the 18th century. Indications of age can also be found in the village of Grappenhall, where the canal winds, Dutch-style, through the centre,

From the west end of the Barnton Tunnel, the Trent & Mersey Canal runs through woods towards its junction with the Bridgewater.

with the church nearby and pretty houses flanking the (recently) cobbled streets.

Next comes Thelwall, famous now for the huge soaring bridge that carries the M6 motorway over the Ship Canal. Before this, a much smaller, but in its time just as important, structure carries the canal over a minor road. Walk down the steps beside this aqueduct, cross the A56, and walk straight on for 1/2 mile to the bank of the Ship Canal. Here, unexpectedly, is a passenger ferry waiting to carry you over to the other side. Once across, a short walk westwards leads to the giant Latchford Locks, 600ft long, a worthwhile detour. Back beside the, by contrast, tiny Bridgewater, the towing path continues, under the towering arches of the M6 viaduct and on to the outskirts of Lymm. Lymm is another real canal town, with the waterway at its heart overhung by earlier houses, and a suitable place to end the walk.

Lymm to Manchester, Portland Basin

GUIDE BOX

PLACES TO VISIT
Little Bollington Dunham Massey – Georgian house with collection of Huguenot silver; working Jacobean mill; large garden.
Manchester An extensive list of sights includes Museum of Science and Industry, hands-on and working exhibits; Air and Space Gallery – flight and space technology; Granada TV Studio Tour; Town Hall – Waterhouse's gothic masterpiece – Ford Maddox Brown murals depicting the city's history; Charles Barry's City Art Gallery – good collection includes Pre-Raphaelites, Adolphe Valette waterways scenes and Lowry; 15th-century cathedral.

CAR PARKING
There is ample public and on-street parking all along the route of this section.

PUBLIC TRANSPORT
Train With the exception of the area around Lymm, the walk is well served by trains and trams on the Metrolink.
Bus The only bus service on this section is that between link Lymm and Runcorn.

ACCOMMODATION
Hotels, guest houses etc Altrincham, Sale, Manchester.

TOURIST INFORMATION CENTRES
Altrincham Stamford New Road, Trafford, Altrincham, Cheshire WA14 1EJ (tel 0161 9125931)
Manchester Visitor Centre, Town Hall Extension, Lloyd Street, Manchester M60 2LA (tel 0161 234 3157/8)

LYMM TO STRETFORD

About 10 miles/16km
OS Landranger 109
Start at Lymm town centre,
where A6144 crosses the canal
(grid reference 683 874)

From Lymm the canal follows a pleasantly quiet route through the low-lying countryside, well protected from the assaults of industry and suburbia. Marinas, boatyards and moored craft abound, the canal creating in the process its own kind of boating suburbia. A long embankment carries it past Little Bollington and the grounds of Dunham Massey. This National Trust house and garden is easily reached from the B5160, which the canal crosses on a hefty stone aqueduct well protected against assaults by oversized lorries. There are several aqueducts along this stretch, one carrying the canal over the River Bollin. This elevated section gives ample opportunity for enjoying the Cheshire landscape and the distant views of church towers. At Oldfield Brow all this comes to an end, and the canal enters Manchester's suburbs, initially salubrious as it passes through Altrincham and Sale, but getting steadily less so as it reaches Trafford and Stretford.

The suburbs may seem monotonous, but the start of this section is more interesting, with old warehouses, cranes and other surviving details of commercial canal life in the Broadheath area. By Timperley the canal starts a remarkably straight run through Sale towards the heart of Manchester, a route followed precisely by the railway when it was built in the 1840s. Canal, and then railway, encouraged the rapid development of hitherto rural farmland into a massive interconnected sprawl. The railway, first electrified in 1931, is now part of the new Metrolink line, and the stations along the route give easy access to the canal and to Manchester. Those wanting a rural walk could, therefore, miss out all the urban section through Manchester and start or finish at Timperley Station. After Sale there is a brief respite as the canal crosses the green valley of the Mersey, with its extensive development of water sports and other leisure activities. The canal goes under the M63 and then is carried over the Mersey on an aqueduct before re-entering the suburbs at Stretford, now rather less appealing.

STRETFORD TO PORTLAND BASIN, ASHTON-UNDER-LYNE

About 11 miles/17.5km
OS Landranger 109
Start at Stretford Metrolink Station
(Grid reference 799 944)

This is the start of an urban canal walk of great interest, rivalled only by the canals of Birmingham. The regeneration of the latter over the last ten years has set a

Near Broadheath, the old Linotype works is a distinctive landmark alongside the Bridgewater Canal.

standard that Manchester now has to emulate, and not before time. A few years ago, Manchester's canals were not only squalid but also downright dangerous, and passages through the city, by boat or on foot, were fraught with hazards. Today, things are very much better, thanks in part to the massive regeneration works inspired by the city's bid for the Olympic Games. New marinas, and leisure and commercial centres created out of derelict warehouses and dock complexes have brought Manchester's waterways back to life in a dramatic way. At the same time, enough of the old survives to add the necessary atmosphere.

After the station, the canal swings away from the Metrolink line, turning north towards the attractively named, but still rather grim Water's Meeting. Here, the main line of the Bridgewater continues towards Manchester, while turning away to the west is the Leigh branch, which meets the Leeds & Liverpool Canal near Wigan. This branch served the coalfields around Wigan, and the Duke of Bridgewater's extensive mines near Worsley, and was a vital source of early revenue for the canal. The main line now passes through the massive Trafford Park estate. Set up from 1896, this was the first industrial estate in the world, housing at its peak over 200 companies, some of which helped to keep the canal in business at least until the 1960s. Next comes Manchester United's famous Old Trafford ground, overlooking the canal, followed, across the water, by the massive Salford Quays redevelopment of the former Ship Canal dock complex. The canal now passes the branch leading to the River Irwell, via the subterranean Hulme Lock, buried beneath the railway viaduct, and then at Castlefield Junction, a complex meeting point of four waterways, the Bridgewater comes to an end, head to head with the Rochdale Canal. Warehouses around the junction echo the Bridgewater's early history as Manchester's first major waterway.

The next section, the famous Rochdale Nine, cuts through the heart of Manchester, below Deansgate and Oxford Street, and within a stone's throw of St Peter's Square and Mosley Street. The route is generally in cuttings, below street level, and the nine locks offer a varied insight into Mancunian life, old and new. The settings are dramatic, with warehouses, railway viaducts, offices and modern developments lining the banks. There is no towing path on the last section, from Dale Street Basin to Paradise Wharf, and so walkers have to return to street level, and walk parallel to the canal

along Canal Street and Ducie Street. At Ducie Street Junction, adjacent to the new Paradise Wharf development, and near Piccadilly Station, the Rochdale meets the Ashton Canal, which branches away to the south. The Rochdale Canal Company still operates from buildings behind the famous battlemented archway, and grand warehouses hint at better days, before car parks replaced canals as the major source of revenue.

From here, the last section of the walk follows the Ashton Canal, first past Piccadilly Village, the last of the impressive new developments, and then through Ancoats, starting the long flight of 18 locks that raise it steadily towards

The canals of Manchester have been extensively revived over the last ten years. The Rochdale runs through the city centre from Castlefields to its junction with the Ashton Canal.

the distant hills and Saddleworth Moor. The surroundings are primarily industrial, but the canal's climbing route also allows interesting views back over the city. Mills, old bridges and traces of former branches and basins line the route. Near the top lock, at Fairfield Junction, is the 18th-century Moravian Settlement, founded by a strict Protestant Sect. From Fairfield the mills continue and then, accompanied by a plethora of railway lines, the Ashton Canal comes to its end at Portland Basin.

In and Around Birmingham

A CIRCULAR WALK FROM LAPWORTH INCORPORATING SECTIONS OF SEVERAL CANALS
36 MILES/57KM

THE walk described in this chapter is along the towing paths of several canals, built by three independent companies whose routes, part of a complex waterway network at the heart of England, came together in Birmingham. It takes in stretches of the Stratford-on-Avon, built from 1793 to 1816, the Worcester & Birmingham, built from 1791 to 1815, and the Grand Union, formed in 1929 by the amalgamation of a number of waterways including the Grand Junction and the Warwick & Birmingham. Also incorporated are short stretches of the Birmingham Canal Navigations.

The towing paths, for years decrepit and frequently hazardous, are now generally in good condition. The walk can be completed in two days, but three days makes it more leisurely and gives more time for visits along the route. The surroundings range from the delightfully rural to the urban and industrial. The whole route is well served by railways and buses, making access fairly easy throughout. No cycling without towpath permit from British Waterways.

At its peak in the late 19th century, the Birmingham Canal Navigations network totalled over 160 miles and as late as the 1940s over a million tons of cargo, mostly coal, was still being carried by boat. It started in 1768 when the Birmingham Canal Company was authorised to build a waterway linking Birmingham and Wolverhampton. Engineered by James Brindley, this opened in 1772. Success brought rapid expansion, with rival companies building routes into the Black Country, many of which were ultimately absorbed into the Birmingham Canal Navigations. From 1846 the whole Birmingham network was owned by the London & North Western Railway, but this resulted in an expansion of the canals due to the localised nature of the traffic. This pattern continued well into this century, with the canal age living on in Birmingham far longer than in other parts of the country. Serious decline started in the 1950s, and by the 1960s about a third of the network had fallen out of use or been closed. At this time the future looked bleak, but in the last 20 years support groups and local authorities working together have rescued and restored much of the surviving network, developing its leisure and amenity potential.

WALKING GUIDES
There are a number of published guides covering the whole route, including *Nicholson's Ordnance Survey Guide to the Waterways Book 2: Central* and Pearson's *Canal Companion to the Birmingham Canal Navigations*. In addition, *A Gas Street Trail* and other local guides are available from the Birmingham Marketing Partnership.

OS MAP
Landranger 139

LINKS
There are more miles of walkable canals in the Birmingham and West Midlands areas than in any other part of Britain, and the canals on this route can be used as a backbone for further explorations.

Lapworth to King's Norton along the Stratford-upon-Avon Canal

LAPWORTH TO WHITLOCK'S END
About 8 miles/13km
OS Landranger 139
Start at Lapworth Station
southeast of Birmingham
(grid reference 188 716)

Lapworth Station, pleasantly set in a quiet suburban location actually known as Kingswood (the village of Lapworth being over 1 mile to the west), is well placed not only for the Stratford-upon-Avon Canal but also for two National Trust houses, Baddesley Clinton to the east, and Packwood House to the west, both about 15 minutes' walk away.

For the canal, turn right from the station along Station Road. At the end, turn right again onto the B4439, walk under the railway bridge and join the canal at the road bridge. Looking southwards, the canal divides into two, the right-hand branch continuing down the locks towards Stratford, the left leading to a junction with the Grand Union, visible to the east beyond the railway line. It was the Stratford's northern section, from Lapworth to King's Norton, that was completed first, in 1802, and this has always carried the heavier traffic. The southern section, genuinely rural and in a world of its own, is well worth exploring and offers another pleasant day's walk. It has many distinctive features, in particular the famous barrel-roofed lock cottages, one of which can be seen by Lock 22, just to the south of the junction.

Despite its proximity to Birmingham, the Stratford-on-Avon Canal has remained delightfully rural. Its heavily locked route has had a chequered history. Taken over by the Great Western Railway in 1856 and then suffering from a steady commercial decline followed by periods of uncertainty and partial closure. Now, however, it is in good condition, with many boats making the 25-mile journey from King's Norton to Stratford, where there is a junction with the recently restored River Avon Navigation.

The walk starts near the bottom of the picturesque Lapworth flight. Densely packed together are 18 locks, interesting to observe with their intermediate pounds and their iron bridges split to allow the passage of the towing rope, but hard work for the boat crews. These form part of an almost continuous sequence of 55 locks that lower the canal down to Stratford. Although the immediate surroundings are quite suburban, the towing path up beside the locks is flanked by trees and there are views out across the fields. The B4439 runs beside the canal for a while, but is rarely intrusive. By the top lock a minor road crosses the canal, leading southwards to Lapworth's 15th-century church, and north towards Packwood House. Lines of moored boats precede Hockley Heath, which the canal skirts to the south, sheltered in part by a tree-lined cutting. On the approach to Hockley Heath two steel counterbalanced lift bridges, operated by boat crew, give the canal a European touch.

Fields and patches of woodland remote from any village accompany the canal until it passes under the M42. It then takes a meandering course through the countryside to the north of Earlswood, where there are two large reservoirs built to keep the canal supplied with water. Plenty of handsome arched bridges in old red brick add interest, while the canal's route remains enjoyably private, well hidden from the encroaching suburbia that becomes much denser after Whitlock's End. The canal passes under a railway, midway between two stations, Whitlock's End and Shirley, both accessible from the following road bridge.

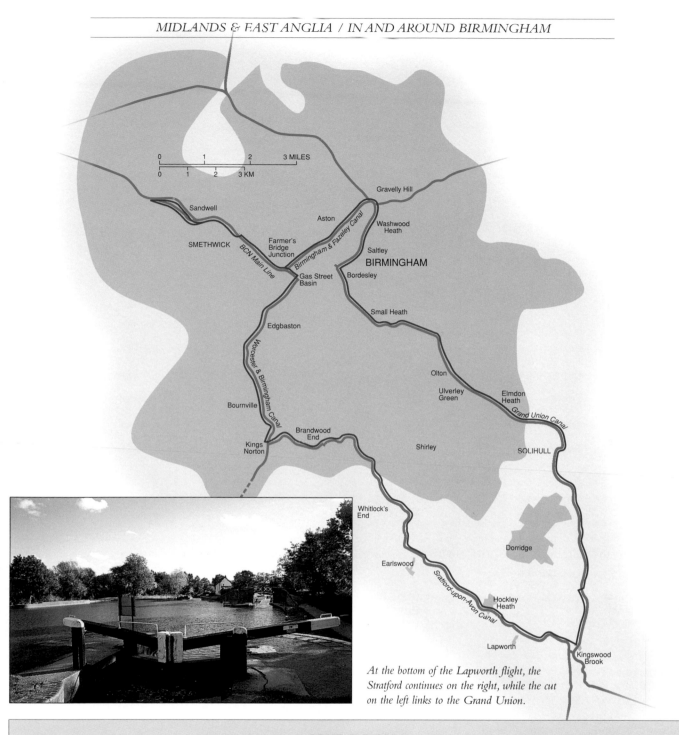

At the bottom of the Lapworth flight, the Stratford continues on the right, while the cut on the left links to the Grand Union.

GUIDE BOX

PLACES TO VISIT

Lapworth Packwood House – Tudor house with fine textiles and furniture; 17th-century yew garden clipped to depict Christ's Sermon on the Mount. Baddesley Clinton – romantic moated medieval house, little changed since 1634; family portraits, priest holes, ponds and lake walks.
Kingswood The Navigation is a classic pub in a tranquil setting with popular riverside garden.
King's Norton Patrick Collection of motoring history; some exhibits in period settings.
Bournville Cadbury World – the story of chocolate from tropical rainforest to packaged sweet; story of Cadbury family, Bournville factory and village.
Barber Institute of Fine Arts, Birmingham University's collection of paintings from 13th century to present day.
Botanical Gardens Delightful oasis with beds, borders, over 400 trees; palm house, orangery, cactus house.
Birmingham Nature Centre British and European wildlife in natural setting; butterfly house, fishpond with underwater viewing.
Birmingham Museum and Art Gallery Collection of Pre-Raphaelite paintings and much more.

Museum of Science and Industry Industrial Revolution to present day with emphasis on Birmingham's contribution to science and engineering; locomotives, aircraft, working engines.
Perrott's Folly Built in 1758, 96ft tower with good views.
St Paul's Church and Square 18th-century buildings; numbered box pews in church were 'sold' to pay for the church; close to Jewellery Quarter with shops and craftsmen's workshops.
St Chad's Cathedral (Roman Catholic) Designed by Pugin, completed 1841.
St Philip's Cathedral (Church of England) 18th-century English baroque, Burne-Jones windows.
Railway Museum Impressive collection of working steam locomotives; saloon carriage from royal train used by Churchill in World War II; travelling post office ambushed in Great Train Robbery of 1963.

CAR PARKING

There is ample public parking in and around the city of Birmingham, and there is on-street parking, sometimes rather limited, in the towns and villages along the route.

PUBLIC TRANSPORT

Train The canals that make up this walk are generally close to railway stations and so access by train is easy, at the start and finish of each section of the walk and sometimes along the route. The starting point for rail services is generally Birmingham's New Street Station.
Bus Comprehensive network.
Local transport services information tel 0121 200 2700.

ACCOMMODATION

The Convention and Visitor Bureau (see below) has information on the full range of accommodation available in Birmingham. For information and reservations tel 0121 780 4321.

TOURIST INFORMATION CENTRE

Birmingham Convention & Visitor Bureau, 2 City Arcade, Birmingham, West Midlands B2 4TX (tel 0121 643 2514)

WHITLOCK'S END TO
KING'S NORTON
About 5 miles/8km
OS Landranger 139
*Start at bridge taking minor road to
Whitlock's End Station
(grid reference 113 769)*

The canal is soon taken over the River Cole on an aqueduct and then wanders along a quiet valley, well sheltered from suburban estates. For parts of the route the canal is in a cutting, overshadowed by trees which ensure its privacy, helped by the tall bridges in this area which often have no access to the roads and houses above. Boats and walkers can therefore proceed in their own secluded world, framed by oaks, willows and alders, taking time to look at the moored boats that flank the canal, boats whose generally somnolent immobility echoes the suburban life of their owners in the real world up above.

Passing between Billesley Common and Highter's Heath, delightful-sounding but completely indeterminate places, the canal reaches the short Brandwood Tunnel. There is no towing path through it, and so walkers follow the old horse path over the top. From here, the canal curves past a chemical works, approached by a swing bridge, the scene of a famous encounter in 1947 between a group of canal enthusiasts who formed the Inland Waterways Association and the railway company owners of the canal. The latter had, illegally, tried to close the canal by fixing the bridge across it, thus stopping all traffic. Subsequent demonstrations and the raising of the matter in the House of Lords became part of a major campaign to give canals the future they now enjoy.

A final stretch of almost French-like canal lined by grand trees leads to the famous stop lock with its permanently raised guillotine gates, built originally to prevent water belonging to one canal company flowing freely into that of a rival company. Beyond is King's Norton Junction, where the Stratford-on-Avon Canal meets the Worcester & Birmingham, their meeting point marked by an elegant bay-fronted former toll house, a classic example of the high quality architecture associated with canals at the end of the 18th century.

For the continuation of the walk to Birmingham, cross the towing path turnover bridge and turn right along the Worcester & Birmingham Canal. For a return to Birmingham by train, leave the canal by the bridge adjacent to the guillotine stop lock and walk northwards into Lifford. Turn left for the $1/2$ mile to King's Norton Station or carry straight on for 1 mile to the next one on the line, Bournville. There is no direct bus or rail link between King's Norton and Lapworth, and so the return trip has to be via Birmingham.

At the end of the Stratford Canal an old stop lock with vertical guillotine gates separated its water from the Worcester & Birmingham Canal.

King's Norton to Gas Street along the Worcester & Birmingham Canal

KING'S NORTON JUNCTION TO
GAS STREET, BIRMINGHAM
About 5$1/2$ miles/9km
OS Landranger 139
*Start at King's Norton Junction
(grid reference 054 794)*

The Worcester & Birmingham, like all other canals leaving Birmingham to the south and west, is heavily locked, underlining the city's position on a plateau over 450ft above sea level. In the canal's total length of 30 miles there are 58 locks, and these occur within a 16-mile stretch. Long tunnels also add to the canal's engineering complexity, and illustrate the problems faced by its builders at the end of the 18th century. Constantly busy during its heyday, the canal is now a pleasantly rural waterway, its route a green finger stretching right into the heart of the city of Birmingham.

Secluded and well sheltered by trees, this route manages to keep at bay all the surrounding Birmingham suburbs, and all those well-known areas, Bournville, Selly Oak and Edgbaston, through which it passes. But for the railway, which follows the route so closely that it and the canal often share bridges, the Worcester & Birmingham would appear to be in the middle of the country.

Soon after leaving King's Norton, the towing path briefly changes to the eastern bank, and then returns to the west after a railway bridge. With the canal swinging to the west, walkers will increasingly be aware of the strong and tempting smell of chocolate that heralds the huge Bournville complex. Cadbury's moved here from the city centre in 1879, creating not only large factories but also a famous estate village built along the lines of a garden suburb, and fully equipped with everything except a pub. Even today there is no pub in the village, and so George Cadbury's Quaker beliefs live on. Instead, there is a massive visitor centre, a kind of chocolate theme park that attracts thousands every week. The factory was established beside the canal for the good reason that there was a belief in waterway transport, and Cadbury's for many years operated a large fleet of distinctively painted boats carrying raw materials and the finished product to and from Bournville. Just beyond the station there was a large wharf, with extensive rail links into the factory, but there is no trace of this today. Those who find the tempting smell too hard to resist have to leave the towing path by the station, for there is no direct access to Bournville from the canal.

Next comes Selly Oak, a less salubrious setting, and the site of a former junction with the old Dudley No. 2 Canal, which until the First World War ran westwards from here to join the Staffordshire & Worcestershire Canal via the notorious, inherently unstable, unpleasant and very long Lappal Tunnel. It was the final collapse of this that brought about the closure of this route. Buried somewhere far below southern Birmingham are the remains of this tunnel, the fifth longest ever built in

Britain, and a hidden memorial to the endeavours and achievements of the canal age. Selly Oak is soon passed, and then the canal's route is through Birmingham University and the pleasant Edgbaston suburbs, partly in a verdant cutting and partly from a raised embankment that offers fine views eastwards across the campus and the parkland of Edgbaston. There is a short tunnel at Edgbaston, equipped with a towing path. The only problem offered by the walk along this part of the Worcester & Birmingham is the shortage of access points. There are several stations adjacent to the canal, but walkers caught out by rain or tiredness will find no easy way of reaching them. It is really a matter of pressing on, and enjoying the extraordinary sense of privacy so near the centre of a major city.

Soon after the tunnel, this illusion disappears, and the city rapidly encroaches, first in the form of the ring road, and then in the echoes of former industry that flank the canal's final stretch. Railways and former railways abound and then the canal makes a sharp turn to the west to cross over the Holliday Street Aqueduct with its elegant cast-iron column supports. Ahead now is Gas Street Basin and the site of the

famous Worcester Bar, for years a physical barrier separating the Worcester & Birmingham Canal from the Birmingham Canal Navigations, and necessitating complex transshipping operations between boats on the two independent waterways. Later, this was replaced by a lock where tolls were collected.

TARDEBIGGE

The sequence of 58 locks southwards from Tardebigge, the longest flight in the country, have always been a kind of mecca for waterway devotees. It was at Tardebigge that the great railway and canal historian LCT Rolt moored his converted narrow boat, *Cressy*, while he worked during the war at the Ministry of Supply in Birmingham, and it was while he was living here that his first book, *Narrow Boat*, was published. This inspired a young waterway enthusiast, Robert Aickman, to get in touch with Rolt and they met at Tardebigge in 1945. That meeting led to the formation the following year of the Inland Waterways Association, and thus to a change of heart about Britain's heritage of canals and navigable rivers.

At King's Norton Junction, a pair of hotel boats pass the former toll house.

Gas Street Basin and the Birmingham Canal Navigations

GAS STREET BASIN AND A CIRCULAR WALK ON THE BCN
About 10 miles/16km
OS Landranger 139
Start at Gas Street Basin
(grid reference 064 864)

In the old days Gas Street Basin was the heart of Birmingham's canals, a secret, highly evocative place, hidden behind towering and gloomy warehouses, and one of the last habitats of the working narrow boat. It was the meeting place of several major canals, the complex hub of an extraordinary and little-known waterway network. As commercial canal-carrying gradually dwindled away during the 1960s, dereliction and decay inevitably took over. The narrow boats remained, by now mostly residential, and the whole area acquired a particular kind of romantic appeal.

During the 1970s an extensive redevelopment programme began to sweep this away and now the Gas Street Basin is the centre of an imaginative and prize-winning urban regeneration scheme. The old warehouses have gone, replaced by hotels, offices, pubs, restaurants and houses, but enough of the old canal architecture remains to create an interesting and challenging balance between past and present.

At any time of day the smartly bricked towing paths are full of people, going about their business or just taking a canalside stroll to watch the boats. In the old days, navigating a boat through Birmingham was a solitary, and sometimes threatening experience, a voyage through an unknown world of picturesque decay. Today, there is constant boat traffic, and many of the towing paths have become official urban walkways. Birmingham from the water may never look like Venice, but it is certainly making an heroic and much appreciated effort to improve its waterway environment.

Gas Street is still the haunt of traditional narrow boats, and the sight of these can be enjoyed from the iron footbridge across the canal, itself a relatively recent arrival.

From the basin, walk northwards under the long Broad Street Bridge and into another world of waterway regeneration. The Brindley Place shopping centre and restaurant complex, the Sea Life Centre, the National Indoor Arena and extensive residential developments all now look out over the canals, bringing to life in a popular way Birmingham's greatest, but hitherto least-known asset. From Farmer's Bridge Junction, a waterway roundabout, canals radiate out in four directions, southeast to Gas Street and towards Worcester, eastwards into the intricacies of the Birmingham Canal Navigations and thus towards Coventry, Rugby, the East Midlands, Oxford and London, north towards Wolverhampton, North Wales, Manchester and the North, and westwards along a meandering route, the remains of James Brindley's original line to Wolverhampton.

To enjoy the flavour of the Birmingham Canal Navigations to the

Old and new meet at Birmingham's Gas Street Basin, still a haven for traditional narrow boats.

full, take the northern route for a while. There are two canals going north. The new main line, carved straight through the landscape with deep cuttings, is a kind of canal motorway, engineered by Thomas Telford in the 1820s and built to replace the narrow, winding, and heavily locked route chosen initially by Brindley, and then later improved by Smeaton. The main line runs straight to Smethwick Junction, not far from Smethwick Rolfe Street Station, but criss-crossing loops of older canals indicate Brindley's original line. At the junction, the two canals divide, the older route turning to the north and climbing to a higher level via a flight of locks while the new main line enters the deep cutting characteristic of Telford's engineering. From here a circular walk of about 4 miles follows the old main line's winding route at a higher level, descends to the lower level through the Spon Lane Locks, one of the oldest flights in the country, and then returns via the cuttings of the new main line. The route is littered with industrial and waterway history, and the two canals underline the differences between the primitive engineering of the 18th century and the more advanced techniques of the early 19th century and the railway age.

Longer and more localised walks, many detailed in JM Pearson's *Canal Companion*, can include other wonders of the Birmingham canal networks, such as the great tunnels at Dudley and Netherton – the latter a huge structure with towing paths on both sides – as well as aqueducts, lock flights, pumping stations and all the other surviving relics of what was probably

The Farmer's Bridge locks drop the canal steadily from the heart of redeveloped Birmingham towards an area of older industry.

the greatest industrial canal complex in the world. In the remoter corners of the network, the spirit of endeavour behind the industrial revolution can still be appreciated.

GAS STREET BASIN AND ITS ENVIRONS

The revitalisation of Gas Street Basin and its asociated canals has been a phenomenon of the last decade, with waterside restaurants and pubs, shopping precincts and smartly presented towpath walkways replacing the legacy of centuries of traditional industry. While this process of urban regeneration is clearly desirable, it is important that the past is not completely obliterated.

The best way to explore the heartland of the BCN is on foot, and there is, fortunately, still plenty to see that can bring the past to life. History is sometimes revealed by signs and descriptive panels, but one of the clearest reminders of the once-dominant role of the canal in the economy of the Birmingham region is the large number of old brick arches that suddenly lift the towpath above the water. These former bridges, generally now

crossing nothing but a brick wall, mark the site of former junctions, branches, basins and factory wharves, all of which add up to something over 50 miles of the BCN closed since 1900, lost for ever beneath subsequent development.

Most of the BCN branches were less than a mile long, but there have been some more significant losses, such as the majority of the Wyrley & Essington Canal, closed in the 1950s, and the Dudley No 2 Canal, which included the horrendously narrow Lappal Tunnel, at 3,795yds the fourth longest in Britain. After a century-long battle against subsidence, this finally collapsed irreparably in June 1917, but its gloomy remains, buried far beneath Birmingham, await the attention of some archaeologist in the far distant future.

Farmer's Bridge Junction (Birmingham) to Lapworth along the BCN and the Grand Union Canal

FARMER'S BRIDGE JUNCTION TO
OLTON STATION

About 7 miles / 11km
OS Landranger 139
*Start at Farmer's Bridge Junction
in the heart of Birmingham
(grid reference 060 868)*

Farmer's Bridge Junction (adjacent to the National Indoor Arena and the Sea Life Centre) is a waterway roundabout, with canals branching off in four directions. Take the eastern arm, the start of the Birmingham & Fazeley Canal, which leads under a couple of bridges to another large basin, Cambrian Wharf, overlooked by a large pub and some domestic tower blocks. The Birmingham & Fazeley, initially a rival to the Birmingham Canal, merged with it

in 1794 to form the Birmingham Canal Navigations. On the left, or towing path side, is a lock, the start of a flight that disappears down into the distance. Walk down beside the flight of 13 locks, initially though a smartly restored area, and then increasingly into a ravine whose walls are formed by towering buildings and decayed warehouses. Access signs from bridges point to the Science Museum and the city's jewellery quarter, just to the north. Ahead is the Birmingham Telecom tower, and shortly the canal disappears into the basement of the adjoining building, a cavernous and gloomy area complete with lock. Next is a vast, brick-lined vault, virtually a tunnel of Piranesian scale carrying the railway and Snow Hill Station. This marks the limit

of regeneration, and ahead is a more traditional stretch of urban waterway lined with warehouses and industrial premises, some derelict, and some still housing inconceivable manufacturing processes. Notable in this stretch is the delicate cast-iron Barker Bridge dating from 1842, and the series of brick-arched bridges that lift the towing path over the former entries to long-abandoned branch canals and factory basins.

Passing under the flying concrete of the Aston Expressway, the canal swings south to Aston Junction. Here, the Birmingham & Fazeley goes straight on, down the Aston Locks to Salford Junction, buried beneath infamous Spaghetti Junction. To continue the walk, cross over this canal on the pretty cast-iron bridge and turn south along the short Digbeth branch. This was opened in 1799 to connect the Birmingham Canal Navigations with the Birmingham & Warwick, now part of the Grand Union's route southwards to London. There are six locks, dramatically overshadowed by old buildings and a muddle of railway lines that incorporate Robert Stephenson's original London & Birmingham route towards its famous Curzon Street terminus. The branch ends at the site of Warwick Bar, originally a stop lock between the two canals to control water supplies and collect tolls.

Warehouses of various periods, hinting at earlier times when canal-carrying was king, flank the Grand Union's route southwards. Many of these were still in use as late as the 1960s, for the commercial life of the canals lived on longer here than in other parts of Britain. At Bordesley Junction go straight on. The branch to the left offers an alternative route back to Birmingham via the Garrison locks and the Aston Locks. Ahead now are the six Camp Hill Locks, gloomy survivors in an area beset by decay and vandalism, that further lift the Grand Union to its summit level by Sparkbrook. This is the start of an 11-mile pound, a kind of linear reservoir to ensure adequate water supplies for the locks at each end, itself fed from nearby reservoirs such as that at Olton. More warehouses and basins recall past glories and the industrial surroundings continue through Small Heath. However, as the city recedes, so the setting begins to improve. An aqueduct carries the canal over the River Cole, with nearby a ski slope and the Birmingham Railway Museum at Tyseley. Next comes Acock's Green, the start of Birmingham's extensive suburbs. Those wanting a shorter walk, or preferring to avoid the industrial section of the canal can take a train to Acock's Green or Olton stations, both only a few minutes' walk from the towing path.

The distinctive style of the wide Grand Union locks, modernised in the 1930s, is first encountered at Knowle.

OLTON TO LAPWORTH STATION
About 10 miles/16km
OS Landranger 139
Start at minor road bridge near Olton Station
(grid reference 134 825)

From Olton onwards the Grand Union spends much of its time in deep, wooded cuttings, virtual wildlife sanctuaries largely isolated from the rich panorama of suburban life hidden above. For the boater and the walker on the towing path it is a private world. Next come Olton and Ulverley Green, but these are merely names on the map for those hidden below. Even the Rover factory at Elmdon Heath passes virtually unnoticed. Those wanting greater variety in their surroundings may find the long cuttings rather tedious, particularly on a gloomy day. On a fine day, with the dappled light filtering down through the trees, and with kingfishers flashing past, it can be very pleasant, with ample time to consider the minutiae of canal and towing path life. Eventually, near Catherine de Barnes, the suburbs and the

cuttings end, and the canal wanders through a gentle landscape of fields and woodland. The canal itself is broad and deep, reflecting the extensive reconstruction work undertaken by the Grand Union Company in the early 1930s, a last and initially successful, attempt at keeping motor transport at bay. Solihull and Knowle lie to the west, but the canal manages to keep to its rural route and avoid both of them. Only the M42 crossing intrudes briefly on the pastoral seclusion.

Knowle is bypassed in another cutting and this ends at the top of the Knowle flight of locks, dramatically placed at the top of a steep slope from which a splendid landscape rolls away into the distance. The locks, rebuilt in the 1930s to a broad gauge to speed up traffic, along with their distinctive enclosed paddle gear set at a slope and large storage pounds, all serve to remind us of what might have been. The locks also underline the smallness of the standard narrow locks of so many English canals, their 7ft width chosen by James Brindley in the middle of the 18th century.

The wide Grand Union cuts straight through the landscape north of Lapworth.

Well maintained, surrounded by flower beds and interesting buildings, the Knowle Locks add great interest to the walk. A helpful sign at the top of the locks points out that it is 13 miles from here to Gas Street Basin. What it fails to say is that there is a further 3½ miles to go from here to the end of the walk at Lapworth, but it is an enjoyable final stretch, through an open landscape of farmland and woods and with only minor roads to intrude on the sense of peace and rural seclusion that the canal engenders.

Even in summer, with the pleasure boats trekking to and fro, it is hard to believe that 50 years ago this was still one of England's major commercial transport arteries. Baddesley Clinton lies to the east, accessible from a footpath across the fields from the B4439 bridge. This bridge is also the end of the walk, and it is a matter of minutes to retrace the route from here to Lapworth Station.

The Fen Rivers Way

CAMBRIDGE TO ELY
17 MILES/27KM

THE Fen Rivers Way, waymarked with a blue eel, follows both banks of the River Cam between Cambridge and Ely. Between the two cities it crosses the chequerboard of the fens, a unique, mysterious and artificially created landscape beloved of many. While at times it may be windswept under the wide open skies, its uncompromising flatness means you can see for miles, and the wonderful cloud formations are something special.

Bridges and a network of paths and tracks to the east of the river make circular routes easy. On the western route, the Haling Way towpath runs from Cambridge to Clayhithe, and the path then continues close to the river all the way to Ely. The eastern route wanders away from the riverbank now and then into villages and across fields (with some muddy sections). The walk described here is the western one. At the time of writing Holt Fen Bridge is derelict and a 2-mile diversion is necessary to cross the River Great Ouse at its junction with the Cam. If you want to avoid this, use the east bank alternative between Bottisham Lock and Ely.

WALKING GUIDE
The Fen Rivers Way (Cambridgeshire County Council) – pack includes laminated route map based on OS Landrangers.

OS MAPS
Landranger 143, 154

LINKS
The Harcamlow Way is a 140-mile, figure-of-eight walk with Cambridge at the top of its northern loop. The *Fen Rivers Way* pack includes details of 4 circular walks that can be followed off the route.

CAMBRIDGE TO BOTTISHAM LOCK
About 8 miles/13km
OS Landranger 154
Start at Midsummer Common
(grid reference 457 591)

From the railway station or town centre, follow the Fen Rivers Way across Jesus Green and Midsummer Common and then along Riverside. Well used by local walkers and cyclists, the towpath crosses to the western bank at Water Lane, Chesterton, while a footpath continues on the east bank across common land. On the stretch of river from here to Baits Bite Lock you may well see rowers in training, accompanied by their coaches cycling along the towpath and calling out instructions. This is where the traditional university 'Bumps' take place every February and June, rowing races that date back to 1824.

Young cattle graze the grassy banks on the final stretch of the walk, with Ely Cathedral riding the horizon ahead.

The well-surfaced towpath continues northwards through the suburbs under overhanging willows while fishermen sit amid their accoutrements, swans glide nonchalantly by and pleasure boats chug up and down. Shortly after the river passes under the city bypass comes Baits Bite Lock, with its guillotine head gate and weir. A bridge takes a footpath over to the eastern bank and back to Cambridge or north through Horningsea to another crossing point at Clayhithe.

Away from habitation now and entering the fens, the river passes through pastureland and peaty ploughed fields, with the railway line to the west striding ahead straight as a die. At Clayhithe pleasure boats moor up alongside the Bridge Inn's riverbank garden. The towpath ends here and for 500yds the Fen Rivers Way western path follows the road towards Waterbeach, turning off just before the station to join the top of the floodbank for ³/4 mile to Bottisham Lock, where there is a bridge and another guillotine head gate.

BOTTISHAM LOCK TO ELY
About 9 miles/14km
OS Landranger 154, 143
Start at Bottisham Lock, near Waterbeach
(grid reference 507 657)

The eastern path now follows the river closely. Tracks lead off across the fenland and alongside the reed-lined lodes, or drainage channels, that feed into the Cam. One of these, Reach Lode, was originally built by the Romans as part of a canal system used to transport supplies to their army bases in Lincoln and York. Much later, in the 18th century, the Fen Lighters were developed and until the end of World War I these flat-bottomed boats, working in trains of five towed by a horse, traded local crops for foreign imports and coal from the North.

Well into the open fens landscape, the western path is now less clearly defined. Isolated and mostly undistinguished farmhouses stick up in flat fields of cabbages and carrots. Poplars act as windbreaks. At River Bank a chain ferry, one of several that

once operated on the river, used to take Waterbeach parishioners to a chapel that can be seen from the river bank.

As it approaches Upware, the path tends to be overgrown in patches, but this is the Cam Washes, land designated an SSSI, and the reward for battling on through nettles and over sometimes rickety stiles is the chance of seeing herons, willow warblers, cormorants and, in winter, numerous duck and geese. To the east of the river, Wicken Fen is managed as a nature reserve. Raised above the fields, with water pumped in to keep it wet, its sedge fields and reed beds provide a unique wildlife habitat similar to that of the fens before they were drained.

The stillness of the Washes is broken only by the sound of motor launches, some of which are heading for the 'Five Miles From Anywhere No Hurry' pub on the east bank at Upware. This replaced an old bargemen's pub after it was gutted by fire and is a popular destination tantalisingly inaccessible to thirsty walkers on the west bank. Just over a mile on, Dimmock's Cote Bridge provides another crossing point.

The western path continues along the floodbank, with bends in the river bringing exciting glimpses of the vast hulk of Ely Cathedral. At Popes Corner the Fish and Duck restaurant and marina is sited at the junction of the rivers Cam and Great Ouse. Here Holt Fen Bridge awaits rebuilding and to cross the Great Ouse you have to take a 2-mile diversion down one side of the Great Ouse and up the other, using the road bridge. From here, it is only about ¹/₂ mile on to Stretham Old Engine, whose engine-house chimney has been visible from the path. Built in 1831 to drain the fens, it stands surrounded by a patchwork of red and green lettuces.

Back on the Fen Rivers Way, the path is closely accompanied for the last 3 miles into Ely by the railway. There is plenty of boating activity, colourful narrow boats heavily outnumbered by white motor launches. But always now the greatest 'Ship of the Fens' sits high on the horizon ahead, beckoning the walker on. After a quick diversion to cross the old Braham Dock, the last section of path comes along the edge of Cawdle Fen to the main road into Ely, beside the station. Follow the Fen Rivers Way over the road to a marina, café and pub. The magnificent cathedral, notable in particular for its wonderful 12th-century west front and octagonal lantern tower, is nearby.

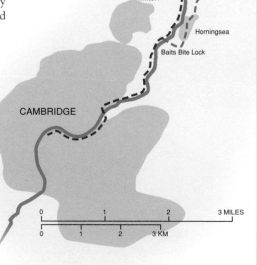

THE DRAINING OF THE FENS

Until the 17th century the Fens were basically a dangerous, peaty swamp. Then in 1630 the Dutch engineer Vermuyden was commissioned to drain the area. By diverting the rivers and digging a system of ditches, he created a valuable network of transport routes as well as 6,000 acres of extremely fertile agricultural land. Once drained, however, the peat began to shrink, soon enough falling below the level of the channels so that water flowed back. Hundreds of pumping windmills had to be installed to take water from the fields up into the rivers. Windmills were replaced by steam pumps from 1819 and in turn these have been superseded by modern electric and diesel pumps. In many places the land is several feet below sea level, entirely reliant on raised floodbanks and feats of engineering for protection.

The River Stour

SUDBURY TO MANNINGTREE & MISTLEY
28 MILES /45KM

THIS section of the River Stour, forming the boundary betwen Suffolk and Essex, meanders through an undulating, agricultural landscape quietly punctuated with pink and creamy yellow colour-washed houses and the towers of rich, wool churches – a landscape still remarkably similar to that immortalised by John Constable. Indeed, the magic of this walk is that you can at several points stop where Constable stood to paint and even now, almost 200 years on, identify landmarks in the pictures. In Constable's day, the river was a busy navigation and many of his paintings show details of its working. The public right to pass along the river still exists, but the rights of way along the Stour's bank lapsed when trading stopped, so for much of the route, in particular the first section, this is not a riverside walk but one that follows the valley with views, close or distant, of the waterway.

WALKING GUIDE
The Stour Valley Path (Suffolk County Council) includes the section covered here.

OS MAPS
Landranger 155, 168 (169 for Mistley to Harwich)

LINKS
The Stour Valley Path is a 60-mile route from Newmarket, near the source of the river, to Cattawade (Manningtree), where it joins the estuary. The walk described here joins this waymarked path at Sudbury. See above for guide (with accommodation details).
The Painters' Way links Sudbury and Manningtree, sometimes coinciding with the Stour Valley Walk (Peddar Publications, Croft End, Bures, Suffolk CO8 5JN).
The Essex Way is a long-distance walk from Epping to Harwich which follows the southern shore of the Stour Estuary more or less closely from Manningtree to Harwich. Guide and accommodation leaflet available from the Planning Department, Essex County Council, County Hall, Chelmsford CM1 1LF (tel 01245 492211).
The Valley Walk follows an old railway line north from Sudbury for about 2 1/2 miles.

Sudbury to Nayland

SUDBURY TO BURES
About 6 1/2 miles/10km
OS Landranger 155, 168
Start at Sudbury Basin
(grid reference 869 407)

Sudbury was the head of the Stour Navigation, and you should start with a look at Sudbury Basin, at the bottom of Quay Lane. There had been regular traffic on the navigation as early as 1705, but this increased rapidly after 1781 when new commissioners dredged the river, rebuilt several locks and built the warehouse in the basin that is now the Quay Theatre. From the end of the 18th century until the railway began to eat into traffic in the 1860s, Sudbury Basin was busy with the activity of numerous barges, known as Stour lighters, which carried grain and bricks (made across the river in Ballingdon) downstream to Mistley, where they were transshipped to Deptford in Thames sailing barges. Lighters returned upriver with cargoes such as coal, horse manure and grindstones for the numerous mills on the river. From the basin there is now access to an extensive network of footpaths, some of which follow the river. The headquarters of the River Stour Trust and the Sudbury Riverside Interpretative Centre are in a restored granary, close to the Basin (refreshments and river trips are available here).

The Stour Valley Path, waymarked with its dragonfly logo, follows the valley southwards from Ballingdon. Running a mile or so west of the Stour, it climbs gently to the church at Great Henny while the river flows on in unobtrusive fashion through the valley cornfields. From Great Henny the path zigzags across lanes, fields and farm tracks with good views over the valley at several points, eventually joining a minor road – and coming close to

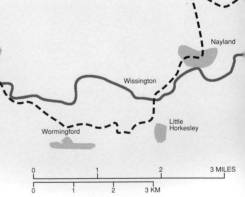

the river – just north of Lamarsh. Notice the church's round tower, unusual for this part of the country.

This minor road from Ballingdon to Bures also makes a pleasant walk or cycle ride and has the advantage of passing right alongside the river at Henny Street, where the Swan Inn has a riverbank garden. A sluice and mill race can be seen close to the road.

Just beyond the Red Lion in Lamarsh, a gravel track leads off to the left down to the railway line. Stiles take the footpath over the railway line and into a meadow that sweeps down to a curl of the river. Were it not for unrelenting pylons and a pillbox – a harsh reminder of a less peaceful modern era – this is a scene that Constable could well have chosen. The path follows the floor of the valley into Bures, from where you can return to Sudbury by train. Alternatively, for a circular walk, retrace steps to Lamarsh and return to Sudbury along the Painters' Way, to the east of the river.

BURES TO NAYLAND
About 6 miles / 10km
OS Landranger 125, 168
Start at Bures Station
(grid reference 902 339)

An important river crossing, Bures was in medieval times a busy trading centre. Today the Stour divides the little town between Suffolk and Essex. From the station go towards the centre and cross the river into the eastern, Essex part and take the Nayland road. A track leads right off this to some old mill buildings, now privately owned, in an attractive grouping beside the millpond. The footpath crosses the former Bures Lock, now a sluice, then veers left across fields as the river loops northwards. The path (waymarked Stour Valley Walk) heads south-east over fields and up a small hill with a plantation of trees on top. There is evidence of an earthwork up here, but more impressive are the wide views in all directions. From here the Walk heads for the landmark of Wormingford Church. Divert off the route for ½ mile along the road leading north from the church to enjoy a lovely stretch of river flowing quietly on between overhanging willows.

The waymarked Stour Valley Path wiggles east from Wormingford Church for

The little steam-powered trip-boat, Firebird, *makes her way downriver from Sudbury Basin.*

about 2 miles before working down to the floor of the valley just north of Little Horkesley and passing through woods to cross the river at Wissington. A short, essential detour left at this bridge takes in the tiny, perfect Norman Wissington (or Wiston) Church. If you are lucky enough to find it open, look closely at its faded 13th-century murals; one depicts a contemporary sailing boat. The main walk turns right along the river bank at the bridge, passes the tall white weather-boarded Wiston Mill, now a private house, and continues to the A134 road on the western side of Nayland. The Anchor Inn, on the river close to this main road, was once a bargeman's wharfside pub. The lockman's cottage survives by the weir that has replaced the lock. Nayland is a pleasant assemblage of colour-washed, brick and half-timbered houses, a former cloth-making town with a church built on the trade. Constable's only religious painting, *Christ Blessing the Elements*, hangs over the altar.

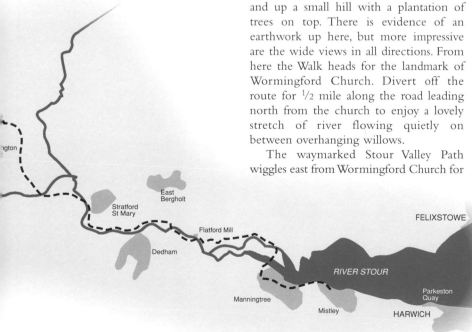

STOUR LIGHTERS

Many rivers and canals had their own distinctive craft, their exact dimensions determined by the size of the local locks, but, thanks to Constable's paintings, it is the Stour lighter, with a narrow central decking dividing the hold and decking at each end, that is the most well-known. During World War I, when trading on the navigation had virtually come to an end, a number of these lighters were sunk in Ballingdon Cut, Sudbury. In the 1970s the River Stour Trust discovered them, buried in the silt, and has done some restoration work on one of them. This is now berthed at Cornard, on the east bank of the river, near the lock which the Trust hopes to restore in the near future.

Nayland to Manningtree & Mistley

GUIDE BOX

PLACES TO VISIT
Stoke-by-Nayland Good 15th-century church.
Stratford St Mary Look for the letters built into the church's exterior stonework.
Dedham St Mary's Church; Alfred Munnings Museum, Castle House.
Flatford Bridge Cottage – Constable exhibition, guided walks, tea room, restored dry dock (as depicted in Constable's *Boat-building near Flatford Mill*); boat hire; Granary Museum of Rural Bygones; Flatford Mill and Willy Lott's House are part of a Field Studies Centre.
Mistley Mistley Towers, remains of a Robert Adam church.

CAR PARKING
Nayland; Stratford St Mary; Dedham; Flatford; Manningtree; Mistley.

PUBLIC TRANSPORT
Trains Manningtree is on the Colchester-to-Ipswich line; connection at Mark's Tey to Sudbury line; Mistley is on the Manningtree-to-Harwich branch.
Buses serve most villages but may be infrequent.

ACCOMMODATION
The Stour Valley Path guide includes B&Bs and inns in Nayland, Thorington Street, Dedham and East Bergholt. Pubs in Manningtree and Mistley.

TOURIST INFORMATION CENTRES
Colchester 1 Queen Street, Colchester, Essex CO1 2PG (tel 01206 282920)
Flatford Bridge Cottage, Flatford, East Bergholt, Colchester, Essex CO7 6OL (tel 01206 298260/298865)

NAYLAND TO STRATFORD ST MARY
About 8¹/₂ miles/14km
OS Landranger 155
Start in Nayland at minor road leading north off B1087 (grid reference 975 345)

There is no footpath close to the river east of Nayland until its approach to Stratford St Mary. The Stour Valley Path follows minor roads and paths for about 2 miles, north from Nayland and then eastwards, to Stoke-by-Nayland, another village with shops, pubs and many lovely old buildings. Set on high ground, with views down into the Stour Valley, the church is a landmark that features in Constable's work.

From Stoke-by-Nayland the Path runs eastwards, down into and up out of the valley of the little River Box, before turning south to cross the B1068 to the east of Thorington Street. Langham Mill Lane leads to the Stour near some waterworks and from here a field track cuts off one of the river's loops, then crosses over it into Stratford St Mary near the lock. Turn left for the town's pubs and shop. An imposing pumping station takes water to a reservoir serving the Colchester area. Constable's *Stratford Mill on the Stour*, painted in 1820, records the large mill demolished shortly after World War II, while *The Valley of the Stour* and *Dedham Vale* show a white wooden bridge across the river on the town's southern outskirts.

STRATFORD ST MARY TO MISTLEY
About 7 miles/11km
OS Landranger 168
Start where Stour Valley Path turns off main street under A12 (grid reference 042 335)

This section of the walk hugs the riverbank and is Constable Country *par excellence*, with numerous views that were, or might have been, the subject of his paintings.

Walk south along Stratford's main street until the Stour Valley Walk turns off left under the A12 bypass and follow the river's north bank for a peaceful mile or so of pastureland to the lock, mill and mill pool beside the bridge at Dedham. Here Constable painted *Dedham Lock and Mill* in 1820; the present mill building, which stands on the site of a mill owned by the artist's father, has – like others in the area – been converted into smart flats. The path continues on the other side of the bridge, where rowing boats may be hired in summer, but there is much in Dedham itself that rewards exploration.

Like other towns in East Anglia, in 1620 Dedham saw many of its residents sail for New England on *Mayflower*, an east coast trading ship built in Harwich. The church, begun in 1492 when the wool town was at its most prosperous, has several features inside that reflect its links with Massachusetts. Dedham's delightful main street is one timber-framed or Georgian gem after another. East of the church is the grammar school to which Constable walked from his home at Flatford, while beyond it Brook Street leads to Castle House where the painter of horses Alfred

A quiet early morning scene near Flatford Mill.

Munnings (1878–1959) lived. Another artist of note, or notoriety, the forger Tom Keating lived at Lower Park.

From the bridge by the old mill the footpath continues for about 1¹/₂ miles to Flatford. The river flows serenely on through watermeadows grazed by cattle, its grassy banks defined with pollarded willows and its waters skimmed by swooping swallows. An alternative path that reaches the river from the eastern end of the High Street passes the spot where Constable stood to paint his *Leaping Horse*, a picture which famously illustrates the necessity for barge horses to jump stiles and hedges where the landowner insisted they should run right to the water's edge, thus blocking the towpath.

In Constable's day, Flatford saw the to-ing and fro-ing of barges carrying wheat ground at his father's mill. Today the hamlet is, at least in high season, a thronging mass of visitors. Rowing boats may be moored or hired here. Flatford Lock was restored by the River Stour Trust with the unusual overhead wooden lintel beam depicted by Constable in *Flatford Mill from a Lock on the Stour* (c1811). Bridge Cottage houses a useful, free exhibition showing the location of the many scenes Constable depicted in the vicinity. A National Trust shop and tea room adjoins. The dry dock in which Golding Constable had barges built and repaired has been dug out, re-creating *Boat-building near Flatford Mill*. Flatford Mill itself is a Field Study Centre and is not open to the public. Beside it is the view immortalised in *The Hay Wain*.

The waymarked Stour Valley Path continues from Willy Lott's House across fields, well away from the northern of the Stour's two streams. The site of Brantham lock is visible, while the Cattawade Barrier marks the start of the tidal reaches of the Stour Estuary. The set of boat rollers at the side of the barrier was constructed in the 1960s so small craft could be hauled over it.

For a circular walk, making a return to Flatford, take the following, southern stream route in reverse.

The alternative route from Willy Lott's Cottage to Manningtree, along the southern stream, crosses Flatford Bridge to the south bank and runs alongside the river, passing the 56 gates of Cattawade Sluice. On a wintry day the seawall makes an exhilarating marshy walk, accompanied by the sounds of swaying reeds and calling sea birds.

Manningtree and Mistley – the two merge virtually into one – are small, pleasant waterfront towns, well worth a look. Until the railway arrived, the two towns, placed where river and sea barges could conveniently exchange cargoes, were thriving ports. Manningtree has good Georgian and Victorian buildings at its heart. Follow the water's edge for ¹/₄ mile to Mistley, where the river widens to over a mile, with exciting views over its tidal reaches. At low tide the channel is very narrow, but at high tide the estuary is busy with commercial shipping, sailing dinghies and, perhaps, a few preserved Thames sailing barges. A colony of white swans has made its home here.

Mistley Towers make an unusual landmark between the road and the river, a rare Robert Adam ecclesiastical commission (1776) and all that remains of a church demolished in 1870. Adam was also involved in the development of Mistley as a model riverport and seawater spa by Richard Rigby, father and son; this never really got off the ground but some Georgian buildings and Adam's Swan

The evening light falls across the tidal reaches of the Stour Estuary at Mistley.

Fountain survive around the Quay. Mistley has been making malt, from barley brought down the Stour, for hundreds of years and its EDME maltings are the largest producers of malt and malt extract in Britain. The whole town smells of Horlicks.

Beyond Mistley, those determined to follow the estuary as far as Harwich on foot can follow the Essex Way, initially along the shore and then on paths and lanes inland. Beyond Wrabness Station, however, the closest views of the estuary are from the train. Near Harwich Town Station is the 1818 High Lighthouse and the unique 17th-century treadmill crane. There is plenty to watch in Harwich Harbour, busy day and night with container ships sliding in and out of Felixstowe and passenger ferries heading for Parkeston Quay.

THAMES SAILING BARGES

With over 2,000sq ft of reddish-brown sail, the occasional preserved Thames sailing barge that ties up at Mistley Quay makes a wonderful sight. These spritsail barges, flat-bottomed with retractable leeboards and often no engines, were designed for use where inland navigations, such as the Stour, met the shallow estuaries of the east coast. Handled by a crew of just two or three, they were commonplace up until after World War II, fleets of them trading along the rivers and coast from East Anglia to the Thames and Medway and beyond. Today, this is a good area to see those that have been updated, the best spectacle being the annual sailing barge races.

North England

The Bounds of Ainsty 108 – 111

The Eden Way 112 – 119

The Esk River 120 – 123

The Weardale Way 124 – 131

Across the Pennines 132 – 139

The Lancaster Canal 140 – 147

The Rochdale Canal, east of Todmorden

The Bounds of Ainsty

A CIRCULAR WALK FROM YORK VIA TADCASTER AND WETHERBY
44 MILES/70KM

IN the centre of Yorkshire there is a series of peaceful walks beside the three rivers, the Ouse, Wharfe and Nidd, that encircle the ancient wapentake of Ainsty. After leaving historic York, the walk meanders along riverside paths and a pastoral landscape with occasional forays into historic villages and towns. There are no long climbs, the highest point on the walk being about 100ft above sea level.

The flora and fauna here is more varied than on the mountains or moorlands where most rivers rise. In the space of a few minutes near Moor Monkton, for example, we saw a flock of goldfinches, a pair of collared doves, a lark singing as it flew across a field, a moorhen, two coots and a grey heron making its ungainly take-off across the River Nidd.

The walk described here starts from York because of its convenient road and rail access and its wealth of accommodation, but as it is circular you could just as easily start at Tadcaster or Wetherby.

WALKING GUIDE
Townson, Simon, *Ainsty Bounds Walk* (Dalesman, 1984).

MAPS
OS Landranger 105

LINKS
The walk links or coincides with the Ebor Way, Jorvik Way, Minster Way, Centenary Way and the Yoredale Way.

York to Wetherby

YORK TO TADCASTER
About 16 miles/26km
OS Landranger 105
Start at Ouse Bridge, York
(grid reference 603 517)

Ouse Bridge is the oldest of York's bridges over the Ouse. In 1154 such a large crowd gathered on it to welcome the new archbishop that the structure gave way and many people were thrown into the river, fortunately with no lives lost. Four centuries later, in 1564, the bridge was washed away by winter floodwater. Looking downstream from today's bridge, take the steps on the left which descend to the riverside at Kings Staith, passing the Kings Arms. This inn has a number of floodmarks inside showing the depth to which it has been flooded. If there is floodwater in the bar you may as well abandon your walk as many of the riverside paths will be under water. Continue beside the river to Skeldergate Bridge and climb the stone steps up onto the bridge. Here there is a good view of Clifford's Tower, the original keep of York Castle, on its lofty grass-covered mound.

Cross over the bridge to the other bank of the river to continue the journey downstream. On this stretch south to Bishopthorpe, you will probably be accompanied by cruise boats, the latest in a long line of vessels to have sailed along the river to the trading centre of York: Romans and Vikings navigated the river to Eboracum and Yorvik, as they respectively called York. Eventually the riverside path passes under the York bypass and approaches Bishopthorpe, where the Archbishop of York's palace overlooks the river. The path then sweeps right to join a road through Bishopthorpe.

After this 3-mile riverside walk, you can return to York by road through Nunthorpe and across York's Knavesmire racecourse, entering the city through Micklegate Bar.

The walk continues past the front of Bishopthorpe Palace and its impressive gatehouse, then turns left and right to rejoin the riverside. Pass a marina and caravan site and continue south to the massive tubular steel legs of the railway swing bridge that now forms part of the

15-mile Selby & York Railway Path and Cycle Route. The riverside path leads into Acaster Malbis, where you follow the road to the left of the Ship Inn to a T-junction. Opposite is the restored village pinfold originally used for impounding stray cattle. Turn left beside the road until it sweeps right, and at that point turn left to rejoin the riverside path to Acaster Selby.

As you approach Acaster Selby, cross two stiles over a ditch then turn right, away from the river, to join a road that continues straight ahead to Appleton Roebuck. The hedgerows may be worth watching for both birds and flowers. At the junction in Appleton Roebuck turn left past the Roebuck Inn and left again down Bond Lane to pick up the Church Lane bridleway to Bolton Percy. Beside Bolton Percy Church is a half-timbered gatehouse. Originally the walk went down to the River Wharfe and followed the riverbank to Tadcaster, but this is not a right of way. Follow the Tadcaster road and then the track past Ouston Farm to reach Tadcaster.

TADCASTER TO WETHERBY
About 7¹/₂ miles/12km
OS Landranger 105
Start at Tadcaster Bridge
(grid reference 487 434)

Tadcaster has been famous for brewing ale for centuries. After a family dispute over one particular brewery, two separate ones were created – John Smith's and Sam Smith's, both of which are still brewing today. A third brewery in the town, founded by a group of baronets' sons in the 1880s, was known as the 'Snobs' Brewery'.

The route to Wetherby coincides with the Ebor Way, leaving Tadcaster past the church. In early spring, when the trees are in full blossom, the churchyard is a riot of colour. The path soon passes the beautiful stone viaduct that carried the former railway and then continues as a pleasant riverside path to Newton Kyme. On approaching the village, bear left past the church and continue through the village to the main road. The path returns to the river

A pleasure boat on the River Ouse passes Bishopthorpe Palace.

along the ancient Rudgate, a crossing point which was guarded in Roman times by a fort on the right.

To return to Tadcaster (a 6-mile circular walk) follow Rudgate south to grid reference 460 431 and take the bridleway past Shaws Farm and back to the riverside.

The walk follows the riverside path along the edge of Boston Spa to the bridge, passing the old spring that was discovered in 1744 and used as a cure for rheumatism. Cross the narrow bridge and follow the road through the pretty village of Thorp Arch. Turn left along the track to Flint Mill Grange Farm, whose original water-powered mill was used to grind flint into a powder for use in the pottery trade. Follow field paths into Wetherby, or to continue on the walk, go up the access road to the farm and cross the edge of Wetherby racecourse to reach the B1224 Wetherby-to-York road.

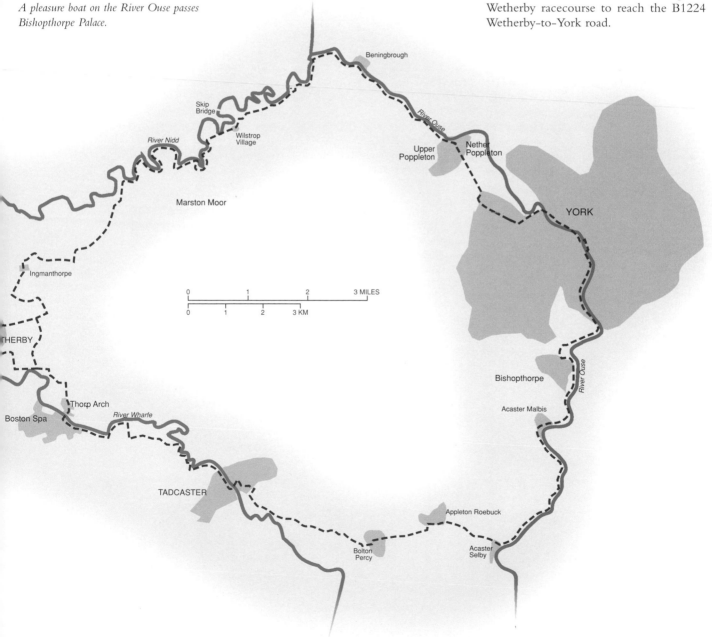

Wetherby to York

WETHERBY TO SKIP BRIDGE
About 10¹/2 miles / 17km
OS Landranger 105
Start at the York road out of Wetherby
(grid reference 406 485)
or from the east side of the racecourse
(grid reference SE 423 491)

Wetherby stands on the old Great North Road and offers accommodation and refreshment just as it did 200 years ago when stage coach passengers were travelling through between London and Edinburgh. The Angel Hotel at that time had stabling for 100 horses. Today the York road out of the town passes the racecourse, where a number of popular meetings are held each year. One and a half miles from the centre of Wetherby, the walk turns left towards Igmanthorpe Park. You are now crossing the low ridge that separates the rivers Wharfe and Nidd.

The track passes across open fields to reach a lane that leads to Cowthorpe. At the junction bear right along the quiet road, bearing left at Lingcroft to Moor Side. Take the old Roman road towards Cattal, then turn right at the public footpath sign to join the riverside path by the Nidd, a river that began its journey on the eastern shoulders of Great Whernside in the Pennines.

To the east of your path beside the River Nidd is Marston Moor, the site of the great Civil War battle. The pleasant riverside path leads round to Wilstrop Hall and passes the site of the deserted village of Wilstrop. In 1377 it was a village with some 50 inhabitants and a water mill, but it was depopulated in the 15th century – possibly as the result of a dispute between three landowners. The walk to Nether Poppleton now coincides with the 65-mile Jorvic Way.

The access road crosses the railway line and leads to the York-to-Harrogate road near Skip Bridge (there is car parking at the crossing place on the River Nidd). In medieval times there was a wooden bridge over the river and on the York side a long causeway with 19 bridges over the boggy ground. Travellers in the 18th century often hired guides to lead them to the next town and there is a tale of one traveller who was fixed up by a York innkeeper with a guide to Harrogate. It was only on his safe arrival that the traveller discovered that his guide was

GUIDE BOX

PLACES TO VISIT
York See page 108 for some of York's many attractions.
Beningbrough Hall Near Shipton – a large house, built in 1716, with fine furniture and National Portrait Gallery paintings; extensive parkland reaches down to the Ouse.

PUBLIC TRANPSORT
Train Station in York.
Bus Services to Wetherby, Skip Bridge and Nether Poppleton.

CAR PARKING
Wetherby; Skip Bridge; York.

ACCOMMODATION
Hotels, guest houses etc Wetherby, York.
Camping Tockwith.

TOURIST INFORMATION CENTRES
York 6 Rougier Street, York YO1 1JA (tel 01904 620557); De Grey Rooms, Exhibition Square, York YO1 2HB (tel 01904 621756/7); also Railway Station (personal callers only)
Wetherby 24 Westgate, Wetherby, West Yorkshire LS22 6NL (tel 01937 582706)

Blind Jack Metcalfe, a famous roadbuilder: 'I would not have travelled with a blind man for £100', stated the traveller, to which Blind Jack replied 'I would not have got lost for £1,000'.

Skip Bridge, where the River Nidd is crossed by the York-to-Harrogate road.

SKIP BRIDGE TO YORK
About 10 miles/16km
OS Landranger 105
Start at Skip Bridge layby on the A59
(grid reference 484 559)

Walk down the road to the former Skip Bridge Inn, now a farm, and turn left on the path to Moor Monkton. Perhaps the inn's busiest day was in the spring of 1807, when the closely contested fight to represent the county in Parliament ended with the defeated member failing by under 200 votes in a poll of 33,000 voters. As the local landowners headed for York to vote they were wined and dined at the candidates' expense: the inn's account totalled over £1,750 for wine and beer and about £250 for food.

The walk continues over the fields to rejoin the River Nidd on its approach to the peaceful village of Moor Monkton. As you cover the last mile of the River Nidd's journey to the Ouse you can look across to Nun Monkton. Beningbrough Hall comes

The confluence of the rivers Nidd and Ouse, on the last stretch of the walk as it approaches York.

into view on the far bank as the path turns right to begin the final leg of the journey back to York. The handsome Georgian House is now owned by the National Trust and its furnished interior includes 100 paintings from the National Portrait Gallery.

A pleasant riverside walk leads to Nether Poppleton. Pass the Lord Nelson Inn and fork right along Millfield Lane, which leads under the bypass and across the railway into the outskirts of York. Follow Boroughbridge Road into the city, turning left to the river at Clifton Bridge. The youth hostel is straight ahead. A riverside path leads into the heart of this historic city. At Scarborough Bridge the railway crosses the river and the walk continues past the Yorkshire Museum Gardens to ornamental Lendal Bridge. Cross the bridge and follow the street beside the river back to Ouse Bridge.

THE BATTLE OF MARSTON MOOR

In the spring of 1644 Royalist-held York was besieged by Parliamentary forces. At the end of June Prince Rupert and his Royalist forces managed to cross the River Ouse at Poppleton and reinforced the defending troops. On 2 July the strengthened forces marched out to Marston Moor to face the opposition, who were under the leadership of Lord Fairfax, but it was seven in the evening before the forces joined battle. Oliver Cromwell was wounded in an early skirmish, went off to have his wounds dressed and, on his return, found his forces in disarray. However, Sir Thomas Fairfax passed around the back of Royalists beside the River Nidd and, joining forces with Cromwell's troops, attacked the Royalists from the rear – an action that by ten o'clock that night had turned the battle in the Parliamentarians' favour. Some 4,500 men were buried the following day and York surrendered on 16 July. Today the battle site is marked by an obelisk near the road between Long Marston and Tockwith.

The Eden Way

AISGILL MOOR TO THE SOLWAY FIRTH
77 MILES/123KM

THE River Eden begins its journey to the Solway Firth at Black Fell Moss, on the lofty ridge that forms the eastern side of Mallerstang. Across the valley stands Wild Boar Fell where, according to tradition, the last wild boar was killed in the 14th century. From this wild and remote dale the river flows into a rich farmland interspersed with villages built of the beautiful local red sandstone. With the exception of the market towns of Kirkby Stephen and Appleby, the only large place is Carlisle – a city which has played its part in the border conflicts between the Scots and English. Several villages on the route are served by the Settle-to-Carlisle Railway.

WALKING GUIDES
Emett, Charlie, *The Eden Way* (Cicerone Press).

OS MAPS
Landranger 85, 86, 90, 91, 98

LINKS
The Eden Way links with the Coast to Coast Walk, Lady Anne's Way, Eden Trail, Hadrian's Wall Walk, Westmorland Way, Cumberland Way, Cumbria Way, Falklands Way, Mallerstang Horseshoe and Nine Standards Yomp, Settle to Carlisle Walk, Yoredale Way.

Aisgill Moor to Warcop

AISGILL MOOR TO KIRKBY STEPHEN
10 miles/16km
OS Landranger 91, 98
Start at Aisgill Moor Cottages, Mallerstang (grid reference 778 963)

From Aisgill Moor Cottages follow a track across a bridge over the Settle-to-Carlisle Railway, the point at which the railway begins its descent into the Eden Valley. The track leads to Hell Gill Farm and continues to the old road from Hawes to Kirkby Stephen. Turn right for Hell Gill Bridge. The ascent to the source of the River Eden, beside Hell Gill Beck and Red Gill, is not a public right of way, so the Eden Way runs north from Hell Gill Bridge, parallel with the valley.

Two miles to the south of the source of the Eden is Ure Head, the source of the River Ure. While the Ure flows out into the North Sea at Spurn Point on the Humber Estuary, the Eden flows into the Solway Firth on the west coast of England over 150 miles away.

Hell Gill is a waterworn gorge above the bridge with the beautiful waterfall, Hell Gill Foss, beyond. There are magnificent views over the Eden Valley to distinctive Wild Boar Fell. The fine green lane then contours the hillside northwards for over 2 miles, eventually descending to a point on the road near The Thrang Country Hotel. Take the public footpath signposted to Deep Gill and cross the river on a pretty stone bridge. From here a return can be made to Aisgill Moor Cottages by following the west bank of the river to Cooper Hill. Then cross back again and continue past Ings Head and Hanging Lund Farms, climbing the hillside back to the start.

The Eden Way follows the path on the western bank to Shore Gill and on to Pendragon Castle. Tradition has it that the original castle on the site was built by Uther Pendragon, father of King Arthur, in the 6th century. The present stone castle was built in Norman times and it was here that Sir Hugh de Morville fled after murdering Thomas Becket in 1170. It was destroyed by raiding Scots in 1341. In 1660 the energetic Lady Anne Clifford (see page 115) restored the building, only to have it fall into decay after her death.

At the bridge follow the road on the western side to pass over a cattle grid and take the bridleway to Wharton. The road continues to Birkett Tunnel on the Settle-to-Carlisle Railway. When it was cut, the workmen encountered shale, limestone, iron, slate, grit, coal and lead ore – all in a 100yd stretch. The path passes ruined Lammerside Castle, a 14th-century peel tower of the Wharton family, and continues to the Kirkby Stephen-to-Nateby road. Take the riverside path to Bollamgate to reach Franks Bridge. Cross over and take Stoneshot into Kirkby Stephen, an attractive town with cobbled squares and a market place.

KIRKBY STEPHEN TO WARCOP
8 miles/13km
OS Landranger 91
Start at Kirkby Stephen market place (grid reference 775 086)

From the market place take the signposted footpath near the Tourist Information Centre to Franks Bridge. Cross the bridge and take the path to Low Mill (ignore the path to Coffin Bridge!). The riverside path leads to the Kirkby Stephen-to-Brough road, where you turn right for ³/4 mile and then resume the riverside walk to the Kirkby Stephen-to-Warcop road. Follow

Having made its descent from Aisgill Moor, the River Eden flows gently on through the unspoiled scenery of Mallerstang.

Pendragon Castle, the home of Uther Pendragon, father of King Arthur.

GUIDE BOX

PLACES TO VISIT
Brough Castle Norman castle on the site of a Roman fort, built to guard the ancient and important route through the Pennines.
The Settle-to-Carlisle Railway One of Britain's most scenic lines. Books and leaflets describe walks from stations along the route. Key stations for Eden Way walkers are Kirkby Stephen, Appleby, Langwathby, Lazonby and Armathwaite.
Pendragon Castle and Mallerstang Scenic moorland valley road through Mallerstang; Pendragon Castle can be seen from the roadside.

CAR PARKING
Near Aisgill Moor Cottages (limited parking in the lane at grid reference 778 963); Kirkby Stephen.

PUBLIC TRANSPORT
Train Station at Kirkby Stephen.
Bus Infrequent services at Kirkby Stephen to Barnard Castle, Darlington, Kendal.

ACCOMMODATION
Hotels, guest houses etc Mallerstang, Kirkby Stephen.
Camping and youth hostel Kirkby Stephen.

TOURIST INFORMATION CENTRE
Kirkby Stephen Market Street, Kirkby Stephen, Cumbria CA17 4QN (tel 017683 71199)

this to Musgrave Bridge, ignoring the road to Little Musgrave, which is narrow and dangerous for walkers. At the bridge turn left along the riverside path into Little Musgrave. It was here that the Eden Valley Railway crossed the River Eden. While the Settle-to-Carlisle Railway descends the full length of the valley, the Eden Valley Railway connected villages from Kirkby Stephen to Clifton Junction near Penrith, passing through a number of places on this walk – Musgrave, Warcop, Appleby, Kirkby Thore and Temple Sowerby. The railway opened in 1862 and closed in 1962. A railway preservation society is hoping to reopen part of the line.

Continue through Little Musgrave on the road to Asby. After ¹/₂ mile turn right over a small plank bridge along the signposted footpath to Ploughlands and Warcop. There are good views ahead to the Pennines, which rise up to their highest point on Cross Fell to the north. The track eventually joins the access road to Ploughlands and when you reach the River Eden follow the riverside path to Warcop's 16th-century bridge. It has remained intact despite many occasions when the river has flooded and destroyed other bridges. Take the road into Warcop, a pleasant village with a maypole on the green topped with a pheasant weather vane.

Warcop to Langwathby

GUIDE BOX

PLACES TO VISIT
Appleby Castle and Conservation Centre – the 11th-century castle grounds are a wildlife conservation centre, while there are fine paintings and porcelain in the Great Hall. *Temple Sowerby* Acorn Bank Gardens – the finest display of culinary and medicinal herbs in the North of England in a walled garden and hot house; also orchards, flower gardens and a wildlife garden. Hazel Dene Nursery – a garden centre with a wide range of garden plants and a tea room decorated with Settle-to-Carlisle Railway memorabilia.

CAR PARKING
Appleby; Langwathby.

PUBLIC TRANSPORT
Train Stations at Appleby, Langwathby.
Bus Services to Appleby and infrequent summer service between Langwathby and Penrith.

ACCOMMODATION
Hotels, guest houses etc Appleby, Langwathby. *Camping* Appleby.

TOURIST INFORMATION CENTRE
Appleby Moot Hall, Boroughgate, Appleby, Cumbria CA16 6XE (tel 017683 51177)

WARCOP TO APPLEBY
About 7 miles/11km
OS Landranger 91
Start at Warcop village green
(grid reference 758 155)

From the village green take the road that leads to the hamlet of Blea Tarn. Cross the bridge over the Eden, and in 100 yards turn right on the bridleway to Blacksyke, where the village of Sandford stands on the north side of the river. (For a 3½-mile circular walk, cross the river to Sandford and return along the road to Warcop.)

The Eden Way continues above the river into Little Ormside and then Great Ormside, a peaceful village standing around a triangular green. Twice treasure has been discovered here: in 1823 a gold and silver cup was found in the churchyard and in 1899 a hoard of Viking weapons was unearthed. In St James's Church, near the former hall, note the lepers' squint, through which lepers could follow the service without mingling with the congregation.

The path passes beneath the 90ft piers of the ten-arched railway viaduct and eventually becomes a riverside path leading into Appleby. Appleby was the county

Bongate Mill, beside the River Eden at Appleby.

town of the old county of Westmorland and has many fine buildings, including the castle, which stands on high ground overlooking the river. The first castle was built by William de Meschines, Baron of Westmorland in the late 11th century. The castle grounds, which once echoed to mail-clad figures bearing arms, is now a conservation centre for rare breeds of farm animals, waterfowl and other birds.

In 1175 Appleby was razed by an army of Scots led by King William the Lion. Over the next century the town prospered until in 1314 and 1319 Scots raiders again devastated the town. The final assault by the Scots was on St Stephen's Day 1388, when they laid it waste once more.

Standing alone in Boroughgate, the main street of Appleby, is the Moot Hall, a meeting place originally for a judicial court in Saxon times. Part of this now houses the Tourist Information Centre. At the foot of Boroughgate, St Lawrence's Church lies in a bend in the River Eden, the burial place of Lady Anne Clifford (see panel on opposite page).

For a week in June each year the town becomes the centre for the Appleby Horse Fair. For hundreds of years travelling people have converged from all over Britain to trade in horses, renew acquaintances and partake in trotting races.

APPLEBY TO LANGWATHBY
15 miles/24km
OS Landranger 91
Start at Boroughgate, Appleby
(grid reference 683 202)

At the top of Boroughgate is St Anne's Hospital, built by Lady Anne Clifford in 1651 as almshouses for 13 poor widows of

the local estate. Turn right at the bottom of Boroughgate and walk towards the bridge over the River Eden. Turn left just before the bridge along the footpath to The Butts and Broad Close. Pass St Lawrence's Church on your left, then the cricket ground and swimming pool. Beyond the playground turn left, then right on the footpath to Colby Laithes – don't cross the bridge over the river. The path also leads to Dowpitts Wood nature trail. At Colby Laithes take the track into the northern edge of Colby and follow the road to New Bewley Castle, a fine white farmhouse, where a track leads over to Bolton Bridge and across the river.

A return can be made to Appleby by taking the track past Redlands Bank Farm to the A66. Turn right, then left towards Long Marton and follow the Roman road back to the outskirts of Appleby.

The Eden Way continues along the riverside into Kirkby Thore, where you cross Trout Beck and return to the River Eden. As you approach Temple Sowerby turn right, away from the river, into this attractive village. Take the road to the National Trust property at Acorn Bank. At the T-junction carry straight on across the field to Acorn Bank. Originally called Sowerby Manor, it was occupied by the Knights Templars in the 11th century and

later by the Knights Hospitallers. In 1930 the house and land was sold to Captain and Mrs McGregor Philips, better known as the poet and writer Dorothy Una Ratcliffe. In 1950 the house was presented to the National Trust and it is now leased to the Sue Ryder Foundation, while the gardens, worth visiting at various seasons of the year, are run by the Trust. There is an excellent display of daffodils in the spring and colourful borders throughout the summer. The two orchards have cherry, apple, quince, mulberry and medlar trees and there is a large collection of herbs for medicinal and culinary purposes.

The route passes to the left of the house, through the car park, and turns right to rejoin the riverside path to Newbiggen. When you reach the road, you can see Newbiggen Hall to the right, for centuries the home of the Crackanthorpe family. Turn left and cross over the bridge that formed the boundary between Westmorland and Cumberland and follow the road uphill. When it turns right take the footpath to the left which climbs into Culgaith. Follow the main road straight ahead through the village towards Langwathby. From this elevated position above the river there are extensive views to the west, including the tree-covered slopes of Penrith Beacon, built to warn of

The river below Appleby Castle.

Scottish raiding parties. Further afield you can see the Lakeland Peaks of Blencathra and Carrock Fell. As you descend the hill you can see the River Eamont flowing down to meet the Eden. Carry on along the broad road into Langwathby.

LADY ANNE CLIFFORD

Born in 1590, Lady Anne Clifford was the only surviving child of George Clifford, 3rd Earl of Cumberland. George Clifford died when Lady Anne was 15, but his land and property passed by trust to his brother. Lady Anne fought for nearly 40 years to regain her estates, until in 1643 her cousin died without heirs and she eventually became the legitimate successor.

From then on for the rest of her life she devoted herself to rebuilding churches as well as the castles at Appleby, Brougham, Brough, Skipton and Pendragon in Mallerstang. Her usual means of travel through the rough Pennine terrain that links these castles was by horse litter and the early part of the Eden Way between Hell Gill Bridge and Pendragon Castle is along an old road that is now named Lady Anne Clifford's Highway. There is a motor trail and a 100-mile long distance walking path connecting Brougham Castle and Skipton Castle.

Langwathby to Wetheral

GUIDE BOX

PLACES TO VISIT
Long Meg and her Daughters A prehistoric stone circle near Little Salkeld.
Little Salkeld Little Salkeld Watermill – a working mill that grinds corn.
Nunnery Walks One of the most scenic parts of the River Eden has no rights of way but you can pay to see the Eden Gorge by taking the Nunnery Walks at the Nunnery House Hotel. They were created 200 years ago by Christopher Aglionby and take in the Croglin waterfall.
Armathwaite Eden Valley Woollen Mill – see a wide range of textiles being designed and woven.

CAR PARKING
Not a problem in any of the villages.

PUBLIC TRANSPORT
Train Services to Langwathby, Lazonby for Kirkoswald and Armathwaite.
Bus Services to Langwathby. There is also Fellrunner Community Bus service.

ACCOMMODATION
Guest houses etc Most of the villages along the way offer some form of Bed & Breakfast accommodation.

TOURIST INFORMATION CENTRE
Penrith Robinson's School, Middlegate, Penrith, Cumbria CA11 7PT (tel 01768 867466)

LANGWATHBY TO ARMATHWAITE
About 11 miles/18km
OS Landranger 86, 90
Start at Langwathby village green
(grid reference 570 336)

Langwathby enjoys a spacious village green, overlooked by the Shepherds Inn. The Eden Way walk leaves the village along the minor road to Little Salkeld. Pass under the railway and across the bridge over Robberby Water. Tucked away in the hollow immediately on the right is Little Salkeld Watermill, where local corn has been ground for many years. British-grown wheat is still ground here, the grain being passed through the burr millstones powered by the small stream (the mill is open to visitors on weekdays). Walk up the road into Little Salkeld, where the Eden Way turns left towards the Settle-to-Carlisle Railway.

A detour to Long Meg and her Daughters, a prehistoric stone circle, can be made by taking the right turn in

Dry Beck Viaduct, near Armathwaite, which carries the Settle-to-Carlisle Railway.

Little Salkeld for just under 1 mile. The daughters are 65 stones that form a circle, while Long Meg is a larger stone standing outside the ring. Set on high ground, it offers far-reaching views to the Pennines and Lake District mountains. A return to Langwathby can made through Hunsonby and along the footpath through Winskill.

The Eden Way follows the railway until it crosses the river at Long Meg Viaduct. Just beyond the viaduct the railway enters a cutting where, on 18 January 1918, a train ran into a landslip and seven people were killed. Just before the viaduct, the path turns right along the signposted footpath on the eastern side of the river to Lacy's Cave and Daleraven Bridge. The cave is named after Lt Col Samuel Lacy, who cut the five chambers out of the sandstone cliff – an idyllic retreat, with the river just a few feet away.

The path leads to the Glasonby-to-Kirkoswald road and after crossing Hazelrigg Beck follows the signposted footpath to Eden Bridge. The village of Lazonby can be seen on the opposite bank as the Way approaches Eden Bridge. At the road bear right into Kirkoswald, an attractive village built in the local red sandstone. The small church stands on the site of an 8th-century wooden structure, built by a well where St Aidan and King

Oswald found local people worshipping the water supply. Walk through Kirkoswald, climbing past the small cobbled market place with three inns nearby, then take the road to Armathwaite.

On the outskirts of Kirkoswald bear left on the footpath that leads through parkland to Staffield Hall. Join the road for 2 miles around the grounds of Nunnery House Hotel, where there is access to the Nunnery Walks (see Guide Box). Turn left just before Coombs Head along the footpath signposted to Armathwaite. The broad track descends through woodland and eventually joins the road near the Fox and Pheasant Inn. Turn left to the bridge, which offers attractive views of the river.

ARMATHWAITE TO WETHERAL
8 miles / 13km
OS Landranger 86
*Start at the bridge over the River Eden, Armathwaite
(grid reference 507 460)*

From the bridge over the Eden look upstream to see Armathwaite Castle. In medieval times this was the home of the Skelton family, but in recent times it has been converted into flats. Climb up into the village and turn right along the road to Wetheral, passing the church. Just over 1 mile along the road Dry Beck Viaduct carries the Settle-to-Carlisle Railway. The Newbiggen-to-Carlisle stretch may have been easier to construct than the section through the wild dales around Ribblehead, but it was not without its problems. In order to reduce the lengths of viaducts, for example, massive embankments were created, using 400,000 cubic yards of material, and there were major problems with the embankment between Dry Beck Viaduct and High Stand Gill Viaduct, a little to the north. As the stone was tipped, it slipped away and the pressure on the surrounding ground was so great that some five acres of land began to move down to the River Eden and additional drainage work was needed to stabilise the land.

Turn right near Dry Beck Viaduct along the road that is signposted to Low House. At Drybeck Farm turn left, passing Low House, to join the delightful riverside path to Wetheral. This is one of the most pleasant sections of the walk, with wooded banks, a steeply rising hillside across the river, Himalayan balsam growing in profusion, and a wealth of other woodland and riverside plants. There are two islands in the river and some rough water in parts as the river tumbles over the riverbed. On the

The 15th-century gatehouse of Wetheral Priory.

approach to Wetheral you may catch a glimpse of the 15th-century gatehouse of Wetheral Priory. Turn left into Wetheral and take the first road to the right to continue on to Carlisle. The road ahead, past the 16th-century church with its octagonal tower, leads to the village green and the priory gatehouse.

THE SETTLE-TO-CARLISLE RAILWAY

The Midland Railway Company was determined to have its own direct line from London to Scotland. The east and west coast routes through England were already in use by rival companies, so, undeterred, the company surveyed a line along the backbone of England, through the remote regions of the Yorkshire Dales and down the Eden Valley. And thus was created the most spectacular and scenic railway in Britain.

The Settle-to-Carlisle Railway threads its way between mountains over 2,000ft high to reach Aisgill summit 1,169ft above sea level. The work of constructing the many tunnels, viaducts, cuttings and embankments took seven years, the terrain causing countless engineering problems. At Crowhill Cutting, south of Appleby, for instance, the gangs of navvies, armed only with picks and shovels, encountered Shap Granite, brought by glaciers in the Ice Age. A ton of gunpowder a week was used to create the cutting.

The first through passenger service took place on 1 May 1876, although trains had been running along the Eden Valley for nearly a year, generating income for the Midland Railway. Despite a number of attempts to close the line, it is still running, serving the needs of the local community as well as visitors and railway enthusiasts.

Wetheral to the Solway Firth

WETHERAL TO CARLISLE
9 miles/14km
OS Landranger 86, 85
Start at Wetheral village green
(grid reference 466 544)

The triangular village green in Wetheral is fringed by fine houses. From here either descend the 99 steps near the railway viaduct or take the road past the church and turn left. (At the point where the steps join the road, near the river, you can detour along a path to St Cuthbert's Well and a former watermill.) The Eden Way then follows the road, which keeps close to the river for most of its length, to reach the busy A69 Carlisle-to-Newcastle road. Turn right and cross the stone three-arched bridge over the Eden. Just downstream, on the west bank, is Warwick Hall where, in November 1745, Bonnie Prince Charlie was entertained by a staunch Catholic family. It was at Warwick Bridge that the prince's army mustered for the march on Carlisle when the Young Pretender rode out on his white horse to take over the city.

Follow the road into Warwick Bridge, bear left on Little Corby Road and continue to Newby East. There is no right of way beside the river here, so continue along the road towards Crosby on Eden until you can join a right of way along the riverbank just before the village. This path leads to Park Broom, where quiet roads lead through Linstock to Rickerby. Here there is a delightful riverside path that follows the meandering river through parkland to Eden Bridge. You can cross the river into the heart of Carlisle, a busy town with a rich heritage of many centuries of border warfare.

The Romans under Agricola built a settlement here in about AD78. This pallisaded fortress was on the site of Carlisle Cathedral, while the civilian settlement was on the site of the castle. When Hadrian's Wall was built to the north of Carlisle the garrison was moved across the river to Stanwix, to create the largest camp along the Wall. Carlisle then became the administrative centre for the western side of Hadrian's Wall.

The Castle saw its share of the border conflicts between the Scots and the English. Following his success at Bannockburn in 1314, Robert the Bruce laid siege to the city. He withdrew after eleven days, but there were at least five further assaults on the city in the remaining years of the 14th century. In 1745 the forces of Bonnie Prince Charlie found Carlisle ill prepared, with just 80 old soldiers with out-dated guns. Nevertheless, they successfully defended their city from

The Eden Way passes through Rickerby Park near Carlisle.

GUIDE BOX

PLACES TO VISIT
Carlisle Castle – well-preserved castle with extensive views from the Norman keep, houses King's Own Royal Border Regiment Museum. Carlisle Cathedral – a magnificent sandstone church, founded in 1122, with many fine treasures, including 14th-century stained-glass windows. Tullie House Museum and Art Gallery – award-winning museum featuring Hadrian's Wall, the Roman town and Border Rivers.

CAR PARKING
Carlisle; Rockcliffe (limited parking at Demesne Farm).

PUBLIC TRANSPORT
Train Station at Carlisle.
Bus Connections at Carlisle.

ACCOMMODATION
Hotels, guest houses etc Wetheral, Warwick Bridge, Carlisle.
Youth hostel Carlisle youth hostel is on the Eden Way.
Camping Blackford, 2½ miles east of Rockcliffe.

TOURIST INFORMATION CENTRE
Carlisle Old Town Hall, Green Market, Carlisle CA3 8JH (tel 01228 511578)

the prince's first attack on 10 November. However, when no reinforcements arrived from Newcastle, the Scots attacked again on 13 November, forcing the mayor and corporation to surrender. The Scottish force continued south to Derby but by 19 December they were back in Carlisle, retreating from the Duke of Cumberland. The Duke laid siege to the city on 21 December and by the 30th the city was back under English control.

CARLISLE TO THE SOLWAY FIRTH
9 miles/14km
OS Landranger 85
Start at Eden Bridge, Carlisle
(grid reference 400 566)

From the north side of Eden Bridge pass through the parkland to the east to rejoin the riverside path which passes under the bridge. Two footpaths lead up into the former Roman settlement at Stanwix. Bear left and continue along the road into Etterby. Turn left immediately before the inn, down to the youth hostel, and just beyond is a signposted footpath down to the River Eden. The way is now clear along the riverside to Rockcliffe. On the way pass St Anne's Well and the Fish House, which carries plaques recording

the visits of four mayors of Carlisle. The Corporation at one time held fishing rights along the river and at times a complimentary fish dinner was served in the building to the mayor and corporation.

Rockcliffe is an attractive village in a remote area that was frequently used by smugglers carrying whisky and other illicit goods into England. In the early 19th century the preventive officer based at Rockcliffe carried a brace of pistols for protection. One trick often used by the smugglers was to have women carry whisky in a belly canteen which made them look pregnant – the preventive man might be suspicious, but he could not search the woman.

The path enters Rockcliffe to the west of the church, whose present spire replaced the original 100ft steeple destroyed by lightning in 1899. Follow the road until you can continue beside the river on to the edge of the Solway Marsh. The best time for the birdwatcher on the Solway Firth is in winter when geese and duck migrate south from the Arctic. The saltmarshes around the firth become the home for 10,000 barnacle geese from Spitzbergen, pink-footed geese, pintail, shoveller and goldeneye duck, red-

Carlisle Castle, in 1596 the scene of the Reivers' raid to rescue Kinmont Willie.

breasted merganser and a rich assortment of waders numbering as many as 175,000. Return along the embankment either to Rockcliffe or Demesne Farm where there is limited parking.

CARLISLE CASTLE AND THE REIVERS

Carlisle Castle was the setting for an audacious raid that became a popular subject for the ballad writers of the time. During the troubled times of the 16th century Scottish and English Reivers frequently raided each other across the border. Regular truces were called to sort out disputes, giving free right of passage to everyone going to the meeting. In early 1596 William Armstrong (Kinmont Willie) was taken by the English when returning from a truce and was detained in Carlisle Castle. On a dark, stormy night 80 reivers, including Kinmont Willie's four sons, rode south to Carlisle. They entered the walled town and forced a side door to the castle. Quickly locating Kinmont Willie, they hurried him away out of the castle and city before the garrison could muster a response to the raid.

The River Esk

THE walk described here follows the waymarked Esk Valley Walk. The first part is a 15-mile loop, beginning and ending at Castleton Station, that climbs up on to the North Yorkshire Moors to find the source of the Esk in a remote area of heather moorland and then follows the river back down through Westerdale. The second half of the walk follows the Esk Valley as the river winds through a landscape that varies from open pasture to wooded gorges, ending up in the seaside town and fishing port of Whitby. This section passes through or near several villages served by the railway.

Castleton to High Blakey to Castleton

WALKING GUIDE
The Esk Valley Walk (published by North York Moors National Park, available from the TIC listed below) has detailed directions and OS Outdoor Leisure mapping.

OS MAPS
Landranger 94 or Outdoor Leisure 26, 27 (North York Moors National Park)

LINKS
The Coast to Coast Walk crosses near High Blakey and passes through Grosmont to Robin Hood's Bay. Lyke Wake Walk, a 40-mile walk across the North Yorkshire Moors, shares part of the old railway trackbed.

CASTLETON TO HIGH BLAKEY
About 6¹/₂ miles/10km
OS Landranger 94 or Outdoor Leisure 26
Start at Castleton Station (grid reference 682 085)

From Castleton Station cross the Esk and follow the Esk Valley Walk signposts (waymarked with a leaping salmon) past the converted Esk Mill, once used for spinning and weaving flax, and through the outskirts of Castleton. The path then enters the lush green pastureland of Danby Dale, running under the steep escarpment of Castleton Rigg through sheep-grazed fields and along farm lanes past Plum Tree Farm and through the yard of stone-built Stormy Hall. At Danby Head, the path goes through Honey Bee Nest farmyard and makes a steep climb straight up through the bracken and heather to the road on the top of the moor. Just as it joins the road, it swings away to the left across the moorland towards Rosedale Head. Here it passes White Cross, or 'Fat Betty', one of a number of stones that have stood on the moors since medieval days. Often at a crossroads or on ancient track, they may have been route markers for pilgrims making their way to the monasteries, or sometimes boundary stones.

Half a mile west, at a junction of several roads, is the 9ft-high Ralph Cross.

Over the road at White Cross, the path crosses Rosedale Head to join the Castleton to Hutton-le-Hole road. In the mid-19th century Rosedale was found to have rich deposits of high-quality ironstone and from then until the General Strike of 1926 finally brought an end to mining in the area, this quiet, isolated valley was buzzing with mining activity and supported a population of some 3,000. Many of the miners' cottages have been demolished, but the area is pitted with disused workings, and the line of the railway that transported the ore to the ironworks of County Durham is clearly visible along the eastern side of the dale. This line, opened by the North Eastern Railway in 1861 and known as the Rosedale Railway, looped round the head of the dale from Rosedale East mines to Blakey Junction, where it joined the line from Rosedale West mines and headed north over the moors to Battersby. Further along the eastern side of Rosedale, a row of arches in a disintegrating brick wall is all that remains of kilns, built next to the goods station, where the ore was roasted to reduce its weight before transportation.

The Esk Valley Walk follows the road along the eastern edge of High Blakey Moor, with views down into and over Rosedale, passing the Lion Inn (meals, accommodation and camping) and High Blakey House (accommodation in summer) to the junction of the Castleton road with a road down to Farndale, a sheltered valley whose meadows are covered in spring with wild daffodils.

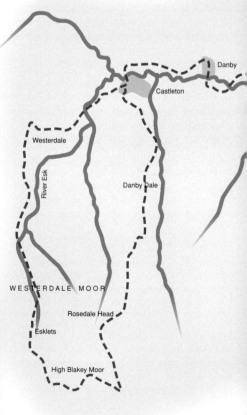

Looking down into Danby Dale. At Danby Head the path leaves this rich pastureland, and makes a steep climb to the moorland above.

HIGH BLAKEY TO CASTLETON
About 8¹/₂ miles/14km
OS Landranger 94 or
Outdoor Leisure 26
Start at car park by junction of Castleton and Farndale roads (grid reference 682 989)

The first 5 miles or so of this section are well away from civilisation, and you should keep an eye on the weather.

The Walk leaves the road near the old stone railway bridge and for nearly 3 miles follows the trackbed of the former Rosedale Railway across high, open moorland. The moor is part of the largest expanse of continuous heather moorland in England and in summer all around, as far as the eye can see, stretch great swathes of purple. In the autumn, the bracken turns to rusty gold. Sheep graze the grassy patches and grouse, bred on the moors for shooting, feed on the young shoots of heather. To the right of the track you may see lines of grouse-shooting butts.

Where a track crosses the old railway, follow the waymarked sign and turn right down to a stream, one of several that come off the moors eventually to form the River

Walkers head across Blakey Ridge with heather moorland stretching beyond them as far as the eye can see.

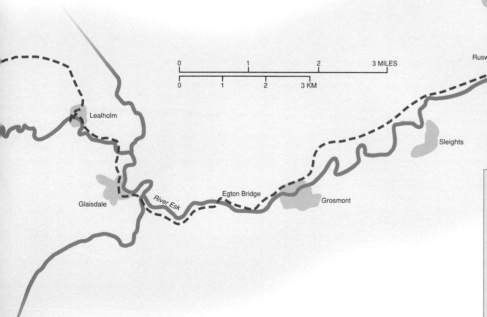

Esk at Westerdale. The path passes the ruined buildings of Esklets, a one-time monastic farm owned by Rievaulx Abbey, and then follows the course of a stream northwards. Waste tips visible to the left are from the jet mines that were worked here in the Victorian era, when jet jewellery was so fashionable. The North York Moors were the country's main source of this form of fossilised wood.

As the path approaches some farm buildings, cross a ford and carry on through fields into Westerdale. The River Esk is now over to the right as the path passes beneath a steep moorland

escarpment of bracken and heather, with fields of grass and drystone walling on the right. A lane leads off the path over the Esk and into the little stone village of Westerdale, where there is accommodation available. Just beyond Hawthorn Farm, the Esk Valley Walk takes a minor road up on to Westerdale Moor and makes its way for a ¹/₂ mile or so through the heather before dropping down to Dale View Farm and continuing through fields to meet the river. For a few hundred yards the path sticks with the river bank, then at Dibble Bridge it turns right on the road into Castleton.

GUIDE BOX

PLACES TO VISIT
Danby Moors Centre A National Park Visitor Centre with exhibitions on the industrial archaeology and natural history of the moors; also book shop, information desk and tea room.

CAR PARKING
Castleton; High Blakey.

PUBLIC TRANSPORT
Trains Several trains daily on the Middlesbrough-to-Whitby line stop at Castleton Moor.
Buses Run through Castleton. A 'Moorsbus' service runs between Castleton and Blakey (Lion Inn) on Sundays and bank Holiday Mondays from end May to end September; also every Tuesday and Wednesday between end July and end August.

ACCOMMODATION
Hotels, guest houses etc The Esk Valley Walk guide includes a leaflet detailing accommodation and food available in Castleton, Danby Dale, Blakey Ridge, Westerdale.
Camping Lion Inn, Blakey Ridge.

TOURIST INFORMATION CENTRE
Danby The Moors Centre, Lodge Lane, Danby, North Yorkshire YO21 2NB (tel 01287 660654)

Castleton to Whitby

CASTLETON TO GLAISDALE
About 10 miles/16km
OS Landranger 94 or
Outdoor Leisure 26, 27
Start at Castleton Station
(grid reference 682 085)

From the station, the Esk Valley Walk runs north of the railway and the river through the woodland of Danby Park, a medieval deer-hunting park. The track continues eastwards with views across the green fields of the valley. The river itself is hidden in trees. Follow lanes through the village of Danby, where there is a station, shop, tea room and pub, and criss-cross the river to reach the Moors Centre at Danby Lodge, an old hunting lodge that is now a National Park Visitor Centre with a tea room, information desk and informative exhibitions on the industrial archaeology and natural history of the area.

From here the path climbs very steeply up Oakley Side and then continues up to Danby Beacon. From the car park and viewpoint, an unmade-up road runs east across Lealholm Moor. This is a lonely and remote stretch of about 3 miles, passing only the stump of a stone cross and some prehistoric burial mounds, but on a fine day there are extensive views to the south, down into the patchwork of green fields and trees in the broad valley and across to fingers of high, purple moors beyond. An alternative route would be along the minor roads that run closer to the river, linking Danby Lodge, Houlsyke and Lealholm.

The Esk Valley Walk drops down from the moor into Lealholm, a small village with a station, shop, pub and a pretty stone bridge over the Esk. The village green alongside the shallow, boulder-strewn river is a popular picnic spot in summer. The walk follows the north bank through fields in the narrowing valley with the railway close by. Shortly before Glaisdale, the path follows a loop of the river into a patch of ancient woodland on a slope that rises sharply from the river. The village was an ironstone mining centre until the ore ran out in the 1880s and the stone terraces of workers' cottages still stand. Half a mile away is the station (the old station building is now a tea-shop). Take a short diversion here and go under the railway bridge to see the cobbled packhorse bridge. Dated 1619 and bearing the initials TF, it is known as Beggar's Bridge, built by one Thomas Ferries (see panel opposite).

GUIDE BOX

PLACES TO VISIT
Danby Moors Centre A National Park Visitor Centre with book shop, information desk, exhibitions on the industrial archaeology and natural history of the area and tea room.
Whitby Ruins of 13th-century Benedictine abbey; Captain Cook Museum.
Grosmont North Yorkshire Moors Railway: steam trains run 18 miles between Grosmont and Pickering; loco sheds at Grosmont.

CAR PARKING
Castleton; Danby Moors Centre; Danby Beacon; Lealholm; Grosmont; Sleights; Whitby.

PUBLIC TRANSPORT
Trains Several trains daily on the Middlesbrough-to-Whitby line serve Castleton Moor, Danby, Lealholm, Glaisdale, Egton, Grosmont, Sleights and Whitby.
Buses Run through Castleton.

ACCOMMODATION
Hotels, guest houses etc The Esk Valley Walk guide includes a leaflet detailing accommodation and food available in Castleton, Danby, Houlsyke, Lealholm, Glaisdale, Egton Bridge, Grosmont and Ruswarp. Wide range in Whitby.

TOURIST INFORMATION CENTRES
Danby The Moors Centre, Lodge Lane, Danby, North Yorkshire YO21 2NB (tel 01287 660654)
Whitby Tourist Information Centre, Langbourne Road, Whitby YO21 1YN (tel 01947 602674)

Danby Beacon gives a good view of the landscape through which the Esk flows, even if the river itself is not always visible. Across the valley are the moors where the river rises.

GLAISDALE TO WHITBY

About 10 miles/16km
OS Landranger 94 or
Outdoor Leisure 27
Start at Glaisdale Station
(grid reference 783 056)

Near Glaisdale Station, just before the railway bridge, the Esk Valley Walk turns right up steps into Arncliffe Woods and along the south side of a steeply wooded gorge with river and railway twisting their way under and over each other below. The stone pathway through the oak trees is an ancient pannierway once used by packhorses and travellers, now lined with wild strawberries and moisture-loving plants. After ³/₄ mile the path emerges from the woods to join the minor road leading to Egton Bridge. At a junction just past the Horseshoe Hotel, steps lead down to a path to stepping stones across the river. (If the river is too high, take the road bridge.) Across the river, turn right on the road and then follow the old toll road opposite St Hedda's Church through the landscaped parkland of Egton Manor (private, but used with the landowner's permission).

At the end of the toll road, the Walk continues to the west of Grosmont, but some will want to divert a short distance along the lane over the ford and into the village, where the Middlesbrough-to-Whitby line shares the station with the North Yorkshire Moors preserved railway. Engineered by George Stephenson, the line runs for 18 miles over the moors to Pickering. With steam trains arriving and departing regularly from spring to autumn, there is plenty to watch and the loco sheds can also be visited.

Back on the Walk, the path continues through riverside pastureland in a more open stretch of the dale, passing through the yard of Grosmont Farm and into a short length of wood with more stone 'trods' again forming a pathway over the sometimes wet land. Beyond Newbiggin Hall, there are more patches of woodland and more stretches paved with stone trods. At Sleights, the Walk crosses the main A169 and takes the B1410 for the next 1¹/₂ miles to Ruswarp. The river now is wide and deep, and liable to flood the flat land on either side. In summer boats may be hired here and picnickers sit under the trees on the bank. An old mill has been converted into flats.

From Ruswarp the Walk takes a footpath to the north of the river and on the outskirts of Whitby crosses the bed of the old Whitby-to-Scarborough railway line. To the right is the monumental Larpool Viaduct, built in 1885 to take this

The old packhorse bridge known as Beggar's Bridge, near Glaisdale Station. Beyond is the bridge that carries the railway.

line over the Middlesbrough railway and the River Esk. The path enters the seaside town of Whitby along the marina, with the 13th-century abbey ruins and Norman St Mary's Church up on the cliff to the right, overlooking the tall orange-roofed houses below. Whitby is still an active fishing port but in summer months it is also a holiday resort and still finds a ready market for the local jet. The Esk finally empties into the North Sea by the pier, near a monument to the town's most famous son, Captain Cook, whose ships *Endeavour* and *Resolution* were built here.

BEGGAR'S BRIDGE

The story goes that Thomas Ferries, a local farmer's son, fell in love with Agnes Richardson, but the only way he could get across the river to see her was to swim. Agnes's father, a wealthy landowner, decreed that Thomas was not rich enough to be her husband, and Thomas therefore determined to set off and make his fortune at sea. Unable to cross the river to say goodbye to Agnes the night before he left, he vowed he would one day return and build a bridge here. Six years later, in 1619, having fought against the Spanish Armada and engaged in piracy in the West Indies, Thomas did indeed return to Glaisdale having made his fortune. He married Agnes and built the single-span bridge.

The Weardale Way

COWSHILL TO MONKWEARMOUTH
79 MILES/126KM

THE River Wear cuts its way through the heart of County Durham. Starting high on the Pennine fells as a moorland stream, the river passes through diverse countryside that will appeal to most walkers before it finally reaches the North Sea at Monkwearmouth.

The high moorland where the river begins its journey is remote, a land for lapwing and grouse. But in the latter part of the 18th century this harsh environment was an important lead-mining centre. The methods used by that hardy breed of men to obtain and process the ore is explained at the Killhope Lead Mining Centre, the highest tourist attraction in England and an essential place to visit for anyone interested in the history and geology of the area.

The river winds its way across the county to the North Sea, passing a number of places associated with early Christianity. Durham Cathedral stands above the loop of the River Wear, the resting place of both St Cuthbert and the Venerable Bede. The walk passes Escomb, with its beautifully simple Saxon church, and Bishop Auckland, where the powerful bishops of Durham had a residence. Finally, it ends near Monkwearmouth, where St Peter's Church stands on the site of a Saxon monastery.

WALKING GUIDE
Piggin, JKE, *The Weardale Way* (Dalesman Publishing).

OS MAPS
Landranger 87, 88, 92, 93

LINKS
The 46-mile Wear Valley Way goes from Killhope to Willington picnic site. The Brandon-to-Bishop Auckland Walk also links with the Weardale Way.

The Lead Mining Centre at Killhope, with the huge Killhope Wheel.

Cowshill to Westgate via Allenheads

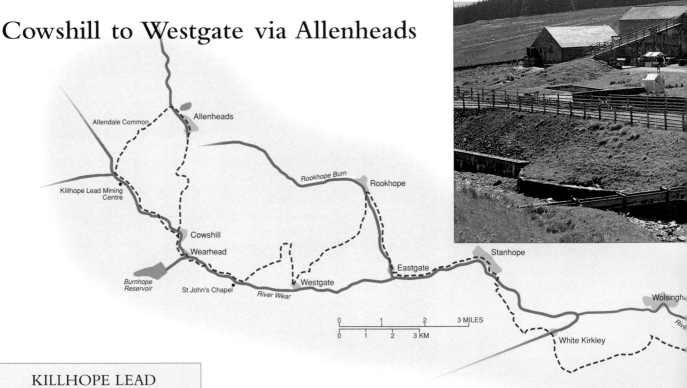

KILLHOPE LEAD MINING CENTRE

Set in the upper reaches of Weardale, the Killhope Lead Mining Centre opened as a lead mine in 1853 and reached its peak in 1875 when 110 men and 30 boys were employed. It closed in 1910.

Groups of visitors are now taken on a 45-minute visit into the Park Level mine. Suitably clothed in helmets and equipped with lamps, they experience life below ground and can see the 18ft underground water wheel used for pumping. Also to be seen is the Killhope Wheel, nearly 34ft in diameter, which powered the crushing machinery, and exhibits on various aspects of life 1,500ft up in the Pennines. There is a woodland walk, picnic site and café.

COWSHILL TO COWSHILL VIA ALLENHEADS
10 miles/16 km
OS Landranger 87
*Start at the car park in Cowshill
(grid reference 856 406)*

Paradoxically, the Weardale Way begins by climbing up out of Weardale and down into Allendale, but the diversion is amply rewarded by the fine Pennine fell countryside. From the village of Cowshill, take the bridleway northwards, climbing on to Burtree Fell, and at the Northumberland-Durham border, turn left to the road and descend to Allenheads.

Allenheads owes its existence to lead.

Between 1729 and 1896 over a quarter of a million tons of lead concentrate was removed from Allenheads mine. Today it is a picturesque, scattered community, surrounded by dramatic moorland scenery. Follow the road past the Heritage Centre, where there is an Armstrong hydraulic engine on display outside. Close by is the Allenheads Hotel, built in 1770; the bar has a remarkable collection of bric-à-brac, some of it adorning the outside walls. Follow the road into the inappropriately named hamlet of Dirt Pot and just beyond the village turn left over the stone bridge to join the Carriers Way to Killhope.

The walk heads southwest past Dodd Reservoir and over the shoulder of

Killhope Law to descend back into Weardale at Killhope Burn. Here, beside the road, is Killhope Lead Mining Centre, where you can learn how the ore was mined and processed. From Killhope follow the moorland road eastwards for a mile, then turn right to join the bank of Killhope Burn back to Cowshill.

COWSHILL TO WESTGATE
About 7 miles/11km
OS Landranger 91 or 92, 87
Start at the car park in Cowshill
(grid reference 856 406)

Having crossed the high moorlands between the rivers Wear and Allen, the walk now sets off determinedly down Weardale heading towards the North Sea.

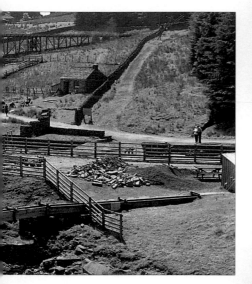

Walk past the church and turn left to the bridge over Killhope Burn and follow it downstream until it merges with Burnhope Burn to form the River Wear. Nearby is the hamlet of Wearhead. Its houses were originally built to house workers in the local sandstone quarries

and later in the lead mining industry. Continuing beside the river, pass the hamlet of Ireshopeburn where at Forge Cottage, the former blacksmith's forge, you can see handloom weavers at work. The nearby Weardale Museum gives an idea of how life was lived in Weardale about a century ago.

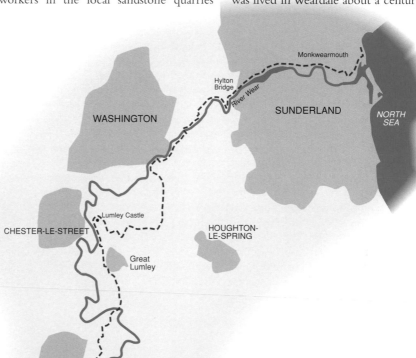

The riverside path passes St John's Chapel on the opposite bank, the largest village in the upper valley. It takes its name from the church, built in 1465, and strangely has a town hall overlooking the village green. The war memorial records not only the local men who gave their lives in two world wars but also seven airmen who died when their plane crashed at Greenlaws in 1943.

From St John's Chapel the walk crosses the river and several stiles to reach a walled lane that climbs the valley side offering excellent views. The route passes through old lead mine workings and turns south to Westgate, descending into picturesque Slit Wood with Middlehope Burn tumbling down the valley side in a succession of small waterfalls.

GUIDE BOX

PLACES TO VISIT
Allenheads Heritage Centre Displays the development of the village and lead mining; blacksmith's shop, café, picnic area and woodland nature trail.
Killhope Lead Mining Centre (see feature box).
Ireshopeburn Weardale Museum – housed in the old manse with kitchen displaying the domestic lifestyle of a local family 100 years ago; superb display of crystallised minerals and rocks; room devoted to John Wesley who preached locally.

CAR PARKING
Cowshill; Allenheads; Killhope Lead Mining Centre.

PUBLIC TRANSPORT
Bus Services available in summer up Weardale as far as Killhope Lead Mining Centre.

ACCOMMODATION
Guest houses etc Limited accommodation in the villages.

TOURIST INFORMATION CENTRE
Stanhope Durham Dales Centre, Castle Gardens, Stanhope, Co Durham DL13 2FJ (tel 01388 527650/526393)

Westgate to Witton-le-Wear

WESTGATE TO STANHOPE
8 miles/13km
OS Landranger 87, 92
*Start at Westgate village centre
(grid reference 906 380)*

Westgate was the western gateway into the Old Park, which was kept as a hunting ground for the Bishops of Durham. To reach Eastgate, at the other end of Old Park, the Weardale Way begins with a steep climb up the northern side of Weardale past Chester House, with wide-ranging views back into the dale. The path eventually follows the bed of a former railway past Smailsburn to Stotfield Burn, south of Rookhope. Turn right and follow the road south for 700yds to a signpost that indicates the delightful path that follows Rookhope Burn as it tumbles over the waterfalls of Holm Linn, Middle Linn and Dunter Linn before its final drop over the horseshoe-shaped Low Linn Falls.

All Saints Church in Eastgate has a large font carved out of the local Frosterley Marble, a limestone which contains large numbers of fossil corals and when cut and polished forms a very decorative stone. Beside the main road in the village is a replica Roman altar dedicated to Silvanus;

the original was removed to Durham University for safe keeping.

Follow the road towards Stanhope and then turn right down to the bridge, where a riverside path between the River Wear and the railway leads into the outskirts of Stanhope. On the approach to Stanhope the stream passes through a small rocky tree-lined gorge. Follow the road straight ahead to join the main road through the dale opposite Stanhope Old Hall, a 12th-century fortified manor house. Turn right into the middle of Stanhope, passing the Durham Dales Centre.

STANHOPE TO WITTON-LE-WEAR
About 16 miles/26km
OS Landranger 92
*Start at Market Place, Stanhope
(grid reference 996 391)*

The church in Stanhope is notable for the trunk of a fossilised tree set in the boundary wall. Formed some 250 million years ago, it was discovered near Edmondbyers during quarrying work. In front of the church is the market place, with Stanhope Castle beyond. The castle was erected in 1798 on the site of a medieval manor house and was enlarged in

GUIDE BOX

PLACES TO VISIT
Rookhope Rookhope Nursery, near Eastgate – a high Pennine nursery and garden 1100ft above sea level with a wide range of alpine plants, heathers, shrubs suitable for northern gardens.
Witton le Wear Low Barns Nature Reserve and Visitors Centre (see feature box).
Stanhope Durham Dales Centre has craft workshops, a tea room and the tourist information centre with books and a good display of information boards.

CAR PARKING
Stanhope (Market Place); parking is not really a problem along the route.

PUBLIC TRANSPORT
Bus Services operate along the Wear Valley to Stanhope and Westgate.

ACCOMMODATION
Hotels, guest houses etc Most of the towns and villages in the valley offer accommodation and there is easy access to Wolsingham and Frosterley.

TOURIST INFORMATION CENTRES
Stanhope Durham Dales Centre, Castle Gardens, Stanhope, Co Durham DL13 2FJ (tel 01388 527650/526393)
Bishop Auckland Town Hall, Market Place, Bishop Auckland, Co Durham DL14 7NP (tel 01388 604922)

1875 to house a collection of minerals and stuffed birds which proved of interest to visiting shooting parties.

A horse and rider beside the stepping stones that take the path over the Wear at Stanhope.

Early in the 19th century the market place and the Bonny Moor Hen Inn were the setting for the Battle of Stanhope. Poaching of game from the moors by lead miners and others had gone on for years and in 1818 the Bishop of Durham's gamekeepers, with the help of men from Bishop Auckland, marched up to St John's Chapel hoping to arrest some of the poachers. Forewarned, most of the men had disappeared but after a chase Charles and Anthony Siddle were apprehended and taken by cart to Stanhope, where they were locked in a room at the inn. However, a large group of men had followed the party down the dale and a battle with the gamekeepers ensued during which the Siddles were released. The group returned back up the dale, to become the subject of a popular ballad.

The route out of Stanhope is down The Butts, signposted 'Riverside Walk'. Turn left on a path that crosses the railway and heads towards Shittlehope. Cross the bridge over the River Wear and follow the road to a terrace of houses where a footpath leads up to Parson Byers farm and on to Hill End, offering good views. Now turn left down

the road to take the junction that leads passed White Kirkley to reach the track above Allotment House. From the edge of the dale you can look back down on the village of Frosterley, which gives its name to Frosterley Marble. The decorative 'marble' can be seen in the parish church where, after a local appeal for money, a Frosterley Marble font was installed, brought here from Gainsborough in Lincolnshire.

For the next 4½ miles the path follows the valley top with Weardale to the left. When the moorland track reaches the road south of Wolsingham, the Way takes the road which goes southeast to Bedburn and Hamsterley.

For a return to Stanhope, follow the road down into Wolsingham and either take a bus or walk along the south bank of the river to Frosterley and then along the road into Stanhope.

Continuing on the main walk, when the Bedburn road swings to the right, carry on along the quieter, unfenced moorland road, enjoying attractive views down into Weardale. At Knitsley Fell turn left downhill to Shipley Moss and

The glorious Pennine hay meadows of Weardale have never been 'improved' for agriculture.

Monkfield Farm, then cross the river and railway to reach Low Harperley. Turn right to pass Harperley Hall and walk along the hillside above the railway to Witton-le-Wear.

PENNINE HAY MEADOWS

In late spring and early summer a rich variety of wild flowers blooms in the hay meadows beside the river. To the older walker it will bring back childhood memories of the rich plant life to be seen before intensive farming and pesticides wiped out these 'weeds'. The hay meadows of northern England are a managed crop with no animals allowed in the fields until after the wild flowers have produced their seeds. The meadow is then cut before the herbage becomes tough and fibrous to provide a rich fodder for the winter months. It is a centuries-old tradition that provides an attractive, colourful landscape and an excellent crop for the local farmer.

Witton-le-Wear to Durham

GUIDE BOX

PLACES TO VISIT
Escomb Church One of the finest Saxon churches in England.
Bishop Auckland Auckland Castle – the residence of the Bishops of Durham since medieval times; Throne Room, Long Dining Room, King Charles Dining Room; 12th-century chapel; nature trail in the Bishop's Park.
Binchester Roman Fort The remains of the Roman fort of Vinovia include the military bath house. The fort is set on the Roman Dere Street and a motoring trail visits the forts at Piercebridge, Lanchester and Ebchester as well as Binchester.
Durham Cathedral – fine example of Norman architecture in a magnificent position overlooking the Wear; tombs of St Cuthbert and the Venerable Bede; cathedral treasury. Heritage Centre – exhibition of the county of Durham and the city, housed in a medieval church.

CAR PARKING
Bishop Auckland (Riverside car park); Sunderland Bridge; Durham.

PUBLIC TRANSPORT
Train Stations in Durham and Bishop Auckland.
Bus Good services throughout the area.

ACCOMMODATION
Hotels, guest houses etc Bishop Auckland and Durham.

TOURIST INFORMATION CENTRES
Bishop Auckland Town Hall, Market Place, Bishop Auckland, Co Durham DL14 7NP (tel 01388 604922)
Durham Market Place, Durham DH1 3NJ (tel 0191 384 3720)

WITTON-LE-WEAR TO BISHOP AUCKLAND
About 4¹/₂ miles/7km
OS Landranger 92
Start at road junction south of Witton-le-Wear (grid reference 146 311)

Take the road or footpath that descends to the River Wear near Witton Castle. The keep dates back to the 14th century, when it was constructed by Sir Ralph de Eure. Cross the river and take the footpath around the northern side of the parkland to Witton Park. Across the river is Low Barns Nature Reserve and Visitors Centre (see panel opposite).

The walk continues into Witton Park, not the most attractive place on the walk but one that holds a place in railway history. On 27 September 1825 George Stephenson drove his *Locomotion* out of the nearby colliery on the inaugural journey on the Stockton & Darlington Railway. Although the 27-mile long railway was primarily built to carry coal to the River

The delightful little Saxon church at Escomb, built with Roman stones, has a 13th-century carving of a knight.

Tees for shipment, the second Act of Parliament in 1823 had granted permission to carry passengers. The first passengers to be carried by a railway completed their journey on this inaugural run.

The next village along the way is Escomb, with its gem of a Saxon church. Set in a circular churchyard, the church may have been built during the life of the Venerable Bede (672–735). The small, simple church appears lofty and spacious inside. Some of the stone had been used earlier in the Roman fort at Binchester, which the walk passes later.

The walk continues beside the river towards Bishop Auckland. You may have left behind the Pennine wild flower meadows, but there are still plenty of wild flowers along the riverside walk and in summer you may encounter wild rose, bird's foot trefoil, common sorrel, white campion, wild strawberry, the tall foxglove or lady's bedstraw.

The route skims the edge of Bishop Auckland, joining a road end near two small car parks. Nearby Auckland Castle and its Bishops Park has been the country residence of the Bishops of Durham since the 12th century.

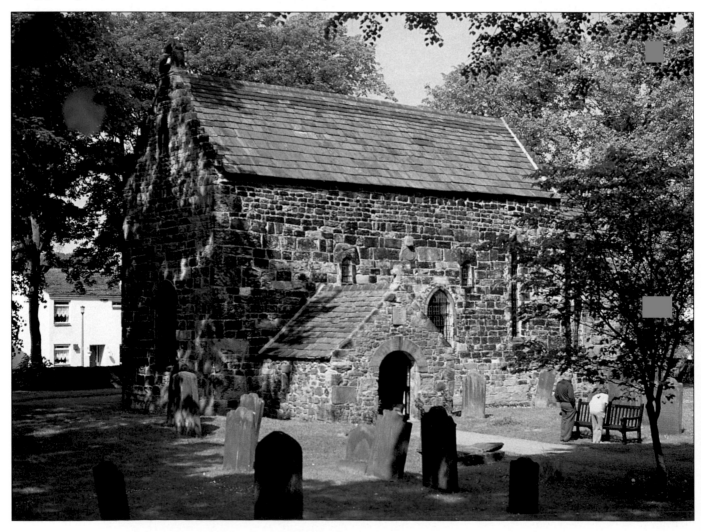

BISHOP AUCKLAND TO DURHAM
About 14 miles / 22km
OS Landranger 92, 93, 88
*Start at Riverside car park, north of Bishop
Auckland (grid reference 199 296)*

From the car park follow the quiet road which is fringed with trees and large boulders. At the junction turn left and cross the 15th-century road bridge. Just downstream is Newton Cap railway viaduct, which is now used to carry the main road. Turn right in front of some houses along the bridleway that passes under the viaduct and turn left, uphill, to join the disused railway track that forms part of the 9½-mile Brandon-to-Bishop Auckland Walk.

Across the river is the site of the Roman fort Linovia at Binchester. The fort guarded Dere Street, which linked York and Corbridge, the supply station for Hadrian's Wall. Follow the former railway track to Sunny Brow on the outskirts of Willington then turn right down the road to reach the Brown Trout Inn where meals are served. On the grass opposite the inn a mineral wagon is set on a stone plinth. Durham has been associated for centuries with coal mining and the monument serves as a memorial to the

men and boys of the local communities who died in the mines. It also commemorates the Rocking Strike of 1863, the forerunner of the checkweight system which operated in the Durham collieries. The track continues down to the river, where you turn left to reach the Jubilee Bridge picnic site at Page Bank.

The riverside path continues, eventually passing under the lofty viaduct that carries the main Edinburgh-to-London railway line. Turn right on the cul-de-sac road that crosses the medieval Sunderland Bridge over the River Wear. In the days of stage coaches this was the route of the Great North Road into Durham. The eight-day journey from Edinburgh to London in the 1750s had been cut to 59 hours by 1818 as the roads and carriages improved. The stone bridge was widened in 1822 not only to improve travel times but – after the mail coach caught the parapet and two passengers were killed by being thrown from the coach into the river – to prevent further accidents.

Just beyond the bridge the walk turns left through metal gates and passes under the road to continue past Croxdale Hall. The track eventually follows the top edge of the wood that drops steeply down to the River Wear until you reach High Butterby

Sunderland Bridge, the scene of a coaching tragedy in the 19th century, was originally constructed in medieval times.

Farm. A stile takes the walk into the wood and the path continues to Shincliffe Hall (part of Durham University) and on to the village of Shincliffe. A delightful riverside path then leads into Durham, with its cathedral and castle standing on the hillside. At the medieval stone Elvet Bridge there is easy access into the city centre.

LOW BARNS
NATURE RESERVE

This former gravel pit was given to Durham Wildlife Trust in 1965 by Tarmac Ltd. The 100-acre reserve now has a rich variety of plants, trees and shrubs which attracts reed buntings, snipe, tree and meadow pipit, while you may be lucky enough to see a dipper, kingfisher or great spotted woodpecker. From the north and south hides you can look across Marston Lake, which has resident mallard, tufted duck and mute swans, while in winter you may see teal, wigeon, pochard and shoveller. Eight species of dragonfly have been recorded on the site as well as red admiral, large and small skipper and peacock butterflies.

Durham to Monkwearmouth

DURHAM TO LUMLEY CASTLE
About 6 miles/10km
OS Landranger 88
Start at Elvet Bridge, Durham
(grid reference 275 424)

From Elvet Bridge – where there are good views of Durham Castle and Cathedral on the lofty promontory surrounded by the River Wear – the route follows the riverside path below the cathedral. This delightful section of the walk passes below Kingsgate Bridge, taking the road up to the North Bailey and the cathedral. The path continues round the point of the headland to Prebends Bridge, where the monks had a ferry to Crossgate Manor. The ferry was replaced by a wooden bridge in 1574, a stone bridge, built in 1696, was swept away by floodwater in 1771, and the present

bridge was erected in 1777. Beside the weir on the river is the Old Fulling Mill, which now houses the Museum of Archaeology. Temporary displays are held in the upper galleries including artefacts recovered from excavations on local Roman and medieval sites. There have been mills on this site since about 1500. One of the mills was being used for carding and fulling in 1792. Carding is a method of straightening the fibres in wool to make spinning easier, while fulling was used to strengthen and shrink the woven woollen cloth by beating it with hammers while it was immersed in water and fuller's earth.

The footpath continues beneath the castle to pedestrianised Framwellgate Bridge. This stone bridge was built about 1120 by Bishop Flambard, William II's tax

GUIDE BOX

PLACES TO VISIT
Finchale Priory A 13th-century Benedictine Priory in a delightful setting beside the River Wear.
Washington Wildfowl and Wetland Trust – set in 100 acres of grounds beside the River Wear with many wildfowl from around the world; an important stop over for migrating birds.
Washington Washington Old Hall - a Jacobean manor house with some excellent panelling; the medieval home of George Washington's family.
Sunderland Monkwearmouth Station Museum - a transport collection housed in the station built in 1848 by George Hudson, the Railway King, and MP for Sunderland; restored booking office, platforms and rolling stock in an Edwardian setting.

CAR PARKING
Durham; Sunderland; near Lumley Castle.

PUBLIC TRANSPORT
Train Stations in Durham, Chester le Street, Sunderland.
Bus Good services throughout the area.

ACCOMMODATION
Hotels, guest houses etc Durham, Chester le Street, Washington, Sunderland.
Camping Finchale Priory.

TOURIST INFORMATION CENTRES
Durham Market Place, Durham DH1 3NJ (tel 0191 3843720)
Sunderland Unit 3, Crowtree Road, Sunderland, Tyne & Wear SR1 3EL (tel 0191 565 990)

collector. It was damaged by floodwater in 1401 and the tolls from a temporary ferry, along with donations from Bishop Langley and others, enabled the bridge to be rebuilt. Here you cross over the bridge and continue along the other side of the river to Crook Hall, a 14th-century manor house. Over the years various owners have modified the building and added wings, the latest restoration having won the owners a Civic Trust commendation.

Continue beside the river, then follow the right of way to Frankland Farm and beyond to pass between Frankland Prison and the Remand Centre. Frankland was originally a park owned by the Bishop of Durham. Turn right then left down the road to Finchale Priory, where there is a camp site.

Finchale Priory nestles in a bend of the River Wear with steep wooded cliffs beyond. It was selected as the site for a hermitage by St Godric in the early 12th century and the appeal of this charming place was known in medieval times when a prior and four monks from Durham Priory ran it as a retreat for up to four other monks on three-week visits.

Cross the footbridge over the River Wear and turn right to climb the steps up the wooded hillside to the road. Take the road towards Great Lumley and when it

The ruins of Finchale Priory stand beside a bend in the river, with wooded cliffs beyond, a fine position no doubt appreciated by the monks from Durham who used to come here on retreat.

The end of the Weardale Way is marked by this memorial to the Venerable Bede on the seafront at Roker.

turns right carry straight on along the signposted track which passes around the western side of the village and then descends to the River Wear. Lumley Castle comes into view with its ivy-clad towers peering over the tops of the trees. When you reach the bridge which leads to Chester-le-Street, cross over the river to a large car park or carry on along the edge of the river to continue on your way.

LUMLEY CASTLE TO MONKWEARMOUTH
About 13 miles / 21km
OS Landranger 88
*Start at car park below Lumley Castle
(grid reference 281 509)*

From the bridge between Lumley Castle and Chester le Street, follow the signposted path that passes between the castle golf course and the river, then later Lumley Beck. The castle was built in the 14th century and incorporates Sir Ralph Lumley's earlier manor house. It is now a hotel which is noted for its medieval banquets. Eventually the path circles the castle grounds to the B1284. Turn left beside the road and fork left on the road which passes the Smiths Arms and goes under the A1(M) in a wooded ravine, continuing beside wooded Lumley Beck.

The route passes around the eastern side of Bournmoor and beside the railway line, turning left to rejoin the River Wear opposite Washington New Town. Pass Victoria Railway Viaduct, cross over the next bridge downstream into James Steel Park and turn right to pass the entrance to the Washington Wildfowl and Wetland Trust Centre. The centre has an excellent display of wildfowl from all over the world.

At the approach to Hylton Bridge, which carries the A19, there is a choice of routes. The Weardale Way passes under the bridge and joins the A1231 to Monkwearmouth Church, or there is now an alternative series of paths along the River Wear Trail on the south side of the river. About 150 yards before Hylton Bridge steps lead up to the A1231, where you turn right. A second right turn takes you over the bridge where a steep path leads back down to the opposite river bank. A River Wear Trail leaflet, available from the Tourist Information Centre, gives a wealth of information about the points of interest in Sunderland. Cross over Wearmouth Bridge to St Peter's Church, Monkwearmouth, set in its own grounds on the north side of the river. This was formerly the Saxon monastery where the Venerable Bede entered monastic life at the age of seven. The final mile of the walk follows the road to Roker seafront, where there is a replica cross, erected in 1904, to commemorate the Venerable Bede.

Across the Pennines

THE HUDDERSFIELD NARROW CANAL: MILNSBRIDGE TO MOSSLEY
15 MILES/24KM
THE ROCHDALE CANAL: ROCHDALE TO SOWERBY BRIDGE
21 MILES/34KM

The walks described here follow sections of two of England's most dramatic canals. The Rochdale Canal, one of the engineering wonders of its day, follows a splendid route through Pennine scenery and along the Calder Valley, while its great trans-Pennine rival, the Huddersfield Narrow, offers the additional challenge of climbing and crossing bleak Marsden Moor, high above the most significant of the canal's many engineering features, the Standedge Tunnel. There are pleasant towns along both routes, access is easy from the accompanying railway lines and the towpaths are in good condition.

The crossing of the Pennines was the greatest challenge facing canal builders in the late 18th century. Many schemes were proposed, including one surveyed by James Brindley in 1765, but it was not until the 1790s that the dreams became reality.

In 1794 work started on the Rochdale Canal, along a route surveyed by John Rennie but under the direction of William Jessop. Completed in 1804, with 92 wide locks and its summit 600ft above sea level, this was a vital connecting link between Manchester and Liverpool. It was immediately successful and its presence encouraged the building of textile and chemical mills along its route.

The Huddersfield Narrow Canal was also started in 1794. This too was a spectacular undertaking, with 74 locks in its 20-mile length, 42 of which lifted the canal 436ft from Huddersfield in under 8 miles, as well as the Standedge Tunnel, cut by hand for over 3 miles through Pennine rock, up to 600ft below ground level. However, this, the longest canal tunnel ever built in Britain, was not completed until 1811, by which time the canal, with its huge costs and its narrow locks, was a white elephant, never able to compete with its well-established rival, the Rochdale.

In the 1840s both canals passed into railway ownership and long-distance traffic across the Pennines declined. Short-haul traffic kept both canals busy until World War I, but after that commercial traffic rapidly diminished. The Huddersfield Narrow was formally abandoned in 1945 and the Rochdale in 1952. Decay and infilling affected both waterways, but since the 1970s a steady programme of restoration has been reversing years of dereliction. By the end of the century, boats may once again be crossing the Pennines on the Rochdale and the Huddersfield Narrow canals.

WALKING GUIDES
The Huddersfield Narrow Canal
Towpath guides have been published by the Huddersfield Canal Society and Kirklees Metropolitan Council. Quinlan, Ray, *Canal Walks of England and Wales* (Alan Sutton) includes parts of the route.
The Rochdale Canal
There are a number of published guides for walkers, historians and for boaters, the latter reflecting the recent restoration and reopening to navigation of the canal from Littleborough eastwards to Sowerby Bridge. Quinlan, Ray, *Canal Walks of England and Wales* (Alan Sutton) includes parts of the route.

OS MAPS
The Huddersfield Narrow Canal
Landranger 109, 110
The Rochdale Canal
Landranger 103, 104, 109

LINKS
The Huddersfield Narrow Canal
The Pennine Way crosses high above Standedge Tunnel, and parts of the route west of the tunnel are linked to the Oldham Way.
The Rochdale Canal
The Pennine Way crosses the canal west of Hebden Bridge and the Calderdale Way crosses it south of Todmorden.

The Huddersfield Narrow Canal

COMPLETE ROUTE: HUDDERSFIELD TO ASHTON-UNDER-LYNE
20 MILES/32KM
SECTION COVERED: MILNSBRIDGE TO MOSSLEY
15 MILES/24KM

The complete route of this canal can be followed, from its junction with the Huddersfield Broad Canal to its meeting with the Ashton Canal near Manchester, but the most appealing section is that described below. The towpath offers an easy walk but the climb onto Marsden Moor is more taxing. The walk can be completed in a day, subject to weather conditions, or in shorter sections, using the railway that closely follows the route. No cycling without permission from British Waterways.

surroundings, but gradually Huddersfield falls away as the landscape opens out.

Locks come more quickly as the canal reaches the outskirts of Slaithwaite, and then it suddenly disappears, the long section through the town having been infilled during the 1950s. The route can easily be followed, however, and just to the west of the town centre the canal starts again, immediately after the site of a lock now buried beneath a little park and picnic site. Slaithwaite has a station, with ample parking close by, and so it can be an alternative starting point for those wishing to avoid the last couple of miles of Huddersfield's industrial and suburban sprawl.

From Slaithwaite the walk improves immediately, with the canal climbing steadily up the wooded valley of the Coln towards the distant moorland hills. It is a route that is both dramatic and attractive, with occasional lock cottages surrounded by pretty gardens, old mills and wharves, and the remaining scars of industry long softened by time. The canal climbs ever nearer to the hills, the views improving as

Milnsbridge to Marsden

MILNSBRIDGE TO MARSDEN
About 6¹/₂ miles/10km
OS Landranger 110
Start at road bridge carrying the B6111
(grid reference 116 160)

It is possible to follow the canal's route from the centre of Huddersfield, but it is rather a gloomy walk, along a towing path flanked by cavernous old mills and urban decay. Milnsbridge makes for a better start, with locks coming thick and fast, lifting the canal towards the Pennine hills, visible in the distance.

At Golcar an aqueduct carries the canal over the River Coln, which then stays close by for the rest of the walk. Old mills still determine the immediate the horizon takes on the distinctive colours of the moorland. Approaching Marsden the canal twists and turns, as though seeking a way through the hills, and lock follows lock in quick succession. Trees overhang the water, shading cuttings that were formed partly by dumped mounds of tunnel spoil. Between the locks, circular pounds allowed for boats to pass. In the grandeur of the setting the canal seems very small, and the narrow locks almost toy-like, underlining the point that in commercial terms this canal was doomed before it had even opened.

The last couple of locks are over-shadowed by the bridges that criss-cross the canal and then at the appropriately named Railway Lock, next to Marsden Station, the summit is finally reached, 645ft above sea level and the highest point of any artificial waterway in Britain. There is parking close by the station. The canal passes under the railway and then comes to a large old warehouse, now a maintenance yard. During the long years when the tunnel was being built, cargoes were unloaded here and transferred to packhorses and carts for the slow journey over the Pennine moors. Ahead now is the mouth of Standedge Tunnel, and nearby are the other railway tunnels bored

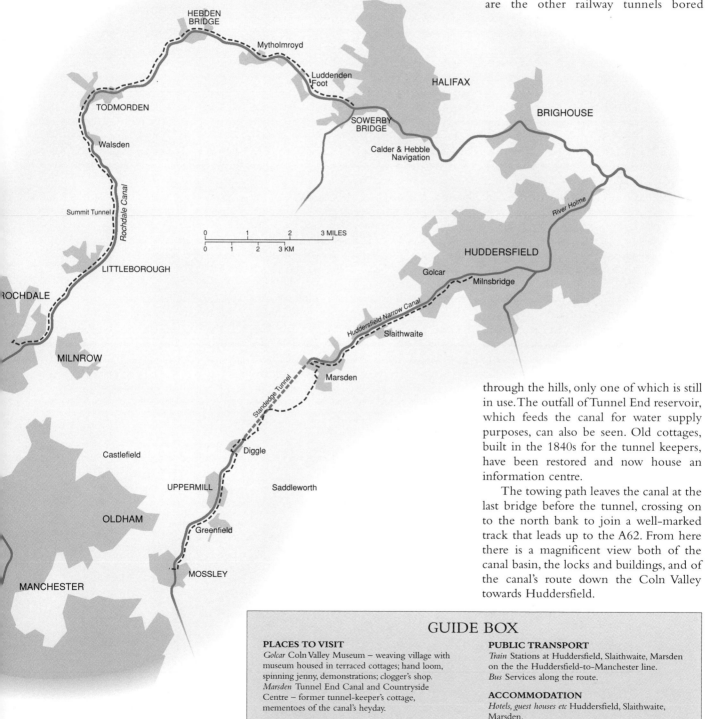

through the hills, only one of which is still in use. The outfall of Tunnel End reservoir, which feeds the canal for water supply purposes, can also be seen. Old cottages, built in the 1840s for the tunnel keepers, have been restored and now house an information centre.

The towing path leaves the canal at the last bridge before the tunnel, crossing on to the north bank to join a well-marked track that leads up to the A62. From here there is a magnificent view both of the canal basin, the locks and buildings, and of the canal's route down the Coln Valley towards Huddersfield.

GUIDE BOX

PLACES TO VISIT
Golcar Coln Valley Museum – weaving village with museum housed in terraced cottages; hand loom, spinning jenny, demonstrations; clogger's shop.
Marsden Tunnel End Canal and Countryside Centre – former tunnel-keeper's cottage, mementoes of the canal's heyday.

CAR PARKING
Ample public and on-street parking at Milnsbridge; Slaithwaite; Marsden.

PUBLIC TRANSPORT
Train Stations at Huddersfield, Slaithwaite, Marsden on the the Huddersfield-to-Manchester line.
Bus Services along the route.

ACCOMMODATION
Hotels, guest houses etc Huddersfield, Slaithwaite, Marsden.

TOURIST INFORMATION CENTRE
Huddersfield Albion Street, Huddersfield, West Yorkshire HD1 2NW (tel 01484 430808)

Marsden to Mossley

GUIDE BOX

PLACES TO VISIT
Upper Mill Saddleworth Museum – old woollen mill showing local textile production, working machinery; rooms from 1890s cottage.

CAR PARKING
Marsden; Marsden Moor (beside A62, at grid reference 018 095); Saddleworth; Mossley.

PUBLIC TRANSPORT
Train Stations at Marsden, Greenfield, Mossley on the Huddersfield-to-Manchester line.
Bus Serve parts of the route.

ACCOMMODATION
Hotels, guest houses etc Marsden, Uppermill, Saddleworth.

TOURIST INFORMATION CENTRE
Saddleworth Saddleworth Museum, High Street, Uppermill, Oldham, Lancashire OL3 6HS (tel 01457 870336)

MARSDEN TO MOSSLEY
About 7¹/₂ miles/12km
OS Landranger 110, 109
Start at Railway Lock,
adjacent to Marsden Station
(grid reference 048 119)

From Railway Lock follow the towing path westwards towards Standedge Tunnel, leave the canal at the last bridge before the tunnel and follow the signs that lead to a track that climbs steeply to join the A62. A number of tracks lead up onto the moor, but the easiest to find are those that start from Marsden village. Turn left on the A62 and walk down the hill towards the village. At the start of the village is a terrace of houses. Between the end of the terrace and a newer house is a narrow, steep path that leads up the hillside behind the village. It is not marked but is easily found. Turn right onto this and follow it up the hillside and through New Hay Farm, where there are barking but friendly dogs. The path becomes a proper track. After a gate, turn left and follow signs to Old Mount Road. This well-defined track crosses Marsden Moor, with fine views of the reservoirs in the valley below, and then gradually converges with two minor roads. The track ends where it meets the road.

If you wish to avoid the farm and the dogs, take the northern of these two roads, leaving the A62 near Marsden Church.

Cross the road and take a marked footpath that leads out onto the moor. Follow this path, initially narrow but soon better defined, as it curves round to the south of Redbrook Reservoir. It is an exposed, though spectacular route, and it is

not hard to imagine the bleakness of the journey faced by the heavily laden packhorses and their drivers as they passed continuously to and fro across the moor before the tunnel was completed, particularly in winter.

The track now curves away to the west and then meets the A62, at the point where the Pennine Way crosses it. (For those wanting to break their journey, there is a pub on the A62, ¹/₄ mile to the right, just by the reservoir.) The point where the track meets the road marks the boundary between Lancashire and Yorkshire. Turn left and walk beside the road for about 200yds and then take a marked track that turns away to the left. This is the Oldham Way. Follow it through a gate, down past a derelict cottage, and right at a signpost. The broad, but irregular track turns down the hill, beside an old stone wall. To the right of the track are huge spoil tips formed when the tunnel was excavated through the vertical shafts that are now marked by tall chimneys and serve as air shafts. The shapes of the spoil tips are clearly defined on the landscape. The track continues down past a house, broadens into a lane and then ends beside the Diggle Hotel, a free house that serves food. For those walking in the other direction, the path is clearly marked Oldham Way. From the hotel, turn right across the railway bridge, pausing to examine the overgrown tracks that lead to the disused tunnels, and then turn left. After some cottages, turn left onto a path that leads to the tunnel mouth and the start of the towing path. From this end the tunnel looks small and insubstantial, and it is hard to believe that this

overgrown culvert was the start of so great a subterranean journey. Only the background of high moorland hills adds the vital sense of reality. Not far away is the first of the 32 locks that lowered the canal 334ft to its junction with the Ashton Canal near Manchester.

The descent is rapid, with the locks, restored from here down to Saddleworth, coming in quick succession as the canal curves round towards the Tame Valley. It is a very different landscape, open, wooded and more rural, with the canal making a vital contribution. In the Tame Valley river, canal, railway and roads are packed tightly together, but the canal still enjoys a kind of privacy, with a particularly attractive section near Uppermill. An old aqueduct carries the canal, and a lock, across the Tame, overshadowed by the striding arches

Bleak landscape by Redbrook reservoir on Marsden Moor, high above Standedge Tunnel.

Near Uppermill a massive railway viaduct strides across the canal, while below, the canal crosses the River Tame on an aqueduct.

of the railway viaduct. The contrast between these huge arches and the tiny opening of the canal bridge far below makes it all too clear why so few canals could survive the coming of the railway.

From here, the canal enters a tree-lined side cutting, with the Tame flowing along at a lower level. Short sections of canal have been infilled, but otherwise it is in good order, and the target of full restoration by the year 2001 seems realistic. By Saddleworth the canal is quite domestic, with a park-like setting. A trip boat is operated here, by Saddleworth Canal Cruises, and nearby is the local museum, housed in a former woollen mill. The local history displays include the interiors of a clothier's cottage. For those wanting to end the walk here, Greenfield Station is a few minutes' walk away, by the A669 to the west of the canal. There is nowhere to leave a car at the station, but street parking is available nearby. Otherwise, there is a public car park by Saddleworth Museum.

From Saddleworth the setting becomes less appealing. Old mills and industrial buildings flank the towing path as the locks continue the descent. The big stone arches

of the Royal George Aqueduct, the largest on the canal, carry it over the Tame again and then it follows a twisting route to Mossley. Shortly before reaching the town, the towing path crosses to the western bank, and then crosses back again. In

Mossley pass the church, and leave the canal to take the road that crosses it. Turn right and this leads to the station, a few minutes' walk away. There is on street parking around the station.

THE STANDEDGE TUNNELS

After years of toil, and the expenditure of huge sums of money – well over £123,000 – Standedge Tunnel was finally opened on 4 April 1811. Apparently, on that day boats carrying over 500 people passed through, to the strains of 'Rule Britannia'. The tunnel, 5,456 yards long, later extended to 5,698 yards by railway building operations, was then, and still is, the longest on any canal in Britain. In the primitive technologies of its day, it must have seemed as wondrous as the Channel Tunnel. It was cut through solid rock by navvies armed only with explosives, picks and shovels, working up to 600 feet below ground, and all the spoil had to be hauled up the series of vertical shafts that mark its route beneath the Pennines. Much of the canal is unlined, and the rough-hewn walls vary continuously. At its narrowest it is 7ft wide, with 7ft clearance above the water, and at its widest it opens out into large subterranean caverns. There was no towing path and boats were legged through, taking up to four hours for the passage. There were three passing places, but the timings of the entry of boats was carefully controlled at both ends.

In 1849 the first of the railway tunnels through Standedge was completed, a single-track bore 3 miles and 66 yards long. It was built by the Huddersfield & Manchester Railway and its construction took only three years, thanks to the presence of the canal tunnel which was used to transport materials and spoil and for ventilation via a series of interconnecting lateral passageways. The effect of these was well described by LCT Rolt, after travelling through the canal tunnel in the late 1940s:

'At the passage of an express the rocks reverberate with a dull thunder of sound and a sudden blast of air is followed by a blinding cloud of acrid smoke which bellies out from the cross galleries. Altogether a closer approximation of the legendary route to the infernal regions by way of the Styx it would be difficult to conceive.'

In 1871 a second, single track tunnel was added, followed in 1894 by a new, double track one. This is the only one in use today, the two earlier ones having been abandoned long ago.

The Rochdale Canal

COMPLETE ROUTE: CASTLEFIELD (MANCHESTER) TO SOWERBY BRIDGE
33 MILES/53KM
SECTION COVERED: ROCHDALE TO SOWERBY BRIDGE
21 MILES/34KM

It is possible to walk the 12 miles of the Rochdale Canal that run westwards from Rochdale, through a changing and often dramatic urban landscape, to Castlefield in the heart of Manchester, but the best section of the canal is that described below. This is a moderately easy 21-mile walk along the towing path of England's earliest, and most successful, trans-Pennine canal. The path is in excellent condition and the railway is never far from the canal. No cycling without permission from British Waterways.

Rochdale to Todmorden

ROCHDALE TO LITTLEBOROUGH
About 4 miles/6km
OS Landranger 109
Start at bridge carrying the
A671 across the canal
(grid reference 903 124)

Rochdale Station, well to the south of the town centre, has seen better days but it is convenient for the canal. Turn left on leaving the station, left again under the railway and then walk along Durham Street until it crosses the former branch to Rochdale Basin, which was filled in years ago. Turn right at the lights on the A671 and join the canal by the bridge. The route is initially by old mills and industrial sites but it soon becomes suburban as the canal makes its way out of the town. A recently restored lock indicates that the long task of re-opening the section from Littleborough westwards to Manchester is under way, but the serious difficulties are soon apparent in the dropped bridges and culverted sections, generally at main road crossing points.

The water in the canal is delightfully clear, and water lilies and other aquatic plants spread across the surface. Wild roses line the path and at one point there is a mass of wild raspberries, at their best in early August. Passing back gardens, the canal leaves the town behind in a landscape marked by the signs of former industry. The railway is now alongside, and from this point it is never far away. Today a quiet and little-used line, this was opened in 1841 by

Old mills are framed by the canal bridge at Clegg Hall.

GUIDE BOX

PLACES TO VISIT
Rochdale Rochdale Pioneers' Memorial Hall commemorates birthplace of the Cooperative Movement.
Blackstone Edge Roman Road (2 miles east of Littleborough) Remarkable length of Roman paved road, best example in Britain.
Todmorden 1875 town hall with striking interior and exterior.

CAR PARKING
Rochdale; Littleborough; Todmorden; and street parking in villages.

PUBLIC TRANSPORT
Train Stations at Rochdale, Smithy Bridge, Littleborough, Walsden, Todmorden.
Bus Towns and villages on the route are well served.

ACCOMMODATION
Hotels, guest houses etc Rochdale, Littleborough, Todmorden.

TOURIST INFORMATION CENTRES
Rochdale Town Hall, Rochdale, Lancashire OL16 1AB (tel 01706 356592)
Todmorden 15 Burnley Road, Todmorden, Lancashire OL14 7BU (tel 01706 818181)

the Manchester & Leeds Railway as one of the greatest engineering achievements of its day. Later, it became part of the Lancashire and Yorkshire network, and stone mileposts marked LYR can still be seen along the route.

A cutting leads to Clegg Hall, a sudden and exciting view of old mills, weavers' cottages with their long, north-facing upper windows and the ruins of the 17th century house, all in dark red stone and framed by the stone bridge. In the distance are the hills and moors of the Pennines, a high and richly coloured backdrop, now always present as the canal climbs towards the narrow pass that has been the route of packhorse ways since the Roman period. At Smithy Bridge there is a little station, and a fine old signal box.

A mile from here the canal stops abruptly, where there used to be a bridge carrying the B6225, and for 200yds the towing path disappears into the roadside pavement before starting again. This is the present limit of navigation.

Littleborough, a moorland village much expanded by Victorian industry, makes a convenient breaking point, with a station close to the canal.

LITTLEBOROUGH TO TODMORDEN
About 6 miles / 10km
OS Landranger 109, 103
*Start at Littleborough Station
(grid reference 939 163)*

A flight of locks lifts the canal up past Littleborough and then canal, railway and road cling together as they wind through the pass. The railway plunges into the famous Summit Tunnel, 2,885yds long. When it was opened in 1841 it was the longest in the world, a point noted with pride by its engineer, George Stephenson: 'It is the greatest work that has yet been done of this kind.' In 1984 a train of petrol wagons was derailed in the tunnel, causing flames and smoke to pour for days on end from the air vents high in the hills above, and the line was closed for over a year.

Just before the tunnel another series of locks, close together, carries the canal to its summit, 600ft above the sea. It is a powerful landscape, made more so by the ever-present stone. Walls, bridges and lock chambers are all made of tough gritstone, wonderfully cut and fitted together. Richly colourful throughout the year, the landscape is at its most dramatic in winter when freezing conditions often brought boat traffic to a complete halt for days, and sometimes for weeks. The summit level is less than 1 mile long, and so the canal needed many reservoirs in the surrounding

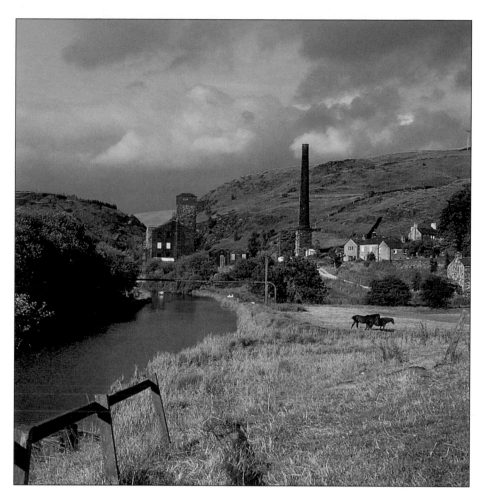

hills to maintain its supplies of water, and to feed the locks with the 70,000 gallons needed every time they were used. On the summit, the canal crosses the boundary between Lancashire and Yorkshire and is soon in Calderdale.

A pretty, white-painted cottage stands by Longlees Lock, the start of the long descent through 36 locks. This is an attractive stretch, along a steep-sided and occasionally wooded valley, dotted with handsome stone buildings, that leaves the wild moorland behind as it descends. It is a popular section, and the towing path is often busy with walkers, fishermen and cyclists. Walsden is set among woods, the village dominated by the tall stone spire of the 19th-century church. A welcome sight is the Cross Keys Inn, set right beside the towing path. From here the canal winds past houses and gardens towards Todmorden, a rather secret route despite the proximity of the A6033. This is a busy road, and care is required when the towing path crosses it on the level.

A flurry of locks drops the canal down towards the town, and beneath two fine railway bridges. The first is part of a long 18-arch stone viaduct, while the second, at Gauxholme, is a spectacular iron bowstring bridge set at a skew between rusticated stone arches with crenellated turrets.

A derelict mill adds classical splendour to the canal near Todmorden.

Designed by George Stephenson, this gothic masterpiece frames the tall spire of the church. Old mills flank the canal as it enters Todmorden along a private route remarkable for the huge wall of over four million bricks built to carry the railway and its sidings high above the water. To break the journey here, leave the towpath close to the station.

A border town with a long history, Todmorden developed into a textile centre alongside the canal. From simple beginnings in the town, the local Fielden family founded one of the world's largest cotton empires. As MP for Oldham in the 1840s, John Fielden championed legislation that controlled the working hours of women and children in the mills. The great wealth of Todmorden in the 19th century, and the lasting influence of the Fieldens, is reflected in its massive classical town hall which totally dominates the town. Completed in 1875 to the designs of John Gibson, it is marked on the outside by the great pediment that contains sculpture emblematic of the industries of Lancashire and Yorkshire, and inside by extravagant mosaics, plasterwork and painted ceilings.

Todmorden to Sowerby Bridge

TODMORDEN TO HEBDEN BRIDGE
About 4 miles/6km
OS Landranger 103
*Start at canal bridge carrying the A6033
(grid reference 935 242)*

From Todmorden the River Calder is increasingly in evidence, flowing down the steep valley often beside the canal, but generally on a lower level. The canal leaves the town quietly past local industry, with a new marina underlining the way restoration is bringing the Rochdale Canal back to life. It then descends into a broader valley towards the towering chimney and decayed classical elegance of a ruined mill, made more striking by its setting and the patterned colours of the stonework. As the locks take the canal steadily downwards, the trees increase and soon it is making its way between wooded banks, a complete change from the Pennine moorland of the previous section. Trees overhang the water, and the hedges and fields are full of flowers. To the south and high above the tree line is the bare peak of Stoodley Pike, marked by a tall stone obelisk. Along this stretch the Pennine Way crosses the canal, by Callis Lock. In an altogether more rural setting, colourful canal boats are numerous, either moored by the towing path or

making their way through the locks. The modern steel canal cruiser, with its traditional lines, strong colours, formalised decoration and flower tubs on the cabin roof, is an essential component of the Rochdale restoration. Also adding to the scene are the new cast-iron mile posts, made in a traditional style by the Rochdale Canal Trust, the driving force behind the restoration campaign. These are a great help for walkers, but not to be overlooked are the old mile posts, with R C Co finely cut into the hard stone, a few of which still survive. The Trust's maintenance yard, marked by tugs and lighters, and piles of old lock gates and other equipment, is passed on the approach to Charlestown, whose canalside cottages sport bright flowery gardens.

Still flanked by trees and with the Calder continuing on its way alongside, the canal passes under the railway and then turns to the south of Hebden Bridge.

Access to the town is easy from the various bridges, but a good starting point is the first one reached, by the Stubbing Wharf pub. From here, the best approach to Hebden Bridge is along the main road, which reveals the town's particular qualities bit by bit. Without any doubt, Hebden Bridge is the most attractive town on the Rochdale Canal. It has many fine

GUIDE BOX

PLACES TO VISIT
Hebden Bridge Automobilia Transport Museum – vintage cars, motorbikes and bikes in restored textile warehouse.
Heptonstall Old Grammar School – 17th-century school building in pretty village just north of Hebden Bridge; early school furniture; displays of local farming and crafts.
Halifax Calderdale Industrial Museum – sights, smells, sounds of local industries through the ages. Piece Hall – story of cloth production. Eureka!, Britain's first hands-on museum for under-12s.

CAR PARKING
Todmorden; Hebden Bridge; Sowerby Bridge; and street parking in villages.

PUBLIC TRANSPORT
Train Stations at Todmorden, Hebden Bridge, Mytholmroyd, Sowerby Bridge.
Bus Towns and villages on the route are well served.

ACCOMMODATION
Hotels, guest houses etc Todmorden, Hebden Bridge, Sowerby Bridge.

TOURIST INFORMATION CENTRES
Hebden Bridge 1 Bridge Gate, Hebden Bridge, West Yorkshire HX7 8EX (tel 01422 843831)
Halifax Piece Hall, Halifax, West Yorkshire HX1 1RE (tel 01422 368725)

buildings, it is lively, and makes a good place for an overnight stay.

The landscape of the Calder Valley near Todmorden, with canal and river sharing the wooded valley.

BOATS ON THE ROCHDALE CANAL

Built as it was with generously sized locks (74ft by 14ft 2ins), the Rochdale Canal was used by a great variety of boats. Regular users were the so-called flats, built for the canal and carrying up to 70 tons, Yorkshire keels, shorter sailing barges with a deeper draught and a similar capacity, and the standard narrow boats, 70ft long and 7ft wide, which carried 25 tons and often worked in pairs. Also to be seen were sailing flats, small coastal trading vessels, the short boats from the Leeds & Liverpool Canal, the curiously named bastard boats of the Manchester, Bolton & Bury Canal, and the high speed packet and fly boats that carried passengers and urgent freight from Manchester to Rochdale in seven hours, and to Todmorden in twelve hours.

Until 1895, all boats on the canal were pulled by horses, but from then onwards steam-powered flats were introduced, followed by motor flats. These carried about 45 tons and often towed one or more unpowered flats. Similarly, motor-powered narrow boats generally towed an unpowered butty narrow boat. Boats were operated by a number of independent canal carriers, and there was fierce competition for the trade in cotton and wool, printed cotton, machinery, salt, timber, cement, sand, coal, stone and chemicals. From 1887 the Rochdale Canal Company operated its own carrying fleet, and bought up several of the smaller carriers. In 1912 the weekly wage for the captain of a steamer was 12/-, augmented by tonnage money based on the amount of cargo carried. At this time many families lived on their boats. The Company fleet was disbanded in 1921, by which time trade was already declining rapidly. Independent carriers continued to use the canal but the last through passage by a laden narrow boat was in April 1939.

HEBDEN BRIDGE TO SOWERBY BRIDGE
About 7 miles / 11km
OS Landranger 103, 104
Start at main bridge
(grid reference 989 271)

A traditional mill town with fine pre-19th-century architecture, Hebden Bridge has a famous packhorse bridge, over Hebden Water. It is also notable for a fine railway station with an array of traditional signs, a huge clog-making enterprise and the double-decker mill workers' cottages, whose distinctive style was determined by the shortage of land in the narrow river valleys. The canal's route to the south of the town centre is pleasant, much of it flanked by a park, and at its centre is a marina where Calder Valley Cruising offers a variety of boat trips. Also appealing is the walk north from the town along Hebden Water to Hardcastle Crags, a secret and densely

wooded valley of tumbling water and dramatic rock formations.

Leaving Hebden Bridge, the towing path passes colourful moored boats and then, at the new Falling Royd Tunnel which carries the canal under the A646, it stops briefly, necessitating a walk across this busy road. Beyond the tunnel is Walkley's famous clog factory and museum and then it runs through farmland to Mytholmroyd, a noisy main road village with a range of shops, a good church and an unusual war memorial. There is a railway station across the bridge, on the south side of the river and canal.

From here, canal and road run side by side, with the canal in a side cutting and the towing path raised above the valley of the Calder, with fine views of distant fields with their irregular stone walls and patches of woodland. By Brearley Locks light industry accompanies the canal and then it returns to the wooded meadows of the valley. Luddenden Foot, a brown stone

Near Hebden Bridge, narrow boats explore the recently re-opened section of the Rochdale Canal.

canalside weaving village with a surprising number of pubs, is quite detached from its better known and more attractive namesake, ½ mile up Luddenden Dean.

From here a lovely long stretch of canal runs through woodland, half hidden in rocky cuttings, all flowers and dappled sunlight. This leads to the outskirts of Sowerby Bridge, a town of towers and mill chimneys. The greatest of these is the famous Wainhouse Tower, a Victorian baroque structure 253ft high, set on a hill above the town and designed to carry the fumes from Mr Wainhouse's dye works away from the town and the Calder Valley. A new deep lock and a dramatic tunnel at Tuel carries the Rochdale Canal beneath the town and down to the huge basin complex that marks its eastern end and its junction with the Calder & Hebble Navigation.

The Lancaster Canal

PRESTON TO KENDAL
57 MILES/91KM

THIS walk follows the towing path of the Lancaster Canal from Preston to Tewitfield, the current head of navigation, and from Tewitfield to Stainton. From here to Kendal the canal has been infilled, but footpaths follow the canal's former route across country. It is a long walk, divided for convenience into four sections, that is an enjoyable exploration of one of England's lesser-known waterways.

With an attractive route through the Lakeland hills and some dramatic engineering features, the Lancaster is a canal that has a character of its own. Today, the towing path and the footpaths of the northern section are in good condition and the going is easy. Although a railway follows the route closely, there are stations only in the largest towns. Local buses link these with the smaller towns and villages along the route. No cycling without towpath permit from British Waterways

WALKING GUIDES
Nicholson's Ordnance Survey Guide to the Waterways Book 3: North has information about the navigable section.
Swain, Robert, *A Walker's Guide to the Lancaster Canal* (published by the Lancaster Canal Trust).

OS MAPS
Landranger 102, 97

LINKS
The Ribble Way passes through Preston about a mile south of the canal terminus.

The Lancaster Canal, surveyed by John Rennie in 1792 and built between then and 1819, was, despite its relative isolation, a successful venture that remained profitable until the end of the 19th century. Despite a number of ambitious schemes, the canal was always detached from the rest of the waterway network, its only link in the early years being a tramway that ran southwards from Preston to meet the Leeds & Liverpool Canal at Walton Summit. However, in the long term the branch canal to the large port at Glasson amply made up for this shortcoming. Under railway control from the 1860s, the canal still managed to retain its share of trade, and limited commercial traffic continued until the 1940s. After that date, decline was rapid and the northern section into Kendal was closed and partially infilled. More infilling followed and in 1968 the M6 motorway was built across the canal in three places. Despite this, the Lancaster Canal remained open to navigation from the M6 crossing at Tewitfield south to Preston and since then an extensive restoration programme has greatly improved the canal's appearance.

Preston to Garstang

PRESTON TO NEWSHAM
About 9½ miles/15km
OS Landranger 102
*Start at canal terminus by Aqueduct Street
(grid reference 527 302)*

From Preston's railway station, walk north through the town centre, and take Fylde Road, the main Lytham and Blackpool road, westwards. Cross under the railway, and turn right into one of the side roads that lead into Aqueduct Street.

The route of the canal into the centre of Preston disappeared years ago, but some of the street names hint at its former presence. Typical is Aqueduct Street, where the former line of the canal across the street can still be detected. The present terminus is on the northern side of the street, hidden from view in a small wooded

The present southern terminus of the Lancaster Canal is hidden behind a park, and back gardens run down to the water's edge.

park approached by a flight of steps. Bullrushes, wild flowers and back gardens make this setting a secret oasis in unremarkable urban surroundings. The towing path begins here, the start of an easy and quite pleasant walk through suburbia to the fringes of Preston. A bridge lifts the path over the entrance to Ashton Basin and then a short built-up stretch with a noisy main road bridge leads the canal to Haslam Park, whose northern edge it flanks. From here it is quickly in open country, setting off on a great westwards meander determined by the need to keep to the contour line and thus avoid expensive lock-building.

John Rennie's typical stone bridges mark the route, a hallmark of this canal but interestingly varied in their form. Swans and the occasional boat break up the rather monotonous flat landscape of the Fylde Plain, dominated in this area by power lines and pylons. The canal runs to the north of British Nuclear Fuels huge Springfields plant and then, near Salwick Hall, it turns north. Salwick Station is nearby, a possible starting point for those wishing to avoid Preston. Here the canal is in an attractive tree-lined cutting for a while, and then the open fields return, enlivened now by a distant view of purple hills to the east.

Passing under the M55 motorway, the canal then swings eastwards and comes to life for a while around Catforth, where there is small marina whose buildings are converted stables and canal cottages. The village lies to the north, typical for a canal whose builders seemed determined to create a route that avoided any significant human settlement.

From here the canal turns gradually northwards, as though having finally made up its mind to go to Lancaster after all. At the same time, the landscape begins to improve as the distant hills draw nearer, although still overshadowed by a flurry of

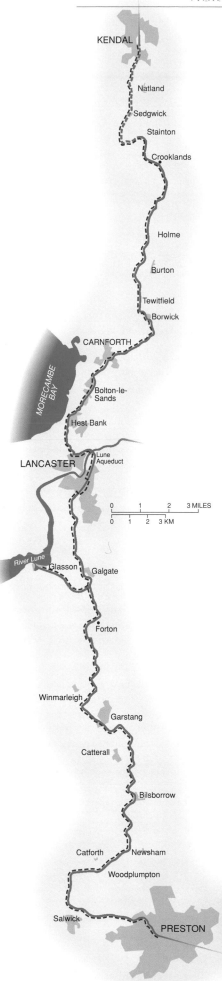

KENDAL
Natland
Sedgwick
Stainton
Crooklands
Holme
Burton
Tewitfield
Borwick
CARNFORTH
MORECAMBE BAY
Bolton-le-Sands
Hest Bank
LANCASTER
Lune Aqueduct

0   1   2   3 MILES
0   1   2   3 KM

River Lune
Glasson
Galgate
Forton
Winmarleigh
Garstang
Catterall
Bilsborrow
Catforth   Newsham
Woodplumpton
Salwick   PRESTON

pylons. To the east is Woodplumpton, where the church is an unusual blend of 15th-century Gothic and 18th-century classicism. A small aqueduct, one of a number along the route, carries the canal over the Barton Brook, and nearby is one of the two surviving swing bridges. The road crossing the canal on the bridge after the aqueduct leads eastwards to Newsham and then Barton, on the A6. Those wanting a shorter walk can take a bus from here to Preston, Garstang or Lancaster.

NEWSHAM TO GARSTANG
About 7 1/2 miles / 12km
OS Landranger 102
Start at Newsham Bridge
(grid reference 507 366)

The canal nows draws nearer to the railway and the A6. At Bilsborrow there is a busy leisure complex with caravans, a hotel and, on the canal, lines of moored boats to enliven the partially tree-lined towing path. Buses are also close at hand here.

A swing to the west takes the canal over the River Brock on a quite substantial high aqueduct, handsomely built in Rennie's familiar classical style, and then it runs briefly beside the A6 before turning away to join the railway and the M6 motorway. There is another aqueduct over the River Calder, and nearby is a feeder taking water from the river into the canal. The hills and moors of the Forest of Bowland now dominate the horizon to the east, a dramatic backdrop to a landscape that gets more exciting with every mile. The canal turns west again as it approaches Garstang, passing to the south of the ruins of 15th-century Greenhalgh Castle, a former Royalist stronghold that in its present rural setting among ambling cows looks more like some 18th-century folly. Curving round to enter the town, the canal passes under the B6430 and crosses the Wyre on another fine classical aqueduct with a broad 34ft span. Beyond is Garstang Basin, a pleasant spot flanked by well-converted old buildings, which include a Lancaster Canal Museum, and convenient for the centre of this old market town and the bus station, a short walk from Kepple Lane Bridge.

Near Garstang, a solitary boat plods northwards, with the Lakeland hills in the distance.

Garstang to Galgate

GARSTANG TO GALGATE
About 18 miles/29km
OS Landranger 102, 97
Start at Kepple Lane Bridge, Garstang
(grid reference 489 450)

The canal quickly leaves Garstang's outer fringes, passes under the A6 and then moves into an open landscape broken by patches of woodland and framed to the east by the Bowland Fells. At this point the canal passes a marina and, close by, the scant remains of the Garstang & Knott End Railway. An obscure branch line started in 1864 and not completed for over 30 years, it had, as a result, a rather chequered career. Its last surviving section, from Garstang to Pilling, lingered on, rather surprisingly, until 1965. In attractively rural surroundings the canal continues northwards in a series of gentle meanders. There is an increasingly dramatic contrast between the low-lying landscape to the west and the hills of the east. The canal's route, avoiding as is its wont, any significant habitation, is marked by a varied selection of Rennie stone bridges, set attractively in the increasingly green but remote countryside. One bridge, number 78, carries a road that

GUIDE BOX

PLACES TO VISIT
Carnworth Steamtown Railway Centre – working museum with impressive collection of British and Continental locomotives, including 'Flying Scotsman'.
Lancaster Lancaster Maritime Museum – 18th-century customs house features restored Long Room and Collectors Office; history of port and Morecambe Bay fishing industry.

CAR PARKING
Garstang; Lancaster; street parking in smaller villages and towns.

PUBLIC TRANSPORT
Train Station at Lancaster for Preston or Carnforth and Kendal (no intermediate stations). *Bus* Services between Preston, Galgate and Lancaster.

ACCOMMODATION
Hotels, guest houses etc Garstang, Galgate, Glasson, Lancaster.

TOURIST INFORMATION CENTRES
Lancaster 29 Castle Hill, Lancaster LA1 1YN (tel 01524 32878)

leads to the little village of Forton. Near the canal is Clifton Hill, a fine classical mansion designed in 1820 by a member of the Gillow family, famous as furniture makers and interior designers.

The canal swings east to meet the A6 again at Potter's Brook. Just beyond the road is the railway and the site of Bay Horse Station, the scene of a railway accident in 1848 caused by rival companies operating trains over the same track without adequate safeguards. Running parallel to the A6, the canal crosses the little River Cocker and continues northwards through attractive stretches of woodland. In the centre of one such stretch is the decorative bridge with its parapet of balusters that carries the drive to Ellel Grange, a Victorian mansion in the Italianate style formerly owned by another member of the Gillow family. This pleasantly wooded stretch takes the canal to the junction with the Glasson Dock Branch, marked by a handsome stone bridge that allowed horses to cross the canal without being detached from their barges. The bridge, the lock, the adjacent canal cottage make this a fine scene, additionally decorated with a signpost, an information board and some seats. For the Glasson Dock Branch, see opposite page.

Moored boats now flank the towing path, leading to Galgate Marina, and then another fine aqueduct takes the canal over the River Conder. Beyond this a bridge carries a minor road into the centre of Galgate, a little town once famous for its silk mills, and rather dominated by the railway and the main road. There are buses from here to Lancaster and Preston.

Woodland flanks the ornamental bridge that takes the drive to Ellel Grange over the canal.

A busy scene at Glasson Dock, with the elegant old canal hotel on the right.

THE GLASSON DOCK BRANCH

Inspired partly by the inadequacy of its links with the rest of the English canal network, the Lancaster Canal Company began to consider other trade outlets and connections at an early date. One of these was the branch canal to Glasson, authorised in 1793, but not actually built until 1825. Glasson Dock had been established in the 1780s to serve Lancaster, but it had had little use prior to the completion of the canal. When the canal was opened, there was also a kind of dock facility and transshipment system at Hest Bank, north of Lancaster, where it runs close to the sea, but this was closed by 1831.

The short 3-mile branch with its six locks ended in the huge basin built at Glasson, with its 14ft of depth protected by a sea lock able to handle vessels up to 98ft long, and allowing direct access into the Lune Estuary. Immediately successful, Glasson Dock made a massive contribution to the Canal Company's fortunes, with coal, timber, grain and slate being typical cargoes. This success continued until the 1840s when silting of the Lune Estuary combined with competition from other local ports, such as Preston, to bring about a slow decline. Nevertheless, the dock continued to operate and the opening in 1883 of a branch railway from Lancaster gave trade a boost. This finally closed in 1964, by which time the canal was largely moribund, and the basin was given over

to pleasure boats. Today, these are the major users of Glasson Dock, its basin and sea lock although small coasters carrying fertilisers and other local cargoes still visit the dock from time to time.

From the junction with the Lancaster Canal south of Galgate, you can walk down the branch to Glasson in under an hour. The branch follows the River Conder to its estuary through a low-lying landscape, with views of the sea beyond. Apart from the locks, there are also eight bridges to add interest, as well as the little Christ Church, built in 1840. The great expanse of the basin, with its variety of moored boats, is both exciting and unexpected, and beyond are the docks, old warehouses and cottages, and the grand Victoria Inn, whose formal façade hints at more prosperous times. Near the Inn is the stop for buses back to Lancaster, but those who prefer to walk can follow the walkway established along the trackbed of the old branch railway. This offers an interesting contrast to the canal, clinging as it does to the side of the broad Lune Estuary with fine views over the mudflats at low tide with their population of waders and seabirds. It crosses the Conder Estuary on the old girder bridge, passes Ashton Hall and the golf course, and then meets a minor road. Turn right here and follow the road to Aldcliffe. Turn left onto a larger road and then carry on until this rejoins the canal just south of Lancaster.

Galgate to Tewitfield

GALGATE TO LANCASTER
About 5 miles/8km
OS Landranger 102, 97
*Start at road bridge on western edge of Galgate
(grid reference 477 553)*

The canal continues towards Lancaster through a remote and increasingly hilly green landscape to the tall Brantbeck Bridge. This marks the start of the long cutting that takes the canal almost to Lancaster. Known as Deep Cutting for good reason, and 1½ miles in length, this is delightfully shaded throughout by tall trees that make it a splendid sight in autumn. Much of it is cut through solid rock, which adds excitement to the route. A cache of important Roman sculpture, found here when the canal was being dug, is now on show in Lancaster Museum. The cutting keeps the canal in its own private world, enabling it to make a rather secret approach to Lancaster without the more usual crawl through suburbia and industrial estates.

As the canal leaves the cutting, the town comes into view, dominated by its castle and the domed Ashton Memorial. There is

A major feature of the Lancaster Canal is John Rennie's great aqueduct over the River Lune.

a quick transition from country to town, with fields of cows giving way to houses, estates and waterside pubs. From Aldcliffe, road and canal run tightly together, passing under the railway. Just beyond the bridge are the remains of a boathouse built for the maintenance of the famous Lancaster Canal packetboats, which for years kept the railways at bay. The boats were hauled up to the first floor by pulleys. Nearby, where the towing path crosses to the eastern side, are a British Waterways maintenance yard, old wharves and a series of old canal buildings which now incorporate the Waterwitch pub. A footbridge gives access from the towing path. It was on the wharf near here that the last commercial freight carried on the Lancaster Canal, several tons of coal, was unloaded in 1947. The next bridge, Penny Street, numbered 99, is the best for access to the town centre, and the bus and railway stations.

Lancaster is a fine stone-built town with plenty to offer visitors. Particularly relevant is the Maritime Museum, housed in the 18th-century Custom House and overlooking the old quays on the River Lune. These quays underline Lancaster's former importance as a port, and made a major contribution to the canal's success in the early 19th century.

LANCASTER TO BOLTON-LE-SANDS
About 6 miles/10km
OS Landranger 97
*Start at Penny Street Bridge, Lancaster, by White Cross Mills
(grid reference 478 612)*

The canal's route through Lancaster gives a good impression of the town's history. Large stone mill buildings, derelict or converted to other uses, tower over the

towing path, along with the great mass of the Roman Catholic cathedral. The towing path crosses back to the western side, where it remains for the remainder of the walk. From the canal's elevated route well to the east of Lancaster there are fine views out across the town and its distinctive buildings. There is a notable lack of the industrial squalor that is a feature of so many urban canals, an attractive quality of the Lancaster Canal as a whole. As the surroundings become more suburban, back gardens become a feature and then, by the golf course, the canal swings sharply west to cross the A683 on a modern aqueduct. The sea, now visible ahead across the fields, becomes an increasingly dominant element of the western horizon. There are not many canals in Britain that offer such splendid sea views.

Running high above the surrounding landscape on an embankment now, the canal reaches the highlight of the walk, the great aqueduct across the River Lune. With its five magnificent classical arches in honey-coloured stone towering 60ft above the water, and its great length of 640ft, this is John Rennie's masterpiece, rivalled perhaps only by his Dundas Aqueduct on the Kennet & Avon Canal. Work started in January 1794 and the great bridge was finally opened in November 1797 after huge teams of men had toiled for 24 hours a day. The towing path crosses the aqueduct, with fine views along the Lune to Lancaster and Morecambe Bay, and eastwards to the Lakeland hills. To enjoy the aqueduct to the full, it is vital to see it from below and this is easily achieved via steps that lead steeply down from the aqueduct's eastern end to meet a footpath that passes beneath one of the arches. This, following a former railway track beside the Lune, goes westwards to Lancaster and eastwards to Halton.

There is a small basin at the western end of the aqueduct and then the canal turns sharply west again to flank Lancaster's northern suburbs before wandering though farmland dominated by the A6 and the West Coast railway line. Next come the outskirts of Hest Bank, the canal's closest point to the sea, and the site of a port and transshipment basin between canal and sea. From here the canal runs parallel to the sea for some miles, in an unusual setting of bungalows and seaside villas. Its elevated route to the east of most of the houses is surprisingly private. There is another swing bridge, number 120, and then the canal runs straight through Bolton-le-Sands. Here, the Packet Boat Hotel is a reminder of the high-speed passenger services that used to operate on the canal before the coming of

the railways. Bolton-le-Sands makes a convenient break point, with access to buses back to Lancaster or on to Carnforth railway station or Kendal.

BOLTON-LE-SANDS TO TEWITFIELD

About 6 miles / 10km
OS Landranger 97
*Start at the bridge taking minor road north
(grid reference 484 681)*

Beyond the village, the still elevated canal and A6 run side by side, and there are fine views out over the tidal marshland and across Morecambe Bay towards Grange-over-Sands and the Cumbrian coast. The dominant hill to the north is Warton Crag, crowned by a prehistoric settlement.

The next town is Carnforth, easily accessible from the canal, which passes to its east. Always a railway and ironfounders' town and still the site of a major railway junction, Carnforth maintains its link with history with the massive Steamtown railway preservation centre, the home of many famous locomotives. There are trains back to Lancaster for those wanting a shorter walk and the wait on the platform offers an opportunity to look at the location where *Brief Encounter* was filmed. After Carnforth the canal swings eastwards and approaches the M6, a noisy and

At Tewitfield the navigable section of the canal ends, cut by a road embankment. The derelict flight of locks raises the canal towards Kendal.

distracting presence for some miles from here. An access link and the motorway cross the canal, and then it continues into quieter, hilly country north of Over Kellet. Swinging north and crossing over the small River Keer Aqueduct and then under a railway, the canal runs through wooded hills to Borwick, passing on the way one of the many quarries that used to supply one of its important bulk cargoes in the 19th century.

Borwick, an attractive stone village, is easily explored from the canal. At its heart is Elizabethan Borwick Hall, richly gabled and battlemented, and built round an older pele tower. Swinging west, the canal comes quickly to Tewitfield, and the new basin that marks the limit of navigation. Moored boats and a pub make this an attractive spot, but it is hard to escape the feeling that the closure of the canal northwards from here by the replacement of the bridge carrying the A6070 with a solid embankment was a completely unnecessary act of vandalism by the Department of Transport. Across the road, the canal, now derelict, continues up the flight of cascaded locks. There is a bus service from here back to Lancaster.

Tewitfield to Kendal

TEWITFIELD TO STAINTON
About 9 miles/14km
OS Landranger 97
*Start at embankment carrying A6070 across
canal just to the west of Tewitfield Basin
(grid reference 519 737)*

Beyond Tewitfield are the remains of the
eight locks that raised the canal 76ft, the
only locks on the whole length of the
Lancaster Canal, apart from those on the
Glasson Branch. Gateless but still in good
condition, these are a sad sight, but the
stone chambers are enjoyed by fishermen.
The towing path, grassy but well
maintained, continues up beside the
flight, but any sense of peace is destroyed by
the M6, which runs immediately parallel to
the canal. Shortly after the top lock, the
motorway crosses the canal, again on a solid
embankment pierced by just a culvert.
Leave the towing path and walk up the
access track that joins a minor road at the
top, turn left onto the bridge across the
motorway and then rejoin the towing path.

The canal now moves away from the
motorway a bit, but its presence continues
to dominate the environment for some

miles. Hills and woods surround the canal
in an increasingly rugged landscape. Half
hidden in the hills to the west are the
villages of Yealand Redmayne and Yealand
Conyers, approached by the minor road
that you used to cross the M6. Both are
pretty hillside villages, the latter with a
17th-century meeting house and two
Victorian churches. Just to the west is
Leighton Hall, an extravagantly gothicised
18th-century mansion housing a range of
interesting collections, and set in a splendid
garden and park.

The canal runs close to but above the
railway for a while, then turns eastwards
towards Burton, crossing an aqueduct over
a minor road. Increasingly taken over by
water plants and overhung by trees, the
shallow canal still enjoys clear water as it
becomes steadily more river-like. After
another aqueduct over a road the canal
reaches Holme, where an old mill stands
complete with its workers' cottages. A
sequence of bridges, eight in a mile, crosses
the canal beneath the steep slopes of
Clawthorpe and Holmepark Fells. The
effects are picturesque, with the bridges set
against the powerful landscape of broken

fields and dramatic hills. North of Holme,
the canal is crossed again by the M6, again
without a bridge. Leave the towing path
and walk along the edge of the field that
flanks the motorway until the path meets a
minor road. Turn right onto the bridge
across the motorway and keep on until the
road crosses the canal. Rejoin the towing
path by Duke's Bridge, enjoying the
towering limestone slopes of Farleton Fell
ahead. Look out for some ruined stables
and a former packet boat staging house. A
series of remote bridges then leads to
another main road crossing, with the canal
forced into a culvert. The towing path
continues under the road. Almost
immediately, there is a further culvert
under a main road. Leave the towing path,
walk along the main road under the
motorway and then rejoin the towing path
on the other side. Thankfully, this is the end
of the M6, which sweeps away to the east
after this point.

Next comes the Crooklands feeder,
which carries water into the canal from the
distant Killington Reservoir, via the Peasey
Beck. The coalyard at Crooklands is a
reminder of the many coke ovens that used
to operate here, keeping the canal wharf
busy in the last century. The canal's route is
now remote and attractive as far as
Stainton. It crosses Stainton Beck on an
aqueduct and then, without warning,
comes to a dead end beneath a bridge just
to the east of Sellet Hall. On one side of
the bridge there is a canal, albeit a shallow
and overgrown one, and on the other there
is just a grassy field.

*Near Holme the canal is still in water, but late
summer weeds have taken over.*

STAINTON TO KENDAL
About 6 miles/10km
OS Landranger 97
Start at road bridge near Sellet Hall
(grid reference 521 855)

From Stainton to Kendal the canal has disappeared, leaving sometimes a shallow depression across the fields, and sometimes nothing at all. However, the towing path continues as a rural footpath, a right of way in the care of Cumbria County Council, and it is easy to follow.

The canal has been obliterated by the A590 crossing, but the path can be picked up again the other side of the bridge that carries this over a minor road. It now leads directly to the eastern portal of Hincaster tunnel, a romantic stone archway half hidden by overgrowth. The tunnel, 378yds long, has no towing path, so walkers should follow the well-marked path over the top, used originally by the towing horses, passing under the railway and two other small bridges on the way. The western portal straddles the still muddy and reed-filled canal bed. The path now goes along beside a minor road for a while, and then it is cut again by the A590. Keep on the minor road and cross the A590, and keep an eye out for a public footpath sign by a

stile that also carries a Lancaster Canal mark. Follow this across the fields and up the slope to a canal bridge in the middle of nowhere. This bridge, crossing nothing, is like some 18th-century garden folly, and from it there are splendid views westwards over the winding River Kent and the Levens deer park and towards Levens Hall, against the backdrop of Whitbarrow.

Closer to hand, and also beside the Kent, is Sedgwick House, which sets the tone for the attractive village of Sedgwick. The canal used to cut through the heart of the village on a high embankment. This survives, carrying the towing path, along with a fine stone aqueduct, buttressed like a fortress. Steps lead down into the village. From Sedgwick the path continues, following the traces of the canal's route high on the side of the Kent Valley, and looking out across woodland to Sizergh Castle. There are more isolated bridges over nothing, and increasingly these, and the scant remains of the canal, make the whole thing seem more like remains from the Roman era than something that was in use within living memory. It is very hard to believe that boats travelled along here just over 50 years ago.

West of Natland, a big side cutting carried the canal in a curve across the

The last few miles of the Lancaster Canal have been infilled, sometimes leaving bridges stranded in the middle of fields. This one is near Natland, on the approach to Kendal.

fields, and this can be traced, culminating as it does in another surviving bridge. From here the path continues, but the traces of the canal itself become less and less distinct as it approaches the outskirts of Kendal.

Lines of trees determine the route which is, in fact, well marked and easy to follow past gardens, factories and car parks. The path crosses the A65, and then comes to Changeline Bridge, the last one on the canal, and so named because at this point the towing path crossed to the eastern side for the last $^1/_2$ mile to Canal Head and the terminus. Originally there was a basin below Kendal Castle, but this has long gone, and it all rather peters out.

The centre of Kendal is easily reached to the west, and not far away are buses back to Tewitfield and Lancaster. Kendal still has a railway station, on the Windermere branch from Oxenholme, and this offers a more interesting way back, but not for those who left their cars at Tewitfield, as there are no stations between Oxenholme and Lancaster.

Wales

The Wye Valley Walk   150 – 159

The Montgomery Canal   160 – 163

The Swansea and Neath Canals   164 – 167

The Morfa Mawddach Trail   168 – 169

The Morfa Mawddach Trail, west of Penmaenpool

The Wye Valley Walk

CHEPSTOW TO RHAYADER
113 MILES/181KM

THE River Wye has to be one of the loveliest rivers in Britain. It is unspoilt and unpolluted, and not surprisingly supports a wide range of wildlife, including salmon and brown trout, otters, kingfishers and flycatchers. Consequently, there are several nature reserves in the valley and much of it has been designated a Site of Special Scientific Interest.

The route starts at Chepstow and finishes at Rhayader, so it is partly in Wales and partly in the English Marches. The lower reaches, where an upward land movement has given rise to deeply incised meanders and gorges, are quite dramatic. In Herefordshire, by contrast, the Walk passes through gentle pastures and orchards, climbing triumphantly to Merbach Ridge before descending to Hay-on-Wye. From here upstream the river is at its best, young and fresh, as the waters cascade over innumerable cataracts. It makes for great walking.

Chepstow to Monmouth

CHEPSTOW TO TINTERN
About 5 miles/8km
OS Landranger 162 or
Outdoor Leisure 14
Start at Chepstow Castle
(grid reference 533 938)

Chepstow's formidable Norman castle stands above the tidal flow of the Wye and is a very appealing attraction, but the town too has a rich history and a nice bustling feel to it. It is ideal for a short stay and makes a good starting point for the walk.

Walk the medieval walls from the Castle up the Dell to Welsh Street, then turn right for a road walk to a school and leisure centre. Here cut right to Alcove Wood. The path leads through the Piercefield estate, woodland set out for local notable Valentine Morris in the 18th century. It is best known now for its nearby racecourse.

After about 1 mile, you catch your first glimpse of the Wye at the foot of Piercefield Cliffs, with the church at Lancaut opposite. You also pass the Giant's Cave, a curious small cavern which is said to have been frequented by all manner of mystical folk. The walk dips beneath Lover's Leap, through thickly set natural woodland, to a collection of beeches at the A466.

Cross here and walk up an access track to a car park. There is a choice of direction at this point. You can make your way left up an easier graded path to the summit of the Wynd Cliff, or you can climb the hard way up the 365 Steps, first set down in 1828, but restored several times since.

Proceed to the Eagle's Nest, where at 700ft the views down the Wye are exquisite. The way to Tintern is gentler, through Minepit and Black Cliff Woods to a long thin enclosure, then following a packhorse route through Limekiln Wood to Tintern Abbey. The ruins are spectacular. No wonder that they have inspired poet and painter alike, including the literary giant Wordsworth and the landscape painter JMW Turner.

Tintern is a useful cut-off point, with buses on Mondays to Saturdays returning to Chepstow or onward to Monmouth.

TINTERN TO MONMOUTH
About 11 miles/18km
OS Landranger 162 or
Outdoor Leisure 14
Start at Tintern Abbey
(grid reference 533 001)

Go right along the main street, and opposite the Wye Valley Hotel bear right to pass between dwellings to Tintern parish church, tucked away in an old quarter. The path nears the Wye for the first time, leading to an embankment of the Chepstow-to-Monmouth railway, built in 1876. Your way is ahead, by the restored station, to Brockweir Bridge, at one time a quayside for goods which were taken by wagon into the Forest of Dean or transferred to smaller vessels and carried further upstream.

Cross the A466 and climb through Coed Beddick Wood to Botany Bay, one of the many names around Tintern that reflect a time when trading with the New World brought a variety of cargoes upriver by way of Bristol. You reach a road by a large dwelling only to leave it again by a camping pitch. Drop down to a road, then climb through forestry again to the Whitestone picnic area (toilets and a playground).

Continue through what seems to be miles of larch and spruce above Cleddon Shoots nature reserve. Emerge by Orchard Cottage, where you follow a route to Pen-y-fan. You are likely to see an array of wild flowers here, possibly including the very rare Tintern Spurge. Pen-y-fan is a maze of lanes, so be watchful for waymarks. Head back towards the Wye at Whitebrook, at one time known for its mills, where you join the railway trackbed to the Boat Inn, a very traditional pub which is not easy to find by road, despite Redbrook village being just across the river. Cross the river on the footbridge by the old rail bridge.

In Redbrook go left to the riverbank for the final 2- to 3-mile stretch of easy walking into Monmouth. Exit at the Wye Bridge, something of a shock after the tranquillity of miles of traffic-free rambling.

Monmouth grew up as a bridging point at the confluence of the Wye and Monnow. The ruins of the Norman castle still remain, but the masterpiece of the town has to be the Monnow Bridge, the only surviving medieval fortified gatehouse bridge in Wales. King Henry V was born at Monmouth and his statue is in Agincourt Square, near to another dedicated to Charles Rolls of Rolls Royce fame. Also associated with the town is Geoffrey of Monmouth, a 12th-century scribe who penned much about king and court.

WALKING GUIDES
The Wye Valley Walk Guide Book is the excellent official guide book produced by the sponsoring authorities. It provides a section by section introduction to the walk from Chepstow to Rhayader and replaces the map pack and set of leaflets that has been available up to now. The book is sold at local tourist information centres and bookshops in the area. A very useful accommodation and access guide is also available for the entire route, giving details of public transport, luggage-ahead services and accommodation in the towns and villages along the route.
Discover The Wye Valley By Bus is another excellent booklet (published by the Wye Valley Area of Outstanding Natural Beauty) available locally at a small charge.

OS MAPS
Landranger 147, 148, 149, 161, 162. Outdoor Leisure 14 (Wye Valley and Forest of Dean) and 13 (Brecon Beacons East) cover some parts of the route.

LINKS
The walk crosses Offa's Dyke at Monmouth and Hay-on-Wye, offering scope for a long circular walk. It also meets Marches Way, an unofficial long distance path between Chester and Cardiff at Hereford.

THE FOREST OF DEAN

The Forest of Dean is much underrated. Not only are there miles of ancient and modern forests laced with footpaths, but it also has many remnants of an industrial past, best discovered at The Dean Heritage Centre. There are also iron mines at Clearwell, the sculpture trail at Cannop, a steam railway at Parkend. Best of all are the miles of off-road cycling routes.

GUIDE BOX

PLACES TO VISIT
Chepstow Castle – one of the earliest stone-built castles in the country. Local history museum has a collection of paintings of the Wye Valley and displays on Chepstow's maritime heritage. 18th-century Gwy House. Stuart Crystal Glass Studios.
Tintern Ruins of the Cistercian abbey in magnificent setting; restored abbey mill. Trails in the Angiddy Valley exhibit earlier iron works. Parva Farm vineyard.
Monmouth medieval fortified Monnow Bridge. Norman castle. Castle & Regimental Museum. Nelson Museum.

CAR PARKING
Chepstow; Wyndcliff; Tintern Station; Monmouth.

PUBLIC TRANSPORT
Train Station at Chepstow.
Bus Between Chepstow and Monmouth Monday to Saturdays. Between Monmouth and Ross-on-Wye daily (Sundays in summer only).

ACCOMMODATION
Hotels, guest houses etc Chepstow, Tintern, Monmouth.
Camping Near Botany Bay.

TOURIST INFORMATION CENTRES
Chepstow Castle Car Park, Bridge Street, Chepstow, Monmouthshire NP6 5EY (tel 01291 623772)
Monmouth Shire Hall, Agincourt Square, Monmouth NP5 3DY (tel 01600 713899)

Tintern, nestled in the valley, was once a hive of industrial activity. The abbey ruins are simply spectacular.

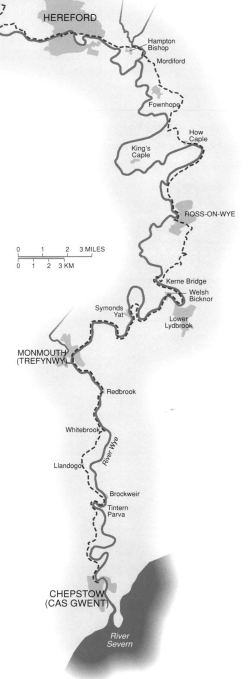

Monmouth to Ross-on-Wye

MONMOUTH TO KERNE BRIDGE
About 13 miles/21km
OS Landranger 162 or
Outdoor Leisure 142
Start at Wye Bridge, Monmouth
(grid reference 513 128)

From the Wye Bridge walk by a boathouse and past the lonely church at Dixton through meadows to the parkland of Wyastone Leys, thus passing imperceptibly into England. This is one of the loveliest and also the most ecologically sensitive parts of the valley. The river has cut its way between Seven Sisters Rock and the Biblins above, and Far Harkening Rock and The Slaughter on the opposite side.

Much of the area is designated part of the Upper Wye Gorge Site of Special Scientific Interest, and Lady Park Wood is a nature reserve which has been left unmanaged for over 40 years. The canopy of oak, beech, lime and sometimes whitebeam trees to be found in the valley makes this all the more splendid. In the late spring and summer months, here, as elsewhere, you will see dragonflies and damselflies in abundance.

There are also many historic sites in the vicinity, notably King Arthur's and Merlin's caves which, despite the allusions to Arthurian legend, are thought to date from the Bronze Age. The artefacts found in early excavations are now displayed in Hereford Museum.

At the Biblins, cross the suspension bridge to join the railway trackbed to walk into Symond's Yat East. At the Saracen's Head you can hail the ancient hand-pulled rope ferry across the Wye to Symond's Yat West, or you can just sit and watch the river boats go by.

Continue through Symond's Yat East to follow a track which skirts Huntsham Hill and then runs beneath Coldwell Rocks, where peregrine falcons nest. The path joins the old railway for a mile again and then leaves it to follow the riverbank to a bridge across the Wye at Lydbrook.

Proceed upstream beneath Welsh Bicknor, where there's a pretty church and old rectory that is now a youth hostel. The riverbank leads to Kerne Bridge, which dates from the 1820s. It replaced a ferry which is known to have operated for centuries, certainly from the days of King Henry IV. Cross on the bridge.

There is a good bus service between Ross-on-Wye and Kerne Bridge, including a Sunday service in summer.

GUIDE BOX

PLACES TO VISIT
Symond's Yat Boat trips and other attractions, mainly based on the west side; Wye Valley Open Farm is a few minutes' from the Walk; Yat Rock is also a marvellous viewpoint. The major problem with Symond's Yat is traffic, so it is not a good place to park.
Goodrich Ancient red sandstone castle on a bluff a mile or so from the river near Kerne Bridge – dates from the 12th century, an important stronghold in the English Civil War.
Ross-on-Wye **House of** 17th-century town planner John Kyrle, 'Man of Ross' in High Street; also 'The Prospect', the walled garden he laid out. Church has fine sculptured tombs.

CAR PARKING
Monmouth (Wye Bridge); Symond's Yat West; Kerne Bridge; Ross-on-Wye (near Wilton Bridge).

PUBLIC TRANSPORT
Bus Daily service between Monmouth, Kerne Bridge and Ross-on-Wye (Sunday service summer only).

ACCOMMODATION
Hotels, guest houses etc Symond's Yat, Kerne Bridge, Ross-on-Wye.
Youth hostel Welsh Bicknor.

TOURIST INFORMATION CENTRE
Monmouth Shire Hall, Agincourt Square, Monmouth NP5 3DY (tel 01600 713899)
Ross-on-Wye **The Swan,** Edde Cross Street, Ross-on-Wye, Herefordshire HR9 7BZ (tel 01989 562768)

The steep gorge near Symond's Yat is very appealing at all seasons.

KERNE BRIDGE TO ROSS-ON-WYE
About 5 miles / 8km
OS Landranger 162
Start at Kerne Bridge
(grid reference 582 188)

From Kerne Bridge turn right to pass an inn and opposite the car park go left but then immediately left to climb the wooded Leys Hill. The route now takes to higher ground and the views across the Wye and Herefordshire are exceptional.

Make a descent towards Walford but before the village follow the path as it sweeps away to Bull's Hill, where you might catch sight of a half-timbered house, Upper Wythall, which dates from the early 16th and 17th centuries, and to Howle Hill. The Walk cuts left down to Coughton across a deep valley that was most probably

The walk crosses Kerne Bridge, which in the 1820s replaced a centuries-old ferry.

a loop in the Wye at one time. Rise out of the valley to the ancient hillfort on Chase Hill, pass Hill Farm and descend from Penyard Hill to Alton Court and Ross-on-Wye. The waymarks lead to Wilton Bridge car park.

Beautifully situated on the Wye, Ross is a favourite with the visitor. The town has been shaped by 17th-century town planner John Kyrle, known as the Man of Ross. The magnificent 14th-century spire of the church is a welcoming landmark and the interior is rich in local history. Most people gravitate towards the Market Place, where the sandstone market hall dating from the reign of King Charles II stands proudly and people set out stalls several days a week.

A CHURCH TRAIL

There are eight churches between Goodrich and Fownhope, each offering an insight into the local community it serves. St Giles Church at Goodrich, for example, stands on high ground above the village, dating mainly from the 13th and 14th centuries. Walford is also of Norman origin with fine interior decorations. All the other churches, including Ross-on-Wye, Foy, Brampton Abbots, Brockhampton, How Caple and Fownhope, are situated on or near the walk. Collectively they represent a fine array of medieval architecture within a day or two's walking. The exception is All Saints at Brockhampton, which has been described by art historian Nikolaus Pevsner as 'one of the most convincing and most impressive churches of its date in any country'. It was built in the early years of the 20th century.

Ross-on-Wye to Hereford

ROSS-ON-WYE TO FOWNHOPE
About 11 miles/18km
OS Landranger 162, 149
*Start at car park near Wilton Bridge
(grid reference 592 239)*

From the car park near Wilton Bridge walk through the underpass to the riverside, passing the Anchor Inn and going by the Rowing Club and under the main A40 road. You reach the trackbed of the Hereford-to-Gloucester Railway, which you follow before descending once more to walk through arable fields to a green track, sometimes overgrown, at Hole-in-the Wall. Across the river is Foy Church, which contains many fine monuments including several from the 13th century. It is possible to cross a suspension bridge here, first built in 1876, for a ½-mile detour to visit the church.

Otherwise walk along the road, past buildings now used for activity holidays, and within 1 mile revert to a riverside path. On the hillside to the right is How Caple Church, and soon there is a group of houses that form part of this scattered hamlet. Cross the road and continue through fields to Totnor, at one time a centre for milling, and then follow the road until you come to a junction at Brockhampton.

Bear left along a green lane through fields to Ladyridge and Caplor Hill. Cross the road to walk through the scant remains of Caplor Camp, an Iron Age hillfort, then to Caplor Farm near the B4224. The Walk regains a path which rises to Paget Wood nature reserve and the scattered settlement of Common Hill, high above Fownhope. In this area you will pass through a number of orchards, many of which bear cider apples. Cider as a beverage has been made in the area since Roman times, and the art of traditional cider making is kept alive by a small number of farms and cideries to be found in the county.

For those detouring to Fownhope it is best to cut left here to descend to a crossroads in the village, a walk which passes between orchards with views down to the church. To stay on the Walk, continue along tracks to the Woolhope Road near Cherry Hill. Fownhope is reasonably well served by bus from Hereford. It has shops and inns. There are also several local walks from the village to the river and into the Woolhope Dome.

The isolated church of Foy is of medieval origin.

GUIDE BOX

PLACES TO VISIT
Foy Church with 17th-century glass and good monuments.
Fownhope Large church with excellent Norman tympanum. Local footpaths are publicised in a booklet available at the village store.
How Caple Delightful church. How Caple Court – sunken Florentine and Edwardian terraced gardens.
Brockhampton 1902 church by Lethaby with central tower and thatched roof.
Hereford Cathedral – of Norman foundation with two particular treasures: the Mappa Mundi map of the world dated 1300 and the chained library. Other attractions include the City Museum & Art Gallery (pavement from Roman town of Magni, Kenchester), Old House Museum, Herefordshire Waterworks Museum, Cider Museum, Bulmer Railway Centre.

CAR PARKING
Ross-on-Wye (near Wilton Bridge); Caplor Wood; Mordiford; Hereford (those south of the river are best for the walker).

PUBLIC TRANSPORT
Train Station at Hereford.
Bus Services to Fownhope and Mordiford Monday to Saturday.

ACCOMMODATION
Hotels, guest houses etc Ross-on-Wye, Brockhampton, Fownhope, Mordiford, Hereford.

TOURIST INFORMATION CENTRES
Ross-on-Wye **The Swan**, Edde Cross Street, Ross-on-Wye, Herefordshire HR9 7BZ (tel 01989 562768)
Hereford 1 King Street, Hereford HR4 9BW (tel 01432 268430)

FOWNHOPE TO HEREFORD
About 7 miles/11km
OS Landranger 149
Start at the Green Man Inn, Fownhope
(grid reference 577 344)

From the Green Man in Fownhope go left to the crossroads and turn right along the Woolhope Road. In ½ mile you meet the Wye Valley Walk. Go left by Nupend Farm and proceed through gentle pastures and orchards, across a section of the Woolhope Dome to a recently restored mill on the edge of Mordiford.

Leave the village over the ancient Mordiford bridge, some sections of which are said to date back centuries. Bear right along the levee to Hampton Bishop, a collection of half-timbered houses nestled around the medieval parish church. Walk through the village to join a path which crosses the Hereford road near the Bunch of Carrots pub. Proceed on another levee, known as the Stanx to the outskirts of Hereford, where you rejoin the B4224.

After the railway bridge, cut left to walk through an old part of town to the General Hospital and Castle Green. Go left over the Victoria Bridge to the Bishop's Meadow. Turn right for the old Wye Bridge. Cross the bridge to the city centre.

Hereford Cathedral is home to the Mappa Mundi exhibition, which should on no account be missed. Walk down the narrow Capuchin Lane to High Town through an old quarter of the city. The Victorian Buttermarket is still very traditional and across High Town you will see the half-timbered Old House, a Jacobean building par excellence.

The ancient bridge at Mordiford spans the River Lugg.

WOOLHOPE DOME

The intricate topography of the area features an eroded dome with an upwards thrust of older Silurian limestone and shales which have been exposed by thousands of years of weathering. A group of early naturalists and archaeologists, who have written much about the Wye Valley, were so impressed by this part that they named their association The Woolhope Society. Try the Mordiford Loop which passes several old quarries; it is a geologist's paradise. At nearby Putley and Much Marcle there is 'The Big Apple', an annual event that celebrates the importance of apple orchards in the area. Also near by is Haugh Wood, which offers several walks through woodlands.

Hereford to Hay-on-Wye

HEREFORD TO BREDWARDINE
About 14 miles/22km
OS Landranger 149
Start at Old Wye Bridge, Hereford
(grid reference 508 396)

Leave the city over the old bridge to follow a town path which runs beneath the new Wye Bridge to a railway bridge. Cross over here to regain the riverside path. On your right you will see the Herefordshire Waterworks Museum.

Walk through rich riverside pastures for over 1 mile up to Lower Breinton, where there is a pretty rural church and earthworks that date from the 12th century. Look for a path which cuts left through an orchard and then runs across fields to the hamlet of Upper Breinton. The Walk passes by Manor House Farm and crosses fields to Breinton Common. Go right along the lane to Sugwas Pool.

Turn left along the A438 road by the Kite's Nest public house. Turn off right for a 2-mile section of road-walking through Kenchester and Bishopstone to the Garnons estate, beautiful parkland set out by the landscape genius, Humphry Repton. Kenchester was once a Roman town known as Magnis. Excavations have revealed pavements and other artefacts, some of which are displayed at Hereford Museum. (It is unfortunately not possible to visit the site.)

At Garnons cross the A438 again and then go next left between the half-timbered dwellings that make up Byford. Bear right after the church along a bridleway which runs through orchards that serve the world's largest cider maker, HP Bulmer. This leads to one of the loveliest corners of the county, Monnington Court and Church. The church contains much fine woodwork which is almost certainly the work of John Abel, carpenter royal to King Charles I. The 17th-century court is simply charming and it incorporates parts which date back to the 13th century. It is associated with the Welsh leader, Owain Glyndwr, who is said to have hidden here on more than one occasion. It is not open to the public but you pass it en route to Monnington Walk, a bridleway lined with Scots pine and yews.

At Brobury Scar are Brobury Gardens, which stretch down to the Wye. There is also a gallery here. Go left and left again along roads which lead to the handsome Bredwardine Bridge. On the left stands Bredwardine's gem of a Norman church, the resting place of parson and diarist Francis Kilvert. The road leads to the Red Lion at the centre of the village.

Near Bishopstone the walk passes the Garnons estate, one of many splendid parklands in Herefordshire laid out by Humphry Repton. The castellated house was built by W Atkinson before 1828, but was much altered in the early 1900s.

BREDWARDINE TO HAY-ON-WYE

About 9 miles/14km
OS Landranger 148
Start at the Red Lion, Bredwardine
(grid reference 331 445)

Merbach Hill, standing at 1040ft, is the high point of the route in England. Leave the Red Lion on the road which climbs steeply to Arthur's Stone. Aim for a road off to the right to Woolla Farm. You soon reach a hilltop clothed in bracken, where the views are magnificent. The path off the hillside reaches a lane which leads to the B4352. Pass near Clock Mills and Castleton farmsteads before you see the old trackbed of the Golden Valley Railway, a no-hope Victorian enterprise that ran from Pontrilas Junction to Hay-on-Wye until its closure in 1950.

At the road go left for Priory Wood, named after a Cluniac monastery. Be careful here for the Walk cuts along several lanes and paths in the village. Leave along a path by a group of houses to skirt Priory Farm. At the next road, signs guide you through fields to the Hardwicke Brook. Cross the next road by a bungalow and proceed ahead to the Dulais Brook to re-enter Wales and Hay-on-Wye. The Walk leads to the left of a house and descends to a bridge and a narrow thoroughfare. Turn left at the Black Lion for Oxford Road.

Until a couple of decades ago Hay-on-Wye was a distinctly Welsh borderland town which came to life only on Thursdays with the arrival of the market. Its fortunes have changed, and it now flourishes as the capital of secondhand books; there are dozens of shops. There is

Bredwardine Church, where diarist Francis Kilvert was once parson.

also an excellent annual literary festival. The town remains as something of a cross-roads for walkers, for Offa's Dyke Path also passes through the town, offering a passage across the Black Mountains.

FRANCIS KILVERT

Victorian parson, Francis Kilvert, lived in the rectory by Bredwardine Church. His diaries reflect life in these parts during the last century and are now considered to be a major literary work. Kilvert also lived at Clyro, near Hay-on-Wye, and is said to have loathed what could be best described as tourists. He lies beneath a marble cross in the churchyard.

Hay-on-Wye to Rhayader

HAY-ON-WYE TO BOUGHROOD
About 9 miles/14km
OS Landranger 161 or
Outdoor Leisure 161
Start at Oxford Road car park, Hay-on-Wye
(grid reference 230 423)

The route out of Hay-on-Wye is easy enough, along the B4351 out of town, then across fields by Wyecliff and along the river edge to the A438 road for a walk along the verge to the village of Llowes. Here turn right opposite the Radnorshire Arms to walk through the village to Brynyrhydd Common, high above the floodplain, and then through Brynyrhydd Farm. A lane leads down to the A438. Walk towards Glasbury on the opposite verge, passing a turn for Maesyronnen before reaching a kissing gate on the left and a path to the riverside. This soon draws away from the river to a sewerage works and into Glasbury by the bridge.

Cross the main road, and the car park, to walk through Glasbury village, past the Maesllwch Arms and other impressive houses. Once out of the village go left along a track which meets the river, then heads west by Glasbury Farm. At the fork keep right to pass Pwll-y-Baw to the B4350. Proceed to Boughrood Brest, where a track on the left leaves the common for the floodmeadows.

Enter a narrow wood above the Wye, following the waymarks down to the riverside and to the B4350 road. Turn left to cross the Old Moat Lane to Three Cocks Junction railway line and go over Boughrood Bridge.

A short distance southeast of Boughrood Bridge is the village of Llyswen, which, like so many Wye Valley villages, was visited by the Romantic poets Shelley and Wordsworth. There are three pubs, a pottery and a shop.

BOUGHROOD TO BUILTH WELLS
About 13 miles/21km
OS Landranger 147
Start at Boughrood Bridge
(grid reference 129 385)

After Boughrood Bridge go right down the lane to pass The Shrubbery and a water

GUIDE BOX

PLACES TO VISIT
Builth Wells 11th-century castle ruins. Mid-July pageant at start of Royal Welsh Show.
Rhayader Centre for walking, pony trekking, mountain biking, angling.

CAR PARKING
Hay-on-Wye (Oxford Road); Glasbury; Broughrood; Erwood Old Station; Builth Wells (The Groe); Rhayader.

PUBLIC TRANSPORT
Train The Heart of Wales line serves Builth Road and Llandrindod Wells daily (but Sundays during summer only). Llandrindod Wells is better for bus connections.
Bus Services Mondays to Saturdays between Llandrindod Wells, Builth Wells, Erwood and Boughrood; also from Newbridge to Builth Wells, Rhayader or Llandrindod Wells.

ACCOMMODATION
Hotels, guest houses, etc Hay-on-Wye, Builth Wells, Rhayader.
Camping Near Newbridge, on east bank near Llanwrthwl, Rhayader.

TOURIST INFORMATION CENTRES
Builth Wells The Groe Car Park, Builth Wells, Powys LD2 3BT (tel 01982 553307)
Rhayader Leisure Centre, North Street, Rhayader, Powys LD6 5BU (tel 01597 810591)

treatment works. The path follows the river through to Trericket mill, passing by a forlorn graveyard and what was an old chapel belonging to Llangoed Hall, across the fields. Shown on earlier maps as Llangoed Castle, Llangoed Hall is a 20th-century mansion designed by Clough Williams-Ellis, better known for his work at Portmeirion.

On reaching the confluence of the Sgithwen Brook, keep left up the tributary to the A470 road. Cross the elaborately engineered Llanstephan suspension bridge, then continue along the road to a T-junction just beyond the railway trackbed. Go left and follow this road (there is a short detour to avoid a little road walking in about 600yds) for Erwood old railway station, which is now a car park. Once through, take a path leading to Bridge Cottage, where you go right over Erwood Bridge, cross the A470 and keep ahead along a road opposite.

The Walk now takes to hill country and there is a fair climb to Twmpath Common. Here you bear right as signposted across the common. The path runs beneath pockets of woodland to join an old track which fords the Fernant Brook. Go left on the road for a climb up Little Hill. This is something of an understatement, but the view down valley is ample reward. Follow the lane ahead for 1 mile, then look for a turn to Old Bedw Farm. This bends left but the Walk keeps ahead through a barred gate onto a common. The track climbs up

The unpolluted waters of the Wye, seen here near Llyswen, support a rich and varied wildlife and are much beloved by fishermen.

to a junction, where you bear right as signposted. It feels quite remote, with not a dwelling in sight.

The path reaches walling and fencing, then descends to join a track that leads down to a junction at Bedw Fach. The views across to Builth Wells are good from here and the route changes character once more, now following lanes and tracks rich in plantlife that on warm summer days is attractive to butterflies. Cross the road and follow the bridleway down to a junction where you keep left. This exits at a lane where you go immediately right, down a sunken track of antiquity, which brings you to Dolfach Cottage and the River Duhonw, one of the quietest spots on earth.

Climb out of the valley and keep ahead for Builth, passing by a few dwellings. Turn right along Castle Road, where on the left you will catch a glimpse of the earthworks of Builth Castle. Go left at the main road to enter Builth Wells.

At one time Builth was renowned as a health spa, alongside Llangammarch and Llanwrtyd Wells, but it has since reverted to being a market town, known primarily as the home of the Royal Welsh Show. The nucleus of the medieval town is around the 12th-century castle but the High Street is decidedly Victorian and on market days bustles with activity.

BUILTH WELLS TO RHAYADER
About 16 miles/26km
OS Landranger 147
Start at Wye Bridge, Builth Wells
(grid reference 043 512)

Go right from the Wye Bridge to The Groe, Builth's major recreational park. Walk through the park to a suspension bridge over the River Irfon. Follow the path back to the Wye. Make your way upstream keeping near to the river for several miles, by Penddol Rocks, then beneath the Heart of Wales railway line, before joining a lane to Rhosferig Lodge. Return to the riverbank and walk through pockets of woodland by the river.

Look out for a fishing lodge in a wood, as you have to bear left before it for Porthllwyd Farm and a roadside lodge. Leave the road to walk through gently undulating pastures, across the Hirnant brook and into woodland again at Estyn. Go right along the road to Newbridge but, just before the bridge and village, turn left for Llysdinam.

Newbridge, as its name suggests, grew up at a crossroads of routes, and trade increased when the railway arrived in 1863. It closed almost 100 years later, in 1962. In the 1840s the area gained something of a reputation when local men joined in the Rebecca Riots, blackening

The walk rises away from the river beyond Erwood to Twmpath Common.

their faces, wearing women's clothes and attacking turnpikes as part of the campaign against increased tolls and tithes.

Back on the Walk, turn right before Dol Cottage to cross fields to the Estyn-gwyn Brook and to the hill farm at Tyn-y-coed. The path soon crosses a delightful dingle. On reaching the road, keep straight ahead to a small stone bridge. Continue along a bridleway through woodland and open ground before the track becomes a lane leading to Llanwrthwl.

Pass by the old school, then by Dolgai Farm, to join a track up to Cefn Farm. Keep ahead through the RSPB reserve of Carn Gafalt, then go right at the junction. There are great views towards Rhayader before you descend to a minor road. Bear right and then left to cross a suspension bridge over the River Elan. After Glyn Farm take the track on the left which runs by the old railway. Keep right at the junction and right again for a track which leads into Rhayader, where you cross the river for the last time.

In Welsh Rhayader means a 'waterfall on the Wye'. A small market town radiating from the Victorian clock tower, it is the gateway to the Elan Valley and a superb centre for walking and mountain biking.

The Montgomery Canal

LOWER FRANKTON TO WELSHPOOL
21 MILES/34KM

A century ago the 35-mile Montgomery canal route from Frankton to Newtown was frantic with activity. Barges carried timber, limestone, coal and textiles along waterways lined with kilns, warehouses, mills, breweries and factories. Work was tough for the 'navvies', or navigators – but there was plenty of it. Then everything changed: competition from the railways, changing demands and a breach in the canal itself all contributed to its decline; in 1944 the Abandon Act ended navigation and the waterway was left to the mercies of nature and the developers. Volunteers started reclaiming the canal in the '60s and in 1987 an Enabling Act gave the official go-ahead for restoration. Work has been slow and piecemeal, depending on the flow of funds, but substantial stretches of the route have already been renovated, and overgrown areas described below may be transformed by the end of the century.

Lower Frankton to Llanymynech

LOWER FRANKTON TO MAESBURY MARSH
About 5¹/₂ miles/9km
OS Landranger 126
Start at Lower Frankton
(grid reference 371 318)

Take the A495 from Ellesmere and follow signs from Welsh Frankton. Just before a hump-backed bridge, turn left down a no-through road and bear right at a group of farm buildings. Cross the bridge and turn right into the car park.

This first stretch of the walk, along a renovated towpath, starts at the junction where the canal from Llangollen to Hurleston meets the Montgomery Canal. The path leads from the car park to a lock-keeper's cottage, at the head of the Frankton Locks, and crosses an iron footbridge to the far bank. Between the third and fourth locks is the dry dock where LTC Rolt converted his boat *Cressy*, the inspiration for his 1944 book *Narrow Boat*, which led to the foundation of the Inland Waterways Association. A grassy footpath follows the canal on its meandering route through the rural Shropshire Plain and across the Perry Moor. Most of this section was dry for 60 years, after its breach in 1936 by an over-enthusiastic vole. At the time repairs were estimated at £400 – ten times the canal's annual revenue – and the branch fell into decline. The surrounding soggy peat bog has caused huge problems for restorers, but in June 1995 most of the canal reopened for navigation. Their triumph is marked with a stone monument dedicated to Graham Palmer, leading light of the Waterways Recovery Group.

The canal flows through open fields and passes under the Shrewsbury-to-Gobowen railway on its approach to the Queen's Head, an old coaching inn and an excellent refreshment stop. Here the path climbs to meet the B5009: walkers must brave the traffic, but the canal passes under the new A5, built to allow headroom for boats. Work is under way to extend this section of the towpath and the Aston Locks; in the meantime the route between Queen's Head and Maesbury Marsh is overgrown and grassy, and the canal water is covered with broadleaved pondweed and water lilies. Maesbury Marsh was once a major transit point for the market town of Oswestry, and most of its canalside buildings survive – with the exception of the grain warehouse, which burned down in 1968. Boats can be hired here for trips along the waterway near the village and The Navigation Inn has information on the canal's walks and wildlife.

INFORMATION AND WALKS
Information on the canal is provided by the Shropshire Union Canal Society, Oak Haven, Longdon-upon-Tern, Shropshire TF6 6LJ. A booklet on *Walks in Shropshire (the Montgomery Canal)* is available from the Queen's Head or the Navigation Inn at Maesbury Marsh.

OS MAP
Landranger 126

LINKS
The route coincides briefly with the 177-mile Offa's Dyke Path, which extends from Chepstow in the south along the Welsh/English border to Prestatyn in the north.

MAESBURY MARSH TO LLANYMYNECH
About 4¹/₂ miles/7km
OS Landranger 126
Start at Maesbury Marsh Wharf
(grid reference 314 250)

The restored waterway runs out here, and the towpath is harder going, but worth tackling for the wealth of wildlife that now enjoys the abandoned canal: swans nest undisturbed among the reeds; primroses and hawthorn bushes straggle over the track, and dragonflies flash along the water's edge. After crossing a minor road leading to a working mill (which once operated its own narrow boats), the canal heads past Granwyn Cottage and is abruptly dammed off at the next bridge. From this point the canal bed is a reedy swamp and the walk becomes a struggle through long grass over a muddy, uneven path, crossed by the occasional cattle track. Presently the towpath climbs to a five-bar

WELSHPOOL
(Y TRALLWNG)

GUIDE BOX

PLACES TO VISIT
Oswestry Transport Museum Displays on the history of cycling and on the Cambrian Railways, with short steam rides most Sundays in summer.

CAR PARKING
Lower Frankton; Queen's Head, Maesbury Marsh; Pant; Llanymynech.

PUBLIC TRANSPORT
Buses Between Welshpool and Oswestry (stopping Llanymynech and Pant) and between Oswestry and Ellesmere.

ACCOMMODATION
Hotels, guest houses etc Ellesmere, 4 miles northeast of Lower Frankton.

TOURIST INFORMATION CENTRE
Ellesmere Meres Visitor Centre, Ellesmere, Shropshire SY12 OPA (tel 01691 622981)

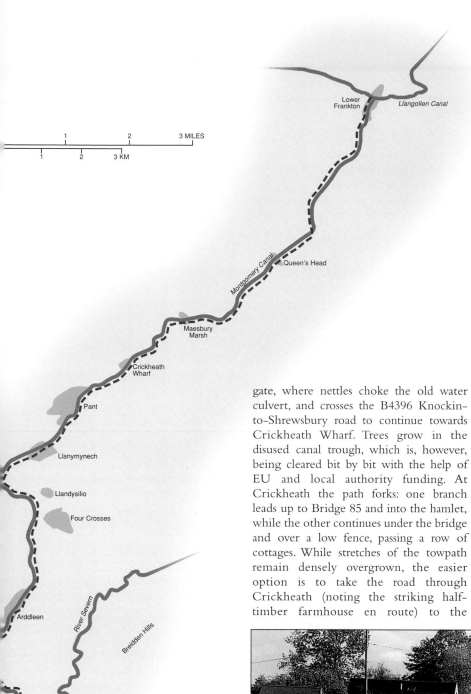

crossroads, turning right to follow the course of the canal or continuing straight ahead to Pant, where Station Road leads off the A483 (at the Powis Arms) back down to the route.

Alternatively, it is possible to battle through the shoulder-high cow parsley to reach the broader, birch-lined approach to Pant, where the towpath gives up altogether, and the canal bed is taken over by brambles and grazing horses. Here the route continues by road, parallel with the canal, with wide views of the Severn Valley to the left and the canal embankment rising to the right.

The towpath can be picked up again as it crosses the Welsh border, straddled by Llanymynech, where traces of a prosperous industrial past mark the route. On the outskirts of Pant, a high bank of kilns recalls the days when rail and canal worked together to carry limestone from local quarries to the Midlands. At Llanymynech Hill, looming above the village to the right, stone was loaded onto railway trucks and carried down to the boats: railbridge remains still flank the canal bed beyond the village. In the 1820s three boats a day would be loaded at Llanymynech Wharf; a hundred or so kilns, placed all along the canal, then converted the limestone to quicklime. But by the time the local quarries closed, in 1914, trade was already in decline. A network of railway lines – all derelict now – had taken much of the waterway's business by the late 19th century, and it suffered even more when the vast Warner kiln was built alongside the railway sidings. The kiln's tall brick chimney still towers above the trees to the right of the towpath.

gate, where nettles choke the old water culvert, and crosses the B4396 Knockin-to-Shrewsbury road to continue towards Crickheath Wharf. Trees grow in the disused canal trough, which is, however, being cleared bit by bit with the help of EU and local authority funding. At Crickheath the path forks: one branch leads up to Bridge 85 and into the hamlet, while the other continues under the bridge and over a low fence, passing a row of cottages. While stretches of the towpath remain densely overgrown, the easier option is to take the road through Crickheath (noting the striking half-timber farmhouse en route) to the

Lower Frankton Junction, where the Waterway Recovery Group has reclaimed the canal for navigation.

Llanymynech to Welshpool

GUIDE BOX

PLACES TO VISIT
Powis Castle A red-stoned mansion with beautiful formal gardens, 1 mile southwest of Welshpool. *The Welshpool & Llanfair Light Railway* Travels into the border hills (weekends daily in summer).

CAR PARKING
Llanymynech; Four Crosses; Arddleen; The Wern Claypit Nature Reserve; Welshpool.

PUBLIC TRANSPORT
Buses Between Welshpool and Oswestry (stopping at Arddleen, Four Crosses).

ACCOMMODATION
Hotels, guest houses etc Welshpool TIC can book places in town or in the borders.

TOURIST INFORMATION CENTRE
Welshpool Vicarage Gardens, Church Street Car Park, Welshpool, Powys SY21 7DH (tel 01938 552043)

LLANYMYNECH TO ARDDLEEN
About 4¹/₂ miles / 7km
OS Landranger 126
Start at towpath below the A483/B4398
(grid reference 267 210)

Beyond Pant, the canal is flooded again (though not yet navigable). As it flows under the main road, crossing the border into Wales, the detritus of canalside yards is left behind and the route passes into open countryside. A mile from Llanymynech are the restored Carreghofa Locks, overlooked by a handsome, three-storey wharfinger's house. This was originally the junction between two canals: the Llanymynech branch of the Ellesmere Canal, and the eastern branch of the Montgomery. Each canal was operated by an independent company, charging its own tolls, and there were frequent disputes between them. The Ellesmere, uphill of the junction, was unhappy about the fact that it was supplying free water to the Montgomery (downhill); so the Montgomery constructed its own feeders to tap the River Tanat. Nevertheless, the bickering continued – even after the two companies had merged into the Shropshire Union – and sometimes broke out into violence: in 1827, 18-year-old John Bagley hurled a brick at the lock-keeper, Edward Perkin, who died of his injuries a week later. Locks and drawbridges were damaged; accusations flew of bribes and dishonest toll-charging, and eventually the canal owners were obliged to raise their lock-keepers' wages and build them sturdy houses.

Nowadays the canal could hardly be more peaceful as it crosses the wide River Vyrnwy and turns to follow the edge of the valley towards the Severn. An embankment cut with flood arches carries it towards the 18th-century Vyrnwy Aqueduct, strengthened with iron bars since its partial collapse in 1823. Views of river, valley and wooded hills ahead are magnificent, and the canal itself is busy with swans, ducks and heron. The towpath continues on its southwestern course, swinging into the Severn Valley past fields of white Charollais cattle on the approach to Four Crosses – a useful refreshment stop – and becoming narrower and rougher as it passes behind the village, pressed in by blackberry and hawthorn bushes. Those who prefer a level walk may choose to stop at Four Crosses, but battling on to Arddleen does bring its rewards: heron (and occasionally kingfishers) swoop down to fish in the canal and, on the far bank, sheep and cattle graze at the water's edge. Appearing sometimes to the right, sometimes ahead, as the canal changes its course, are the rocky ridges of the quarried Breidden Hills, with the distinctive silhouette of the Rodney Memorial, commemorating the admiral's naval victory against the French in 1782, with a fleet built largely from Montgomeryshire timber.

Canal and towpath are interrupted by the A483, before moving again into open fields. Considerable care is needed here, as the path narrows between the water and a bank of bushes and trees. At Arddleen the trunk road crosses the canal again; on the far side is the village, where there is a pub and bus services to Welshpool and Llanymynech.

Carreghofa Locks once marked the meeting of two independent canal operations.

ARDDLEEN TO WELSHPOOL
About 7 miles/11km
OS Landranger 126
Start at The Horseshoe pub, Arddleen
(grid reference 261 158)

From The Horseshoe pub in Arddleen, turn right to follow the A483 (with care) to a barrier and stile, leading to the towpath. The canal heads along an embankment towards the Severn Valley, dropping over 16ft at the Burgedin Locks (currently under restoration) and reaching its lowest level at the site of the Wern Mill. At this point a leat carries away the canal's excess rainwater, which was used to drive the old corn mill, whose pool and sluices still exist. A brickworks and tileworks also stood here at the turn of the century, using the 'puddling clay' trampled by cattle to create lining for the canal.

Unfortunately the clay was less successful in brick-making: the bricks burst in the kiln. The wet-clay pits are now part of a small nature reserve.

From here the canal forms a wide arc around the valley and dips under a bridge at Bank Lock, before beginning its ascent towards Pool Quay. Here a wicket gate leads to the imposing roadside church of St John, built in 1860, when this was a busy industrial centre. A stone in the graveyard marks the resting place of young Alexander Grey, a builder who fell to his death during the church's construction.

After following the road for ½ mile, the canal loops round to the right, past a metal swingbridge, and emerges high above the valley, with clear views of the three main routes to Welshpool: the Severn, the A483 and, in the distance, the Shrewsbury to Aberystwyth railway line. About a mile

Vyrnwy Aqueduct was built in 1796 by John Dadford, a contemporary of Telford, and had to be shored up 30 years later.

from Welshpool, a track leads from the path to the Moors Collection of birds, beasts and rare breeds. Further on, the towpath reaches Buttington Wharf, where the remains of lime kilns can be seen and a causeway leads to the wall where carts would be backed up to unload their cargoes onto the boats. Heading into Welshpool, the route crosses the A458 and continues through a housing estate, where boats are moored to fenceposts and garden gates open onto the towpath. It climbs into town at the Powisland Museum and Canal Centre, where boats can be hired and a display traces local history. From here the walk can be extended by another 12 miles along the towpath to Newtown.

The Swansea and Neath Canals

THESE two separate walks follow the towing paths along the surviving sections of the Swansea and Neath canals, some of which have been fully restored and some of which are still in an abandoned state. The fully restored sections are known respectively as the Swansea Canal Towpath Walk and the Neath Canal Towpath Walk.

The two canals, related but independent, share a common history in the industrial development of South Wales. First to be completed was the Neath Canal, whose 13-mile route was opened in 1795. Its 19 locks carried it up the valley of the River Neath, and enabled coal and iron ore to be brought down, initially to the port of Neath and from 1824 to the larger port of Swansea via the connecting Tennant Canal. Busy and prosperous initially, the Neath Canal suffered from increasing railway competition in the latter part of the 19th century and most of the trade had disappeared by the First World War. It was formally abandoned in 1934. The parallel Swansea Canal, also heavily locked, was opened in 1798 with a 15-mile route up the valley of the Tawe. Its principal cargoes were coal and limestone and by the middle of the 19th century it was the backbone of an extensive network of short branches and tramways that supported its continued success and made it the most profitable of the canals of South Wales. From 1824 the Neath and Swansea canals were connected at their southern end by the Tennant Canal. The Swansea Canal was taken over by the Great Western Railway in 1873 and trade on its upper section soon diminished. However, the lower section remained in use at least until the 1930s.

Following a period of complete dereliction when some lengths were destroyed and infilled, both canals have recently been the subject of ambitious restoration schemes. Sections of towing path are now in good condition but others are still hard to follow. The best are those described below. The routes of both canals are well served by buses.

WALKING GUIDES
Information about the Swansea Canal Towpath Walk and the Neath Canal Towpath Walk is available from local Tourist Information Centres.

OS MAPS
Landranger 160, 170

LINKS
The St Illtud Way follows the northern part of the Swansea Canal.

The derelict locks of the Trebanos flight south of Pontardawe offer an idyllic escape from Swansea.

The Swansea Canal

CLYDACH TO CILMAENGWYN
About 5 miles/8km
OS Landranger 170, 160
Start by Coedgwilym Park, east of Clydach, where the B4603 crosses the canal (grid reference 701 017)

Although far more successful and profitable in its heyday than its neighbouring waterway at Neath, the Swansea Canal has suffered greatly since its closure in the 1930s. Long stretches have vanished completely and it is quite hard to trace the route southwards from Clydach to Swansea. North of Clydach it is a different story and the restored canal makes a pleasant walk, with a wide and well-surfaced towing path and plenty of interest along the way.

From Clydach the setting is initially suburban, but the canal maintains its privacy down one side of the valley, below the road, as it makes its way past back gardens and through clumps of woodland. The Tawe, fast-flowing in stretches, is close by, but at a lower level. Surprisingly, the canal also flows quite

quickly, with plenty of water coming over the cascaded locks, and for long stretches its winding, narrow course through the trees is itself more like a river than a canal. Never short of water, the canal was able to increase its revenues by supplying its surplus to power over 40 factories and mills adjacent to the banks.

A series of locks lifts the canal past Trebanos, a particularly attractive stretch with plenty of wild flowers and views out over the valley, and then it comes to an abrupt end as the canal disappears into a pipe underground. The path continues, and it is easy to follow the route across the fields as the Tawe swings away to the east. The path ends by a roundabout outside Pontardawe. From here it is necessary to cross the road and then pick the path up again as it drops down through the supermarket car park, goes along a short pedestrian tunnel and then finds the canal as it reappears again just before an aqueduct over the River Clydach. With plenty of water, and a well-made towing path that is almost overzealous in its neatness, the canal winds its way through

the town and under a series of bridges in the shadow of the church's tall spire. East of Pontardawe trees flank the route as the canal makes its way along the valley side, high above the river, and through a lovely stretch of woods that are reflected in the clear water. After about 1 mile, it passes under a fine stone bridge and then comes to an abrupt stop again, near another roundabout by Ynysmeudwy.

This is the end of the official towing path walk, but the canal continues on the other side of the roundabout past Cilmaengwyn. The start of the path, now rather overgrown and richly supplied with brambles but waymarked the St Illtud Walk, can be found just beside the bus shelter. This section, left in the wild as a nature reserve, continues for about 1/2 mile and then it stops again, this time for ever.

The canal's route north from here through the valley past Ystalyfera and Ystradgynlais has been almost totally obliterated. There was a terminal basin south of Abercraf linked to a complex network of tramways serving quarries and collieries. Much of this too has vanished.

GUIDE BOX

PLACES TO VISIT
Swansea Maritime and Industrial Museum – exhibits recall the city's great seafaring days and local industries; working woollen mill; veteran vehicles, locomotives and floating boats. Swansea Museum. Glynn Vivian Art Gallery.

CAR PARKING
Clydach (street parking north of the canal); street car parking along the route.

PUBLIC TRANSPORT
Train Station in Swansea.
Bus Regular services along the roads that follow the canals along the Tawe Valley.

ACCOMMODATION
Hotels, guest houses etc Swansea, Pontardine.

TOURIST INFORMATION CENTRES
Swansea Singleton Street, Swansea SA1 3QG (tel 01792 468321)

The Swansea Canal Path comes to an end near Ynysmeudwy, shortly beyond this old stone bridge.

The Neath Canal

NEATH TO RESOLVEN
(OR ABERDULAIS)
About 4¹/₂ miles / 7km
(or 1³/₄ miles / 3km)
OS Landranger 160, 170
Start at road bridge over
the canal near castle ruins
(grid reference 755 978)

Join the well-surfaced towing path and walk eastwards away from the town centre. The towing path continues for a while in the opposite direction as the canal swings round Neath, passing close to the railway station, to enter the broad estuary of the River Neath, but the industrial landscape south of the town has little appeal. Canal hunting in this area requires real dedication. Running due east, the canal is flanked by new housing estates but it soon leaves the town behind as it takes up its position on the steep southern slope of the Neath Valley.

River and canal are side by side for a while, and from this point are never far apart. Across the other side of the valley is the Tennant Canal, and jammed between them is a busy highway and a railway. Other roads flank the valley on both sides and so it is a busy scene. Despite all this, the canal's route manages to remain both quiet and private, thanks in part to the surrounding trees.

As the route approaches Tonna, the setting becomes more urban, with the B4434 close by, but the canal soon turns away, passes a huge bottled gas depot, burrows under a road and a large railway viaduct and then reaches the wooded privacy of Aberdulais Basin. Recently restored, the basin is a wide expanse of ochre-coloured water with a fine stone towing path bridge set at a dramatic angle across its mouth. The Neath Canal passes to the side of the basin, with acccess to it via this bridge.

From the other end of the basin the derelict Tennant Canal sets off on its journey towards Swansea across the 11 stone arches of its aqueduct over the Neath. Built in stages between 1790 and 1824, this canal was the creation of George Tennant, a local landowner and entrepreneur, who could see the benefits of a waterway linking the rivers Tawe and Neath, and thus the towns of Swansea and Neath (see panel opposite). Today the Tennant Canal survives, in use as a water supply channel, but it is private and its towing path is not accessible.

Shaded by trees and well-supplied with benches, the basin is a restful place. It also has a car park, accessible from a track beside the Railway Inn, and so makes an alternative starting point for the walk. Beyond the basin, the towing path becomes little more than a track, often overgrown in places, but it can be followed up the valley. However, the canal's character and its formerly rather private route have been radically changed by the new highway that runs all the way along the Vale of Neath. This major road is never far from the canal and at times they run side by side. Ironically, the presence of this road may enhance the chances of full restoration for this section of the canal, for its route along the valley is now far more visible. In the meantime, the effect of the road inevitably make this part of the walk rather unappealing. In addition, a section south of Resolven has been filled in, and the route is sometimes hard to follow. As a result, it is probably preferable to leave the canal at the basin and walk into Aberdulais to take the bus along the valley to Resolven, where things take a dramatic turn for the better.

At Aberdulais the old basin, recently restored, marks the junction between the Neath Canal, on the left, and the private Tennant Canal, which is now derelict.

RESOLVEN TO GLYNNEATH
About 3¹/₂ miles/6km
**OS Landranger 170, 160
(160 for last ³/₄ mile in
Glynneath only)**
*Start at Resolven Canal Basin,
near B4434 crossing
(grid reference 872 031)*

In Resolven a new basin has been created just beyond the B4434 crossing, complete with picnic seats and a launching ramp for small trailed craft. From here the canal has been fully restored for about 2¹/₂ miles towards Glynneath. There are seven locks, all in working order, and the canal's wooded route along the narrowing valley is very attractive. From Resolven the canal runs close by the road for over 1 mile, but trees soften the impact of the traffic. There are good views across the valley to the densely forested hillsides. Another lockside picnic site is near an old iron bridge that used to carry one of the many colliery railways. Beyond this, at Rheola, an aqueduct carries the canal over a little tributary of the Neath. This is the larger of two in this area, made in the local Neath Abbey ironworks early in the 19th century.

After Rheola the canal's route moves into the centre of the valley. The former seclusion of this section has been ended by the new Vale of Neath road which is right by the canal here, but the walk is still attractive, thanks in part to the surrounding trees, the old bridges, the surviving buildings and the locks, all in perfect condition and waiting for the streams of boats that may be some time coming. After a while the new road swings away to the east, leaving the canal to quiet seclusion for the last ¹/₄ mile of the restored section. This ends where it is crossed by the A465. Nearby is a large layby, allowing ample parking for those wanting to walk the canal in the other direction. A short piped stretch follows, and then the canal and the road run side by side towards Glynneath, with the former disappearing into an industrial estate to the south of the town. The old canal basin can still be traced in the town, but the remains give no sense of the busy life the canal enjoyed in the 19th century, when boats loaded with coal and iron ore queued up to make their way southwards through the locks that carried the canal down the Vale of Neath.

This bridge is north of Rheola, where the canal is in the centre of the valley, in an open landscape.

GEORGE TENNANT

The canal age in Britain produced many extraordinary characters. Best known are the engineers, but their achievements have often overshadowed the contributions made by landowners and industrialists. Typical of the latter was George Tennant (1765–1832), the son of a Lancashire solicitior, who in 1816 acquired estates in South Wales with waterway interests. He proposed a new canal to link the rivers Tawe and Neath and, undaunted by lack of support from local landowners and industrialists, and despite considerable engineering difficulties and financial costs, his junction canal was finally opened in May 1824, amid great celebration and the publication of a 19-verse poem by Elizabeth Davies, a Neath sweetshop keeper. The Tennant Canal had a successful life, quickly carrying over 100,000 tons a year, and this led directly to the development of Port Tennant at Swansea. Commercial traffic flourished through the 19th century and the canal remained in use until the early 1930s. Still privately owned today, it survives as a water channel.

The Morfa Mawddach Trail

DOLGELLAU TO BARMOUTH
9¹/₂ MILES/15KM

FOR nearly a hundred years, the north Wales gold-mining town of Dolgellau was linked to the Mawddach Estuary by railway. Trains made the 9¹/₂-mile journey towards the sea along the course of the river to Morfa Mawddach, and joined the Cambrian coast line to cross a ¹/₂-mile viaduct to Barmouth on the far shore. The branch was closed in 1965, after floods washed away part of the line, and the trackbed was bought by the Snowdonia National Park, who transformed it into a level walk past sandbanks, sheep farms and oak forests, with the high peaks of Snowdonia providing its dramatic backdrop.

DOLGELLAU TO PENMAENPOOL
About 2 miles/3km
OS Landranger 124
Start at Dolgellau car park, on the south bank of the River Wnion (grid reference 179 727)

Dolgellau seems an unlikely spot for a gold rush, but this thoroughly Welsh town, with huddled, dark-stone houses, has been the centre of the nation's gold-mining industry since the 1860s, when a haul worth £5 million was dug out of the nearby mountainside. The Mawddach Trail is reached by crossing the recreation ground from the car park to the River Wnion, where a footbridge gives access to its northern bank. A stile just before the A493 underpass leads to the old railway track. After crossing the A493 Tywyn Road, the route continues over the Wnion as it loops round to meet the wider waters of the Mawddach. To the south is the long ridge of Cader Idris ('Idris's Seat'), nearly 3,000ft high. Legend has it that anyone who falls asleep on its peak, Pen y Gadair, wakes up either a poet or a madman. To the north is the 1069ft Foel Cynwch, where the ancient Nannau estate and its 18th-century mansion (the fifth, at least, to stand here) overlooks the fertile Mawddach Valley.

Silver birch and elder trees line the path as it continues to Penmaenpool, where the river opens out and a toll bridge crosses the head of the estuary, leading away to the oak woodland of Farchynys. An old signal box beyond the bridge serves as an RSPB observatory, giving views of whimbrel, greenshank, ringed plover, oystercatcher and curlew.

Penmaenpool is now a tiny hamlet, but in the 17th and 18th centuries it was a busy shipbuilding centre, providing square riggers to carry oak bark and wool to foreign markets. Coastal trade survived until the 1860s, with coal, limestone, slate and timber loaded onto Mawddach ships, before the railway took over. The George III hotel, sitting on the estuary's edge, dates back to the maritime industry's heyday. Until 1890 there were two separate buildings here: a pub and a ship chandlers, both established in about 1650. Among the George's visitors was the Victorian poet Gerard Manley Hopkins, who is credited with the ode (not one of his best) found in an old guest book:

> *Then come who pine for peace*
> *and pleasure,*
> *Away from counter, court and school,*
> *Spend here your measure of time*
> *and treasure,*
> *And taste the treats of Penmaenpool.*

INFORMATION AND WALKS
Details of walks in the area are available at the Information Office, Station Road, Barmouth. The brochure *Natural Heritage*, about wildlife in Snowdonia, is available from the South Gwynedd LEADER network, Parc Busnes Penamser, Porthmadog, Gwynedd LL49 9GB.

OS MAPS
Landranger 124 or
Outdoor Leisure 23 (Cader Idris)

LINKS
The circular Precipice Walk, around Foel Cynwch, can be reached from Dolgellau. Walks from Barmouth include a circular route to Fairbourne and the Blue Lake, and the Panorama Walk over the mountains to Dinas Oleu.

PENMAENPOOL TO BARMOUTH
7¹/₂ miles/12km
OS Landranger 124
Start at the George III Hotel (grid reference 695 185)

Beyond the George, the river swings briefly out of view as the track passes between high slabs of rock and into gentler, sheep-farming country. Much of

BARMOUTH
(ABERMAW)

BARMOUTH
BAY

Fair

The George III hotel has in its time served as a pub, a chandlers and a station house.

the surrounding land has been drained to provide good grazing, and the reedbeds that once covered the area are now limited to field borders and narrow stretches alongside the route – but they still attract nesting birds such as reed bunting, sedge bunting and reed warbler.

After about 1 mile, the estuary widens out to the right of the track, and banks of mixed woodland and wild rhododendrons rise to the left. Beautiful as they are, these rapidly spreading *Rhododendron ponticum* bushes have been a persistent problem for the Snowdonia National Park authority, which has to work hard to keep them from invading its footpaths.

As the track turns to follow the river, it provides the first glimpse of the railway bridge stretching along the horizon from Morfa Mawddach to Barmouth (Abermaw) on the opposite headland. The route now changes character, emerging from rural pastures on to the old stone railway embankment, at the edge of the estuary's broad tidal waters and sandbanks, often cloaked in sea mist. Lapwing and redshank nest on the saltmarshes here, and the rivers flowing down from the hills attract heron, kingfisher and dippers. From Abergwynant, where the footpath crosses a stream and a track to Coed y Gribin

woods, the walk has a distinctly seaside feel: gorse and bracken line the track, water laps against the embankment, and seagulls call overhead. The path becomes a causeway across the marshes as it approaches the outcrop of Fegla Fach, and then loops inland towards the Cader foothills. A tarmac road to the south leads across fields to the village of Arthog and the tranquil Cregennen Lakes, overlooked by standing stones and the ancient hillfort of Pared y Cefnhir.

The main route continues through birch woods, parallel with the A493, before crossing the road to Fairbourne and leading to the disused branch line platform and rail buffers of Morfa Mawddach. Trains still run from the station's other platform along the Cambrian line to Barmouth, and pedestrians can cross the bridge alongside the railway (a small toll is charged at the other end). Ahead is the beach resort of Barmouth, with its seafront cafés, handsome 19th-century buildings straggling up the rock, and a busy harbour full of yachts and fishing boats.

GUIDE BOX

PLACES TO VISIT
Gwynfynydd gold and silver mine Special buses run from Dolgellau for underground trips (not recommended for the infirm or small children).

CAR PARKING
Dolgellau; Penmaenpool – car park near bridge; Morfa Mawddach Station car park; Fairbourne; Barmouth.

PUBLIC TRANSPORT
Trains The Fairbourne narrow gauge railway (April–October) links with ferries to Barmouth at Porth Penrhyn.
Buses Hourly between Dolgellau and Barmouth.

ACCOMMODATION
Hotels, guest houses etc Penmaenpool, Dolgellau, Barmouth. TICs can book accommodation in the Snowdonia countryside.

TOURIST INFORMATION CENTRES
Dolgellau Eldon Square, Dolgellau, Gwynedd LL40 1PU (tel 01341 422888)
Barmouth Station Road, Barmouth, Gwynedd LL42 1LU (tel 01341 280787)

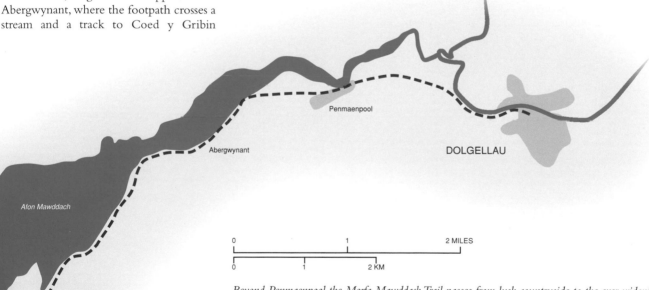

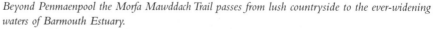

Beyond Penmaenpool the Morfa Mawddach Trail passes from lush countryside to the ever-widening waters of Barmouth Estuary.

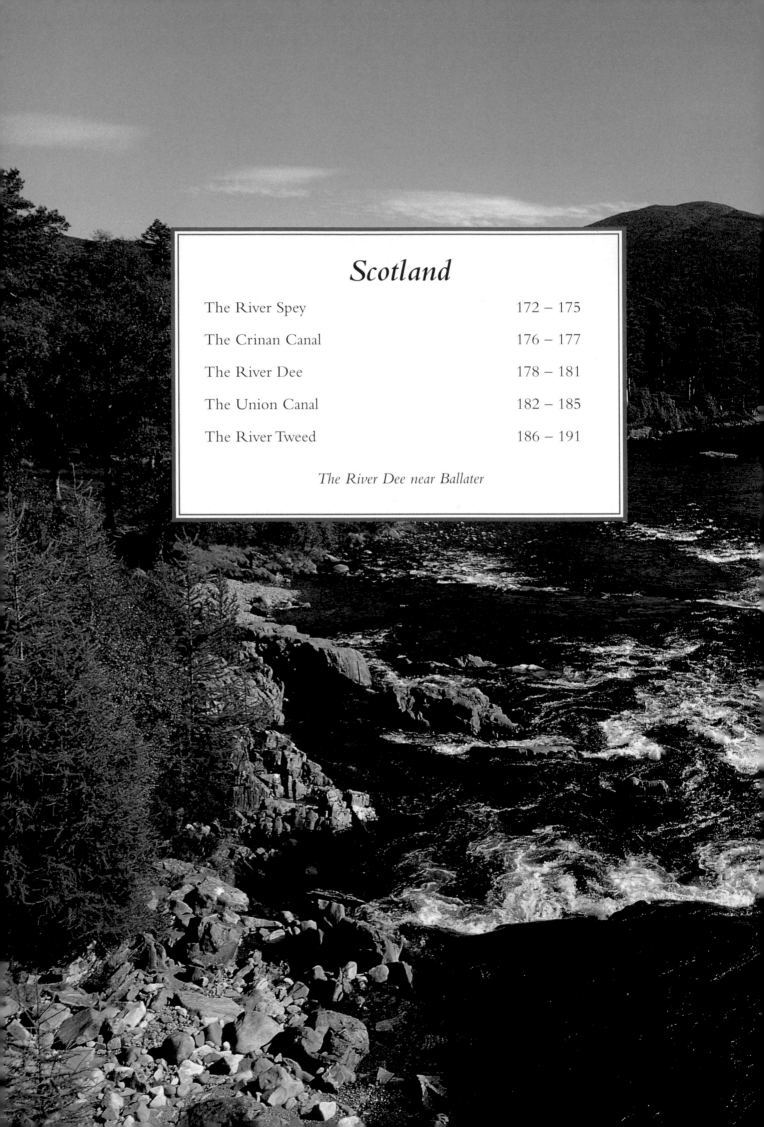

Scotland

The River Spey   172 – 175

The Crinan Canal   176 – 177

The River Dee   178 – 181

The Union Canal   182 – 185

The River Tweed   186 – 191

The River Dee near Ballater

The River Spey

SPEY BAY TO BALLINDALLOCH
28 MILES/44KM

THE Speyside Way was opened as far as Ballindalloch in 1981. The original intention was that the route would follow the River Spey from its mouth all the way to Aviemore, but the last section was never completed, and instead the Way currently swings inland to end at Tomintoul. The section to Ballindalloch, described here, is mainly very easy walking along an old railway track, and is notable for the number of distilleries passed or nearby – this is very much whisky country. A short spur from the route leads to Dufftown, an attractive place with yet more distilleries.

The route has plenty of interest, with good wildlife, and passes through a number of pleasing villages and small towns where accommodation and other facilities can be found. It has been a popular walk since it opened.

WALKING GUIDES
There is no full guide to the walk, but information leaflets can be obtained locally or from Moray Council, High Street, Elgin.

OS MAP
Landranger 28

LINKS
There are at present no links with other paths.

Spey Bay to Craigellachie

SPEY BAY TO BOAT O'BRIG
About 8¹/₂ miles/14km
OS Landranger 28
Start at Tugnet Ice House
(grid reference 348 656)

The Speyside Way starts at the mouth of the river where it empties into the Moray Firth. Here you will find the Tugnet Ice House, the largest of its kind in Scotland, built in 1830, when refrigeration meant storing food in layers of ice inside thick stone walls.

The shingle beach at the mouth of the Spey, known as The Lein, is a wildlife reserve, and is the second-largest system of its kind in Britain; only Chesil Beach in Dorset is more extensive. Habitats vary from marsh to heath, and the plants include some beautiful orchids. As you would expect, there is excellent birdlife, including many waders.

It is typical of the Speyside Way's somewhat eccentric early progress that the first signpost points away from the river. Before long it is on its way back, and in a mile or so reaches the Spey Viaduct. This typically confident piece of Victorian engineering, opened in 1886, was designed by Patrick Barnett to take the Great North of Scotland Railway. Its size and strength were necessary because of the power of the river, which is liable to regular floods. The supporting piers are buried 52ft below the river bed. A path leads across the viaduct to Garmouth.

The Way continues to wander about, through woodland, one minute alongside the river and the next away from it, until the B9104 is joined for 1 mile to reach the outskirts of Fochabers, passing the policies of Gordon Castle, former home of the Dukes of Richmond and Gordon (not open to the public), and going under the A96 road. Baxters Visitor Centre is just across the river.

The older bridge crossing the river here, dating from the 1850s, replaced one seriously damaged in a great flood in 1829. An eyewitness spoke of the bridge 'falling with the cloud-like appearance of an avalanche' as the river rushed on, 'its thunderous roar proclaiming its victory'. Dramatic stuff indeed.

The Way goes through a pleasant riverside park before leaving the river again. It does not really enter Fochabers, but a diversion into the town is well worth taking. This is a planned town, started in 1776 on the order of the 4th Duke of Gordon, the original village being in the way of improvements he wished to make to the castle and policies. The basic street pattern laid down by John Baxter is a grid;

a handsome central square includes the imposing Bellie Church. There is an excellent local museum on High Street, as well as a good range of shops and accommodation.

South of the town, the Way follows Fochabers Burn rather than the Spey for a short distance, then wriggles through some woods to Ordiequish. From here to Boat o'Brig it follows a quiet minor road with little traffic. For much of this stretch the Spey is out of sight, the exception being Aultderg ('red stream') where a path leads to a good viewpoint.

The road eventually drops down to Boat o'Brig. The name is said to derive from a time when an earlier bridge was swept away and a ferry was provided – the 'boat of the bridge'. The fine railway bridge was the work of the great engineer Joseph Mitchell, and was opened in 1858. The approaches are original, but the central section was replaced in 1906.

BOAT O'BRIG TO CRAIGELLACHIE
About 7 miles/11km
OS Landranger 28
Start at Boat o'Brig car park
(grid reference 320 518)

The attractive little building with the Doric columns was a toll house. The Way climbs up behind it to join a track leading to Bridgeton Farm, passes through the farmyard and enters a large area of forest on the western slopes of Ben Aigan. The route climbs steadily here, joining a broad forestry track and making a substantial diversion around the deep side valley of the Allt Daloy.

A little further on a short diversion leads to a viewpoint with a seat. In clear conditions the view from here is magnificent. The whole of the lower Spey is spread out before you, with a wide area of coast also in view. The river winds through farmland and woods, making a most attractive picture, and if the visibility

---

GUIDE BOX

PLACES TO VISIT
Spey Bay Tugnet Ice House – exhibitions on the Spey and its wildlife and on the ice house itself.
Fochabers Baxters of Speyside, Visitor Centre – factory tour, audio-visual show, souvenirs, café, woodland walk. Folk Museum – fascinating collection relating to local history, plus some veteran motor vehicles, in a former church.
Craigellachie Speyside Cooperage, Dufftown Road – see barrels and casks for the whisky industry being made.

CAR PARKING
Spey Bay; Fochabers; Boat o'Brig; Craigellachie.

PUBLIC TRANSPORT
Bus Good services to Fochabers from Elgin and Aberdeen. The rest of the route has less good cover.

ACCOMMODATION
Hotels, guest houses etc Reasonable choice in Fochabers and Craigellachie.
Camping Fiddich Park, Ballindalloch (pre-booking required).

TOURIST INFORMATION CENTRES
Elgin 17 High Street, Elgin IV30 1EG (tel 01343 542666)
Dufftown Clock Tower, The Square, Dufftown, Keith AB55 4AD (tel 01340 820501)

is at its best, on the far northern horizon you can see the distinctive mountains of Sutherland and Caithness.

The forestry track continues to be followed, the trend being downhill, until a minor road is reached leading towards Craigellachie. This is part of the Arndilly Estate which has long been noted for fine trees, both coniferous and broadleaved. Arndilly House has a neat double row of stone toadstools lining the driveway. The house was built in the 1830s for David McDowall Grant, who was one of many land 'improvers' of his day, introducing new agricultural practices and planting many thousands of trees.

This section of the walk ends by crossing the River Fiddich at the Fiddichside Inn, to enter Fiddich Park. A small campsite for walkers can be found here, and a triple-armed signpost indicates the Dufftown Spur of the walk. This provides a pleasant 4-mile stroll towards Dufftown, beside the Fiddich, and the opportunity to see how whisky is made at the famous Glenfiddich Distillery, where there are full visitor facilities.

The shingle beach at the mouth of the Spey, the second largest system of its kind in Britain.

The main path heads right, under a bridge, to reach the ranger's office at Boat o'Fiddich. Information can be obtained here and the rangers are always glad to help walkers. Craigellachie is popular with fishermen trying their luck on the Spey, the Fiddich and other waters. It has several hotels where refreshments can be obtained, and also its own distillery, though this one is not open to visitors.

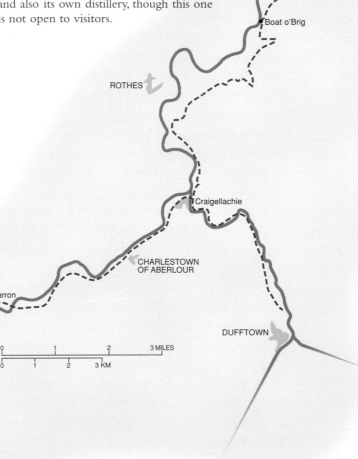

Craigellachie to Ballindalloch

CRAIGELLACHIE TO KNOCKANDO
About 7 miles / 11km
OS Landranger 28
*Start at Craigellachie car park
(grid reference 293 451)*

Before leaving Craigellachie, take the short walk to look at Telford's magnificent bridge. Built in 1814, this is the oldest iron bridge in Scotland, and shows to the full Telford's genius as an engineer and designer. He took maximum advantage of the lightness and airiness facilitated by the new material to create a structure that is both graceful and strong. The bridge cost £8,200 and at its west end abuts onto the crag called Craig Ailichidh ('strong rock') from which the place takes its name.

From here all the way to Ballindalloch, the Speyside Way follows the trackbed of the former Strathspey Railway. This gives very easy, level walking, and directions are hardly necessary. You may have noticed a curious dichotomy of nomenclature. The more usual and perhaps more accurate local name for the river valley – also a popular dance form – is Strathspey, but Speyside often appears, and is used for the walk. Perhaps it does not matter.

Between Craigellachie and Aberlour, the path goes through a short tunnel about 150yds in length, carved from a steep slope. The visibility is good and the path surface firm. Walk on with the river to your right and the A95 not far away on your left to reach Aberlour.

This is another planned village, built at the direction of Charles Grant of Wester Elchies in 1812; its full name is Charlestown of Aberlour, after its founder. It is an attractive place with a broad main street and a neat central square with a church. On its southern edge is a distillery which is open to visitors, and the village, like others along the Spey, is popular with fishermen.

The Speyside Way continues behind the houses to reach the former railway station, nicely preserved and open for teas and snacks in summer. This service is run by local ladies on a voluntary basis and the proceeds go to charity. The station is part of

GUIDE BOX

PLACES TO VISIT
Tamdhu Distillery, near Knockando – tours, tasting, exhibition, café, gift shop.
Dufftown Glenfiddich Distillery – visitor centre, tours, tasting, café, gift shop.
Ballindalloch Glenfarclas Distillery – tours, tasting, gift shop. Ballindalloch Castle, home of the Macpherson-Grant family for over 400 years.

CAR PARKING
Craigellachie; Aberlour; Ballindalloch.

PUBLIC TRANSPORT
This section of the route is not well served. There are regular buses from Craigellachie to Aberlour.

ACCOMMODATION
Hotels, guest houses etc Reasonable choice in Craigellachie and Aberlour. Details from the Tourist Information Centre in Elgin (see below) or from Inverness Tourist Information Centre, Castle Wynd, Inverness IV2 3BJ (tel 01463 234353).

TOURIST INFORMATION CENTRES
Elgin 17 High Street, Elgin IV30 1EG (tel 01343 542666)
Dufftown Clock Tower, The Square, Dufftown, Keith AB55 4AD (tel 01340 820501)

Thomas Telford's iron bridge at Craigellachie, revolutionary for its time, now carries foot traffic.

the Alice Littler Park, named for the wife of a noted local benefactor, Sydney Littler.

A graceful suspension bridge crosses the river, but the Way continues on the east bank. Once out of the village, the tree cover and frequent cuttings limit the views. The river is crossed by the last cast-iron bridge made in Scotland, dating from 1863, then the path parallels a road to the small village of Carron, passing the Imperial Distillery, where Black Bottle whisky is produced. This one is not normally open to visitors. The Carron Inn offers refreshments and accommodation.

After Carron, the path follows the sinuous curves of the Spey, again with plenty of tree cover and a good variety of woodland birds usually to be heard if not seen. The next distillery to be reached is Knockando, a famous malt. It was founded in 1898 and has an attractive sign at the entrance (not usually open to visitors).

KNOCKANDO TO BALLINDALLOCH
About 5 miles/8km
OS Landranger 28
Start at Knockando Station
(grid reference 193 418)

After crossing the Knockando Burn, the path reaches the former station at Tamdhu, now transformed into a visitor centre for the distillery of the same name. This one has just celebrated its centenary, having been opened in 1896, partly because of the pure waters of the Knockando Burn and partly because of the convenience of the railway line. Tamdhu's own fine malt can be sampled after visiting the distillery (admission free: café, toilets and gift shop).

Having enjoyed a taste of the 'water of life', return to the path – perhaps fortunately with little chance of losing it, as it continues along the railway line, close to the river, all the way to Ballindalloch. As well as the birdlife you may well see rabbits, foxes and perhaps even a flash of white rump indicating a roe deer in the trees.

Blacksboat is the next stop, two miles from Tamdhu. Picnic tables are provided at the former station. The road bridges here were completely realigned in 1991 to eliminate a very awkward double bend. The name derives from the brothers John and James Black who at one time in the 18th century ran a ferry across the river – naturally enough known as Black's Boat.

A final two miles of easy walking brings you to Ballindalloch. The fine viaduct across the river was built by G McFarlane of Dundee, who has his name at both ends. He would be pleased to see that his sturdy bridge, erected in 1863, looks fit for another 150 years at least. Across the viaduct is the

former Ballindalloch station, now a hostel used mainly by canoeing groups but also available for walkers if pre-booked.

The Speyside Way leaves the river here – for the time being, at least. There are current plans to extend it right down to Aviemore. For now, it heads off across the hills and moors to Tomintoul. To round off your journey through the land of whisky,

The path between Craigellachie and Aberlour.

a short diversion of ¼ mile from Ballindalloch would take you to Cragganmore Distillery. Or if you continue with the Way for ½ mile, you can visit Ballindalloch Castle, the seat of the MacPherson-Grant family since the mid-16th century.

THE RIVER SPEY

The Spey is Scotland's second longest river, flowing for 107 miles from its source in Loch Spey to its mouth at Spey Bay. The river is renowned for the quality of its fishing, particularly the salmon.

The salmon season runs from February to October. Fishing in the early part of the season is done by spinning, but later on, when the water is lower and warmer, 'flies' (brightly coloured baits) are used. There has been great concern over the deline of the wild salmon stock in recent years, and much effort is being paid to conservation in an attempt to restore the salmon runs to their former glory.

The Spey is also notable as a whisky-producing area. The purity of the water enables the distilleries in the area to produce a lighter malt whisky than is the case in areas where peaty soils predominate. Whisky smuggling was rife before an Act of Parliament in 1823 legalised the industry. Glenlivet, a few miles from the Spey, was the first distillery to be licensed, in 1824. Many distilleries now offer tours for visitors and have shops where souvenirs can be bought.

The Crinan Canal

CRINAN TO ARDRISHAIG
10 MILES/16KM

THE Crinan Canal was built to allow ships an easier passage from the west coast waters to the Clyde Estuary, saving a long and often difficult haul of 80 miles round the Mull of Kintyre. An excellent towpath runs on its east bank for the full length, and the canal provides a delightful short day's walking with plenty of interest along the way.

The canal runs through attractive scenery with well-wooded hills to the west and a large nature reserve, the Moine Mhor, to the east for much of the way. This area is rich in birdlife. Watching boats passing through the 16 locks is always diverting, and if you walk the full length of the canal you may well become involved in opening or shutting lock gates at some stage – all part of the fun.

WALKING GUIDE
There is no full guide to the walk, but British Waterways publishes a very informative free leaflet, available locally or from British Waterways, Canal House, Applecross Street, Glasgow G4 9SP.

OS MAP
Landranger 55

LINKS
There are at present no links with other paths.

Crinan to Ardrishaig

CRINAN TO CAIRNBAAN
About 4¹/₂ miles/7km
OS Landranger 55
Start at the Crinan Hotel
(grid reference 788 945)

Watching the busy and efficient operation of the Crinan Canal today, it is hard to imagine the severe financial and constructional difficulties that beset the project in its early years. Construction began in September 1794, but good labour was hard to obtain and the work soon slipped badly behind schedule. By 1799 a government loan of £50,000 was needed. The canal was partly opened in July 1801, but there had been difficulties in rock-cutting and piling, and in 1804 yet more money was raised.

The canal was finally completed in August 1809, but after a severe gale in January 1811 it was closed again and the great engineer Thomas Telford was called in. Repairs went on until autumn 1817, but in 1835 there was yet another closure. After that matters finally settled down.

Unlike other canals, the Crinan was not threatened by railways, and has remained a useful link to the present day, though nearly all of its traffic now is for pleasure rather than business.

Start at Crinan, the west end of the canal. There is a basin here for boats either leaving or entering the canal, a hotel, coffee shop, toilets and a craft shop. Before the canal was built the settlement was called Portree. The initial section – one of those that gave difficulty during construction – is quite narrow. There is a lovely view to the north across Loch Crinan, with Duntrune Castle prominent. The castle, once a Campbell stronghold, has been owned by the Lairds of Poltalloch since 1792.

The canal soon turns to head southeast, its main direction. In summer the path is richly lined with wild flowers including ragged robin, buttercups, orchids and dog roses, making a riot of colour.

The Bellanoch Basin is soon reached and then Islandadd Bridge. To the left is the Moine Mhor – the 'great moss' – a

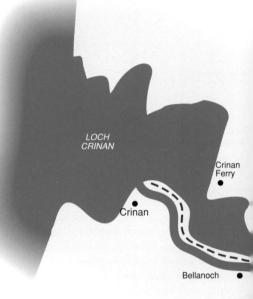

National Nature Reserve of 1,200 acres, one of Britain's best examples of a raised bog. Birdlife includes warblers, hen harrier and curlew, and you can often see heron fishing the pools.

Across the moss is Dunadd, a rocky knoll with a long, distinguished history. It was an Iron Age fort, has Pictish carved rocks and was the capital of the ancient kingdom of Dalriada. It is allegedly the original site of the Stone of Scone, recently returned to Scotland from Westminster Abbey.

The first five locks are encountered at Dunadry. The bridge over Lock 11 runs, most unusually, on rails. A little further on, by Loch a'Bharain, there is a notice proclaiming the 'summit' of the canal – at just 68ft surely the lowest named summit in Scotland.

Fishing boats in the basin at Crinan, the western end of the canal. This is always a busy place as boats enter and leave the sea lock.

GUIDE BOX

PLACES TO VISIT
Cairnbaan Inscribed rocks, a short signposted walk from the canal.
Dunadd Iron Age fort and centre of the ancient kingdom of Dalriada.
Kilmartin Glen (on A816 6 miles north of Cairnbaan) Wealth of ancient monuments, including standing stones and cairns; Kilmartin Church has collection of early grave slabs and crosses.
Crarae Gardens (off A83 at Minard 10 miles north of Lochgilphead) Include many specimen trees and magnificent rhododendrons.

CAR PARKING
Crinan; Cairnbaan; Lochgilphead; Ardrishaig.

PUBLIC TRANSPORT
Bus Intermittent service from Lochgilphead to Crinan. No Sunday service. Alternatively, a taxi can be hired in Lochgilphead to take you to Crinan.

ACCOMMODATION
Hotels, guest houses etc Wide choice along the route. Details from the Tourist Information Centre in Lochgilphead (see below) or from West Highlands and Islands of Argyll Tourist Board, Boswell House, Argyll Square, Oban PA34 4AN.

TOURIST INFORMATION CENTRES
Oban Boswell House, Argyll Square, Oban PA34 4AN (tel 01631 563122)
Lochgilphead Lochnell Street, Lochgilphead, Argyll PA30 8JN (tel 01546 602344)

The basin at Bellanoch, where the canal broadens out. Boats often moor here before heading west to the open sea.

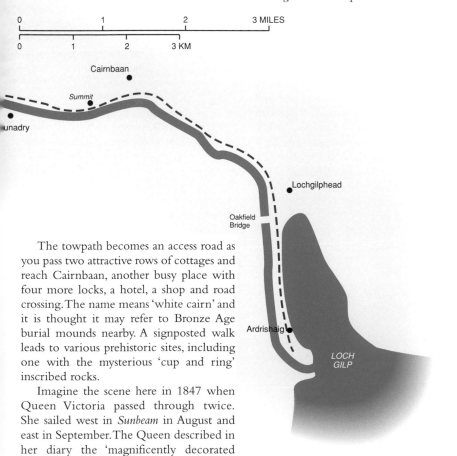

The towpath becomes an access road as you pass two attractive rows of cottages and reach Cairnbaan, another busy place with four more locks, a hotel, a shop and road crossing. The name means 'white cairn' and it is thought it may refer to Bronze Age burial mounds nearby. A signposted walk leads to various prehistoric sites, including one with the mysterious 'cup and ring' inscribed rocks.

Imagine the scene here in 1847 when Queen Victoria passed through twice. She sailed west in *Sunbeam* in August and east in September. The Queen described in her diary the 'magnificently decorated

barge, drawn by three horses ridden by postillions in scarlet'. Cheering crowds lined the banks, and it did wonders for the tourist trade.

CAIRNBAAN TO ARDRISHAIG
About 5¹/₂ miles/9km
OS Landranger 55
Start at Cairnbaan Locks
(grid reference 840 908)

After Cairnbaan the character of the canal changes. It becomes more peaceful, swinging away from the road and well wooded to the south. As Lochgilphead is neared, the distant silhouette of the Arran hills becomes clear on the southern horizon. Nearer to hand, a massed bank of rhododendrons provides a blaze of colour in spring and early summer.

After Oakfield Bridge the canal starts its last 1¹/₄ miles to the sea lock at Ardrishaig. On the way you pass a building with the date 1895 inscribed on it. This is the 'auto water waster' and is worth a closer look. It operates on a very simple principle of alternate huge tipping buckets, operated by a chain and lever arm, filling with water in order to maintain the canal level.

At Ardrishaig you reach the last three canal locks, then the sea lock. The village grew greatly in size and importance after the canal was built and is today an attractive tourist centre.

The River Dee

BALLATER TO ABOYNE AND BANCHORY TO ABERDEEN
29 MILES/47KM

THE River Dee is renowned for several things: its superb fishing, especially for salmon; the beauty of the surrounding area; and, of course, its connections with the Royal Family, dating back 150 years to the time when Queen Victoria and Prince Albert first fell in love with Deeside. Upper Deeside in particular is a great place for hillwalking, but here we explore the riverside area lower down.

The walk is described in two sections, the first from Ballater to Aboyne and the second from Banchory to Aberdeen. The section in between is not easy to walk at present, but is simply covered by a hop on the frequent buses that go up and down Deeside. The walk uses the former railway line, which is being converted to a footpath and cycleway, as much as possible, but there are inevitably a few road stretches. The beauty of the landscape should compensate for them more than adequately.

WALKING GUIDE
There is no guide to this walk, but parts of it are described in various local guidebooks.

OS MAPS
Landranger 37, 38

LINKS
There are at present no links with other paths.

Ballater to Aboyne

BALLATER TO DINNET
About 5¹/₂ miles/9km
OS Landranger 37
Start at Ballater Station
(grid reference 370 959)

Ballater is a handsome town with many well-proportioned buildings and an air of spaciousness about it. The town has long enjoyed a close association with the Royal Estate of Balmoral, but it owes its growth to the development 200 years ago of nearby Pannanich Wells as a spa based on the discovery of mineral-rich water there. The healthful association continues today with the luxury Craigendarroch Hotel, lodges and leisure resort close by.

There are many links with Queen Victoria. The Queen opened the Royal Bridge over the Dee in 1885 – the fourth bridge at this point – and once the 'new' Balmoral was completed in 1855, she was a frequent visitor. After 1866, Victoria came by train. An extension of the line to Balmoral was considered but never completed, and Ballater remained as the terminus until the line closed in 1966, after exactly a century of use. In 1900 Queen Victoria left Balmoral for the last time to take the train from Ballater south to Windsor. She died a year later.

Today, the station building houses a tearoom, while across the square is the Tourist Information Centre, which has a display on the history of the railway. The trackbed is gradually being developed as a walkway and cyclepath, and you go between the station buildings to gain access to the platform and thus the path.

Turn east and follow the walkway, which soon becomes a delightful fenced path, with the wooded hill of Craigendarroch (meaning crag of oaks) to the left. In summer there are masses of wild flowers. In 1 mile or so the A93 is reached. Cross with care and continue a further ¹/₂ mile to the ruined 15th-century church and kirkyard of Kirkton of Tullich. There was a chapel here long before that, founded by St Nathalan. An interesting 7th-century character, Nathalan was an agricultural innovator and visited Rome. He had chained his right arm to his side as a penance and thrown the key into the Dee. While in Rome he bought a fish and in its stomach he found the same key. He is said to be buried at Tullich. At the time of writing, access from the walkway to the kirk is not easy, but it should impove.

The path continues, birch-fringed. On a low wooded hill on the right is a slender monument to William Farquharson of Monaltrie, who died in Switzerland in 1828, aged 75. The Farquharsons have long been important landowners on upper Deeside.

Shortly after this, the Dee appears on the right, your first sight of it since Ballater. It stays with you for the stretch to Cambus o'May around a marked right-hand bend (cambus means a bend), with a clear view of the elegant suspension bridge which crosses the river here. It was built by Abernethys of Aberdeen in 1905 and renovated in 1988.

Pass the colourful Cambus Cottage, with its lovely hanging baskets of flowers. There is a fine view of the wide sweep of river with heathery hills beyond. The path continues, becoming a broad, dead straight sandy track crossing the Muir of Dinnet, out of sight of both river and road. The track is fringed by birch and pine trees with at one point a glorious sweep of heather on the left. The road rejoins at Dinnet.

DINNET TO ABOYNE
About 6¹/₂ miles/10km
OS Landranger 37
Start at Dinnet crossroads
(grid reference 460 988)

The developed path currently ends here and there is a choice of routes. You can either go right to cross the Dee and follow

GUIDE BOX

PLACES TO VISIT
Kirkton of Tullich Ruined 15th-century church
and kirkyard close to walkway. Access currently
difficult from path but easy from A93 road

CAR PARKING
Ballater; Dinnet; Deeside Gliding Club (2 miles
west of Aboyne); Aboyne.

PUBLIC TRANSPORT
Bus Good service along the A93 linking
Aberdeen and Braemar via Banchory, Aboyne
and Ballater.

ACCOMMODATION
Hotels, guest houses etc Ballater, Aboyne. Details
from Grampian Highlands and Aberdeen
Tourism, Freepost AB320, Aberdeen AB9 7AR
(tel 01224 632727).

TOURIST INFORMATION CENTRES
Banchory Bridge Street, Banchory ABC1 5SX
(tel 01330 822000)
Ballater Station Square, Ballater AB35 5QB
(tel 01339 755306)

*Looking down on Ballater from the nearby
hills. A compact town with many fine stone
buildings, Ballater is rich in royal associations.*

the South Deeside Road (B976) which is
not unpleasant, or carry on north of the
river using such sections of the old railway
as are walkable. The latter option, which is
worth pursuing, is now described.

Cross the B9119 and walk past the
garage before picking the old line up again.
For the next ½ mile it is rougher than
before but still walkable. The bridge at Mill
of Dinnet is missing, and after this the
trackbed is badly overgrown, so you need
to take to the road verge as far as the access
track to the gliding club. Short sections of
track are walkable but the road verge is not
bad and makes for good progress.

Take the Deeside Gliding Club access
track (signposted) and then turn left. The
graceful craft may be seen being towed
into the air, circling above, or returning to
land. This is an excellent area for gliding,
the topography of the mountains helping
with the 'thermals' needed for lift. Indeed,
the British altitude record, a spectacular
38,000ft, was set in this area in recent years.

The club offers a trial flight and, who
knows, after that you might be hooked.

At the far end of the airfield there is a
car park and picnic area. At its east end a
stile gives access back onto the old line. It
is again a little rough but you can follow it
without undue difficulty as far as the next
track, after which it rather disappears. Take
to the road verge again for a short distance.

One feature of Aboyne is that the
roadside pavement starts a very long way
out of town! Pass the town sign and turn
right into Rhu-na-Haven Road, a long
straight. In ½ mile, when the road bends
sharply left, go right onto a footpath which
in a short distance leads to the Dee.

Here at last a true riverside path is
found, giving a delightful end to the day.

Walk past Rhu-na-Haven House. Across
the Dee, the Water of Tanar empties in.
River and path curve left to give a most
enjoyable walk along to the bridge
carrying the B-road into the town. You
need to cross *under* the bridge, then go up
to the left to gain the road. Turn right and
walk along to Aboyne's very large central
green. Shops are at its far end, with an
excellent tearoom, and also the bus stop if
you are staying overnight elsewhere.

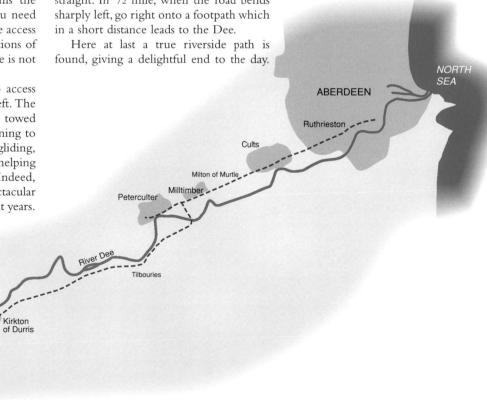

Banchory to Aberdeen

BANCHORY TO PETERCULTER
About 11 miles/18km
OS Landranger 38
Start at Bellfield Park
(grid reference 697 953)

Banchory is a busy place, both a commuter town for Aberdeen and perhaps the first true up-valley Deeside town as well. Recent development includes the very attractive Scott Skinner Square, named for the famous fiddle player, who was born in Banchory in 1843. From the traffic lights in Banchory, turn right and then left across the car park to Bellfield Park. Note the monument to Dr Francis Adams (1796–1861), Banchory's first GP and also 'a renowned polymath'.

Cross the park to the track on its right edge. Follow it as it winds through some houses then becomes tarmaced through a neat housing scheme, reaching a car park. Go down steps here to a remarkable riverside path that runs below a high wall. The fine view back upriver encompasses Scolty Hill, with its monument to General Burnett prominent.

At the end of the wall, go up left and then turn right onto a track – the old railway line again. Pass behind the inevitable sewage works and then a large sawmill. The track jinks left and right and then runs straight and true with the river

Looking back up the Dee from the riverside path at the eastern end of Banchory.

visible through trees on the right. After a cross-path, the track becomes narrow with the A93 road close by to the left.

Cross the entry to the Crathes Gallery (open weekend afternoons) and continue on the path, with the main entry to Crathes Castle on the left. The castle is well worth the diversion. Owned by the National Trust for Scotland, the 16th-century building, formerly the home of the Burnetts of Leys, has remarkable painted ceilings and many other treasures. The extensive grounds include some fine examples of topiary.

Follow the path to the next road, go right and left on a track over an old stone bridge, then ahead on a wide sandy track, keeping left of large sandpits. Pass the half-hidden platform of Crathes Station, with the signalbox still in place. Walk through some houses and past the Crathes Emporium – a grand name for a village shop! – and reach the Stonehaven Road, known as The Slug, from the Gaelic word 'slugain', which means a throat or a narrow way.

Here again there is a gap in the walkable railway. To continue the walk, turn right on the Stonehaven road, cross Durris Bridge over the Dee, opened in 1977 and offering a grand view of the river, and then go left along B9077. This road is never too busy as it winds along the south side of the Dee, passing through Kirkton of Durris and Tilburies, with the river close by to the left. The alternative to

GUIDE BOX

PLACES TO VISIT
Banchory Town museum, Bridge Street.
Crathes Castle and Garden – fine 16th-century baronial castle, open Apr–Oct daily; garden open all year.
Maryculter Storybook Glen – landscaped grounds with many characters from childrens' stories.
Aberdeen Several museums and attractions, including Art Gallery – 18th- to 20th-century painting and sculpture; Provost Skene's House – fine painted ceilings; Duthie Park Winter Gardens.

CAR PARKING
Banchory; Peterculter; Cults; Aberdeen.

PUBLIC TRANSPORT
Bus Good service along the A93 linking Aberdeen and Banchory.

ACCOMMODATION
Hotels, guest houses etc Banchory, Peterculter, Aberdeen. Details from Grampian Highlands and Aberdeen Tourism, Freepost AB320, Aberdeen AB9 7AR (tel 01224 632727).

TOURIST INFORMATION CENTRES
Banchory Bridge Street, Banchory ABC1 5SX (tel 01330 822000)
Aberdeen St Nicholas House, Broad Street, Aberdeen AB10 1DE (tel 01224 632727)

walking the road would be to hop on the bus again in Crathes, as far as Peterculter (usually shortened to Culter and pronounced 'Cooter' locally).

At a junction the B9077 becomes the B979. Go left with this road back across the Dee and just before the A93 is reached at Milltimber, turn left for 1½ miles to Peterculter, if you wish to take a break here, or right to rejoin the walkway (probably with some relief). The path is now clear all the way to Aberdeen.

PETERCULTER TO ABERDEEN
About 6 miles/10km
OS Landranger 38
Start at Peterculter old station
(grid reference 840 005)

To pick up the walkway from Peterculter, go down Station Brae and turn left at the old station. You are close to the river here, but after this stretch you will not get a clear view of it until Aberdeen.

At the B979 crossing notice the seat presented by members of Grampian Fire Brigade in recognition of their fundraising walk from Aberdeen to Ballater, 12–13 May 1990. Tough guys, to do it all in two days. Your progress will be more leisurely. The next ½ mile or so is quite narrow. This whole stretch is very popular with mountain bikes, which rarely either give way or warn of their approach – due care is needed. The path sides are thick with bramble bushes, giving great berry-picking in the late summer.

Pass through the charmingly named Milton of Murtle, with an old halt half-hidden in the bushes and the neat station building now a red-painted house. A fine iron bridge across the line here was the

work of the same firm, Abernethys, which made the suspension bridge back at Cambus o'May.

Shortly after this, the river can be glimpsed across the expanse of the golf course to the right. There are more houses around now, but the walkway itself, mostly sunk in a cutting, has a surprisingly rural air about it. The next place reached is Cults, which nowadays is more or less a suburb of Aberdeen. If you need any facilities here, take any of the roads which cross the line, up to the left for a short distance to find shops, pubs etc.

The line from Aberdeen to Culter was known as 'The Subbie', and Cults was a busy station as people waited for the 20-minute ride into the city. Down on the Dee are the remains of Morison's Bridge, known locally as the Shakkin' Briggie. In time it shook too much and most of it fell into the river.

The path runs on through Garthdee to Pitfodels, lined with trees and with some fine town mansions on the left. Go under Auchinyell Bridge, and Ruthrieston Station is reached. Here the scene is rather more urban, but the path is clear ahead to Holburn Street. The bridge carrying the

The former station building at Crathes, east of Banchory, now almost hidden in the trees.

railway has gone, but steps are provided on each side of the road. In 1906 King Edward VII travelled by train from Ballater to Holburn Street to open an extension to Aberdeen University.

The final mile of the old railway leads to Polmuir Road and the entrance to Duthie Park, a beautiful riverside space. It contains the Winter Gardens, where there are many tropical plants and other exotica. The park was opened in 1883 and is named for Elizabeth Crombie Duthie, who gifted the land to the city of Aberdeen. She is commemorated by the tall column topped by a statue of the Greek goddess of health, Hygeia.

That seems somehow a very appropriate place to end a walk. Despite the interruptions, it has been a grand progress down the Dee, which here, near its mouth, is a slow and stately river, unlike the rushing turbulence of its upper reaches. A ½ mile walk beyond Duthie Park, if you want to close the bracket, so to speak, the river empties into the North Sea at Aberdeen Docks.

The Union Canal

FALKIRK TO EDINBURGH
34 MILES/54KM

THE Union Canal originally linked with the Forth & Clyde Canal to provide a crossing from the Forth to the Clyde, Edinburgh to Glasgow. A major project, the Millennium Link, aims to restore this route. Meantime, the Union makes a very satisfying walk in its own right, with a great deal of historical and natural interest along the way. It is a 'contour canal' – in other words, there are no locks, so while the route is winding it is also flat. On the way you pass through Scotland's only canal tunnel and over three superb, high aqueducts.

WALKING GUIDE
There is no guide to the walk as such, but helpful leaflets can be obtained from British Waterways, Union Canal Office, Broxburn, West Lothian.

OS MAPS
Landranger 65, 66

LINKS
The Water of Leith Walkway, used for the final part of this walk, can be walked to Balerno.

Falkirk to Winchburgh

FALKIRK TO LINLITHGOW
About 10 miles/16km
OS Landranger 65
Start at Falkirk High Station
(grid reference 883 791)
or Falkirk Grahamston Station
(grid reference 888 903)

It is convenient to start the walk at Falkirk High Station, just a few yards from the canal. However, for completeness, you can start at Falkirk Grahamston Station, taking in a short stretch of the Forth & Clyde Canal. From Grahamston walk up to the town centre and turn right (west). Walk along to the Rosebank Distillery building, now a restaurant, and turn left up the Forth & Clyde locks to the Union Inn, formerly the meeting point of the two canals.

Cross the road left and walk uphill. In 400 yards pass under the railway bridge and then turn left up a rough track which leads to the start of the Union Canal. There were considerable arguments about the route of the canal, some people wanting a complete route through to Glasgow. However, the shorter link to Falkirk was eventually settled on, and the canal opened in 1822.

Like others of its kind, it suffered serious loss of traffic once the adjacent railway line opened, and reached its nadir in the 1970s when road construction cut it in several places. Since then there has been a great revival of interest in the canal and a number of stretches have been reopened to navigation.

From the first section of canal there are good views north to the Ochil Hills and also, nearer at hand, the petrochemical complex at Grangemouth, where the F&C ends. Masses of daffodils and narcissi brighten the scene in spring. You soon pass a new building belonging to the Seagull Trust, which does outstanding work providing boat trips for disabled people.

Just past Falkirk High Station you enter Falkirk Tunnel – an exciting walk! Water drips from the roof, and the path is usually wet underfoot. There is a handrail but take

care, sections can go missing. The far end of the tunnel is reassuringly always visible. The tunnel is 696yds long, and was made because William Forbes, then owner of Callendar Estate, did not want the canal passing through his land.

Shortly after leaving the tunnel you reach the Laughing and Greeting Bridge (greeting is Scots for crying), the carved faces said to represent either two contractors whose areas met at this point, or the fact that the work was much more difficult on the tunnel side of the bridge.

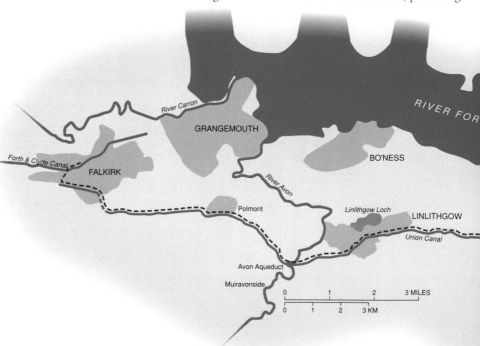

The next stretch is very peaceful and rural, with birds singing, plenty of woodland, marsh irises in summer and no traffic noise. In time the railway is rejoined just to the left, though not visible at first.

Join a road with a travellers' site on the left and then a small industrial estate. In spring you see here the first swans nesting, a regular feature all the way along the rest of the canal and a beautiful sight. A word of warning, however – they are very protective birds, so don't get too near.

Past Bridge 56 you reach the Young Offenders Institution on the right with its high fence, at Polmont, then some attractive new housing. The canal swings sharp right, and Polmont Station is just ahead on the left. Bluebells and marigolds mass in colour on the bank.

The stretch before the A801 is again very attractive. This road provides the first interruption, with the canal culverted below it. Cross with extreme care. On the left is a car park with picnic tables. Beyond is the extensive Manuel Works, producing

brickwork, terracotta and so on, with at its centre the derelict tower of Almond or Haining Castle, once the seat of the Earls of Linlithgow.

The short diversion to Muiravonside Church is worth taking. The church itself stands out among more prosaic buildings and around it are many interesting old gravestones which repay exploration. At the next road bridge (another culvert) a

The east portal of the canal tunnel at Falkirk – an exciting stretch of the walk!

link footpath is signed to Muiravonside Country Park, 1/2 mile away. Cross under the B825 then continue in a very leafy cutting. Walk round a bend and suddenly ahead you see the highlight of this section, the magnificent Avon Aqueduct.

The aqueduct, product of the genius of Thomas Telford, is second only to Pontcysyllte in Wales for size. It has 12 arches which reach 82ft above the River Avon and is as graceful as it is impressive. Its lightness was made possible by using an iron trough to carry the water. Downstream, the equally impressive 23-arch railway viaduct over the river helped speed the decline of the canal.

On the approach to Linlithgow you pass the old stables at Woodcockdale. In the early days, relays of horses using for towing barges would be changed here. As you near the town you pass Milestone 22, showing the distance still to be covered before reaching Edinburgh.

Bridge 45 is new, with a sign showing that the West Lothian Canal Project is a partnership between a number of public agencies and Europe. The canal basin at Linlithgow deserves a stop. As well as the boats moored here (trips in the summer), there is an interesting small museum and display run by the Linlithgow Union Canal Society, who have done a tremendous amount to restore the canal and make it better known.

Linlithgow itself should not be passed by. As well as the superb Palace, birthplace of Mary Queen of Scots, there are many other fine historic buildings (a town trail explores them), and the walk round Linlithgow Loch always reveals a rich diversity of birdlife.

LINLITHGOW TO WINCHBURGH
About 6 miles/10km
OS Landranger 65
Start at Linlithgow Station
(grid reference 004 771)

The section from Linlithgow to Winchburgh is surprisingly rural, and provides a tranquil and easy walk of 6 miles. At first the scenery is open with fine views northwards towards the Ochils. The banks gradually become more wooded and the canal more weedy. As the path nears Winchburgh the vast shale bings, a fascinating part of our industrial history, come into view. The shale oil industry, developed by James 'Paraffin' Young, employed 13,000 people in 120 separate works at its peak. The pollution must have been disastrous, but at least there were jobs. Production declined from the 1880s onwards, but the bings, holding all the waste material, remain and are very slowly being reclaimed by nature.

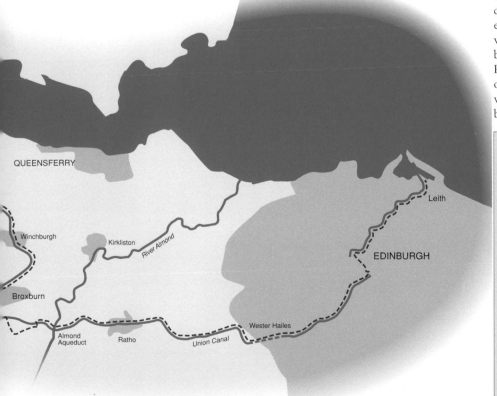

GUIDE BOX

PLACES TO VISIT
Muiravonside Country Park Signposted from canal west of Linlithgow.
Linlithgow Linlithgow Palace, birthplace of Mary Queen of Scots, a superb building on the shore of its loch.

CAR PARKING
There are car parks close to the route at Falkirk High and Grahamston stations; Polmont Station; Linlithgow. Street parking elsewhere.

PUBLIC TRANSPORT
Train The canal roughly parallels the main Edinburgh-to-Glasgow railway line, with stations at Falkirk (High and Grahamston), Polmont and Linlithgow.
Bus Good services from Broxburn and Winchburgh to both Linlithgow and Edinburgh.

ACCOMMODATION
Hotels, guest houses etc Wide range in Falkirk and Linlithgow. More limited elsewhere.

TOURIST INFORMATION CENTRES
Falkirk 2-4 Glebe Street, Falkirk FK1 1HX (tel 01324 620244)
Linlithgow Burgh Halls, The Cross, Linlithgow EH49 7AH (tel 01506 844600)

Winchburgh to Edinburgh Haymarket or Leith

WINCHBURGH TO WESTER HAILES
About 9 miles/14km
OS Landranger 65
Start at Canal Bridge, Winchburgh
(grid reference 087 751)

The section of canal between Winchburgh and Broxburn is dominated by the great bings. Instead of following the canal directly out of Winchburgh, take the signposted walk around the golf course and past the restored Niddry Castle. Built in 1490, it was the home of Mary Seaton, one of the 'Four Maries' who served Mary Queen of Scots.

Cross the Edinburgh-to-Glasgow railway by a bridge and rejoin the canal to walk through Broxburn. The canal's contouring means that you actually walk *west* here for a while! After leaving the town, head east again, but a diversion (signposted) is needed as the canal is blocked by the M8.

Leave the canal at the British Waterways office (if open, helpful literature is available here) and walk down the minor road, under the motorway and railway. Take the next minor road left to pass the intriguingly named Lookaboutye Farm.

There are views left over the bings to the distant Ochils and right to the Pentlands. Go left with the road at Muirend Farm and in 200 yards rejoin the canal at Bridge 28.

The motorway is never far away on the next stretch, but it is forgotten as you reach another great feat of engineering, the Almond Aqueduct. Reaching 128ft above the river, the superb brickwork is best appreciated by going some steps to view it from below. An 1834 handbill offered 'fruits, confectioneries and varieties of refreshments' here: today you must wait until Ratho. Among the Irish navvies who worked on the canal here were two named Burke and Hare, who later achieved greater fame as body-snatchers in Edinburgh.

Back on the canal, continue through a quiet wooded section to the basin at Ratho (excellent pub, canal display and boat trips). Ratho Church is worth the short diversion. One grave records the death of farmer William Mitchell, killed in 1800 by 'an instantaneous stroke from a threshing machine'.

Past Ratho, another motorway, the new M8 extension opened in late 1995, accompanies you to the Edinburgh City Bypass, which is crossed by the Scott Russell Aqueduct, named for a 19th-century scientist. It is an odd sensation to walk beside the peaceful canal over the maelstrom of roaring traffic.

The canal swings right and then left before coming to a halt among the houses of Wester Hailes.

Looking west along the canal at Hermiston, just outside Edinburgh. Despite its proximity to towns and villages, the canal retains a rural feel.

GUIDE BOX

PLACES TO VISIT
Edinburgh There is a vast array of visitor attractions in Edinburgh. Close to the path are St Mary's Cathedral, Palmerston Place, and the Royal Botanic Gardens, a magnificent collection of plants, trees and shrubs from all parts of the world.

CAR PARKING
There are car parks close to the route at Linlithgow; Broxburn; Ratho; Wester Hailes; Slateford; Haymarket; street parking elsewhere.

PUBLIC TRANSPORT
Train The canal roughly parallels the main Edinburgh-to-Glasgow railway line, with stations at Linlithgow and Haymarket. Suburban stations at Wester Hailes, Kingsnowe and Slateford are all close to the canal.
Bus Good services from Winchburgh to Edinburgh, and within Edinburgh.

ACCOMMODATION
Hotels, guest houses etc Very wide range available in Edinburgh; more limited elsewhere.

TOURIST INFORMATION CENTRE
Edinburgh 3 Princes Street, Edinburgh EH2 2QP (tel 0131 557 1700)

WESTER HAILES TO HAYMARKET OR LEITH

*About 4¹/₂ miles/7km to Haymarket or
8¹/₂ miles/14km to Leith*

OS Landranger 66

*Start at Murrayburn Drive, Wester Hailes
(grid reference 196 703)*

There is a gap of about ¹/₂ mile in the path at Wester Hailes, and careful directions are needed. Take the left edge of the large open space, then take Murrayburn Drive under Wester Hailes Road. At Murrayburn Road go right and first left into Hailesland Road. Turn right into Dumbryden Drive and then right again (Hailesland Park). Follow a fence round to the left, go up some steps, cross the road, left and right to regain the towpath.

This is a quiet, reedy section alongside Lanark Road before the eight-arched Slateford Aqueduct over the Water of Leith. Ahead is a fine view of the city centre with the castle and Arthur's Seat prominent. Slateford Road is crossed by the concrete Prince Charlie Aqueduct

and then you pass Meggetland, home of Boroughmuir Rugby Club.

Cross over a railway and under Ashley Terrace. On the other bank is the HQ of the Edinburgh Canal Society; on your side is a helpful information board. There is still good birdlife on this increasingly urban stretch, with moorhens and young prominent in early summer.

Enter the final section with flats either side. Reach a large basin, usually accompanied by a strong smell from the Fountainbridge Brewery. This is the home of well-known beers such as McEwan's Export and Tartan Special. Ahead is the Leamington Lift Bridge, which was moved here from Fountainbridge when that section of canal was filled in.

This is effectively the end of the canal. The short section beyond it, the Lochrin Basin, is used as a canoe slalom course and is a dead end. One odd fact is that George Meikle Kemp, the somewhat eccentric designer of the Scott Monument on Princes Street, fell in here and was drowned. Do not follow his example.

The Scott Russell Aqueduct carries the canal over the roaring traffic on the Edinburgh City Bypass – tranquillity above and a maelstrom of noise below.

Although this is the end of the Union Canal, it need not be the end of the walk. A much more satisfying conclusion is to link up with the Water of Leith Walkway, and finish at the Forth in Leith. To do this, walk down Gilmore Park, turn right past the brewery and left into Grove Street. Cross the Haymarket junctions and go up Palmerston Place, past Sir George Gilbert Scott's fine 1879 Cathedral of St Mary.

Go left over Belford Bridge and left again down to the river. It can be followed right down to Leith, a lovely walk which passes near the wonderful Royal Botanic Gardens (well worth the diversion) and eventually leading to the redeveloped waterfront area at Leith. This is still a busy commercial port, but now has plenty of cafés and pubs where you can sit and reflect on the splendid walk you have just completed.

The River Tweed

GALASHIELS TO KELSO AND COLDSTREAM TO BERWICK-UPON-TWEED
43 MILES/68KM

THE Tweed is the major landscape feature of the Scottish Borders region. It runs for near enough 100 miles from its source close to the Devil's Beef Tub in the hills north of Moffat to its mouth at Berwick. Many splendid Border towns have grown up along its banks; the only one of any size not passed on this walk is Peebles, which is certainly worthy of a visit and has its own fine riverside walks. The walk described here does not stick to the river, as access is not continuous, but is never too far away. The section from Kelso to Coldstream is negotiated by bus; the sections described here give the best walking. Access should improve in the years ahead as more stretches of path are opened. Meantime, there is plenty to see with magnificent 12th-century abbeys, castles, towns and villages, many a graceful bridge and splendidly varied birdlife. A walk down the Tweed is an expedition to be savoured to the full.

WALKING GUIDE
There is no full guide to the walk described here, but various walks leaflets describe sections of it, and there is a guide to St Cuthbert's Way. For more details contact the Scottish Borders Tourist Board, Murray's Green, Jedburgh TD8 6BE (tel 01835 863435 or 863688) for the walks publications leaflet.

OS MAPS
Landranger 73, 74, 75

LINKS
The route coincides with the Southern Upland Way (Portpatrick to Cockburnspath) between Galashiels and Melrose; with the St Cuthbert's Way (Melrose to Lindisfarne, opened in 1996) between Dryburgh and Maxton. A coastal path from Berwick to St Abbs may be opened in 1997.

Galashiels to St Boswells

GALASHIELS TO MELROSE
About 5 miles/8km
OS Landranger 73
Start at Tourist Information Centre, Galashiels (grid reference 493 360)

Although Galashiels is on the Gala Water, not the Tweed, it is a convenient place to start the walk. The town has plenty of accommodation and eating-places, and a short walk on the Southern Upland Way leads to the Tweed.

From the town centre, walk south across Scott Street to head for the swimming pool. At the entrance to Scott Park, pick up Southern Upland Way signs to walk across the park and out by the drive of Galashiels Academy. The route continues along Barr Road, with good views east towards the Eildon Hills, before crossing fields and dropping down to the Tweed across the busy A7 road.

The river is joined almost opposite Abbotsford, the home of Sir Walter Scott, who wrote most of his best-known works here. The house is worth a visit if you can manage the diversion. It contains much of interest, including a collection of Jacobite mementoes, a fine library and splendid gardens graced by peacocks.

The route now follows the Tweed downstream, under the high Galafoot Bridge and along a short road section before crossing the river on an old railway viaduct. This section is tarmaced and is much used by cyclists. After about ½ mile the route swings left and rejoins the Tweed for a true riverside walk into Melrose. Instead of crossing the river again by the suspension bridge, as the Southern Upland Way does, continue along the lane and turn right at the T-junction to go up to Melrose Abbey.

This magnificent ruin in its glorious setting has a wonderfully peaceful atmosphere. The foundation is Cistercian and dates from 1136, at a time when King David I brought peace to much of Scotland, and a number of important religious houses were established. The abbey contains much fine carving and also, in a lead casket, what is reputedly the heart of Robert the Bruce. The ruins cover a large area today but they were originally even more extensive, and the monks controlled land over a very wide area.

Melrose has much else of interest, including a good exhibition on the Romans (in the Ormiston Institute), an intriguing Teddy Bear Museum, and the National Trust for Scotland's Priorwood Garden, which specialises in dried flower sales. Half a day can easily be spent in the town. There is a particularly good selection of tearooms, which will no doubt gladden the walker's heart.

MELROSE TO ST BOSWELLS
About 5½ miles/9km
OS Landranger 73
Start at Melrose Abbey (grid reference 548 342)

Take the paved footpath immediately south of the abbey, heading east, to cross a small burn and then a playpark. This path leads out through housing to run along a shelf to the attractive village of Newstead, which sadly lacks both pub and shop. Walk through Newstead and at its east end, take the lane (now closed to traffic) which continues east towards Leaderfoot. The new bypass recently opened here may not be on your OS map.

The lane passes the site of Trimontium, named after the Eildon Hills and the

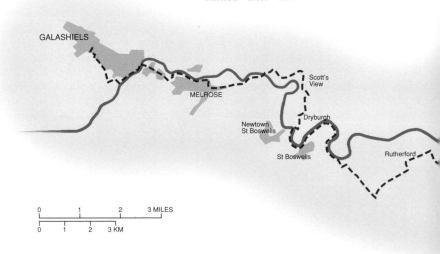

Romans' most important fort and staging-post in the whole of southern Scotland, covering a large area south of the road. Dere Street heads south from here and eventually leads all the way to York. A monument marks the site but, although there has been extensive excavation, there is at present nothing visible above ground.

Continue to pass under the elegant Leaderfoot Viaduct, which formerly carried a railway line across the Tweed on 19 arches reaching a height of 120ft above the river. Opened in 1865, it has carried no traffic since 1948. At the time of writing there are plans to provide a path up to it and public access across it.

Cross the river by Alexander Stevens' fine old bridge of 1780, now happily spared the strain of vehicles, and turn right to cross the Leader Water and climb a steep hill. Take the first road on the right and at the next junction go right again, signed for Scott's View. This road winds along above the river, passing Bemersyde, for long the home of the Haig family. The original central tower, very typical of its time, dates from 1581, but there is much later addition. The gardens are open in summer.

Scott's View gives a magnificent panorama westward with the three Eildon peaks as the central feature. It is said that the horses pulling Walter Scott's hearse stopped here without command, as they had so often done while their master was alive. In a further ¹/₂ mile, leave the road as signed to take the path leading down to the Wallace Statue. This massive 26ft sandstone figure, carved by John Smith in 1814 on the commission of the Earl of Buchan, was

hidden in trees for many years, but now stands proud again following repair and renovation. Since the issue of the film *Braveheart* it has attracted many more visitors than ever before.

GUIDE BOX

PLACES TO VISIT
Melrose Melrose Abbey – magnificent ruin of 12th-century abbey founded by David I. Priorwood Garden – intriguing small garden and orchard with unusual varieties of apple trees and dried flower shop. Trimontium Exhibition, Ormiston Institute – display of artefacts from the Roman era with interpretive material on the Romans. Teddy Bear Museum – exhibition on the history of teddies; you can see them being made, and buy one from the large stock. Abbotsford House – Sir Walter Scott's romantic mansion, full of mementoes.
Dryburgh Abbey Superbly peaceful site on a bend of the Tweed; ruins include the graves of Sir Walter Scott and Field Marshal Earl Haig.

CAR PARKING
Galashiels; Melrose; St Boswells.

PUBLIC TRANSPORT
Bus Reasonable bus services link the towns along the route with each other, and with Edinburgh.

ACCOMMODATION
Hotels, guest houses etc Galashiels, Melrose, St Boswells. Details from Scottish Borders Tourist Board, Murray's Green, Jedburgh TD8 6BE (tel 01835 863435 or 863688).

TOURIST INFORMATION CENTRES
Jedburgh Murray's Green, Jedburgh TD8 6BE (tel 01835 863435 or 863688)
Galashiels St Johns Street, Galashiels TD1 3JX (tel 01896 755551)
Melrose Abbey House, Abbey Street, Melrose TD6 9LG (tel 01896 822555)

Continue along the path to Dryburgh village and follow the signs for Dryburgh Abbey. Its setting on a bend of the river is if anything even more peaceful than Melrose. A Premonstratensian house dating from 1150, it is a wonderful place to spend a contemplative hour, and it is little wonder that Walter Scott chose to be buried here.

Walk back through the small village and cross the Tweed by the splendid suspension bridge of 1850. Turn left to pick up St Cuthbert's Way signs and follow the river along a pleasant path for a mile or so. The Tweed carries a varied range of birdlife and you should see heron, swans, moorhen and

mallard along here at the least. The path follows the river round a sweeping bend before climbing to the village of St Boswells, where this stage ends. The name is a corruption of St Boisils, commemorating a 7th-century abbot of Old Melrose, described by Bede as 'a man of remarkable piety'.

The village offers accommodation, a shop, toilets and other facilities. It is noted for its large green extending to 40 acres, the venue for a fair of travelling people each July. The 1892 village hall and parish church of 1835 are both impressive.

Looking back upriver to the Eildon Hills from the viewpoint on the path at Dryburgh.

187

St Boswells to Kelso

ST BOSWELLS TO ROXBURGH
About 9 miles/14km
OS Landranger 74
Start at St Boswells Village Hall
(grid reference 594 309)

From the centre of St Boswells, head down Braehead Road to the golf clubhouse to pick up St Cuthbert's Way signs again. St Boswells Golf Club was established in 1899. Walk across the golf course, keeping close to the fence as requested. The path is clear all the way and the Tweed is close by on your left.

Continue on the path when the golf course ends, swinging right with a number of striking red sandstone cliff pillars across the river, to reach Mertoun Bridge. This handsome structure, also in red sandstone, dates from 1841 and replaced a former timber bridge. It was designed by James Sleight.

The path continues, right beside the river on a particularly beautiful stretch, with shingle spits that attract a good variety of birdlife from dippers to heron

Floors Castle seen across the Tweed from a fragment of the much older Roxburgh Castle.

and a remarkable double row of tall poplars across the river on the Mertoun Estate. This is a stretch to savour before the path enters woodland below Benrig, rising and falling several times on well-made flights of steps and passing an old well.

Eventually the path climbs to reach Maxton Church, a finely proportioned building of the mid-18th century, on the site of an earlier church, as is evidenced by the bell, which is Dutch and dates from 1609. The church is still used for regular worship and there is a car park nearby.

From here to Kelso, Tweedside access is at present restricted, so the remainder of this section is of necessity something of a compromise. There is a longish stretch on roads, but they are very quiet roads, and there is compensation in the fine views to be had. Walk up the lane into the village, which currently has neither shop nor pub, turn left and then first right (signed to Fairnington), and continue heading south along this road for 1 mile to Muirhouselaw. Turn left here. Muirhouselaw has a fine range of late 19th-century farm buildings and a really splendid group of cottages, formerly occupied by farmworkers.

On the next stretch there are expansive

views across the valley of the Tweed and back to the distinctive triple peaks of the Eildons. Go sharp left with the road after a mile and turn right at Rutherford Farm. Continue to the next junction at Rutherford Mains, and turn right. The former St Boswells-to-Kelso railway crosses the road here. It closed in 1964 but there is no public access to the trackbed at present.

Pass Rutherford Burnside and turn right at the next T-junction. Take the next

GUIDE BOX

PLACES TO VISIT
Kelso Kelso Abbey, smaller than the other Abbey ruins but still impressive. Floors Castle, home of the Duke of Roxburghe, the largest inhabited house in Scotland; superb furniture, porcelain and paintings, extensive grounds beside the Tweed.

CAR PARKING
St Boswells; Roxburgh; Kelso.

PUBLIC TRANSPORT
Bus Reasonable services link the towns along the route with each other, and with Edinburgh.

ACCOMMODATION
Hotels, guest houses etc St Boswells, Kelso. Details from Scottish Borders Tourist Board, Murray's Green, Jedburgh TD8 6BE, tel 01835 863435 or 863688.

TOURIST INFORMATION CENTRE
Kelso Town House, The Square, Kelso TD5 7HE (tel 01573 223464)

turn right in 400yds and go right again at a T-junction in a further ¾ mile to walk to the neat village of Roxburgh. On this stretch there are grand views looking south to the Cheviot Hills.

Roxburgh is a 'new' village in the sense that it was moved here from the original site further north overlooking the Tweed, which will be passed later on in the walk. But this happened centuries ago, and today the quiet village has a settled look to it. It sits on the west bank of the River Teviot, one of the Tweed's main tributaries. The Teviot flows southwest through Hawick and on into the high hills that mark the Border itself.

There are many charming houses in Roxburgh, and the school is also attractive, but the village is rather dominated by the soaring arches of the 1847 railway viaduct. Designed by John Miller, it is every bit as fine as Leaderfoot. Again, there is regrettably no public access to the top of the viaduct, but it can be admired from below, and a footbridge has been cunningly slung from it to cross the river.

ROXBURGH TO KELSO
About 4¹/₂ miles / 7km
OS Landranger 74
*Start at Roxburgh village
(grid reference 697 306)*

Walk down to the viaduct and turn left to join the path alongside the Teviot – a relief after all the roadwork, no doubt. The path keeps close to the river, heading north past Roxburgh Mill. Caves passed here were, it is said, used to hide horses during the 1745 Jacobite rebellion. In nearly 2 miles, just as the river bends abruptly east, there are high grassy mounds on the left, with fragments of masonry. This is all that remains of the once Royal Burgh and Castle of Old Roxburgh.

Its importance in early medieval times can hardly be overestimated. In the 13th century this was one of only four Royal Burghs in Scotland, the others being Edinburgh, Stirling and Berwick. The castle was a royal residence and saw its share of warfare. The old burgh held the royal mint, where coins were made.

Through the 14th century Roxburgh's importance decayed and in 1369 it and Berwick (now ceded to England) were replaced as Royal Burghs by Lanark and Linlithgow. The castle was still strategically important until 1460, when it was razed to the ground during a siege that saw the death of King James II, killed when a cannon exploded. From the top of the mounds there is a grand view of Floors Castle, home of the Duke of Roxburghe, across the river.

The remains of Kelso Abbey. Founded in 1128, this was once the largest of all the great Border abbeys. It was sacked by Hertford's army in 1545.

Originally Fleurs, the castle was designed by William Adam and built in the 1720s for the first Duke. William Playfair made substantial alterations and additions in the 1840s. Floors is open to view in the summer months and contains many treasures.

Continue round the bend and go up to the stile at the road. Walk along the road over the lovely old bridge of 1795, designed by Archibald Stevens. Continue with the road. On the left, at the confluence of Teviot and Tweed, is Junction Pool, one of the most prestigious salmon beats on the river.

Turn left at the junction to cross Rennie's outstanding bridge of 1803. At its far side, a short walk brings you to Kelso Abbey. The foundation moved here from

Selkirk in 1128. When complete this was the largest of all the great Border abbeys, but today it is perhaps the least impressive site, being rather hemmed about with other buildings. It is still worth taking time to explore.

There are many other fine buildings in Kelso, and a Town Trail leaflet is recommended to explore them. The cobbled, rather French-looking main square includes the 1816 Town Hall with octagonal belfry and the Italianate Cross Keys Hotel, an 1880 reworking of a 1761 building. Blair's jeweller's shop is in a building dating back to around 1750.

Coldstream to Berwick-upon-Tweed

GUIDE BOX

WHAT TO SEE
Coldstream Guards Museum – the story of the regiment that takes its name from the town.
Norham Castle Impressive fortress beside the Tweed.
Berwick-upon-Tweed Barracks Museum – excellent material on the history of the town and its military garrison.

CAR PARKING
Coldstream; Berwick.

PUBLIC TRANSPORT
Bus Reasonable services link the towns along the route with each other, and with Edinburgh.

ACCOMMODATION
Hotels, guest houses etc Coldstream, Berwick.
Details from Scottish Borders Tourist Board, Murray's Green, Jedburgh TD8 6BE (tel 01835 863435 or 863688).
Camping Coldstream.

TOURIST INFORMATION CENTRES
Coldstream High Street, Coldstream TD12 4DH (tel 01890 882607)
Berwick-upon-Tweed Castlegate, Berwick-upon-Tweed TD15 1JS (tel 01289 330733)

COLDSTREAM TO NORHAM
About 9¹/₂ miles/15km
OS Landranger 74
Start at Coldstream Bridge
(grid reference 848 402)

Cross Coldstream Bridge, thus walking into England, and take the signposted footpath on the south side. It runs close to the river through woodland for about 500yds then heads off uphill to cross a track and pass under power lines before meeting the A698. Getting back to the Tweed means crossing the Till and to save taking a convoluted route, or following the main road, it is easier to head east across fields from Harper Ridge to Stickle Heaton and then turn left down a lane to rejoin the A698 at the entrance to the Tillmouth Park Hotel. From here the road must be walked to Twizel Bridge.

Take the signed footpath which says 'Norham 5' at a gateway. Old Twizel Bridge dates from the 15th century and played a significant role in the Battle of Flodden in 1513. The Earl of Surrey crossed his troops here and thus trapped the northern wing of the Scots force.

The path runs pleasantly along beside the Till through woods and in 1 mile passes under the impressive former railway viaduct crossing the river. Across the Till is St Cuthbert's Chapel, a 19th-century reconstruction. Shortly after this the Tweed is rejoined, and there is a seat to watch the river go by if you wish. Turn right along the riverbank. This stretch is well fished and you will usually see anglers out in small boats trying their luck. The river here is broad and slow-moving with sandy spits – at least in summer.

Pass the cottage at Ord. After another small building, the path swings inland to enter a wood. Turn left at the fingerpost by a house and follow the path – quite rough here – at the top of the wood, where there is a good view across the river to Milne Graden House. Designed by James Gillespie Graham, this was built in 1822 in neo-classical style and was originally called Kersfield.

The path winds up and down, narrow and overgrown at times and passing through a forest of giant hogweed, towering up to 15ft high. Fortunately eradication measures are countering their threat. Hogweed can inflict a nasty sting and should be scrupulously avoided. It is a relief to escape from this section – a bit of a struggle at times and rather claustrophobic – just before West Newbiggin. There are often remarkable assemblies of swans on the river here, a beautiful sight.

Another wood is entered, but this time with a good clear path. Pass a house with two statuettes of cherubs. The next house has lions as a contrast! After joining a lane, you can either take the signposted riverside path to Norham Bridge or continue into Norham village, which offers shops, pubs and public toilets. There was a ford here

The Tweed at West Newbiggin, near Norham.
Swans often congregate in this area.

long before the river was bridged and Norham saw more than its fair share of conflict during the Border Wars.

The parish church is dedicated to St Cuthbert, not surprising as all this land was once farmed by the monks of Lindisfarne, and includes 14th-century work in the chancel. The weathervane on the village cross is a salmon. At the east end of the village is the powerful keep of Norham Castle, a typical Border stronghold. It was started in the mid-12th century by Richard of Wolveston after Henry II had recaptured Northumberland from the Scots. For the next 400 years it saw regular action, and was taken by the Scots force before Flodden in 1513. Although much is ruinous, Norham is still an impressive place. It is cared for by English Heritage and though entrance is free, there is a strange lack of interpretation at the site.

NORHAM TO BERWICK
About 9¹/₂ miles/15km
OS Landranger 75
Start at Norham Castle
(grid reference 907 477)

From Norham Castle go down to the river and continue along the path, through more woodland called Hangman's Land, perhaps a reminder of more troubled times, then in the open round a broad bend. In 2¹/₂ miles from Norham steps go down through a tangly wood, across a burn and then the path rises into Horncliffe, a pleasant if straggly village. Work your way through it,

trending right, noting the plaque on the old school dated 1833. Pass the Fishers Arms and the United Reformed Church. The memorial shows that 16 men of the village died in World War I but only one, an airman, in the 1939–45 conflict.

Turn left at the T-junction and walk past the front of Horncliffe House, an early 19th-century sandstone Palladian mansion built for William Alder. Turn left again. The sign says 'Union Bridge 1' but it is less than half that distance. On the way you pass the Chain Bridge Honey Farm, where you can see how honey is made and perhaps buy some to take home with you.

The Union or Chain Bridge is at the point where the Tweed becomes non-tidal, and there was a ford here before Captain Sir Samuel Brown designed the suspension bridge, which opened in 1820. It was repaired and strengthened in 1902–03. Continue east on an excellent grass path. Paxton House peeps over the trees across the river. This superb Palladian mansion was built in the mid-18th century to a design by James Nisbet, with interior work by Robert Adam. It includes magnificent furniture and paintings, and is an outstation of the National Galleries of Scotland. The extensive grounds were laid out by Robert Robinson, who was trained by Capability Brown.

It is hoped that before too long you will be able to cross to the north bank at the Union Bridge and walk down to Berwick on that side. At present this route lacks a bridge over the River Whiteadder. For the

moment then, continue on the south bank, the river now very broad and majestic.

Just past Low House the Border makes its odd jerk northwards and no longer runs down the centre of the Tweed. After a very good section the path runs below woodland and deteriorates to the point where it is sometimes hardly visible. Eventually it leaves the river to climb a steep flight of steps – tough going but at least you get a better path at the top, across fields with fine views.

The A1 bypass is reached. Cross the road with extreme caution, go left and cross the river on the 1984 bypass bridge. At the far side, go right to join the riverside path. As the river curves right, the view ahead is dominated by the 28 soaring arches of the Royal Border Bridge carrying the railway. Achieving both grace and strength, the bridge was designed by Robert Stephenson and opened in 1850. Over 2,700 men were employed in its construction.

Turn left before the railway bridge to enter the town. Berwick has much to offer, including a fine Barracks Museum and of course the Town Walls, a grand walk in themselves. It is worth going down towards the pier to see the old bridge across the Tweed. It dates from 1634 and has 15 low arches with cutwaters.

You have come a long way from Galashiels, and so has the Tweed, which ends its journey here as it empties into the North Sea.

Old Berwick Bridge at the mouth of the Tweed.

Acknowledgements

Creative director Julian Holland
Editor Sue Gordon
Cartography and page make-up LP&TS Ltd

The authors would like to thank the following individuals for their help in preparing this book:
Richard Attwood of the Cotswold Canals Trust, Roger Lambert of Kent County Council Planning Department,
Frank Haskew for his assistance on Helen Livingston's walks, Blodwen and Dick Evans for help and
hospitality given to Nia Williams and, last but not least, Jackie Jennings for assistance
given to Paul Atterbury, Julian Holland and Sue Gordon.

Photographic acknowledgements

AA Photo Library: 35, 49, 151, 170/171, 173

Paul Atterbury: 7, 10/11, 13, 14, 15, 16, 17, 18, 19, 69, 70,
71, 72, 73, 74, 75, 76/77, 82, 84, 86, 87, 88, 89, 93, 94, 95,
96, 97, 98, 99, 107/107, 134, 135, 136, 137, 138, 139, 140, 141,
142, 143, 144, 145, 146, 147, 164, 165, 166, 167

Richard Attwood: 34, 36, 37

Malcolm & Hazel Boyes: 109, 110, 111, 112, 113, 114, 115, 116,
117, 118, 119, 124/125, 126, 127, 128, 129, 130, 131

Ian Burgum: 24, 25, 148/149, 163, 168, 169

Sue Gordon: 65, 66, 67, 100, 103, 104, 105, 120, 121, 122, 123

Frank Haskew: 38/39, 40, 42, 43, 44, 45, 46, 47, 48, 50, 51, 52,
53, 54, 55, 57, 58, 59, 60, 61, 62, 63

Julian Holland: Title page, 8/9, 20, 22, 23, 27, 28, 29, 30, 31, 33

Chris Rushton: 78, 80, 81(t), 81(b), 85, 90, 91, 152, 153, 154,
155, 156, 157, 158, 159, 161, 162

Robert Smith: 179

Roger Smith: 174, 175, 176, 177, 180, 181, 183, 184, 185, 187,
188, 189, 190, 191